Applied Healthcare Economics

A wide range of managerial challenges in healthcare, from decisions on what reimbursement levels to accept to how to deal with social determinants of health, could benefit from economic insights. This book for managers of medical services, insurance, and public policy emphasizes intuition and common sense, making the concepts of health economics more relatable and actionable. It also challenges conventional wisdom, debunking myths and suggesting innovative solutions to industry challenges. For each problem, the book suggests actions managers should or should not take, when to seek new information, and how to interpret it. Economic analysis and research suggest novel answers to questions like whether to raise private insurer prices when Medicare cuts what it pays, when to accept a particular reimbursement offer, or how to manage patients with high-deductible insurance. The book highlights the impact on healthcare costs and efficiency of issues such as moral hazard, cost-sharing, and price-setting.

MARK V. PAULY is Bendheim Professor Emeritus of Health Care Management and Economics in the Wharton School at the University of Pennsylvania. He has taught courses in health economics and healthcare management for 55 years at Northwestern University and at the Wharton School. As one of the nation's leading health economists, he has made significant contributions to the fields of health economics and insurance.

Applied Healthcare Economics

Unexpected Insights for Management and Policy

Mark V. Pauly

University of Pennsylvania

CAMBRIDGE
UNIVERSITY PRESS

CAMBRIDGE
UNIVERSITY PRESS

Shaftesbury Road, Cambridge CB2 8EA, United Kingdom

One Liberty Plaza, 20th Floor, New York, NY 10006, USA

477 Williamstown Road, Port Melbourne, VIC 3207, Australia

314–321, 3rd Floor, Plot 3, Splendor Forum, Jasola District Centre, New Delhi – 110025, India

103 Penang Road, #05–06/07, Visioncrest Commercial, Singapore 238467

Cambridge University Press is part of Cambridge University Press & Assessment, a department of the University of Cambridge.

We share the University's mission to contribute to society through the pursuit of education, learning and research at the highest international levels of excellence.

www.cambridge.org
Information on this title: www.cambridge.org/9781009606974

DOI: 10.1017/9781009606967

When citing this work, please include a reference to the DOI 10.1017/9781009606967

First published 2026

Cover image: YAY Media AS / Alamy Stock Vector

A catalogue record for this publication is available from the British Library

A Cataloging-in-Publication data record for this book is available from the Library of Congress

ISBN 978-1-009-60697-4 Hardback
ISBN 978-1-009-60698-1 Paperback

Contents

Figures

Boxes

Exhibits

Preface: What Managers Should Do

The purpose of this book is to help managers address economic challenges that occur in the health and medical environment by offering insights from economics research – and the economic view of the world in general. My view is that economic problems require economic solutions (rather than slogans or rage), and that sometimes economic theory or data can help managers avoid dead ends as well as open new doors to a greater extent than if they relied on their best judgment alone. Not all challenges that arise from the current environment can be addressed, but many can – and knowledge of which others are still open cases can help managers avoid jumping too soon or seeming too defensive. It is sometimes said that the US healthcare system is a nonsystem; it is also sometimes said it is a system perfectly crafted (by someone) to produce the outcomes it does. The second observation is closer to the truth but fails to recognize that systemic relationships can and do develop organically. There always is an invisible hand – though sometimes it can be all thumbs. But tracing these relationships to their consequences and then back to their causes is what economists are supposed to be good at doing, so I will offer up what we have so far, in the hope that it can both explain and guide.

My approach here differs from the usual books that explain health economics, mostly to economists or economics students. They do not try to tell managers things they did not already know or might have been mistaken about – while my hope is to do just that. Most of management, everybody knows, is a combination of personal attention and common sense; I am going to assume my readers already have that. (I actually believe it is true of students as well.) What I can add is that both theory and evidence from health economics tell you things beyond common sense (and surely beyond the much but appropriately maligned conventional wisdom). Some points I will make are counterintuitive – cost-shifting cannot happen in a world of profit-maximizing firms, better health insurance is not always good for you, nonprofit hospitals are no different from investor-owned ones. And Malcolm Gladwell is wrong about why people use hospitals. Often the message is counsel of caution when what people need to know to make the best decisions does not exist (despite widely accepted beliefs), so you need to hedge your bets. As well, sometimes economics does agree with common sense, even when it is uncomfortable to do so (physicians need financial incentives to be more thoughtful).

My hope is to supply punchlines that not only are clear but also pay off for managers in terms of insights they would not otherwise have, assumptions they would not otherwise make, and conclusions that might otherwise follow the crowd. I do hope to surprise a little, reassure some, and warn a lot.

My strategy in assembling these topics was largely looking for the union between two circles – what my management students have told me they would like to understand and what economic research tells you that is unexpected (even if it makes you mad). I start with a reassuring macroeconomics point: The medical care industry in the US is not ruining the economy, and we do not always have to apologize for high health spending. Then I dip into a chapter on efficient managerial decision-making based on the counter-anatomical theory: Use your head, not your gut feelings or the seat of your pants. I show how to use information that shows up on your desk and how to decide whether to get more. Then a pair of chapters on coordination of care and caregivers: physicians and nurses, physicians among each other, physicians and hospitals. Speaking of hospitals, I display some economic approaches to determining your costs for services you supply that are far superior to accounting or bean-counting methods.

Then on to real economics: how to set or predict prices for medical goods and services when you know what you want and how to structure (and cope with) insurance when some agents do not know the effectiveness of care or the risk level of prospective insurance buyers. One way to deal with imperfect information is patient cost-sharing, another way is to use managed care, and a third way is to use value-based payment policy; I cover what economics has to say (cheering and disparaging) about each. Then a detour to an important destination: How does it work out when your boss picks your medical insurance (and how much to pay you in cash)? Finally, a laundry list of four important topics that help to determine the cost of care and the outcomes of it: (1) competition and monopoly in healthcare and health insurance markets, (2) the sobering story about efforts for cost containment (so far), (3) markets for prescription drugs, and (4) the impact of social determinants on the level of and disparities in health outcomes for the American population.

This will cover most of the known universe in healthcare, I believe – at least the parts of it that economics can illuminate. I close with hopefully sage observations on how to manage in an economic-constrained healthcare world. I admit to having an economist's affection for markets as a way of deciding who should get what – as opposed to politics – but I try to be fair in indicating when markets fail. In those cases, I offer advice to managers on how to cope gracefully and also some thoughts to policymakers on how to clean up the bad situation or prevent it from happening in the first place. I make the humble assumption that the goal of any health system ought to be to supply those services whose health benefits are worth their cost – and not ones that are worth less. This is sometimes dangerous if you face someone who wants to ignore cost; the economist Code of Conduct does not allow me to do that, but I try to show how to do the best you can when doing more for health uses up resources that could be devoted to other things that people value. I hope you will be kind in interpreting my well-intentioned remarks.

In what follows, I offer two kinds of insights from economics applied to healthcare. One type is a positive or descriptive analysis of what we think agents will do when faced with changes. For example, if a large fee-for-service insurer reduces what it pays a provider of that service, what will the response be – less of the service because it is now less lucrative or more of the service (and all other services) to make up for the lost income? The same issue arises if the seller can set prices for some buyers but must take what it can get from others: If Medicaid pays a hospital less than before, will the hospital change prices (in which direction) to its commercial network partners – will it reduce prices to bring in more of their profitable business or increase prices to make a smaller amount of business more profitable? Can a drug firm with a popular patented product increase its prices whenever it chooses? If so, why would it not do so?

The other type of analysis is normative or prescriptive: Is some change a good idea from the viewpoint of economic welfare? Although we economists are especially good at making the concept of welfare confusing, I will try to take the applied approach and ask whether the change is likely to do more good than harm overall – and if so, is there a way to distribute those benefits and costs to make everyone better off?

In the book, I cite Plato (I majored in classical Greek in college; don't ask why) who hypothesized that we humans know everything at birth and life is just a process of remembering what we forgot. As a professor, I am used to playing the absent-minded role. Plato or not, I know that much of what I now know, and all the questions I still wonder about, came not from me but from others who have helped me – first of all my students, then my colleagues, and then my tolerant friends and family. For this book, I had the great good fortune to sign up two graduate students in health economics, Alejandra Benitez and

Aidan Crowley, who helped me to remember what I was trying to say, but even more importantly contributed their own ideas, knowledge of the literature, and criticism to help make what is here much better than I could have done on my own. I also owe boundless thanks to my assistant Tina Horowitz who has had to put up with a lot and always makes things better.

I am also very grateful for helpful comments on parts of the early drafts from Claudio Lucarelli, Rob Burns, Guy David, Atheendar Venkataramani, Jeff Goldsmith, Richard Scheffler, Lou Garrison, Bill Comanor, Kate Bundorf, Mary Naylor, Roger Feldman, and Richard Frank. I paid attention to their advice, even when (especially when) we disagreed.

1 Management Mission Impossible

My Care Is Okay, but the System Is Broken

Americans have a layered perception of the country's medical care system, and the layers do not align. At base, their view of their own care in terms of quality, convenience, and consumer sensitivity is good: They generally like physicians and other health professionals who care for them, view the hospitals they use as satisfactory most of the time, and feel they can get care when they really need it. If we overlay this perception of individual satisfaction with the map of insurance arrangements, verdicts become somewhat darker. Consumers are not ecstatic about private insurance coverage or about the behavior of private insurance companies or their employers who generally determine those options.[1] There is still a preponderance of sentiment for having choice among different private plans rather than a single payer, though this preference is strongly influenced by political affiliation. The best one could say about the private insurance system is that it is generally decent if sometimes maddening. For the Medicare program that covers the elderly and disabled, feelings are generally more positive, but behavior suggests that most people are uncomfortable with the original government Medicare plan from 1966. They almost all modify it either by purchasing private Medigap insurance to cover cost-sharing or by opting for private Medicare Advantage plans with better coverage and lower cost.[2] Seniors love Medicare, but not enough to accept it on its own terms; they supplement, trim, and add private options. Finally, there is a third layer of perception of the American health system which is unfavorable. The system is regarded as both excessively costly and especially ineffective in improving the health of the population, especially (but not only) lower-income people and minorities. It is also regarded as unfair to lower-income people and to

[1] "Americans sour on U.S. healthcare quality." Gallup Poll Social Series: Health and Healthcare. (2023). Gallup News Service. https://news.gallup.com/poll/468176/americans-sour-healthcare-quality.aspx.

[2] Freed, M., Biniek, J. F., Damico, A., & Neuman, T. (2023). *Medicare advantage in 2023: Enrollment update and key trends.* Kaiser Family Foundation. www.kff.org/medicare/issue-brief/medicare-advantage-in-2024-enrollment-update-and-key-trends/.

those with above-average health risks. Compared to what would please people evaluating system performance for political choices, the system costs too much and does too little that is effective.

My goal in this chapter is to present an economically correct and clear picture of the system, both what we know and what we do not know. The system, I will argue, has substantial benefits as well as costs compared to the past or compared to no care. It is surely not ideal, but there is no rigorous theory and evidence on what would improve it – and "improve" itself is a subjective judgment on which so far there is no consensus. I also offer advice to those who work within it about how they can defend or at least provide reasons (but not excuses) for what happens.

The most fundamental issue is whether there is some alternative system or some set of adjustments to the current system that would do more additional good than additional harm. Be forewarned, economics will neither fuel outrage nor offer unstinting praise, in large part because the alternatives people talk about are either hypothetical or oversold. Identifying bulletproof measures of additional benefits and costs (which is what economists are supposed to be good at doing) not surprisingly turns out to be complicated, and not as yet capable of a final verdict – not even on which direction to go, much less on how far to go in some direction. But we can identify the places where there is evidence of a potential for improvement, and we can offer advice to managers (the point of this book) about the prospects and the tasks that might lead to gains.

Who Cares about Cost?

The economic perspective imagines that a good or efficient outcome is a situation in which all actions (producing a good or service, having a given person consume that good or service) which yield benefits greater than their cost should be undertaken, and no actions which yield cost greater than their benefits should be undertaken. This idea is the essence of the notion that all care which is cost-effective should be rendered, and no care should be supplied which is not cost-effective. To make this a little more concrete, imagine there is a given set of resources available to a population, and these resources (smart people, land, and physical capital) can be used to produce medical services which people value but also other things that people value. If a decision is made to divert some of those resources to medical services, what those diverted resources could have done elsewhere is, in a fundamental sense, the cost of the medical services. The diverted resources can be converted into a cash measure by attaching a dollar value to their use in the alternative to medical services. If we think the other use (call it "making good stuff") has a value per unit of $1 and that it takes one unit of resources to make one unit of stuff, we will have a dollar measure of the true cost of medical services.

This abstract discussion makes two important points. One is that the economic cost of anything is its value (measured by some metric) in its next best use – this is called "opportunity cost." The other is that if an economy is currently at some level of production of medical services, it will be a good thing for medical costs to be increased from that point if the value of medical services is greater than the opportunity cost – the benefits foregone from the other use. The system should be cost-effective.

The last point means that there is no special reason to want to have low-cost medical services; it all depends on what you get for the money. It also means that using medical services to improve health outcomes or consumer satisfaction needs to provide not just positive benefits but benefits larger than their opportunity cost. Some beneficial care will be foregone in an efficient outcome – but those who might have benefited from it may complain.

What Managers Should Say: Take One

This last point is the key for managers who need to respond to general claims about high or out-of-control medical spending. The first step is to change the conversation away from spending or cost per se and talk about value for money. In any other industry, rising revenues (and their usual complements, rising employment and rising profits) are regarded as a good thing, contributing to GDP growth and increasing opportunities for good investment. In healthcare, rising spending in and of itself is not necessarily a bad thing – it is bad only if it is not accompanied by a concomitant rise in what we are getting for that spending. But rising medical spending is almost always felt to be a bad thing.

The positive if theoretical economic view has some evidence behind it. Studies show that, despite their cost, innovations in pharmaceuticals have added high-value health outcomes for the American (and the global) population. Macro studies show that rising real incomes will prompt consumers to spend much of the increment on improvements in health that are worth it to them.[3] They will not, in the modern era, want to spend on more potatoes or more salt (or even that much more meat). And relatively high US medical care spending has not so far been shown to deter either economic growth or beneficial international trade.

One implication of this economic view is that the indicator of the performance of or burden from a country's health system most often cited by journalists and others, the fraction of GDP spent on medical care, is one of the most misleading measures ever developed. For one thing, if people in healthcare muddle through this year just like they did last year, but GDP tanks, the burden measure will leap but with no blame owed to the healthcare sector. More seriously, without knowing the value of whatever improvements in healthcare that are associated with an increase in spending, and without knowing the value of other parts of GDP that might have been displaced, you cannot even tell from changes in this measure if things are getting better or worse.

There is, it should be obvious, no intrinsic merit in slow growth of medical spending – it all depends on how much good the growth does. That is, evaluation depends on value. It is ironic that an organization created to lobby for better value and measurement of value in healthcare – "The Health Care Transformation Task Force," with representation from major insurers and other worthy groups – has as one of its missions making sure that "the growth in health care costs should ideally be at or below the growth of GDP."[4] What if somebody invents something costly that cures cancer? Perhaps only economists have a basis for saying that cost should not be the highest priority.

What about Other Countries?

A common topic of discussion compares the American healthcare and insurance system with those in other countries.[5] If the US and the UK are two countries linked only by a common language, matching the US against Singapore or Spain is even harder; culture matters. Still, in anticipation of

[3] Hall, R. E., & Jones, C. I. (2007). The value of life and the rise in health spending. *The Quarterly Journal of Economics*, *122*(1), 39–72.

[4] Guiding principles. Health Care Transformation Task Force. https://hcttf.org/about-us/guiding-principles/.

[5] Emanuel, E. J. (2020). *Which country has the world's best health care?* Hachette UK; Reid, T. R. (2010). *The healing of America: A global quest for better, cheaper, and fairer health care.* Penguin.

what we will be able to say with some confidence in the following chapters, here is my opinion about variation in spending and its causes after several decades of exploring many systems: To begin with, the share of this country's labor resources used to provide medical care in the US is about the same as in the Scandinavian countries, Germany, France, and Australia, but larger than in the rest of Europe. From that pool of inputs, medical care in the US does not displace a larger share than in many other countries. (I will explain why spending varies so much more in Box 1.1.) Differences in health outcomes across middle-class countries are not large and are not explainable by differences in their healthcare delivery or financing systems; culture matters, and poverty kills. So do racism and the uneven distribution of wealth, a more serious issue in the US than in most other developed countries. Still, we can come away with some nuggets from comparisons: We will know that many different arrangements are possible and that the main difference in spending or outcomes depends on income. Beyond that, we will see what we can see.

Box 1.1 Theory: How to use exchange rates to correct cross-national comparisons of medical care spending

It is widely believed that US healthcare expenditures per capita are higher than those anywhere else in the world, even compared to other developed countries. But how do we know that? We know what spending per capita is in the US; it was $11,600 in 2019, the most recent pre-Covid year for which we have data on a large sample of countries. Take Japan as a comparator. For the same year, we know that healthcare spending per capita in Japan was about 660,000 Japanese yen. Obviously, we cannot compare yen to US dollars. To do that, we need an exchange rate – how many yen are equivalent in purchasing power to $1?

The easy way to do this would be to use the published rate, averaged over the year, at which yen could be bought with or sold for dollars – approximately what you would see as a tourist if you exchanged your greenbacks for yen (minus commission). Economists do not do it the easy way, because this "spot" exchange rate bounces around and can be affected by the monetary authorities in different countries – their interest rate policies, their accommodation to government budget deficits, and so on – which have nothing to do with healthcare. Instead, what is usually used is the "purchasing power parity" (PPP) exchange rate. That is supposed to reflect (averaged over a year) what it would cost to purchase a typical basket of goods and services in one country compared to another.

If the hypothetical basket cost $1 in the US and 150 yen in Japan, the PPP exchange rate would be $1 = 150 yen – or each yen is worth 2/3 of a cent. That is what is used to convert Japanese healthcare spending in yen into dollars, and the conclusion is that such spending per capita in Japan is much lower (at $4,400 per capita using this figure) than in the US. The PPP standard is sometimes called the "Big Mac" standard because, both in theory and in practice, it is pretty close to the comparison of what it costs to buy a hamburger and fries in the currency of most countries – and a hamburger is a hamburger. (As I write this, the cost of a Big Mac in Japan is about 600 yen – equivalent to a little over $4 at the round number of 150 yen per dollar, a pretty good deal given recent US food inflation. If you are going to order carry out, you might prefer to order from the Osaka branch, but then you would really have to wait and pay a big tip for Door Dash.)

However, a hamburger is not a doctor visit, a hospital admission, or a bottle of pills. This uncontroversial observation matters if the relative price of healthcare (compared to a Big Mac meal) is different in the countries you are trying to compare. The problem is that, as far as we can tell, in most countries, healthcare is priced much lower relative to a hamburger meal or a basket of goods than in the US. If you had to pay for a doctor visit in the US, you would have to give up many more Big Macs than in Japan. You might have to give up 20 Big Macs in the US – which would translate into 3,000 yen at the Big Mac rate – but only 10 hamburgers in Japan, which would cut the yen price in half. So, if we translate the yen price of healthcare in Japan using the healthcare PPP rate (75) rather than the usual Big Mac rate (150), we will get a much higher number of dollars.

I picked Japan because by the usual PPP measure it has a much lower level of spending than in the US and because it also has very low medical care prices relative to other prices in Japan (such as apartment rent or even food). Using the medical care rather than the all-commodities exchange rate, Chris Conover has shown that the dollar measure of medical spending in Japan is approximately doubled, from 38% to 75% of US spending per capita.[6]

If you are a manager, you can at least use this argument to confuse your critics. It is a more technically correct version of the slogan, "It's the prices, stupid": Medical spending is higher in the US because we pay doctors, hospitals and their employees, and drug companies more for comparable products than other countries do. Later in this book I will offer what economists think are some of the reasons why.

What Managers Can Say: Take Two

This is supposed to be enough economic theory to move critics away from useless cross-country comparisons. But within the US, medical spending has been rising, in most years more rapidly than GDP. So how can a manager defend an industry that absorbs an ever-larger share of spending? Zoological insults abound: "you are custodians of a rathole down which unlimited resources are being poured, feeding the tapeworm that is eating away at our international competitiveness." The most fundamental (though not the snappiest) comeback has already been proffered: Look at the benefits from better healthcare and tell me they aren't worth the money. Then there is

6 Conover, C. J. (2012). *The American health economy illustrated.* American Enterprise Institute (AEI) Press.

a divide and conquer strategy: Much of the growing spending represents higher payments to workers in healthcare – do you begrudge nurses their raises? That still leaves out some suppliers who are viewed less favorably: the owners of drug firm stock or your friendly neighborhood urologist (though they are mostly Americans too).

But these ripostes do not answer the feeling that almost if not all of the progress in health outcomes could be achieved at lower cost, and not all of those groups who have collected more money deserve it. At this point we can at least get down to cases – what can practically be done to remove waste and excessive payments, or (the mirror image of healthcare costs) to cut health worker wages, jobs, and wage growth – if that is what you want to do? I would argue that there is not a long list of practical changes, and most of the items on the usual list are a little soft in terms of evidence of mattering enough to matter. Chapter 13 deals with this issue in more detail, but the best summary here is that controlling medical spending or its growth is a challenge, not something easy to do right before your very eyes; it is a challenge to find something that will reduce inefficiency in ways guaranteed to do more good than harm. That discovery process is what we try to do every day, and we even use economics to help guide us. Then take your lumps.

What Managers Should Do

The purpose of this book is to help managers address economic challenges that occur in this environment by offering insights from health and medical economics research – and the economic view of the world in general. My argument is that economic problems require economic solutions (rather than slogans or outrage). Not all challenges that arise from the current environment can be addressed, but many can – and knowledge of which others are still open cases can help managers avoid jumping into action too soon or seeming too defensive. It is sometimes said that the US healthcare system is a nonsystem; it is also sometimes said it is a system perfectly crafted (by someone) to produce the outcomes it does. The second observation is closer to the truth but fails to recognize that systemic relationships can and do develop organically. There always is an invisible hand – though sometimes it can be all thumbs. But tracing these relationships to their consequences and then back to their causes is what economists are supposed to be good at doing, so I will offer up what we have so far, in the hope that it can both explain and guide.

My approach here differs from the usual books that explain health economics, mostly to economists or economics students. They do not tell managers things they did not already know – while my hope is to do just that. Most of management, everybody knows, is a combination of personal attention and common sense; I am going to assume my readers already have that. What I can add is both theory and evidence from health economics, which tells you things beyond (or counter to) common sense (and surely beyond the much-maligned conventional wisdom). Some points are counterintuitive – cost-shifting cannot happen in a world of profit-maximizing firms, better health insurance is not always good for you, nonprofit hospitals are no different from investor-owned ones. Often the message is counsel of caution when what people need to know to make the best decisions does not exist (despite widely accepted conclusions), so you need to hedge your bets. And sometimes economics does agree with common sense even when it is uncomfortable to say so (e.g., physicians perform differently based on economic incentives).

My hope is to supply punchlines that not only are clear (hard for an economist) but that also pay off for managers in terms of insights they would not otherwise have, assumptions they would otherwise make, and conclusions that might otherwise follow the crowd. I am not bold enough to imagine that this book will be a version of *Freakonomics* meets health economics, but I do hope to surprise a little, reassure some, and warn a lot.[7]

The most fundamental idea in welfare economics is that the best situation in any part of the economy is for activity to be carried to the point where the benefit from doing more of it just equals the cost of doing so. The mantra in economics is that "marginal benefit should equal marginal cost." This is common sense personified and simplified: If you can get more benefit than cost by doing more of something, you should do more of it – whereas if you get positive benefit but it is less than cost, you should do less. Obviously doing less, or stopping altogether, is what you should do if you get zero or negative benefit (harm) from more of some activity.

This self-evident truth has actually gotten a lot of play in health economics. As a theoretical concept, one can think of an economy starting with no resources devoted to healthcare and adding more. Up to a point, the improved health from doing so will be large enough to cover the cost, but

[7] Levitt, S. D., & Dubner, S. J. (2005). *Freakonomics: A rogue economist explores the hidden side of everything*. William Morrow & Co.

there will eventually (and often quickly) be diminishing returns, so marginal benefit (though positive) falls as more is done. Beyond some point, more resources devoted to care may do almost no good for the health of the population getting them – this is the famous law of diminishing returns, rechristened for health economics as "flat of the curve" (that plots health outcomes as a function of inputs) before going over the top and hitting the range where excess care actually can make people sick. Where to stop adding inputs (say, to improve the quality of care)? Not at the top or flat where more inputs have a cost but do little good, but at a lower level of spending where the additional health benefit is just worth the additional real resource cost. For most services we do not need this belaboring of common sense, but for health care we need an antidote to slogans like "the best possible health outcomes" – and this is it.

One reason why this idea has gotten so much play is partly because many observers feel that, as a whole, the US healthcare system may be at the flat of the curve, where more spent on care does almost no good. What has gotten less play among the general public (though well known to economists) is that an ideal system should stop adding resources well before the flat of the curve is reached. The awkward implication of this conclusion is that it is not economically efficient for a system to maximize health – precisely because the maximum (the peak of the mountain) occurs, as any climber can tell you, at the top where it is flat. The same kind of debunking applies to slogans about the "maximum possible quality of care" or the "maximum prevention of disease." All are foolish goals.

You can make even more trouble with economics. Another implication of what has just been said is that there are bound to be situations in which more care has positive health benefits, but not enough of such benefits to justify its cost. People talk about "necessary" care as if they knew what it meant – but is care of positive benefit but high cost "unnecessary"? Economics abhors the concept of "need": We think that people should get what they want, not just what they need. For many goods and services there are unequivocally better versions that just are not worth their cost to most people – and we do not fault them for walking away. If I do not add the lane change assist option on my new car, I will be at greater health risk but too high a cost can be a good excuse. We have a harder time living with the conclusion that even in healthcare some good must be left undone.

Managers generally have a keen awareness that some things are good but not worth doing. Healthcare managers have the difficult challenge of explaining that this is sometimes the case for what they manage. It is hard to find graceful language to explain why – and economists are no help with soothing words here. Sometimes you just have to say "no" and brace for the incoming. A little good news: This is not the case for most healthcare interventions, so managers need not worry about continuous complaints. But there will be some.

Getting Down to Brass Tacks and Real Inputs: Where Are All Our Smart Young People Going?

Healthcare is a labor-intensive industry; hospitals and physician practices employ many people, and even some things purchased from the outside (like clean hospital bedding) primarily use labor to produce them. Producing healthcare services does not require high heat, huge machines, or smoking chimneys. Because prices and wages vary so much over time, across the US, and across countries, rather than use that nasty percentage of GDP statistic, it is more realistic to think of the percentage of the workforce going into healthcare. Obviously, someone who works in a clinic when they could have taught in a school, sold shoes, or worked as a cook deprives the economy of the value of whatever else they might have done. The Organisation for Economic Co-operation and Development (OECD) collects data on the workforce in healthcare in different countries. That data is a little soft; the healthcare share of Sweden's workforce dropped dramatically when the government moved nursing homes from the healthcare to the housing sector in the national accounts – and Italy only counted people who worked in government hospitals. Still, what Exhibit 1.1 shows is that the US healthcare workforce share has been growing over time but is still lower than some of the other countries; our healthcare labor "cost" is not the highest in the world. The reason why our cost is the highest is

Exhibit 1.1 Percentages of labor force in medical care, 1993 and 2004

	Physicians		Nurses		Total health employment	
	1993	2004	1993	2004	1993	2004
US	0.42	0.47	1.51	1.53	6.6	7.5
Canada	0.43	0.40	2.23	NA	7.3	7.5
France	0.73	0.74	1.32	1.65	6.9	7.1
UK	0.35	0.47	1.66	1.87	5.7	6.8
Switzerland	0.51	0.64	NA	2.40	8.8 (1995)	9.9
Norway	0.53	0.68	NA	2.90	NA	10.6

that US healthcare wages (not just the wages of physician specialists) are both high relative to other countries and high relative to the average wage in the US – compared to that ratio in other countries. The reason is, in the first instance, higher prices here, but those prices largely support higher wages – especially in the production of medical services (rather than devices and drugs).

So, if managers succeeded in reducing real healthcare costs, they would have to fire many workers – or let them leave voluntarily – and these workers would get other jobs elsewhere in the economy, doing things of greater value than what they had been doing in their healthcare jobs. That is what economic theory would say, but I personally would not try to prove that their alternative job was more valuable than healthcare – what if they became lawyers? More seriously, analysis shows that the growth in health employment in the US was largely matched by shrinkage in manufacturing employment over time – not from other service industries.[8] Did those workers who laid down their hammer and picked up their stethoscope (metaphorically speaking) jump into healthcare, or were they pushed by the hollowing out of US manufacturing employment caused by higher productivity and foreign competition? Far from depleting the manufacturing sector in the US by attracting away its workforce, the medical care sector probably provided them with a new home when foreign competition reduced the demand for their products. Had it not been for growth in good healthcare jobs, the Great Recession of 2008–10 would have had a much more harmful effect on total employment and wages for labor. No final verdict can be rendered on how these changes all worked out (compared to some other scenario) but it is clear that the "burden of healthcare costs" on the US economy is easy to overstate.

The Limits of Economics

Compared to critical views of the US healthcare sector as a drain on the economy and the welfare of citizens, health economics can offer some consolation. The true cost of medical services and goods provided has not been proven to be an unsustainable burden on the economy. The international comparisons of spending per capita (in dollars converted at the PPP exchange rate or relative to GDP) use an estimate for the US that is significantly biased upward – all because our medical prices and health

[8] Pauly, M. V., & Saxena, A. (2012). Health employment, medical spending, and long-term health reform. *CESifo Economic Studies*, *58*(1), 49–72.

worker wages are higher than elsewhere in the world. We could have costs relative to GDP like those of western Europe if we chose to pay not only doctors but other healthcare workers less. (The greater governmental control of healthcare in those countries permits the government to force down wages for workers in the sector.) From the viewpoint of economics, the relative burden of US medical care is much lower than comparative spending data suggests – and almost all of the difference represents payments to our fellow Americans. In their role as custodians of scarce resources, managers do not have to be so embarrassed.

These soothing words apply to marginal cost, but what about marginal benefit? The relatively poor health outcomes in the US suggest that the effectiveness of care delivered here is not high – and managers have some responsibility too, though the blame also rests on clinicians. The full answer is more to a question of epidemiological causation; the cross-national data is certainly consistent with the hypothesis that the health productivity of US medical care compares unfavorably with that in other countries – but they do not prove it. This is not primarily an economic issue, although (as we will see in this book) economists have used their statistical techniques to illuminate it.

The most obvious thing to say about the cause is that health outcomes depend on much more than formal medical care use. They are affected by socioeconomic deprivation, which can influence citizen lifestyle behaviors that also can have a large effect on health outcomes. I will deal with this issue in more detail in Chapter 15 on the social determinants of health. For the present, it is enough to note that the aggregate health outcomes in any country (such as mortality) are affected by the level and distribution of resources across various segments of the population – beyond some point more resources cannot make you immortal, but few resources can shorten your life. Both the more uneven distribution of income and wealth in the US and the stronger effects of race-related disparities cause worse health outcomes than in more homogeneous countries. The role of medical care in alleviating these disparities, even if it was taken as a positive goal in the US, has to be limited. Not all data is adverse; middle-aged men live longer in Minnesota than across the border in Manitoba, evidence either that the Canadian healthcare system is inferior to the system in some parts of the US or that much more is going on. Whatever the resolution of this question, there is no proof in the data that managers in the US are responsible for overall health outcomes. The absence of proof does not let them off the hook, but it does mean that more research is needed.

What to Say about Healthcare Spending: Past, Present, and Future

We are used to confronting a dystopian vision of "out of control" medical spending. There is a reason for that. Using the journalist-favored measure of national health expenditures as a share of GDP, that metric has increased substantially over the last 50 years, from about 7% in 1974 (which President Nixon declared to be unsustainably high) to about 17% in 2023. For reasons which no one (including yours truly) understands, the share took a big jump after 1980,[9] as spending outpaced GDP growth thereafter by about 2%, year in and year out for decades. However, this horror story is old news; it is no longer true. The healthcare share in 2022 at 17.3% of GDP was actually lower than the recession-affected 2010 share of 17.9%. There have been some bumps since then – in 2016 when the expensive but curative treatment for hepatitis C came online, and in the COVID year of 2020 when the economy and GDP tanked, health services use actually fell but the government flooded the sector with bailout money.

Things apparently have changed lately from the old gloomy story. It is always dangerous to predict, especially about the future, but more than 10 years of stability suggest that things may have stabilized at about a 17%–18% share, still higher than anywhere else in the world but no longer growing. Here again we do not know why. We can narrate the developments – drug spending actually fell in the early 2010s as new introductions fell, physician real incomes have been falling, both Medicare and Medicaid now tell hospitals how much they will pay rather than pay what a hospital's charges or costs are, and higher deductible insurance grew. Perhaps as healthcare spending rose, in line with economic theory, citizens noted it was biting more and more into what they could spend on other things, and so as private insurance purchasers and as taxpayers for public insurance, they decided "Enough!" and conveyed that message in a subtle way. Perhaps managers actually helped.

In what follows I offer some insights on pockets of success in lowering the level of cost. I also preach the message of needing evidence of effectiveness before going ahead with new spending. I am an optimist about this sector: I think it has reached a stable level where it can support a reasonable flow of effective new treatments and other ways to improve quality of care. I am even optimistic that the adverse social determinants of health, surely one of the

[9] Frakt, A. (2018). Medical mystery: Something happened to US health spending after 1980. *New York Times*, May 14.

main causes of poor health outcomes in the US, can finally be addressed, although doing so will require effort from agents in addition to healthcare managers. There have been (as there will doubtless continue to be) disappointments as changes which sound good do not work. Read on for an overall bright picture about what economics advises can be done to hold our own and move forward.

2 Ideal Decisions with and about Evidence

The ancient Greek philosopher Plato, as noted in the Preface, believed that we do not really learn anything; instead, we gradually remember concepts embedded in our spirit before we are born. He had in mind concepts such as "justice" or "equality," but he might have said that, when it comes to good methods for making decisions, learning comes from remembering what we already knew about how best to make informed choices. So it is with adult decision-making (though usually better than our more impulsive two-year-old selves): We have built-in ideas about how to choose important things, such as where to go to school, whom to marry, and what career to pursue. In healthcare management especially (but also in almost any other job), the greatest challenge often is how to decide among several courses of action to deal with a problem. In this chapter, I will first go up the ivory tower and talk about what economists and decision scientists (who chose careers to study people making choices) have said about those choices, especially with regard to how to use evidence (broadly defined) you already have but also how to decide whether to go with what you know or seek further evidence. Much of what I will say about rational decision-making you probably will not find surprising. However, you may find it surprising that, coming down from the ivory tower, there is good evidence that managers often do not decide in this rational way and so fail to make the best bets that lead to the best outcomes on average for themselves and their organizations. Often a little bit of thinking before you leap (along the lines of what we will discuss) is itself a good decision.

Managerial Decision-Making, in General and in Healthcare

Perhaps unsurprisingly, business school researchers have studied (and second-guessed) the decisions of managers and leaders of large firms and organizations.[1] The general conclusion is that managers rely too little on external evidence and too much on their own experiences (especially more recent ones), as well as on the logical appeal of the argument that the chosen intervention should make a difference in the expected direction.[2] As well, decisions often depend on poorly remembered experiences or just on events which had the best (or sometimes the worst) outcomes.[3]

For example, research on healthcare manager decision-making does not find that managers with more recent experience make decisions with better outcomes than those who have less recent experience. This is because managers fixate on recent extreme outcomes (disasters or triumphs) rather than more run-of-the-mill causes and effects, a phenomenon known as "availability bias."[4] Reliance on experience or feelings (whether in the gut or the seat of the pants) does not seem to produce on average as good a set of outcomes compared to an alternative which I will outline.

That alternative, it should come as no surprise, will be one that conditions decisions (about whether or not to proceed with an intervention) on evidence broader than a manager's remembered recent experiences. Management treatises say that the way to proceed is to "use the best evidence available." However, this nostrum is not very useful without some way to judge what evidence is "best" and what "available" means. Most people know that an expectation based on one example is less good than predicting outcomes from multiple settings or experiences; there is safety in numbers. They also know that "available" means more than what is on your or your staff's desk at the moment; evidence must be gathered or dug out of sources in some way. But how much, and when should you stop digging and start doing?

The idea that decisions should be based on evidence is a cliché that nevertheless has caught fire in public policy and some management circles. If you don't use evidence for some decision, you are already judged to be in

[1] Raiffa, H., & Keeney, R. L. (1975). Decision analysis with multiple conflicting objectives, preferences and value tradeoffs. IASA Working Paper. WP-75-053; Meltzer, D. O., Hoomans, T., Chung, J. W., & Basu, A. (2011). Minimal modeling approaches to value of information analysis for health research. *Medical Decision Making, 31*(6), E1–E22.

[2] Perkins, W. S., & Rao, R. C. (1990). The role of experience information use and decision making by marketing managers. *Journal of Marketing Research, 27*(1), 1–10. https://doi.org/10.1177/002224379002700101; Pauly, M., Winston, F., Naylor, M., Volpp, K., Burns, L. R., Muller, R., . . . & Chartock, B. (2022). *Seemed like a good idea: Alchemy versus evidence-based approaches to healthcare management innovation.* Cambridge University Press.

[3] Tversky, A., & Kahneman, D. (1973). Availability: A heuristic for judging frequency and probability. *Cognitive Psychology, 5*(2), 207–232; Ludvig, E. A., Madan, C. R., & Spetch, M. L. (2014). Extreme outcomes sway risky decisions from experience. *Journal of Behavioral Decision Making, 27*(2), 146–156.

[4] Kahneman, D. (2013). *Thinking, fast and slow.* First paperback edition. Farrar, Straus and Giroux.

error. In healthcare this idea got its first push from "evidence-based medicine" (EBM).[5] The problem clinicians faced was that in a large number of cases, different physicians were treating similar patients with similar diseases in different ways. This fact was awkward, to say the least, for physicians who wanted to claim superior knowledge on how to treat disease effectively. If they could not agree on how to treat something, how effective could any treatment be? Variation was the bad guy here – if different doctors are doing different things, how can they pretend to know what they are doing? Evidence was supposed to be summarized and gathered to settle on the one best way to treat. The EBM movement was both a revolt against medical experts (the med school professors) who wrote textbooks on their views on how to treat that came to different conclusions because they had different views (rather than evidence) and a plea for a more knowledge-based set of uniform protocols about what to do in a given clinical situation.

The movement did make some clinical headway and led to some useful studies that sometimes settled things (though not always). It also helped to avoid embarrassment: If physicians cannot agree on how to treat some condition, why should patients pay for treatment at all?[6] However, the fundamental reason why practice varied was usually because the evidence was absent or inconclusive – so it could not logically yield support for one particular course of action. What was needed was better evidence. Sometimes this was the solution, but often there was a drive toward consensus even though evidence was imperfect. To this day, the promise of EBM remains brighter than evidence on the effectiveness of EBM would suggest.

More to our point, the EBM movement led to envy on the parts of management researchers. We scholars of how to manage likewise did not have a uniform evidence base for what we advised managers.[7] Advice was either conflicting (pay this way! pay that way!) or anodyne (do what is best on the one hand or on the other). Could health managers and managers in general be more "scientific" in basing their advice and conclusions on evidence, and be apologetic when they could not?

The idea of evidence-based interventions took strongest hold in governmental settings and programs. At a minimum, the leaders started to say,

[5] Sackett, D. L., Rosenberg, W. M., Gray, J. M., Haynes, R. B., & Richardson, W. S. (1996). Evidence based medicine: What it is and what it isn't. *BMJ*, *312*(7023), 71–72.

[6] Pauly, M., Winston, F., Naylor, M., Volpp, K., Burns, L. R., Muller, R., . . . & Chartock, B. (2022). *Seemed like a good idea: Alchemy versus evidence-based approaches to healthcare management innovation*. Cambridge University Press.

[7] Pfeffer, J., & Sutton, R. I. (2006). Evidence-based management. *Harvard Business Review*, *84*(1), 62. https://hbr.org/2006/01/evidence-based-management.

costly programs should be required to gather evidence on whether or not they made a difference. Cass Sunstein, the administrator of the White House Office of Information and Regulatory Affairs in the Obama administration, argued strongly for this approach and was proud that the administration implemented it on his watch.[8] Ron Haskins, who wrote the welfare reform bill, and Greg Margolis, his research assistant, published a history of the Obama initiatives in a book titled *Show me the evidence.*[9] This movement meant that managers in the public and private sectors who wished to be in step with public policy needed in some way to clear their decisions with the "Evidence Police."

We therefore have two polar models of decision-making from which to choose. One is the informal evidence/anatomical "gut feeling" model and the other is the heavily documented and reviewed evidence-based model. If you are a modern manager attentive to the public good, which way should you go? It turns out that there is a theory that allows a middle road between these two (caricatured) extremes that I will now present.

Going with What You Ought to Find Out

Here is one way researchers answer this imponderable question. They begin by imagining that you, the decision-maker, have some prior belief about the probability that the action you are contemplating will do more good than harm – if it weren't for its bad reputation, we would call this your initial "gut feeling." If you only used that information, and you have to make a choice now, you will decide on some action or inaction. The question really is how confident you are that your best choice based on your current feelings and knowledge is really the best. One way to answer this question is to decide whether there is key information or evidence you currently do not have which could reverse your choice. If you guess that there is little chance of conflicting evidence, you might as well go with what you have (and there is no point in seeking evidence confirming what you would have done anyway). If on the other hand, there is some evidence, say, the result of a test or a measure of something, that could cause you to think your original preference would do much more harm than you thought, or that the alternative you were not going to do would provide much more benefit than you thought, it

8 Sunstein, C. R. (2018). *The cost-benefit revolution*. MIT Press.

9 Haskins, R., & Margolis, G. (2014). *Show me the evidence: Obama's fight for rigor and results in social policy*. Brookings Institution Press.

will be worthwhile, up to a point, to seek that evidence before going ahead. Then, once you have decided to pull together as much evidence as makes sense from this perspective, you see what it says, and, based on that, you decide what to do. You look for where the tiebreaker might be found; you look for the evidence that might prevent you from making a big mistake.

If it is helpful, you should know that behaving this way has a noble historical name – Bayes' rule – and a mathematical formulation.[10] The mathematical formulation of how to change your probability estimate based on evidence says that you adjust your initial probability *p* that a program will succeed *S* based on the observation that a metric or evidential experience takes on the value *X* based on two other probabilities: your estimate that, if you looked, you would observe X regardless (or p(X)) and your estimate of the likelihood that when you observe X, S is going to happen (or p(X given that S is true)). Having observed X, you then adjust your estimate of the probability of success by the ratio of p(X given that S is true) to p(X).

In plain English, the idea is that evidence should be sought the more uncertain you are to begin with, the better at predicting outcomes is the evidence you might find, and the greater the consequences of making a mistake in choice.

Bayes' rule and the cost of getting evidence better than what you started with tell us something important: Sometimes evidence beyond what is "available" is worth it, but sometimes it is not. The first case argues that always going with your gut feeling may not be a good idea, but the second tells you that requiring that a manager get rigorous and convincing but costly evidence for a decision (or be punished for not doing so) may not be so great either.

So, you know to stay away from either using pure visceral decision-making or waiting forever for an evidence-based and unequivocal sign. Where to settle in between all depends, as usual, on where you start and the specifics of the case. Beyond that common sense, however, I hope this excursion into theory has convinced you to consider and respect evidence and to look at (and think about) what evidence there is or could be before you decide. If you want to be noted as a critic or admired as a reviewer of decisions, it never hurts to ask what evidence there was around a decision. Did the person or people who made the decision have evidence, did they get what additional evidence they should have, and did they at least mop up afterward with new evidence on whether what they decided did more good than harm? We now provide an example of that kind of activity applied to a choice in healthcare policy.

[10] Joyce, J. (2021). Bayes' theorem. In Edward N. Zalta (ed.), *The Stanford Encyclopedia of Philosophy*. https://plato.stanford.edu/archives/fall2021/entries/bayes-theorem/.

The Value of Evidence

More often than not, just because prediction is hard, conclusive evidence is not available on the benefits and costs of some intervention which management must consider whether to start or wait to enact. The Bayesian decision model in the previous section tells you as a manager to seek evidence on the factual question which, if answered (or even given better odds), would indicate changes in behavior that help avoid the worst outcome. See Box 2.1 on the value of information in decision-making. David Meltzer, a physician and economist at the University of Chicago, has pursued this idea most vigorously.[11]

Box 2.1 Theory: The value of information

New information which tells a decision-maker what the consequences of alternative actions will be is clearly of value. If there is information that tells you what is going to happen, you pick the action that yields the highest payoff. But how much is it worth for you to find out the future? What is the demand curve for fortune telling? Here is the way economists think about this issue:

Suppose there are two mutually exclusive actions you could take whose chances of success are equally likely, as far as you now know. The payoffs if successful are inversely correlated: If the future takes on one scenario, action A will lead to the highest payoff while action B would lead to lower payoffs or losses. In the other equally likely scenario, action B will lead to higher payoffs than action A. Without information, suppose action B has a higher expected value of payoff than action A, so you would choose B if you were risk-neutral. If instead you could get information that told you for sure which scenario would happen, your payoff would be a 50–50 chance of getting the highest payoff under either scenario, a larger amount than if you just chose B. The difference between your expected payoff with perfect information and the payoff if you chose the best option is the value of information. Getting information allows you to know whether or not to go for action A in the best scenario for it and reap larger rewards than if you had taken action B. It allows you to avoid the after-the-fact mistake (and loss in payoff) of choosing B when the scenario that occurs is the one where A would be the best choice.

Exhibit 2.1 is a numerical example to explain the previous paragraph (although it seems perfectly clear to me). There are two scenarios of payoffs 1 and 2 with a 0.5 probability of happening each, and two actions A and B. With no further information, you would choose action

[11] Meltzer, D. (2001). Addressing uncertainty in medical cost-effectiveness analysis: Implications of expected utility maximization for methods to perform sensitivity analysis and the use of cost-effectiveness analysis to set priorities for medical research. *Journal of Health Economics*, *20*(1), 109–129; Basu, A., & Meltzer, D. (2007). Value of information on preference heterogeneity and individualized care. *Medical Decision Making*, *27*(2), 112–127.

B if you were risk-neutral, since it has the higher average payoff (6,750 for B vs. 5,000 for A). Suppose you could get complete information to tell you which scenario actually would happen – but you obviously have to pay for the information before you knew its content. If the information was that 1 would happen, you would choose action A, and if the information was that 2 would happen you would choose action B. Since there is a 50–50 chance that the information will say 1 or 2, the expected value with information would now be the average of 5,500 and 12,000, or 8,750. So, if you would have gone for B without information, the value of information to you would be 8,750 minus 6,750, or 2,000. (Things would be different if you were extra cautious and would have chosen action A without information; then the value of information would be even greater.) The key insight here is that you have to bet on what you think the information will tell you and then whether you will do something different with it. You will not win all good bets.

Exhibit 2.1 Expected payoffs of Actions A and B under Scenarios 1 and 2

	Scenario 1	Scenario 2	Expected payoff
Action A	5,500	4,500	5,000
Action B	1,500	12,000	6,750

The most general question for a manager is to judge the quality of evidence – either evidence already present or evidence the manager wants to see produced. In the world of statistics and epidemiology, there is a hierarchy of evidence. At the top are randomized controlled trials (RCTs), in which a policy's impact on some outcome measures is determined by randomly assigning some people to the treatment and the others to some nontreatment alternative, without telling anybody which is which. Then a statistician can attach odds (though never a guarantee) to a measure of the impact of the treatment on outcomes. Other studies that use control groups (not necessarily randomly assigned) rank lower, but there are some techniques to control for selection. Further down are before-and-after studies of a single program introduction with no control group. At the bottom of the pile are anecdotes or case studies.

One problem with this story is that it is hard to tell how much difference quality of evidence makes. If you already have before and after measures, how much more would you pay for an RCT? Bayes' theorem, previously described, answers this if you can fill in the blanks – but the hardest thing often is to determine how much of a difference to your decision better evidence would make. An RCT properly done will give you evidence of effectiveness that will only be wrong 1 in 20 times (significance level 0.05) but how much of a difference will that make compared to a before-and-after observational study (significance level unknown)? Here is one consoling thought. If you choose a program that might make no difference to outcomes, you only waste money. If you choose one that affects health outcomes, you might kill people. The best counsel obviously is to think on these things, but there is no magic 8-ball that will tell you what to do.

What Do Managers Do?

Generating top-quality evidence that intervention A definitely causes a specific outcome is a pain. Aren't there shortcuts that would save the time and money needed to conduct an RCT? Managers certainly behave as if there are. In addition to the "gut feelings" test described earlier in the chapter, there is the "wisdom of crowds" approach and the consulting firm approach (which often end up being fairly similar). In the wisdom of crowds approach, when you do not know what is best to do, you look at what other people are doing and copy them. This is how you learn to behave in fancy society. It also apparently is often used by physicians in gray area cases where there is as yet no proof. Research shows that physicians sometimes tend to copy what other physicians are doing in their town, especially when evidence is uncertain.[12] This would be fine except that some physicians in the other town are also doing what others in their town are doing – but it can be completely different from the first town.

Physician practices in areas yet to be touched by EBM often show these "similar within, different across" patterns. I think it likely that the same is true in management. After all, if you can blame others for doing the same thing you were doing that led to disaster, you can be safe (even in court). And in some circumstances, the average of individual judgments is a reasonably accurate measure of the true value.[13] However, this works best when individual agents do not talk to each other and copy each other but just guess based on their own data and experience (whatever that may be).

Another way managers get and use evidence is to obtain it from consulting firms. The problem here is somewhat similar; consultants talk to each other and usually recommend whatever is the going fashion – but they do it with

[12] Wennberg, J., & Gittelsohn, A. (1973). Small area variations in health care delivery: A population-based health information system can guide planning and regulatory decision-making. *Science, 182*(4117), 1102–1108.

[13] Fleenor, J. W. (2006). The wisdom of crowds: Why the many are smarter than the few and how collective wisdom shapes business, economics, societies and nations. *Personnel Psychology, 59*(4), 982–985.

style. They are subject to bandwagon effects (everybody is going with managed care; everybody is going with value-based pricing) even when the bandwagon takes its riders to a destination they do not prefer.

We have reviewed some consulting firm reports on a question on which we think we know the evidence well: the best way to transition patients from hospital stay to home.[14] The jury included experts on the evidence on transitional care.[15] The best evaluation of those consulting reports is that they provide "the sizzle, not the steak." That is, they present final conclusions in understandable and persuasive language and with excellent graphics. But the quality of the research summaries – or even the distinction between evidence and opinion – is lacking. Research from multiple sources (peer-reviewed journals, lobbying group white papers, and *Harvard Business Review* articles) all get the same treatment – with emphasis on the most recent not necessarily the best or most thoughtful design.

When we looked at such reports on better ways to facilitate the transition of high-risk Medicare patients from a hospital stay back to home, we judged the evaluation to be superficial, not discriminating between plans with stronger and weaker evidence or designs (e.g., RCTs and before-and-after studies were treated as equally valid). They failed to answer the key questions: the business case for particular versions of these interventions. Box 2.2 presents a real healthcare example that shows the importance of having adequate evidence in decision-making.

Box 2.2 Evidence: A case study – Medicare's decision on the Hospital Readmissions Reduction Program

The political and bureaucratic entities that manage the Medicare program made a decision in 2011. Based on advice from a committee of experts on the Medicare Payment Advisory Commission (MedPAC) and others, the Department of Health and Human Services designed a program that was included in the Affordable Care Act to impose financial penalties on hospitals that had high readmission rates for Medicare patients. The goal was both to save

[14] Pauly, M., & Winston, F. (2022). Driving innovation in health care: External evidence, decision-making, and leadership. In Pauly, M., Winston, F., Naylor et al., *Seemed like a good idea: Alchemy versus evidence-based approaches to healthcare management innovation* (pp. 369–397). Cambridge University Press.

[15] Naylor, M., & Werner, R. (2022). Evidence-based programs to improve transitional care of older adults (pp. 132–160). In Pauly, M., Winston, F., Naylor et al., *Seemed like a good idea: Alchemy versus evidence-based approaches to healthcare management innovation.* Cambridge University Press.

money on balance because readmissions use up real resources (are costly) and to improve the quality of care by inducing hospitals and their doctors to get treatment right the first time.[16] The average 30-day Medicare readmission rate was about 20%, but if a hospital's readmission rate exceeded a predicted rate (based both on the average for all hospitals and then on adjustment for the clinical riskiness of their patient mix) a financial penalty was imposed.[17]

One issue was that hospitals that treated patients who were similar clinically but who were of lower socioeconomic status had higher readmission rates but were subject to the same penalties as hospitals whose Medicare patients were more middle class.[18] Even though there is some evidence that hospitals used by minorities really are lower quality than others, this aspect raised political issues. The rationale for the program, however, was that all hospitals should be providing high-quality care regardless of nonclinical patient characteristics; treating more poor patients is no excuse, and quality is quality. The financial penalties were not large for most penalized hospitals, but most hospitals were penalized because they were above average in terms of readmissions.[19]

What evidence did MedPAC, Centers for Medicare and Medicaid Services (CMS), and Congress have for the hypothesis that this program of financial penalties for Medicare readmissions would be safe and effective? Data showed considerable variation in readmission rates across hospitals, especially for serious conditions like pneumonia or heart failure, with no obvious clinical differences in the patients: Some hospitals were able to do better (or at least differently) than others.[20] There was rigorous evidence that some programs, including some on which I was a researcher, were able to reduce readmissions by using specially trained nurses to assist patients discharged after a first hospitalization.[21] Compared

[16] CMS. Hospital Readmissions Reduction Program (HRRP). www.cms.gov/medicare/payment/prospective-payment-systems/acute-inpatient-pps/hospital-readmissions-reduction-program-hrrp.

[17] MedPAC. (2007). Payment policy for inpatient readmissions. In June 2007 Report to the Congress: Promoting Greater Efficiency in Medicare. www.medpac.gov/wp-content/uploads/import_data/scrape_files/docs/default-source/reports/Jun07_Ch05.pdf; Jencks, S. F., Williams, M. V., & Coleman, E. A. (2009). Rehospitalizations among patients in the Medicare fee-for-service program. *New England Journal of Medicine*, *360*(14), 1418–1428.

[18] Barnett, M. L., Hsu, J., & McWilliams, J. M. (2015). Patient characteristics and differences in hospital readmission rates. *JAMA Internal Medicine*, *175*(11), 1803–1812; Joynt, K. E., & Jha, A. K. (2011). Who has higher readmission rates for heart failure, and why? Implications for efforts to improve care using financial incentives. *Circulation: Cardiovascular Quality and Outcomes*, *4*(1), 53–59. https://doi.org/doi:10.1161/CIRCOUTCOMES.110.950964; Joynt, K. E., & Jha, A. K. (2013). Characteristics of hospitals receiving penalties under the Hospital Readmissions Reduction Program. *JAMA*, *309*(4), 342–343.

[19] Rau, J. (2021). 10 years of hospital readmission penalties. Kaiser Family Foundation. www.kff.org/health-reform/slide/10-years-of-hospital-readmissions-penalties/; Rau, J. (2013). Armed with bigger fines, Medicare to punish 2,225 hospitals for excess readmissions. *Kaiser Health News*, August 2. http://kaiserhealthnews.org/news/readmission-penalties-medicare-hospitals-year-two/.

[20] Krumholz, H. M., Merrill, A. R., Schone, E. M., Schreiner, G. C., Chen, J., Bradley, E. H., . . . & Drye, E. E. (2009). Patterns of hospital performance in acute myocardial infarction and heart failure 30-day mortality and readmission. *Circulation: Cardiovascular Quality and Outcomes*, *2*(5), 407–413.

[21] Naylor, M., Brooten, D., Jones, R., Lavizzo-Mourey, R., Mezey, M., & Pauly, M. (1994). Comprehensive discharge planning for the hospitalized elderly: A randomized clinical trial. *Annals of internal Medicine*, *120*(12), 999–1006; Gonçalves-Bradley, D. C., Lannin, N. A., Clemson, L., Cameron, I. D., & Shepperd, S. (2022). Discharge planning from hospital. *Cochrane Database of Systematic Reviews*, *24* (2), CD000313.

to usual discharge planning, these specific programs reduced readmissions, saved on Medicare spending, did not reduce survival, and improved quality of life for patients who survived. Some expert physicians and hospital managers believed that hospitals could and should change their behavior to produce similar outcomes.

Was the decision that Medicare should put this program into effect a good one? As evidence goes for new federal programs, this evidence base was good. It was not bullet-proof, but it was reassuring. However, there was one major gap – the program assumed that financial penalties would induce managers and physicians to adopt the programs that would reduce readmissions without harm, either the ones demonstrated in the literature or others they would dream up for their own hospitals. That gap could have been closed had there been a prior demonstration or test of the specific design and financial incentives in the Medicare Readmission Reduction Program, but there was not. As a result, different hospitals used different programs, many of them home-made, and did not gravitate toward what was proved to be tried and true.

After the implementation of the Medicare program, the first results were encouraging: The national Medicare readmission rate fell by a statistically and practically significant amount, and penalized hospitals did not shut down or refuse Medicare patients.[22] They did, however, complain, especially if their patients had low socioeconomic status; their complaint was that lower patient and caregiver education and less favorable housing and transportation conditions meant that readmission often was the best option if something started to go wrong after the patient got home from the hospital – and that their more limited financial resources meant both that they could not invest in the effective programs and that lost readmissions often cost them more in revenue than the penalties they would save.

This incipient backlash was supported by evidence gathered after the program began that was negative. For one thing, the measured fall in risk-adjusted readmissions coincided with the introduction of a new way to measure risk that allowed hospitals to report their patients were sicker than before – so actual readmissions stayed more or less the same, but the risk adjusted measure fell.[23] For another thing, more patients died at home after the program who might have been readmitted and their life prolonged in the hospital; the program might have been unsafe.[24] None of this negative evidence was itself totally conclusive, but it raised concerns.

Given this scenario, we now want to consider the decisions about both program implementation and use of evidence by two classes of decision-makers: a hypothetical Medicare decision-maker and a hypothetical manager of a hospital subject to penalty. If you were the

[22] Medicare Payment Advisory Commission. (2019). Chapter 1 (revised): Mandated report: The effects of the Hospital Readmissions Reduction Program. *June 2018 report to the Congress: Medicare and the health care delivery system*; Lu, N., Huang, K. C., & Johnson, J. A. (2016). Reducing excess readmissions: Promising effect of Hospital Readmissions Reduction Program in US hospitals. *International Journal for Quality in Health Care*, *28*(1), 53–58.

[23] Ibrahim, A. M., Dimick, J. B., Sinha, S. S., Hollingsworth, J. M., Nuliyalu, U., & Ryan, A. M. (2018). Association of coded severity with readmission reduction after the Hospital Readmissions Reduction Program. *JAMA Internal Medicine*, *178*(2), 290–292.

[24] Wadhera, R. K., Joynt Maddox, K. E., Wasfy, J. H., Haneuse, S., Shen, C., & Yeh, R. W. (2018). Association of the Hospital Readmissions Reduction Program with mortality among Medicare beneficiaries hospitalized for heart failure, acute myocardial infarction, and pneumonia. *JAMA*, *320*(24), 2542–2552. https://doi.org/10.1001/jama.2018.19232.

Medicare czar, what would you have done in 2011, based only on the evidence available at the time? You were under financial pressure to find cost savings to fund the subsidies to younger people in the Affordable Care Act, the MedPAC experts said that three-quarters of readmissions were avoidable, and there was good evidence that there were cost-effective tools that could achieve cost savings in a way that both lowered cost and improved quality. So far so good. What was missing, however, was evidence that financial penalties would cause medical providers to do the right thing, as opposed to some other possibly harmful or useless way to reduce those penalties. You could have waited for a demonstration program that changed payment for a few hospitals and then see what they did compared to others on the old system. On balance, I don't know about you, but I probably would have gone ahead. Perhaps that is because my prior judgement (in the absence of evidence) is that financial incentives would move hospitals to adopt effective programs.

What if I had known beforehand about the negative results of less benefit and more potential harm that were generated after the fact? Would that have changed my decision? I don't know.

Now let us consider decision-making by a hospital or health system administrator whose hospital would be penalized. The first thing to think about is whether cutting readmissions to avoid a financial penalty would be worth it. If my hospital had a low occupancy rate and so readmissions would bring in more revenue without much additional cost, I might conclude that it is better to pay the penalty than to try to change readmissions. If the financial tea leaves went the other way, however, I would still be puzzled, since hospital administration does not directly control readmissions nor can it refuse readmissions for legitimate medical reasons. I might have figured out that by recoding all my Medicare patients' severity measures in the new way I could turn off the penalty. If not, I could send a memo to nurses and physicians affiliated with my system. I would not claim their previous pattern of decisions about readmissions had been wrong, but I would ask them to be more thoughtful about readmissions, especially when patients call with problems or come to the emergency room with them. The profit effects of readmissions might influence their decisions. A more nefarious option might be to turn away the sickest patients with the highest likelihood of readmission in the first place. I would if I had the time try to understand and possibly implement some of the effective programs described in the literature now that they became top of mind, but I would wonder if they would be guaranteed to work so well at my hospital. It would be hard because, no matter what I might contemplate doing, adequate evidence on effectiveness and safety would not exist, and timely predictions of their effects on my finances would be hard to come by.

Conclusion

What advice for managers does the economic theory of decision-making have to offer? One piece of advice is the idea that there is an accepted hierarchy of evidence on the effects of interventions in terms of reliability. Randomized controlled trials (RCTs) are at the top, and surmises based on a manager's own experience and/or appreciation of the inner logic of the intervention are at the bottom. The ranking of strength of evidence is almost perfectly but inversely matched by a ranking of cost. An RCT can take forever to plan and complete, while consulting your managerial feelings can be instantaneous. The Bayesian theory gives you a checklist of the parts to weight (and wait for): how much harm from a mistake, how predictive will the evidence be, and how much might it change what you would have done without it.

I have some advice to offer; I hope it is not too filled with bromides. One is to assemble a portfolio of evidence of various types to review and to judge according to the hierarchy. Another is not to fixate on cost or delay, or to assume that other settings are necessarily different from yours in ways that will matter. A third consideration is whether you will need evidence to back up your decision if it goes wrong.

For the rest of this book, I will try to follow my own advice: ask questions about evidence, provide evidence where it exists and highlight where it does not, and make my best guess on what it all adds up to. In some cases, there is evidence from economics that managers may not know about (I will show two such examples in the next chapter). In other cases, we can say what is out there but have to conclude that it is a gamble. But at least we can get an idea of the odds.

Summary: What Are the Poor Managers to Do?

Perhaps this chapter has overdone the obvious. It provides mostly a set of "don'ts." Don't make decisions thoughtlessly, in a hurry, based on rules of thumb, or like we always do. Don't have confidence in your ability to outguess the rest of the world (or even the market) unless you have some inside and special information. Don't think that recent good luck implies you are on a roll or that recent bad luck means you are about due. Use evidence when it makes sense, but don't be terrorized by the need for evidence-based health management.

The "dos" are the tried and true: hedge your bets and hold a diversified portfolio. Keep gains and losses in perspective and plan for the long haul. Use economics when it helps.

3 The Managerial Problem with Primary Care

Coaching the Quarterback of a Team of Cats

Introduction: Something Needs to Be Done

There has been discussion and debate for years about primary care. The health policy and organization literature imagines that there is an obvious problem with recognizing the merits of primary care in improving coordination of care and health outcomes: Primary care should play a more prominent role than it currently does. Behind this discussion is an assumption that there is some external evaluation entity whose job it is to pronounce whether one way of organizing the delivery of medical care is better than another. Typically, this body is supposed to have the "triple aim" of lowering cost, improving outcomes, and increasing access to medical care. (Sometimes a fourth aim is added: maintaining healthcare team well-being by slowing the pace of work and paying better; more on this in the section "Supply Side: The Economics of Burnout and the Pace of Work.") The ideal arrangement to achieve the triple aim often is alleged to be a new organization of physician practices in which primary care physicians have control or power over all aspects of care and especially over medical specialists, with commensurate incomes and prestige within the profession. Sometimes the discussion is also aimed at advancing equity across disadvantaged patient populations through primary care (in addition to equity across medical specialties), especially racial minorities, or based on the assumption that providers of care should be happy with their jobs. The spokes unit for this body is usually the National Academy of Medicine but sometimes the Commonwealth Fund, the Institute for Healthcare Improvement, and even the National Academies of Sciences, Engineering, and Medicine (NASEM) assume the mantle.

Of course, in the US there is no entity charged by the public with the responsibility of organizing the delivery and financing of medical care, or one given powers of enforcement. Power in our current medical care and financing system is distributed across multiple insurers (Medicare and private), delivery systems, government bodies (the Agency for Healthcare Research and Quality within the Department of Health and Human Services), and to a lesser extent professional associations such as the American Medical Association, the American College of Physicians, and the American Board of Internal Medicine. Perhaps this is why, despite boosters in high places, primary care has yet to assume a prominent role in the system. The fraction of total spending and physician spending represented by primary care has been shrinking and is just above 5%, smaller than in most other countries. The power and prominence of primary care physicians has not increased and often takes a back seat to specialist care.

In this chapter, we will identify the managers of health systems as the audience and potential immediate executor of actions to deal with primary care. We then ask, from the viewpoint of those managers, what potential changes in primary care organization or outcomes will contribute to their organizational goals, and what financial and other resources might they be able to deploy to bring about changes that they desire.

We also postulate that managers must deal with a market for what they have to sell. That means that this market, rather than some external powers-that-be, will decide what arrangement among physicians it prefers. If consumers and employers prefer a primary care–dominated model to the currently more diffuse (and less organized) setup, the ideal mentioned at the end of the first paragraph can be realized. However, at present it is quite unclear what buyers and patients now really want, or what they would really want if only they could experience it, in terms of the role of primary care. What would be preferred by most buyers in the ideal patient-directed world is a puzzle we will consider in this chapter.

What Would Be Perfect Care Coordination, and How Would It Compare with Current Patterns?

The primary care prototype for what right-thinking experts have in mind is that the driving force behind care coordination should be a regular primary care physician (with some helpers). Much like the general contractor for a house, this person should direct electricians (neurologists), plumbers (urologists), carpenters (orthopods), and other tradespeople to use their skills to assemble the parts into a coordinated, functional, attractive, and economical whole. Control is necessary, as Atul Gawande has noted.[1] Otherwise, the

[1] Gawande, A. (2009). The cost conundrum. *The New Yorker*, June 1, 36–44.

electricians will put in too many outlets and the plumbers will install gold-plated fixtures. Care coordination and control are needed, and a trusted and knowledgeable primary care physician or team of such physicians should orchestrate the activity.

One of the challenges is that not all persons need or want care coordination. People with no chronic conditions, especially young males, have little need for medical services beyond keeping their immunizations up to date. In contrast, coordination is most needed for those with multiple and complex chronic conditions. There is no bright line that separates people into two separate groups. The need for a "regular doctor" varies across patients, and it is hard for physicians to avoid driving away some independent-minded patients and bothering others. Not all people want healthcare providers to feature so prominently in their lives.

There is a different kind of tension for the chronically ill. As noted by Burns and Muller, there are multiple definitions used in policy discussions of what care coordination for this population might mean and how one could measure it if one could find it.[2] The discussion begins with the observation that such patients often obtain care from several different providers in different organizations. One main differentiation is that between primary care physicians and specialist physicians. Opinions differ (and old-fashioned hearts are breaking), but it seems inevitable that modern physician care will require more and more division of labor for chronically ill complex patients, dictated largely by the proliferation of medical knowledge that is so great that no one physician can know well and be able to perform well for all tasks for all diseases patients have.

The Norman Rockwell ideal of a kindly general practitioner (GP) who can service you from birth until death is no more. Some physicians even blame one of the patron saints of economics, Adam Smith, for developing the idea that productivity can be improved by the division of labor. [3] Of course, Smith explained this idea in the parable of the eighteenth-century pin factory where cutting, heading, and sharpening pins made them available to the masses. A key issue here is that pins have no personality or differential needs; indeed, making objects all come out the same with precisely the same dimensions as interchangeable parts was one goal of the Industrial Revolution, to the

[2] Burns, L. R., & Muller, R. W. (2008). Hospital–physician collaboration: Landscape of economic integration and impact on clinical integration. *The Milbank Quarterly*, *86*(3), 375–434.

[3] Rourke, E. J. (2021). Continuity, fragmentation, and Adam Smith. *The New England Journal of Medicine*, *385*(19), 1810–1814.

detriment of craftsmen who made bespoke but unique products, even pins to hold your cloak together. When mass-produced buttons and buttonholes came, it was all over for the pinmakers' guild.

In medicine, on the other hand, patients are both different from each other and present at the moment of consumption; some customization is required. They may not get the most benefit from the same uniform commodities, especially service. In the idealized history, physicians knew their patients well enough to manage this coordination; such a connection with patients as persons is what many physicians lament as lost in the era of specialization.

The status of primary care physicians in the sociology of the medical profession is ambiguous. Is my primary care physician the coordinator in chief, making Solomonic decisions on when I need care and from whom? Or is she like the Transportation Security Administration (TSA) agent directing patient traffic to the shortest line according to some predetermined rules or protocols? And how often do patients decide to escape coordination, cutting the line or bolting to somewhere of their own choosing (that they saw on the internet)? If primary care physicians are so important, why are their average incomes so much below that of the specialists they are to control? The answers, of course, to all of the above limit primary care to different degrees, which we will characterize presently.

Probably the best known and least useful mantra for ideal coordination is the goal of "the right care, to the right patient, at the right time." An economist would add "at the right cost," but that is usually left out. Although some physicians believe they know intuitively what is "right," it has no technical definition, as far as I know. If we think of any care procedure having potential benefits and harms compared to doing nothing, we could think that "right" must surely mean that benefit exceeds harm. But that constraint may not be unique – there are often many different ways to treat a sick person that do more good than harm compared to doing nothing. A more refined approach would be to say that ideal coordination occurs when the excess of benefits over harms, or net benefit, is *maximized* in the pattern of care delivered. The problem with this version is that medicine has no accepted formal metric for adding up benefits and harms. If you let some health economists into the act (and how could you keep them out), they might advocate a pattern in which all cost-effective treatments are provided to the patients for whom they are most cost-effective at the time that they are most cost-effective.

What Is a Manager to Do?

We need to set the stage. We are thinking about the manager of a health system with a flagship teaching hospital. It has a dozen outpatient facilities in its service area away from where its main hospital is located, and it owns several smaller hospitals geographically separated in its target service area. It maintains a separate professional practice with salaried primary care physicians; it also has salaried specialists primarily at its teaching hospital but also at its other sites. It has a good reputation as a tertiary care health system; the reputation of its primary care practices is still developing in competition with other health systems and private practice primary care groups. Analysis based on both accounting costs and statistical cost analysis (of the type to be described in Chapter 4) indicates that its marginal cost for health system primary care services (primarily physician visits) is no lower than prices charged by private groups and possibly higher; its average costs with overhead loaded in are definitely higher. Coordination of primary care patients is accomplished by primary care physician referrals and advice to patients by physicians and advanced practice providers, but it currently has no physicians and nurses organized as patient-centered medical homes (PCMHs). Its patient mix by demographics and insurance coverage (some network and some fee-for-service, or FFS) is average for urban and suburban areas in the US. It competes with three other health systems in its market area and with unaffiliated hospitals and physician groups.

The head of the hospital may or may not be a primary care physician (it does not appear to matter which), but that person obviously has to delegate coordination of care for individual patients to other physicians. We assume (as many do) that primary care physicians will be best at this task, although the evidence base for this assumption is weak. This is the problem of coordinated care. This task of coordination is not unique to healthcare but occurs in many large organizations with complex production processes providing services to individuals. Starbucks cares about how you get along with your barista, and American Airlines hopes you and your luggage get where you want to go on time. Some element of face-to-face custom tailoring has to go on within this healthcare organization, and (as you doubtless already know) that is a heck of a problem.

Economists have a name for this kind of managerial dilemma (which actually occurs all over the place): It is a "principal-agent" problem in which one actor has goals to be achieved but not enough time or knowledge to achieve them alone. Therefore, the principal actor must get someone else, an agent, to use their time and knowledge in the best way to achieve that goal. We have theories on how to incentivize the agents for various versions of knowledge differential and risk, but nothing off the shelf for all seasons. The general goal is to deploy both real inputs (to help and monitor the agent) and incentives for the agent to produce what the principal (the health system) would have done had the principal known as much and had as much time as the agent. Whew! The ultimate principal should be the patient or the consumer – but the health system management must guess what is best for that actor and what that actor wants, a daunting task to say the least.

What gains could the health system anticipate from changes in care coordination? If it could succeed in developing the fact and the reputation for better than average primary care coordination it might see improved patient satisfaction and better health outcomes. At present, the improved health outcomes will not generate additional revenue or higher prices from insurers, but the greater patient satisfaction might increase market share modestly. If it could lower unit cost of primary care or specialty services by better coordination, that could add to net income. If it could reduce the volume of services by avoiding duplication and low-value services, any financial gain would be limited to its capitated or bundled patient populations but would potentially harm revenues and profit margins (depending on the profitability of the foregone services at current prices).

These considerations suggest a frankly underwhelming business case for system investment in care coordination for the bulk of its population. There is little that will be sure to pay off and little support for the potential for high-cost investment to give it a try.

Here again, however, it may be difficult for a health system to benefit financially or even reputationally from better care coordination. Such coordination could be valued by specialist providers and patients with multiple chronic conditions but not known to the market. Moreover, in a healthy population, the main task of primary care would not be one of coordination but rather of ensuring the use of cost-effective preventative care and making any multisite process of treatment convenient. Beyond recommended cancer and chronic disease screenings by the US Preventive Services Task Force, day-to-day monitoring of the health of a well population is not likely to be cost-effective, though it may be reassuring.

Supply Side: The Economics of Burnout and the Pace of Work

It is a common complaint among primary care physicians that they find their work anxiety-provoking, exhausting, and unsatisfying, some to so great an extent that they leave practice or worse.[4] The aspect of practice that is most irritating (for public consumption) is the demand of the electronic medical record that everything be documented and every box checked even though only a few facts about the patient are relevant for managing their care.[5] The less frequently cited but probably more substantive is the pace of work, the scheduling of patients in the outpatient setting to achieve high throughput of billable visits and other services, with the resulting limitation on time per patient. More time might have helped with both better treatment for the patient and better satisfaction on a job properly done for the physician. The advent of virtual messaging from patients added on top of phone calls to be returned has made things worse.[6]

You do not need to be an economist to realize that there is a direct solution to this problem – reduce the size of the primary care physician's patient panel, along with a more modest reduction in hours of patient contact. The net effect can be shorter hours, fewer patients, and more time with each one that will reduce stress. Yet suggesting as a burnout solution still lower primary care incomes will probably not make you popular among physicians.

The downside to this solution is thus economic – under an FFS system, less volume of patients seen means less income either directly for the physician or to the health system paying their salary. Economists call this trade-off a "compensating differential" and see it in many occupations. Lest the analyst be tarred and feathered for pointing out that a physician (and many other workers) can have more pleasant work experiences if only they are willing to

4 Schaufeli, W. B., Maassen, G. H., Bakker, A. B., & Sixma, H. J. (2011). Stability and change in burnout: A 10-year follow-up study among primary care physicians. *Journal of Occupational and Organizational Psychology*, *84*(2), 248–267.

5 Adler-Milstein, J., Zhao, W., Willard-Grace, R., Knox, M., & Grumbach, K. (2020). Electronic health records and burnout: Time spent on the electronic health record after hours and message volume associated with exhaustion but not with cynicism among primary care clinicians. *Journal of the American Medical Informatics Association*, *27*(4), 531–538; Willard-Grace, R., Knox, M., Huang, B., Hammer, H., Kivlahan, C., & Grumbach, K. (2019). Burnout and health care workforce turnover. *The Annals of Family Medicine*, *17*(1), 36–41.

6 Salisbury, C., Murphy, M., & Duncan, P. (2020). The impact of digital-first consultations on workload in general practice: Modeling study. *Journal of Medical Internet Research*, *22*(6), e18203; Lieu, T. A., Altschuler, A., Weiner, J. Z., East, J. A., Moeller, M. F., Prausnitz, S., . . . & Awsare, S. (2019). Primary care physicians' experiences with and strategies for managing electronic messages. *JAMA Network Open*, *2*(12), e1918287–e1918287.

give up income, one should note that physicians themselves understand this trade-off between money wages and the conditions of work. In the landmark 2013 RAND survey of physicians, they report that "some of the physicians we interviewed had joined practices in which payment did not rely on the number of patients seen but, in doing so, they reported accepting lower incomes."[7]

The limitation on physician supply is the economic reason why FFS payment does not necessarily create a system that incentivizes clinicians to focus on limitless increases to the number of visits and procedures. Higher volume may be what managers want, but disutility of work and other rising costs prompt doctors to say no.

In an ideal world, physicians would match with practice arrangements whose rewards were consistent with their desired pace of work and work–life balance. The frequency of complaints suggests, however, that there is some glitch in this matching: Apparently many primary care physicians are condemned to a faster pace of work (even with high monetary incomes) than they prefer. If this is so, it suggests that managers who offer the less frantic mix of work and money can gain: They should have more applicants and a balance between revenue and physician salaries that is as good as when they paid more for more relative value units.

Is this frictionless physician market a pipe dream? If individual physicians could deal with individual insurance company plans, it might not be. A physician who wants a slow pace of work and hassle-free dealings with an insurer could agree to a lower fee and accept fewer patients into their practice. If consumers have a variety of health plans and the market is small, the physician (or for that matter the physician group) might be challenged to match enough patients to such an insurance plan to earn a reasonable income. But in large metropolitan areas there should be scope for what is effectively a kind of product differentiation – on the consumer as well as the physician side – where those consumers who prefer physicians who take more time with them and physicians who prefer to do the same can match with a health plan set up in that fashion. We do not know that there is variation across physicians in their taste for pace or work versus financial incentives and that the size of the market for primary care in big cities is large. There may be a limited number of academic opportunities but not a limited number of group practices to permit such differentiation.

[7] Friedberg, M. W., Chen, P. G., Van Busum, K. R., Aunon, F., Pham, C., Caloyeras, J., . . . & Tutty, M. (2014). Factors affecting physician professional satisfaction and their implications for patient care, health systems, and health policy. *RAND Health Quarterly*, *3*(4). www.rand.org/pubs/research_reports/RR439.html.

So, what is a manager to conclude? One possible conclusion is that complaints about pace of work and stress are only that – complaints that will not turn into sacrifices of money income. The other is that there may be a missed opportunity. Breaking the nearly unbreakable tie between work output and income may be a solution but, as we will see in Chapter 6, dumping FFS for something else at the individual physician level is easier said and rarely done.

Demand Side: Competitive Advantage and Coordination

We can all agree that better coordinated care than at present would be a good thing. Automatic transfers of information about your condition from one provider to another, minimal delays in seeing different people when that is needed, and a feeling that there is someone in charge of your care who makes the patient's problem their problem are sought by almost all consumers. Convenience is desired as much as technical excellence. A now-traditional model delegates the task of achieving this pattern to the patient's primary care physician (see Box 3.1 for evidence). With greater specialization, the task has become harder as different body parts and bodily systems are parceled out to various specialists with better but narrower information than the regular doctor would have. For example, coordinating a single chronic condition for a single patient can require up to 50 interactions with the patient and other care providers over a three-month period.[8] However, in

Box 3.1 Evidence: Primary care physician care coordination – why evidence on how to do it best is not conclusive

Researchers have tried to investigate whether more care coordination changes patient outcomes and costs. There is no direct measure of care coordination that can capture all the pulls and tugs that affect patients with complex or chronic conditions as they move through the system, but the usual proxy measure is the number of other physicians a primary care physician refers to. This number does vary across primary care physicians. A primary care physician's list can be as large as 90 referral partners. There are two key questions for managers: (1) does care coordination matter and (2) how do you change things to cause more

[8] Press, M. J. (2014). Instant replay: A quarterback's view of care coordination. *New England Journal of Medicine, 371*(6), 489–491.

or better care coordination? We have some circumstantial evidence on the first, but no conclusive evidence on the second.

When researchers examined the use of care overall by patients with more referrals, they found large numbers of referrals were indeed related to outcomes like emergency department use (more) and patient satisfaction (less).[9] When they looked across primary care physicians and compared those with more or fewer referral partners, they found the same thing: Physicians who referred to fewer others had better patient outcomes and lower use of emergency rooms and avoidable hospital admissions. You might conclude that this is evidence in favor of the care coordination hypothesis, and indeed it is a more supportive finding compared to the opposite. However, to economists and to those in search of truth, the problem is that patients and primary care physicians were not randomly assigned to high or low coordination conditions. Perhaps the patients with more referrals were sicker. Perhaps the physicians who passed on doing work themselves and sent patients to others were less competent or less productive at those tasks. You really want to know why the observations differed – why some referred more than others – and that is not known. This "endogeneity" problem is almost always present in observational data, and it is a real pain, but not one to be ignored.

On the other question, there seems to be no research on direct interventions to produce more care coordination. Instead, cheerleaders for the hypothesis point to care arrangements like accountable care organizations (ACOs) or virtual coordination efforts during the pandemic that we will discuss in Chapter 9 on value-based care. Here we have the usual lukewarm findings of small reductions in cost and improvements in those outcome measures that come with financial rewards. Moreover, the evidence over time does not suggest a highly beneficial role for primary care (or harm from its absence). We just don't know and can't prove it.

What seems both clear and daunting is that improved care coordination cannot be introduced in small doses, with a tweak to reimbursement here and an information seminar there. It probably requires an overhaul of the relationships between primary care physicians and specialists within the health system – perhaps within a single health system or maybe at the market level. It probably also requires a wholesale switch to capitation payment of the system (and probably of physicians in it), a monumental task. The Kaiser system is an example of a different structure that may have better coordination (not proven but claimed as a result of focus on those patients with chronic conditions where coordination was needed),[10] but a system like this requires revolutionary change. The implication is that managers had better be sure of benefit before starting down a road whose final destination they do not know.

many settings, the task of coordination has itself been farmed out to care coordinators, often nonphysicians. Medical school does not train professionals who necessarily know better how to work referral networks and

[9] Agha, L., Frandsen, B., & Rebitzer, J. B. (2019). Fragmented division of labor and healthcare costs: Evidence from moves across regions. *Journal of Public Economics*, *169*, 144–159.

[10] Pearl, R., & Madvig, P. (2020). Managing the most expensive patients. *Harvard Business Review*, *98*(1), 68–75.

patient scheduling than, say, experienced nurses who know everybody and everything about a healthcare system.

We have the most evidence on care coordination from the multiple efforts to make the "patient-centered medical home" model work. The name of the plan describes its objectives, but the evidence on its ability to achieve them is mixed. The model envisions the task of coordination as one for a team of nurses and doctors, not for one manager-in-chief. Where the model has been tried, its most positive outcome has been a modest improvement in patient satisfaction (compared to the mixed bag of the usual primary care practice model of coordination).[11] But it has not shown better health outcomes, and it has not shown lower costs.[12] The empirical evidence can confidently be labeled "decidedly mixed." Nor has it caught fire away from targeted and stylized demonstration projects.

There have been statistically significant but practically modest at most (4%) cost reductions to adults at high initial morbidity from PCMHs, although the number of studies looking at cost (as compared to some measures of quality) is small.[13] For managers, it is important to note that the primary vehicle for such savings was a reduction in inpatient admissions and associated revenues paid on a diagnosis-related group (DRG) basis to health systems. We will revisit this issue in more detail in Chapter 9 on value-based payments, but for the present, note that this kind of cost savings (and the necessary reductions in hospital employment associated with them) may not be attractive to managers of health systems – this would mean fewer patients in their hospital beds. In contrast, insurance managers covering populations with larger proportions of high morbidity members may seek to network with health systems that emphasize PCMHs. Those insurers who cover primarily working adults and their dependents may have less to gain.

[11] Maeng, D. D., Davis, D. E., Tomcavage, J., Graf, T. R., & Procopio, K. M. (2013). Improving patient experience by transforming primary care: Evidence from Geisinger's patient-centered medical homes. *Population Health Management, 16*(3), 157–163.

[12] Flieger, S. P. (2017). Impact of a patient-centered medical home pilot on utilization, quality, and costs and variation in medical homeness. *The Journal of Ambulatory Care Management, 40*(3), 228–237.

[13] Sinaiko, A. D., Landrum, M. B., Meyers, D. J., Alidina, S., Maeng, D. D., Friedberg, M. W., . . . & Rosenthal, M. B. (2017). Synthesis of research on patient-centered medical homes brings systematic differences into relief. *Health Affairs, 36*(3), 500–508; Nielsen, M., Buelt, L., Patel, K., & Nichols, L. M. (2016). *The patient-centered medical home's impact on cost and quality: Annual review of evidence, 2014–2015.* Patient-Centered Primary Care Collaborative and Milbank Memorial Fund; Grumbach, K., & Grundy, P. (2010). *Outcomes of implementing patient centered medical home interventions.* Patient-Centered Primary Care Collaborative.

The Economics of Physician Referrals and Conflicts of Interest

Often, a primary care physician will refer a patient to another physician who will also care about rewards and effort. If I as the patient am now the principal in the principal-agent problem, how do I get my primary care physician to do this in the way that is best for me? Normal human beings know that one thing I will want is a referral partner I like; primary care physicians run a dating service (with the mutual concerns that entails) to match patients with certain characteristics with specialists with complementary characteristics. Economists know that the relative cost of different specialists should also matter, with lower being better than higher. The specialist physician in turn both needs referrals and wants to be paid for them – directly if the specialist is in a separate firm from the primary care physician (the olden days model) or indirectly if both are employed by the same group or hospital.

Often this process is complicated by rules or customs that forbid money changing hands, at least to the knowledge of the principal (patient). You worry that your guide may not take you to the rug seller in the souk who offers the best deal for you; you worry that your primary care physician may not send you to the best dermatologist in town but rather one from which they stand to personally gain. Politicians worry too; they have passed laws forbidding independent physician practices from paying kickbacks for referrals. If both physicians are employed by the same group, however, these laws are not effective since the group can set incomes however it wants and reward whatever its management or partners want. The buyer should beware.

Economists are conflicted but know when to be most afraid. If insurers set reimbursements for specialists very high relative to their costs, it is obvious that getting ever more referrals will pay – fee splitting can lead to excessive volume. However, the lowest-cost specialist can pay the largest kickback, so at least referrals will go to the "right" person. The solution is to lower the fee to reduce temptation – good advice if you are an insurance manager.

However, the ultimate reward for good referral practice will be better consumer satisfaction and lower insurance premiums in one network compared to another. Hence competition among networks and patient knowledge are both ways of doing the best you can in a tough situation.

Conclusion on Coordination

In their estimate of the total waste in the US health system (almost $1 trillion, 25% of the total) Shrank and coauthors do not expect much in terms of lower cost from changes in care coordination.[14] They expect reduced admissions to make up the bulk of any savings, and even they would add up to only about 7% of total hospital spending – billions to be sure but a tiny fraction of total medical spending. Some primary care advocates do not worry about short-term savings; system redesign, they argue, will improve quality and therefore should be pushed regardless. Care coordination could substantially improve health outcomes and patient satisfaction, especially for socially vulnerable populations. But how is our health system manager to turn such gains into rewards for the system? Better health outcomes are usually not paid for directly, and their role in shifting market share (assuming other systems in town cannot easily copy the changes) is bound to be small.

Primary Care Effects

While there is a strong constituency advocating for primary care as a vehicle to achieve the triple or quadruple aim associated with health outcomes and costs, what is the evidence? To take the economic indicator first (as is appropriate in an economics book), would (or how would) more spending on primary care in the US affect overall population health outcomes, their distribution, and total resource cost? The prestigious NASEM have pronounced on part of this: They claim that "primary care is the only health care component where an increased supply is associated with better population health and more equitable outcomes. For this reason, primary care is a *common good*, making the strength and quality of the country's primary care services a public concern."[15]

This is a strong statement. The study did not investigate all other components of healthcare supply to determine they had no association with population health; for example, it is generally thought that an increase in the supply of

[14] Shrank, W. H., Rogstad, T. L., & Parekh, N. (2019). Waste in the US health care system: Estimated costs and potential for savings. *JAMA*, *322*(15), 1501–1509.

[15] National Academies of Sciences, Engineering, and Medicine. (2021). *Implementing high-quality primary care: Rebuilding the foundation of health care.* https://nap.nationalacademies.org/catalog/25983/implementing-high-quality-primary-care-rebuilding-the-foundation-of-health. (Italics added.)

new drugs, especially for cardiovascular diseases, lowered mortality from that cause. The evidence in support of the proposition appears to be one journal article from 2019,[16] which only showed an association between increased primary care supply and reduced mortality, not causation. (Since the period studied was one in which mortality rates fell, this study showed that they declined more in US counties with more growth in primary care physician supply.) In their most rigorous specification, the changes in supply were predicted using changes in consumer spending, problematic because economically depressed counties probably would have had higher mortality because of falling incomes. It would be impossible to run a national experiment in which the long-term decline in the primary care workforce caused by retirement of older GPs was reversed and the market was flooded with new physicians trained in care coordination. It would be feasible in a smaller market, but the advocates for rebuilding primary care would probably not wait for it. Managers of health systems and insurance plans will have to hedge on this one. I do review careful research on specific primary care interventions later in this chapter. See Box 3.2 for a discussion about value-based payments in primary care.

Box 3.2 Theory: Value-based payment and the redemption of primary care

There is in principle no economic reason why FFS payment cannot be used to increase primary care incomes and incentivize behaviors that could help with care coordination. Payments per visit could be increased, and explicit payments could be made for patient contacts (calls, messages) and reviews of patient care plans. However, many primary care physicians (and the NASEM committee) feel that alternative payments mechanisms somehow based on value would work better.[17] What is the economic argument here, and what is likely to happen?

I discuss value-based payment (VBP) in more detail in Chapter 9; it generally takes the form of a capitation payment per patient coupled with some metrics of desired outcomes or quality. So, think about paying the primary care physician practice a capitation payment intended to cover the cost of all care their patients receive. Given some level of this payment, if primary care physicians can improve coordination or otherwise change the process to care to yield lower costs, the amount of the capitation payment they can retain will be larger. In

[16] Basu, S., Berkowitz, S. A., Phillips, R. L., Bitton, A., Landon, B. E., & Phillips, R. S. (2019). Association of primary care physician supply with population mortality in the United States, 2005–2015. *JAMA Internal Medicine*, *179*(4), 506–514.

[17] American Academy of Family Practice. (2024). Establishing accountability in value-based payment models for primary care. Position Paper. www.aafp.org/about/policies/all/accountability-value-based-payment.html.

terms of economic incentives, this would be the strongest push toward lower cost; if there was a way to achieve that cost and still satisfy (or even improve) the outcome metrics, the four-way triple or quadruple aim of health system improvement could be achieved.

However, counting on such changes in payment to be offered by insurers selling products attractive to buyers requires some things so far unproven: that primary care physicians can bring about changes in the patterns of care and that those changes reduce cost and improve outcomes. So far evidence does not exist to demonstrate that this can be done. Insurers should require such evidence to support changes both in the form of reimbursement (i.e., capitation versus FFS) and, if capitated, in the level of capitation payment. Medicare has recently funded some new demonstration projects for primary care payment reform in selected sites (e.g., Primary Care First), but preliminary evidence was mixed and the program was ended early.[18] Moreover, the level of the capitation payment (which will determine how much is left over for primary care physicians) would be expected to be determined in a competitive process which could lead to capitation payments that yield little more than current FFS-based incomes if primary care physicians are willing to work for less. Chapter 9 explains how capitation or bundled payments will be determined in a market (along with any FFS payments in a hybrid model) – the punchline is that primary care physicians will receive more only if they provide more demonstrated value and if they are only willing to supply that value if paid higher prices. That they currently are willing to accept lower incomes suggests the absence of a supply-side constraint that would boost payment. If VBP is so successful that there is a demand for more primary care services and providers, that could bid up prices and incomes.

Coordinating Primary Care Doctors and Hospitals

Embedded in the problem of how to coordinate care for the benefit of the patient (which should by all rights be the primary objective) is a question of how to coordinate physician and hospital behavior. I deal much more intensively with this general problem in the next chapter, but here we briefly consider the relationship of primary care physicians and hospitals. Are there better ways of coordination and sharing that might save some money and cheer up some downtrodden doctors? Historically, and puzzlingly, the US (and Canadian) medical care systems were organized with the key decision-makers (physicians) and the suppliers of inputs (hospitals) organized into two separate organizations: the medical staff with privileges at hospitals and the hospitals themselves which provided tools for procedures and hotel services for patients afterward. This arrangement included primary care physicians who usually would make hospital rounds to visit their patients

[18] Mathematica. (2025). *Evaluation of the Primary Care First model: Third annual report.* www.cms.gov/priorities/innovation/data-and-reports/2025/pcf-third-eval-rpt.

who had been admitted. Other countries were organized in different ways, with doctors who treat hospitalized patients as salaried by the hospital. Primary care doctors are left outside the hospital to do whatever they can for ambulatory patients.

The US health system has been moving in the direction of this alternative model. This transformation to salaried physicians appears not to have much affected the functioning of the combined physician–hospital organization in the US. However, it has affected what primary care physicians do and the roles they are expected to play (see Boxes 3.3 and 3.4 for further discussion). Most obviously, if care is handed over to specialists or hospitalists, whether hospital salaried or not, the primary care physicians' role during this period is limited to one of consultation rather than direct management of services the hospital provides to inpatients (as in the past).

The most important consequence of this break is that the patient is handed back to the primary care physician upon discharge, but this is a transition which poses some serious challenges. The patient may still seek care or advice from hospital physicians or specialists. The primary care physician has to be updated on the patient's need after hospitalization, including changed medications and instructions to the family about who to contact if something unexpected happens. Models of transitional care relying on nurses who follow patients from hospital to home have been developed and proven effective in this process – but one of their main tasks is to reconnect the patient with the primary care physician.[19] Sometimes things fall through the cracks.

Box 3.3 Theory: NASEM report and physician supply

The elementary economics of supply curves, as every freshman economics major knows (or should know), is premised on the assumption that suppliers have as their goal the maximization of profits. In the world where they take price as given, the amount they will supply depends on price but *is not unlimited*. The reason is that rising marginal cost eventually means that you would reduce your profits even though you collected revenue for one more unit if the price falls below marginal cost. It also implies, by the way, that a profit-seeking firm will not want to maximize revenue (sell an infinite amount if the price does not fall).

This lesson has apparently not been learned by experts who comment on physician payment, not even by the committee convened for this purpose by the NASEM. In their report, they state correctly that "practices organized in response to FFS payment maximize

[19] Naylor, M., & Keating, S. A. (2008). Transitional care. *AJN The American Journal of Nursing, 108*(9), 58–63.

revenue-producing in-person visits."[20] However, they do not explain why a physician practice would want to maximize revenue rather than profit. Economists would suggest that both rising practice costs as output expands and increasing disutility of work by physicians would mean that real physician net income and the desired volume will be limited by the price. With costs rising with volume, at some point the price will not be high enough to cover those costs.

We only need look to physician behavior for patients covered by low FFS-paying Medicaid to see that this is true; when the price is low, physicians limit what patients they will accept and what they will do. This economic error of focusing on gross revenue rather than net income shows up often in criticism of FFS payment, and it is wrong. The NASEM go on to say that practices will maximize visits rather than have "a high proportion of preventive and chronic care tasks," which is a non sequitur. The proportion will depend on how preventive and chronic care services are paid; if they are paid poorly compared to visits, the proportion will not be "high" (whatever that means), but the reason is that the FFS payment structure is poorly designed, not the fault of FFS per se. Economists believe that, most of the time, you get what your pay for, and if you want more of something you only need pay more for it.

Box 3.4 Evidence: Incentives to improve primary care coordination – evidence from Hawaii Blue Cross

Hawaii Medical Services Association, an independent licensee of Blue Cross Blue Shield of Hawaii, changed payment for a large fraction of the privately insured population in Hawaii from FFS to a hybrid system with high levels of capitation plus some FFS payment, pursuing the goal of providing incentives for primary care coordination. This change did not in the end affect spending but did result in improvement in some quality measures, including the proportion of patients with advanced planning directives and breast cancer screening, along with an improvement in blood pressure control.[21] Because thousands of patients were affected by the change in payment, the subsequent changes in quality metrics were statistically significant with a magnitude (on a composite score) of about 2%. These results are consistent with a general trend of primary care payment reform leading to improvements in quality at no increase in spending but no reduction either. Care coordination and movement away from FFS to partial capitation was associated with a small reduction in primary care visits being replaced by telehealth encounters. Managers of insurance plans and health systems will have to judge whether these changes are large enough to seek similar substantial changes in payment mechanisms.

[20] National Academies of Sciences, Engineering, and Medicine. (2021). *Implementing high-quality primary care: Rebuilding the foundation of health care.* https://nap.nationalacademies.org/catalog/25983/implementing-high-quality-primary-care-rebuilding-the-foundation-of-health.

[21] Navathe, A. S., Emanuel, E. J., Bond, A., Linn, K., Caldarella, K., Troxel, A., . . . & Volpp, K. G. (2019). Association between the implementation of a population-based primary care payment system and achievement on quality measures in Hawaii. *JAMA*, *322*(1), 57–68.

Competition in Physician Markets

Primary care physicians compete among themselves for the services they supply. They also compete on the basis of who has access to the best network of referral partners and the ability to coordinate such direction as those partners need.

Viewed only by the numbers antitrust regulators use to characterize competition across markets, the market for primary care physician services appears to be highly competitive. In the areas where people live, there are many of them, and none have large market shares. However, this head count measure may be misleading because consumer-patients have problems searching for both price and quality among all the primary care doctors in a town.

Interestingly, there is empirical evidence that greater market concentration leads to higher hospital revenues and prices, but there has been no effort to look at physician income variation with hospital competition. Higher hospital average prices will allow payment of higher physician salaries, but the research may have been looking at the wrong thing.

Economic Interpretation and Advice on Primary Care Coordination

The main burden of both the discussion and the evidence on primary care coordination reviewed in this chapter is that the magic formula for ideal care coordination, or even the best path forward, is still unknown. It seems that primary care physicians have a major role to play here, but often they are still waiting in the wings for some cue, yet to be discovered. Medicare made a major effort with two demonstration programs called Comprehensive Primary Care (CPC) and CPC Plus (CPC+) that paid explicitly for care coordination, offered financial rewards to physicians for good outcomes, and paid them a monthly retainer. While CPC+ reduced emergency department visits, hospitalizations, and acute inpatient expenditures, these reductions were not sufficient to reduce total Medicare expenditures or achieve net savings.[22] It has not been copied by private insurers in either Medicare Advantage or commercial business. Evaluators speculated that the problem

[22] Mathematica. (2023). Independent evaluation of comprehensive Primary Care Plus: Final report. www.cms.gov/priorities/innovation/data-and-reports/2023/cpc-plus-fifth-annual-eval-report

was the lack of control by primary care physicians over the full set of services. Medicare continued to run population-based primary care payment demonstration projects into the future with Primary Care First, which began in 2021, and Making Care Primary, which began in 2024, until they were cancelled by the new presidential administration in 2025.

The discussion of care coordination in my view is more confusing than it should be because it often starts in the middle of the story – we have a patient with complex needs already under care and are trying to figure out the best plan moving forward. It is like catching an episode of a soap opera; you can tell that the issue is whether Lance is the grandfather of Bethany's baby, but you do not know how it came to this or why it is important. My comment, based in part on some economic research on cost-sharing in insurance which we shall review in Chapter 6, is that it would be better to start at the beginning. What prompts patients to enter the system (or not), what are they expecting or hoping, and how are they led from the point of managers further into the system? If the initial diagnosis could be hard and fast – this is what you have, this is what we do for people like you, these are what outcomes and cost you can expect – there would obviously be less of a problem. Patients know something about symptoms that trigger appropriate contact, but usually neither they nor their physicians who then care for them know precisely what should happen next. The decision tree and value of information discussed in Chapter 2 should be part of the framework. There are care protocols and decision path models available to physicians – and perhaps more and better will come from artificial intelligence. To the extent that machines substitute for humans, the outlook of primary care physicians may remain dour.

The general contractor metaphor can be helpful here. If you want your general contractor to deliver a final product with all the characteristics you desire, and to do so on time and on budget, you will have to provide a generous payment and budget and specify carefully what you want. Economics cannot specify the ideal production model (though it can comment on any proposal), but it can specify the incentives needed for it. Current low payment for primary care physicians and their lack of organizational control over all activities and the budget for them suggest that improvement is possible. But the lack of evidence on effective alternatives suggests that improvement will be challenging.

At this point, I fall back to the economic answer to anything: Let there be competition among alternative models and we will see what ends up winning. That does mean that heavy-handed external direction of roles and procedures would be premature. Managers as usual can be advised to be on the lookout for whatever works best (not necessarily whatever sounds best). A good bet would be that the winning system will figure out a way for physicians to do the coordinating (and not be tasked with record-keeping or finance). Something may emerge but probably not any time soon.

4 Doctors and Hospitals

Can We Please Get Along?

By definition, care coordination involves a multitude of linkages and relationships among multiple actors in the medical care system. In this chapter, I will focus on one of the most complex challenges of care coordination, one with a long history: physician–hospital relationships.

I begin with the financial relationships between physicians and hospitals. In the US, there have been two very different versions of this. One is the more traditional approach in which physicians have admitting privileges in a hospital as members of the medical staff but are not employees of the hospital. The other is the increasingly more common arrangement in which the physician is a salaried employee of the hospital or health system. (In most European countries, this model is used, with some physicians seeing patients only in outpatient settings, handing over their patients to different physicians staffing – and employed by – hospitals.) The economic difference between the two arrangements is that payments for physician services flow directly to the physician practice in the first case, usually as fee-for-service but possibly bundled or capitated. In the second case, the payments first go to the health system or hospital, and then presumably are parceled out among physicians. There are a number of different potential forms of this health system payment of salaried physicians, because salaries can vary with the volume of physician services or any other mutually agreeable indication of performance. Ultimately the health system controls how reimbursements for physician services are allocated among salaried physicians or to other uses. In this case, the way individual physicians are paid as a function of the volume of their services can be different from how the health system is paid. The health system may be capitated for physicians' services but then divide payment among physicians based on volume or productivity – or in whatever way it and its physicians choose.

Primary care physicians and some specialties like dermatology and ophthalmology generally provide most care to outpatients. Other physicians treat many patients who are sick enough to benefit from inpatient hospitalization. This latter case, and the physician–hospital relationships it entails, is the one most commonly discussed by health economists, in large part because those physicians direct the inputs used in that inpatient care. Since revenues from inpatient care are larger than physician payments, physicians in the first case serve primarily as feeders of patients (and their subsequent revenues) to the inpatient service. In the second case, physicians can also direct much of the cost of inpatient care. From a financial perspective, both gross and net health system revenues can be affected.

Here is where economic analysis begins. Physicians who provide services to hospitalized patients interact with the personnel and facilities in hospitals – with nurses, technicians, attendants, cooks, administrators, and others. In many cases, physicians have the authority to direct that labor be applied to the patients they treat. The institutional-organizational framework in which this interaction has historically taken place in the US is an odd one from an economic perspective, because the physicians who could order the deployment of hospital resources were not employees of the hospital; instead, they were organized as an attending staff with treatment privileges at a hospital as a separate organization. Moreover, in the great majority of cases, this hospital organization is not owned by investors but instead is a not-for-profit firm with no stockholders.[1] Over time, physicians who treat patients in a hospital have become salaried employees of a health system – to a greater extent than physicians who treat outpatients – but hospitals have remained largely nonprofit. To say the obvious, this structure does not easily fit the traditional economic model of a profit-maximizing firm with owners supplying equity capital and directing labor with the objective of maximizing profits, nor can an equilibrium in a market largely populated by such firms be assumed to reproduce the equilibrium of competitive profit-maximizing firms. (The setting of a market where both types of firms coexist is even more confusing.)

How might an economist model both the internal behavior of this physician–hospital enterprise and the market equilibrium when this form is dominant? (As with all economic models, the answer to this question is not necessarily going to sound like a realistic description of what managers in the industry experience.) The unusual issue in this case is that, although buyers presumably are interested in services or products produced by hospitals and physicians together, in many cases in the US, hospitals and doctors are in separate firms. Other professional services are not organized this way; we professors are part of

[1] Malani, A., Philipson, T., & David, G. (2003). Theories of firm behavior in the nonprofit sector: A synthesis and empirical evaluation. In E. L. Glaeser (ed.), *The governance of not-for-profit organizations* (pp. 181–216). University of Chicago Press.

university firms, are salaried by them, and (we like to think) work in cooperation with the university administration. Students do not get separate bills for professor services and use of classroom facilities.

There is a famous economic theory of the firm from my advisors' former professor and Nobelist Ronald Coase.[2] His idea was that productive inputs would be combined in a firm rather than produced by separate enterprises if it is more efficient and/or lower cost to do so. Rather than have to have a transaction with each worker that specifies payment and the task to be done every day, workers are salaried by firms and in turn agree to be directed to perform whatever task the firm wants. On the one hand, there is in Coase's model of the firm both vertical integration (of production) – inputs linked and moved within the organization – and financial integration – payments that flow from a single collection point to the persons within the organization, usually in the form of prespecified wages for prespecified activities. If, on the other hand, some inputs into the production of some final good are produced in a separate firm, the power of the "final good" firm is limited to contracting with the "upstream" firm. Usually, its interaction is limited to specifying what it wants to buy and then paying for it. Moreover, when the dust clears and all revenues are collected and bills for inputs paid, the owners of capital in the firm are the residual claimants of whatever is left over; they have these profits as an incentive.

However, this "boss-worker" model is not the only form of organization which exists. If you are seeking a new house to be built for you, often you will engage a general contractor who will pull together architects, plumbing firms, electricians, and others to supply the pieces of your building. The general contractor will give you a price in advance for the completed structure, though there can be adjustments as things move on. The contractor may have some employees, but most of the workers who will build your house are employed by separate organizations who contract with the coordinator. I dwell on this story because the general contractor model is, in certain circumstances, a metaphor for care coordination by your primary care physician, a topic in the preceding chapter. In the patient-centered medical home or concierge practice model, the primary care doctor plays the same role at the top of the organizational apparatus as a general contractor. In the more traditional model, the primary care physician is still in charge, but now the individual suppliers send separate bills to the customer rather than the contractor. Having dealt with home remodels over many years, I know that

2 Coase, R. (1937). The nature of the firm. *Economica*, *16*(4), 386–405.

sometimes you the customer get the bills and sometimes your contractor pays. Either way, this general contractor concept is an alternative organizational model to the Coase model – one which often involves a contractor trying to coordinate separate legal "firms" – that has some parallels in US healthcare history and current performance.

The traditional hospital–medical staff separate firm model can be different from Coase's upstream–downstream story. In particular, the downstream physician or surgeon firm (either a separate doctor practice or practices organized as the medical staff) has the power to order the deployment of inputs in the upstream hospital that will provide facilities and care without bearing any of the cost of those inputs. The attending doctor can order nurse services, use of procedure rooms, tests, and medications in the hospital – all of which will be covered by a separate hospital reimbursement or price. This peculiar organizational arrangement for care for hospitalized patients straddles the bounds of Coase's theoretical firm with more than one management team getting into the act. This will call for a novel model of this hybrid firm, which I will present shortly. Whether these different organizational models really matter in terms of cost, price, and output is going to be an open question.

An Economic Story about American Hospitals

For services produced by or in hospitals, this odd two-firm combination is still often present. So how might it work ideally, what happens in practice, and are there alternatives? What the combination needs to settle are the supply/production issues of how to combine and manage inputs and the demand/pricing issue of what price(s) to charge.

Among the possible production relationships, a good example would be the relationship of physicians and hospitals in supplying inpatient surgical care. We will assume that the set of surgeons at a hospital acts as a group or a single unit in pursuing objectives shared in common; later we deal with the possibility of uncooperative behavior among the separate physicians. (Even within a nominally unified health system, separate departments often operate as independent baronies, so this latter concept has general applicability.)

Production of a surgical treatment requires both surgeon input and hospital input. A surgeon uses hospital facilities (the operating suite and staff) and gives orders to nursing staff for postoperative care of the patient. None of these activities are of value without the others, and we assume that surgeons have authority (whatever their organizational relationships) to direct some hospital inputs in the care of surgical patients. (Although metaphors always break down, it is like the general contractor telling the plumber to do the job.) While it is still common for insurers to make payments separately designated for surgeon services (procedure and postoperative care) and hospital services (use of the operating suite, room and board during convalescence, nursing, and anesthesia), the patient or the patient's insurer presumably demand the complete service, without regard to the breakdown into separate parts. (Surprise billing by doctors uncontrolled by hospital management does sometimes occur, but this is a surprise precisely because it is an anomaly.) The price relevant to the quantity demanded by the insurer on behalf of the consumer is thus the sum of physician and hospital payment; it is this sum that an insurer network will consider in choosing a hospital for its network, and which a patient who has cost sharing will consider in deciding whether to have surgery and where to have it.

On the upstream supply side, physicians are willing to devote time, expertise, and effort to provision of surgical services for a share of the total amount paid for the procedure, while other parts of it compensate hospitals for their workers and capital used. The ideal arrangement for production efficiency then would be one in which patient-consumers' demands for both volume of care and quality of care were matched by a supply of care that used the cost-minimizing quantities of both physician and hospital inputs. A physician input is not an undifferentiated commodity that the hospital can purchase in a market but rather represents the time, effort, thoughtfulness, and coordination of other inputs that physicians choose to supply. Output here reflects both the marginal health benefit from the patient encounter with the hospital–physician combination and any dimensions of the process of rendering that service (such as comfort, attentiveness, and reassurance) that patient-consumers seek.

Given the revenue that could be collected for surgical treatments at a given total price, and given the cost of hospital inputs, any inputs in the surgeon's office practice, and the opportunity cost of surgeon time, we can define a net income or profit generated by the supply of such care as the difference between total revenue received and these costs for both firms. The hospital and/or physicians may also have the power to set prices. If they have market power, and seek profits, presumably their ideal price is the profit-maximizing monopoly price given the demand (from patients as transmitted by insurers) for the surgical treatment.

One benchmark model we will use throughout (without necessarily claiming it is always realistic) is to assume that the physician–hospital combination chooses prices (if it has market power) and inputs to maximize total profits of both organizations as if they were one firm. This benchmark is exactly the textbook model of a profit-maximizing firm. Whether it holds for the more modern model of a salaried medical staff is discussed later in the chapter.

In principle, this profit could be divided in many ways. In the US, the constraint that the hospital be nonprofit solves this problem: The group of physicians can collect the maximized profit. They are the de facto recipients of residual income.[3] (The law prevents the nonprofit hospital's management staff from paying itself what would have been profit in a for-profit firm, though there can be bonuses and emoluments.) If physicians have enough leverage to do so, aligning with a nonprofit hospital will also be in the physician group's interest, since it should reduce conflict or rivalry with the hospital owner who has promised not to seek profits; perhaps this is one of the reasons why US physicians predominantly prefer to practice in nonprofit hospitals. They do so even if they are salaried by that hospital.

What comes out of this model that may be of interest to managers of hospitals, insurers, and medical groups? The standard economic model of a firm with market power is that it sets its output and price at the point where marginal revenue equals marginal cost. We can assume that a hospital–medical staff combination will garner more business the more reasonable its price – so there will be downward sloping marginal revenue (see Box 4.1)

Box 4.1 Theory: A model of a physician cooperative

This section provides a diagrammatic description of how price and quantity would be determined by an organization that combines physician and hospital services to produce surgical treatments.

On the demand side, we assume that potential buyers of some surgical treatment provided to hospitalized patients will be willing to buy a larger volume of such treatments from a given physician–hospital organization the lower the price. The demander-buyer is most likely to be an insurance plan on behalf of an insured person or an administrative services only (ASO) organization managing care for a self-insured group of consumers. Alternatives to purchasing this service from this organization are buying it from another organization, choosing a non-surgical treatment, or going without treatment.

A hypothetical organization-level demand curve is shown in Figure 4.1, along with its associated marginal revenue curve. There are assumed to be positive and constant marginal costs for both surgeon practice and hospital-supplied services as indicated in the figure.

[3] Pauly, M., & Redisch, M. (1973). The not-for-profit hospital as a physicians' cooperative. *The American Economic Review*, *63*(1), 87–99.

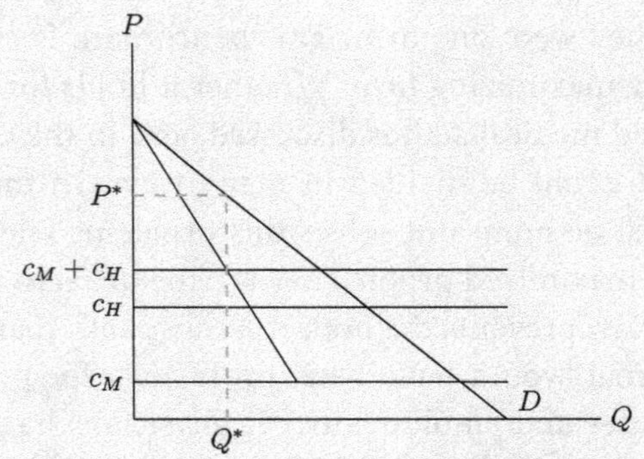

Figure 4.1 Hospital–physician firm equilibrium.

Surgeon costs include time and work in performing the surgery and any associated care, as well as surgical practice costs per patient (generally associated with follow-up visits). They have a constant marginal cost, C_M. Hospital costs include room and board, costs of hospital staff in the operating room and later in the hospital stay, tests and drugs, and capital costs. These services are purchased in fixed proportion at a constant marginal cost of C_H.

The diagram shows an intersection of the marginal revenue curve with the sum of the marginal costs $C_M + C_H$ (the derivation of the marginal revenue curve is shown in Box 10.1 in Chapter 10). The profit-maximizing quantity of this treatment to be sold by this organization is thus Q*, with associated price P*. How that revenue (P*Q*) is distributed among surgeons and the hospital is determined by the objective of the organization. If its goal is to maximize surgeon practice net income, the payment to the hospital will be set at the hospital's cost (so it breaks even) and the payment per surgery to the surgeon will be the difference between the total price and the payment to the hospital. Other divisions of net income are possible depending on the arrangement between hospital and surgeon.

This very simple story shows how the standard economic model of price and quantity determination can be used to solve for targeted behavior. It also explains why surgeons prefer hospitals to be nonprofit with breakeven as their long-term goal, and why both surgeons and hospital management will seek to minimize total cost in the production of the jointly produced service. It applies to patients covered by private insurance; when Medicare and Medicaid set prices they will pay, the model is that of price discrimination discussed in Chapter 10 in which the private insurer price is still set in the way the model describes.

for the combination. Assuming (fairly realistically) that the long-run marginal costs of hospital- and surgeon-furnished inputs are constant over output, the relevant marginal cost for the combination is the sum of physician and hospital marginal cost per surgical admission. Following the simple economic rule determines the profit-maximizing quantity, and the price is the one associated with that quantity on the demand curve.

Historically, physicians were organizationally separate from the hospital and billed separately. They even had a separate insurance company (Blue Shield, now often combined with the hospitals' Blue Cross). This model has a simple interpretation of that phenomenon: The nonprofit hospital should set a breakeven price just enough to cover the costs of the inputs it provides, and the physician group then sets its price to maximize profits after the payment to the hospital. As physicians and hospitals have become more organizationally integrated, with physicians being salaried by the health system or with parts of the medical staff organizing into firms that effectively get a hospital's franchise for pathology or orthopedics, price setting can be different. However, the physician group can legally collect all of the profit, based on the level and change in physician salaries or payments from the hospital to the franchisee. The combined firm may sometimes want to allow the hospital to price above its cost as a way to raise funding for investment (from retained earnings) that will benefit physicians in the future. The legal limits on nonprofit enterprises forbid the management of the nominally nonprofit enterprise to earn incomes that vary with potential profitability, but so far this has not been a constraint for the medical staff. Separating the staff back out into a different firm is always possible as a way to avoid legal challenges.

This caricature obviously does not capture the power or financial relationships in modern health systems where system management is not necessarily limited to pursuing the breakeven strategy that maximizes physician surplus. Empirically, the relative numbers of physicians versus hospitals in a market should matter – physician power will be limited if there are many of them and few hospitals to choose from in a market. We are not sure how this works out.

Another element is the extent of competition between health systems in the local market, which affects the firm-level demand curve. The less concentrated the industry, the lower the summed price for surgery in that market because the firm-level demand curve will be made more price-responsive when there are other alternative sellers. As in usual competitive models, the group in whose interest an organization maximizes profits does not necessarily end up with unfairly high profits if there is competition.

Interestingly, there is empirical evidence that greater market concentration leads to higher hospital revenues and prices, but there has been no effort to look at physician income variation with hospital competition. Higher hospital average prices will allow payment of higher salaries to employed physicians but will cut into the profits of other physicians.

The conclusions from this simple model are made complicated when there are few hospitals in a market area even with many physicians. It is more likely, as I will discuss in Chapter 12, that hospitals will merge and collude than individual physicians. This fact raises the tricky question for important medical services which require both hospital and doctor inputs, like surgery: What will happen when one of the input markets (hospital care) becomes monopolized while the other complementary part (surgeon services) remains competitive in structure? More thoughts (but no conclusions) on this later in the chapter.

How might health system managers help these physicians to better coordinate among themselves to achieve their shared goals? I have already argued that physicians as a group (e.g., the surgeons who practice in a hospital) should have a shared goal of improved efficiency leading to lower hospital costs and prices (as well as lower practice costs) and better patient coordination to improve their hospital's position in the local market. One implication of the model of physician cooperative is that physicians should have an incentive to police themselves and everybody else; they should want to help the hospital avoid waste and inefficiency – to cost-minimize. They should want to help the hospital to deal with the stubborn surgeon who wants operating room access in the amount and time they prefer, and who dumps postsurgical care on nurses and residents. An implication is that physicians as a group should want their members to accept responsibility for efficient use of shared hospital resources; the hospital should be run as a physicians' cooperative. A potentially troubling implication, if the hospital market is not competitive, is that the medical staff might try to coordinate pricing of physician services in the private market to achieve the same market power.

Either way, coordinating physician behavior is easier said than done; it means either incentives or rules to limit individual physician behavior that commandeers hospital resources without regard for stewardship of the amount and cost of those resources. Another implication is that, to the extent that better care coordination will improve outcomes and the reputation of their hospital–physician combination, they should expect to gain from doing so in addition to their concern for the health outcomes of their individual patients. In both cases, incentives and protocols, even ones that irritate individual physicians but improve overall outcomes and lower costs should be implemented if effective versions of them can be found.

How might we modify this model regarding hospital profits? Could physicians be persuaded to let "their" hospital keep some of the money? The health system management may have goals beyond this set of individual or collective physician goals. One obvious management goal is to grow the size of the system through investment; this may be good for physicians as well even if some of them, myopically, do not see it that way. While a nonprofit system can borrow, it cannot issue equity, so investment that will not be supported by debt may be financed by retained earnings by the hospital. If the physician group expects to benefit from the intended investment, it may support positive hospital net income (by collecting lower prices for its services), especially because that net income if held by the hospital will be tax-free. Investment that will not benefit physician income sufficiently will only be undertaken if management has the power and desire to achieve other goals, such as prestige, community benefit, research, or emoluments for management. Sometimes health system managers have pursued such strategies, but many of them have not ended well, if neither the market nor the medical staff supports these objectives to a large enough extent to make them able to cover their costs.

From an economic viewpoint, a nonprofit health system run to maximize physician income would set the total price for a surgical service, its quantity, and its cost at the same level as its profit-maximizing twin. Empirical evidence does indeed suggest little difference in these parameters (price or cost) as a function of hospital ownership type. We defer further discussion of this point to Chapter 12 on hospital reimbursement.

The separate medical staff model used for decades in the US is shrinking as more physicians become salaried employees in more hospitals. Despite the surprisingly static nature of the country's health system as a whole, there has been a notable transformation in hospital–physician relationships, with larger and larger shares of physicians becoming hospital or health systems employees.[4] (This change has been accompanied by a movement from solo ownership to salary in separate physician group practice, so whatever is causing the change is larger than just physician–hospital relationships.) There has thus been a substantial increase in financial integration between physicians and hospitals, supported by a view that there will be substantial benefits from such integration accompanying production. However, managers need to know that the evidence supporting the hypothesis that financial integration matters – in terms of effects on overall cost, quality, or market performance – is exceedingly weak. Why that is so is a puzzle in theory for health economists as well as a cautionary tale for managers.

[4] Muoio, D. (2024). Nearly 80% of docs employed by hospitals, corporate entities in continued shift away from independent practice. *Fierce Healthcare*, April 12. www.fiercehealthcare.com/providers/more-and-more-physicians-are-working-under-hospitals-corporate-entities-report-finds.

Outpatient and Primary Care: Outside the Hospital Walls

In this model of hospitals and physicians, physicians who furnish care in outpatient settings so far have not played a major role. However, physicians who provide primary care, whether individually or organized collectively, often have the power to direct or influence patient use across all types of care. At a minimum, then, a hospital and its medical staff do have an interest in influencing extra-hospital primary care physician choices that might affect the use of the hospital and the inpatient services of physicians. Here is another case of complementarity: Primary care physicians and hospital-based specialists need each other to be able to offer a good package of care to a patient population, and neither group in this vertical chain (from primary care to specialist care) has an a priori grip on power to control the situation. In such a setting, relative numbers may matter – scarce orthopedic surgeons may be able to dictate conditions of access to many primary care doctors with patients with bad joints, but a surplus of cardiac surgeons may lead them to cede control to primary care physicians and outpatient cardiologists.

It will be a major leap to get from this power and influence game to an outcome of ideally coordinated inpatient and outpatient care. Here the form of payment may matter substantially. The closer the payment system is to capitation and the more primary care physicians are held accountable for total cost of care, the more need for them to coordinate care and avoid permitting (much less recommending) costly specialist services of low value relative to their price or cost. In addition, the more loyalty patients have to their primary care physicians, the more power that group will have. (It is striking that in the longest-running capitated systems such as Kaiser, patients often historically received outpatient care in clinics from varying physicians rather than having a regular primary care physician – why was that?) There are a few population-based medical systems in which primary care physicians do seem to have control, and they seem (as a sweeping generalization) to function better than systems where hospital executives or specialty department chairs dominate.

There are three kinds of coordination that would potentially involve primary care physicians. One is care for patients who are unlikely to use a hospital but have ongoing chronic conditions such as diabetes. The second is care before a potential hospitalization that may be able to prevent the hospitalization, such as care for a person with heart failure. The third is care for someone treated in the hospital but then discharged back into the community.

In the first case, the issue is in large part one of timely patient access and patient satisfaction. Patients need to be called in for needed tests that can detect more serious illness early. They want to avoid delay when they feel they are in need but avoid useless and time-wasting care. Usually, a nonphysician care coordinator is involved in this process, but it seems to work best when the primary care physician gets to know the patient and can spend time with them. A growing minority of consumers are willing to pay extra for concierge care to get more time and easier access. Paradoxically, this kind of more intensive involvement would probably do the most good for the more socially vulnerable patients but their location, the low fees from Medicaid, and imperfect information make it so far more common among the well-off.

For the potentially hospitalized patients, the main problem at present is that there is no incentive or reward for keeping them out of the hospital while still maintaining their health and avoiding patient-initiated emergency room visits that lead to inpatient care. Research shows that lowering out-of-pocket cost for outpatient care or covering the uninsured does lead to more outpatient care, but it also leads to more ER visits and hospitalizations.[5]

Finally, primary care physicians need to play a better role in assisting patients with the transition from hospital to home or nursing home. There are models which do this effectively and help avoid readmissions, but they are not commonly used.[6]

Incentives to system managers to cultivate lower cost physician care – and coordinated physician behavior that leads to lower use of other services – are strongest when payment is via capitation – since errors in coordination can lead to more services that generate more revenue under fee-for-service. It seems clear that physicians alone cannot handle this management task but the organizational design and the incentive structure for improved performance has yet to be discovered.

Right now, health systems do not have a single metric for their clinical effectiveness in managing primary care or care coordination for a patient

[5] Finkelstein, A., Taubman, S., Wright, B., Bernstein, M., Gruber, J., Newhouse, J. P., Allen, H., Baicker, K., & Oregon Health Study Group (2012). The Oregon health insurance experiment: Evidence from the first year. *The Quarterly Journal of Economics*, *127*(3), 1057–1106; Manning, W. G., Newhouse, J. P., Duan, N., Keeler, E., Benjamin, B., Leibowitz, A., Marquis, M. S., & Zwanziger, J. (1988). *Health insurance and the demand for medical care: Evidence from a randomized experiment.* RAND. www.rand.org/pubs/reports/R3476.html.

[6] Naylor, M. D., Brooten, D., Campbell, R., Jacobsen, B. S., Mezey, M. D., Pauly, M. V., & Schwartz, J. S. (1999). Comprehensive discharge planning and home follow-up of hospitalized elders: A randomized clinical trial. *JAMA*, *281*(7), 613–620.

population – only indirect or partial measures such as the Hospital Readmissions Reduction Program. There are measures of diabetic care where clinical metrics of control exist. There are simple patient satisfaction scores borrowed from other industries (would you recommend this health system to a friend on a scale of one to five?) but nothing that links satisfaction to choice of system or market share.

Nonprofit Motivation: Does It Make a Dime's Worth of Difference? And Who Gets the Dime?

The great majority of hospital beds and hospital physical capital in the US is owned by nonprofit firms.[7] There are competing for-profit or investor-owned hospitals, and both kinds of private firms have been growing their market shares at the expense of publicly owned hospitals. It seems obvious on its face that nonprofit hospitals should be different. By law, they cannot pay out net revenue or assets to owners, managers, or anyone else. They are supposed to engage in some activities for the public good (broadly and imprecisely defined). They definitely do engage in activities for the private good (like one's hernia repair), collect revenue for those services as well as accept donations, and buy and sell themselves and other enterprises. How should a manager of such an enterprise behave, and how should other firms (insurers, employers) who are customers approach this odd beast?

There is a long and fascinating history of nonprofit hospitals and other private nonprofit firms in the US which I will not detail here. Suffice it to say (by someone who has worked for nonprofit firms all his life) that I favor the theory proposed by the economist Burton Weisbrod: Nonprofits emerge when there are collective or public goods that some people in a population desire but that government does not adequately supply.[8] In colonial times, education of Native Americans (Dartmouth), of members of the clergy (Harvard), or of poor but industrious boys (University of Pennsylvania) was not a tax-financed activity of government, so better-off citizens made philanthropic donations – often in response to the pleas of nonprofit entrepreneurs otherwise known as college presidents – to provide equity and

[7] Sloan, F. A., Picone, G. A., Taylor, D. H., & Chou, S. Y. (2001). Hospital ownership and cost and quality of care: Is there a dime's worth of difference? *Journal of Health Economics*, *20*(1), 1–21.

[8] Weisbrod, B. A. (1975). Toward a theory of the voluntary nonprofit sector in a three-sector economy. In E. S. Phelps (ed.), *Altruism, morality and economic theory* (pp. 171–195). Russell Sage.

growth capital and to get the enterprise going. The same story applies to many of the nations' historical hospitals, along with (in the nineteenth century) the desires by ethnic groups (Jews, Catholics, and Methodists) to provide care for the poor sick in their community and access to facilities for physicians of the same background who were often frozen out of the earlier arrivals.

While both colleges and hospitals originally offered free or low-priced products to the poor and disadvantaged, once they got established, the technical excellence of their offerings and the change in social customs eventually meant that they were able to develop a paying middle-class and even upper-class clientele who paid full price and whose revenues became essential to the organizations' growth and prosperity. The charity care clinic merged with bespoke care for the well-to-do in the form of the modern nonprofit hospital. A key link between the two roles was the physician staff who worked on patients in both private rooms and charity wards. Over the years, the tax advantages intended to foster charity care have become mixed with the "cash model" for the middle class. The resulting blurry organizational lines seem, however, not to have yet posed a serious managerial dilemma, because care of a patient once admitted to a nonprofit hospital is not usually means-tested; rich or poor in embarrassing hospital gowns all get more or less the same treatment: not perfect equity within hospitals, and surely not across hospitals depending on their Medicaid–commercially insured mix, but still workable. It is only in the emergency room and at discharge that the question of who has resources for follow-up care comes into play – some people can go home while others have no suitable home to go to.

Public policy toward these private firms could (optimistically) be interpreted as attempts to integrate their public good activities with what taxpayers/voters would have wanted anyway if only their local governments had acted. In recognition of their provision of goods valued by the community, they were exempted from taxes other firms had to pay. In recognition of their narrower and often religious focus, they were allowed to remain private and free from direct taxpayer control – so they did not necessarily do exactly what voters or politicians wanted. Friction was inevitable, as we will discuss later in the chapter, but this framework of private production and ownership of the means of production has so far proven politically acceptable in the US – compared to the full socialization of hospitals in the UK and de facto government control elsewhere.

Later, in Chapter 12, I will try to use economic theory to straighten out what was inevitably a confusing equilibrium among various supplier groups, taxpayers, and their representatives. Here I first turn to evidence on how (or if) coordination between private nonprofit hospital goals works.

Breaks for Nonprofits: Why Haven't They Capitalized on Them?

At first thought, it would seem that nonprofit firms if well-managed ought to have current-period dominance and a golden future. They pay none of the real estate or income taxes that their for-profit competitors would owe. Much of their capital is donated with no quid pro quo. They should be able to use these advantages to help their middle-class business as well as help the poor. They should be able to underprice or undercut any for-profit competitors in private insurance markets, get warm feelings from some actions for the public good, and offer a happy (and pretty lucrative) life for their managers. Ask any nonprofit hospital administrator in a big city and you will instead get a tale of woe. What has spoiled paradise?[9]

There are some nonprofit managerial imperfections which have let in viable for-profit hospitals in some markets. One is that they cannot sell stock to raise equity if donations fall short. But the main constraint that economists note – and that managers recognize but need help to deal with – is competition. In large cities, many nonprofit hospitals compete for business. The version in our story here will be competition to be in the biggest insurer networks in town. To get in and stay in – unless you run a premier children's hospital, which seem to have vast market power – you will need to offer a lower price than your potential replacement a few miles away. We already know from economics that, in competitive equilibrium, all incumbent firms will earn zero economic profits. So, in competitive markets all firms will end up nonprofit, whether they want to be or not – even if they strive mightily for profits and behave exactly like their capitalist twin.

Not only will competition squeeze out the profits you would have wanted to use for various nonmarket activities – unselfish or selfish – but it gets even worse. Those tax breaks that are supposed to help you provide free care for the poor? Those donations from dead rich people for the same purpose? If all of your competitors have the same subsidy, but if you have to have paying customers to survive, all of that subsidy will be competed away in the form of lower prices paid by networks and ultimately by the consumers in them.

[9] Malani, A., & David, G. (2008). Does nonprofit status signal quality? *The Journal of Legal Studies*, *37*(2), 551–576.

This discouraging conclusion at least offers you an excuse for bad behavior. If your hospital is on the thin financial edge because of competition, as my colleague Amol Navathe has astutely noted, you are not going to have the wherewithal to be very merciful.[10] You will be criticized for trying to collect on costly services, hounding bad debts, and sneaking in charges wherever you can. Not only that, when your city asks you to show what you did rather than pay taxes on the valuable real estate you occupy, you will have a hard time making a genuine case for having done more than the bare minimum. As already noted, if you have to transfer the value of much of the tax breaks to commercial insurer customers, you do not have a money pump to pay for a lot of good works. Weisbrod's private provision of public goods is hard to do by firms that must compete on price to survive. You might get away with paying for a fire engine or two, but you will be limited in the amount of good you can put toward your mission if you do not have a high margin. Of course, if your benefactors uniformly require costly activities from you as a condition for keeping tax breaks or donations flowing, in equilibrium you and your fellow hospitals will have to do what you must. But only because, and as much as, you have to.

Hospital–Physician Integration: How Does It Work Now, and Will Its Time Ever Come?

The economic theory so far says that hospitals and physicians engage in joint production and, for this reason, will do best if and when they can cooperate in the process. As we will see, however, the actual performance on coordinated care – even within the hospital and more so outside in an ambulatory setting – leaves a lot to be desired. Part of the sour feelings about hospital–physician relationships at present is because of a (mostly faulty) memory of a golden age in which physicians had privileges in moderate-sized hospitals, in which they could individually and collectively, with affable colleagues, get whatever resources they wanted, and in which they alone were the judges of the effectiveness of their performance. I will invoke this benchmark (or straw man) in what follows. To some extent, I will blame the physician victims of change – though there is a lot of blame to go around.

[10] Navathe, A. (2023). Why are nonprofit hospitals more focused on dollars than patients? *New York Times*, November 30. www.nytimes.com/2023/11/30/opinion/hospitals-nonprofit-community.html

In this section, the focus will end up being on a model of physician–hospital integration that really and truly combines them into one firm à la Coase. Physicians will be employees of the hospital, paid a salary, and subject to management from the hospital as an organization. That organization will measure their performance in many dimensions and will use those metrics to make decisions on changes in compensation and continued employment. While there will be some clinical leeway for these workers, they will be controlled.

This variant seems to be the one emerging in the first quarter of the twenty-first century. Most physicians are now salaried employees, especially in specialties like anesthesiology strongly associated with inpatient care or care of patients with day-to-day clinical needs. The model of an independent community physician visiting patients in the hospital and leaving orders for their care is being replaced by hospital-employed physicians (hospitalists or specialists). However, this endpoint is coming after several intermediate stages of hospital–physician integration on which we do have evidence, most of it discouraging.[11]

I will discuss one such version here – the closed-panel health maintenance organization (HMO). The poster child here is the Kaiser health system, still an important player in its California birthplace, but which has not so far been able to spread to the rest of the country. That model retains the "two-firm" approach, with physicians in a separate firm (Kaiser Permanente Medical Group) from Kaiser hospitals. This model did succeed in lowering the level of cost, as consumers moved into managed care plans that discouraged inpatient care, but not in lowering its rate of growth. More importantly, it engendered consumer (and employer) backlash against the idea that the doctor and patient would be told by someone else what they could not do.

Kaiser combined not only hospitals and physicians but all providers with insurance. Such group staff model HMOs which furnish insurance retain a small but still significant presence in some areas, ready to march out again if the managed care revolution ever restarts, but that does not seem likely anytime soon. Other acronym-based approximations to integration (e.g., physician–hospital organizations, or PHOs) have also been tried and failed to thrive. Accountable care organizations (ACOs), which do not formally provide insurance, have yet to demonstrate effectiveness – and operate as de

[11] Burns, L. R., & Werner, R. M. (2022). Care coordination. In Pauly, M., Winston, F., Naylor et al., *Seemed like a good idea: Alchemy versus evidence-based approaches to healthcare management innovation* (pp. 64–131). Cambridge University Press.

facto insurers if they receive capitated payments. So, what do we know about how to manage today's fully vertically integrated production model?

We know some things not to do.

Argue over money. While some services are paid on a bundled basis that combines hospital and doctor inputs into a single price, many public and private insurers still pay separately for physician fee and hospital payment – even if the hospital system collects both and then dispenses some funds toward physician salaries. When insurance markets are competitive and determine the combined price, higher hospital prices mean lower physician prices. Either way, management must supervise a cutting and division of the pie. This action is intrinsically contentious and in economics there is no natural (or unnatural) law that governs how to split the proceeds from joint production. If doctors did nothing there would be no payment, so they could hold out for the total. But if the hospital contributed nothing, there would also be no output and no payment. What other hospitals in town pay their doctors might set a benchmark for the physicians' payment; another benchmark might be the net profits if the doctors split off and opened a surgicenter to furnish most of the hospital inputs. Both will be hard to establish and hard to make persuasive. We can fall back to the obvious and say that it will be best to settle this division beforehand – and then stick with it without griping.

Focus on the money, not the care. In those settings that have converted to an employee salary model, operable mechanisms of financial integration have been developed. Prices are set, revenues are collected, and money is dispensed to different kinds of workers (including doctors on a regular basis). There seems to have been much less clinical integration to accompany rearrangement of payment flows. While we do not have large sample data, it does seem that features of clinical integration such as protocols, guidelines, and other services to coordinate patient care have not changed appreciably from what they were under the two-firm model. Changing how people work is always harder than changing how you pay them, so this is not surprising but is regrettable.

Ignore culture and goals. The ideal integrated system would have a culture in which physicians and management work together to achieve mutual goals. Kaiser is sometimes said to have achieved this, but few other integrated systems have. The production function for organizational culture is even more puzzling and challenging than clinical integration. The search goes on.

Dredge up past slogans. In previous efforts to achieve integration, there was high productivity in generating aspirational slogans. Continuum of care, physician alignment, population health, and reduction in care variation – they were all there 30 years ago. Nothing happened with them. Unless and until someone finds a lever for change in the hoped-for direction, talk about such things will not help.

Deal with a dysfunctional family. If physicians do not automatically get along with hospital management, they usually do not get along well with each other either. Across specialties, envy and blame limit cooperation, and within each specialty it only takes a few actors to disrupt agreement. Ideally, management would work with a medical staff already with internal peace, but in practice there may need to be some refereeing of conflicts to bring about a good outcome.

Risk-Bearing and Risk-Sharing

One hallmark of conventional wisdom about healthcare provision, reinforced by the usual view of fee-for-service payment as intrinsically flawed, is the view that providers will perform better if they are at risk for the cost of the inputs for the care they provide. "Risk" here does not necessarily mean uncertainty, but it does mean that they are to some extent recipients of any residual payments after care is provided and paid for. Capitation is the acme of this idea with 100% financial risk for deviations in actual cost above or below the capitated amount. Insurers and healthcare organizations, pushed aggressively by Medicare, have developed many ways of penalizing or rewarding both the firm and the physician for cost variation from some target. There is a trade-off here: Under fee-for-service, the provider is at risk that not enough sick patients will show up; under capitation, the risk is that too many will.

How have these approaches worked? One challenge has been getting physicians to agree to "downside risk," the chance of losing a lot of money, either from lack of physician attention to cost or if some patients needed much more costly care than expected. The goal of downside risk is to offer financial disincentives to slacking off or failing to prepare for sicker patients, but it will also penalize providers for treatment of sicker or riskier patients who just happened to be there. According to economics, even very risk-averse people would agree to such a bet with a potentially bad outcome if paid enough up front, but the required payment may exceed any gains from the intervention. There has been progress with a mixture of rewards and punishments in getting some physician groups and providers of all types organized in ACOs to accept downside risk or two-sided risk.[12] Medicare is proud that a large minority of its providers and beneficiaries are now in risk-based payment contracts, and more are taking downside risk, although many of them are still fee-for-service with some add-ons or takeaways related to a few cost targets. Private insurers have been much less aggressive overall, since they have neither the market share nor the political clout to induce provider participation, but there have been some examples of high-powered payment systems physicians accept in return for upfront money. And of course, capitated providers such as Kaiser are the granddaddies of risk-based payment.

From an economic viewpoint, any gain in efficiency from putting providers at risk does not come from the fact of a different payment arrangement that may be grafted onto financial integration; gain has to come from changes in provider behavior induced by the higher chances of reward or punishment for certain decisions, especially those by physicians about other costly non-physician services or goods. From a managerial perspective, whatever the risk corridor and formula for the organization, translating that financial incentive into rules or rewards for physician behavior and physician decisions will be important. The organization can put in place capacity constraints to hold down volumes of low-value processes, but such heavy-handed tactics may result in congestion and frustration for doctors and patients. Moreover, any gains if they occur are likely to be one-time in the sense that costs will fall as the new payment method is put in place but then continue to grow at the same rate as if it had never happened. That is what happened with HMOs, but it is too soon for the new payment models.

Medicine Isn't Fun Anymore: Who or What Is to Blame?

The general malaise among physicians who now deal with health system management as employees tends to transfer anger to that management. Economics does offer some cures for this problem but not without side effects. However, these approaches may be better than unionization of physicians (a movement already underway by nurses, residents, and fellows).

[12] McWilliams, J. M., Hatfield, L. A., Landon, B. E., Hamed, P., & Chernew, M. E. (2018). Medicare spending after 3 years of the Medicare Shared Savings Program. *New England Journal of Medicine, 379* (12), 1139–1149; Wang, A., Debab, S., Muhlestein, D., McStay, F., Bleser, W. K., McClellan, M. B., & Saunders, R. S. (2023). Medicare accountable care organizations in 2022: Renewed growth and improved savings show small rebound from the COVID-19 pandemic. *Health Affairs Forefront*. https://doi.org/10.1377/forefront.20231017.282343.

Burnout. Physicians dealt with a surge of unpredictable and unexpected work during the coronavirus pandemic, and they are upset that the same pressures to do more with less time are still present in their jobs, especially in the provision of office visits. In the (kind of) good old days, physicians regularly reported more and more inconvenient hours of work than the average worker, but in those days, they could control their time and had deeper relationships with patients.

The epitome of a treadmill-burnout model at present is acquisition of practices by (and ceding management control to) private equity investors. Of course, these acquisitions are voluntary; physicians who take the money (and do not retire) should recognize that what they got themselves into is their own fault. There is as yet no evidence on the sustainability of this model – buying up medical practices bankrupted Wall Street firms in the late 1990s – and so this move may fizzle.[13]

As discussed in the previous chapter, economics (as opposed to smart money) provides an unsympathetic diagnosis and a way to select a solution: The reason for productivity pressure at work is that high volume is needed to cover the cost of the salary you receive. If you were willing to accept lower pay (what economists call a "compensating differential"), you could have a lower workload and more time with each patient – either that or demand higher prices and risk a loss of patients to other health systems. The hamster has to be paid to get on the wheel. The discussion of physician burnout in the preceding chapter summarizes this.

Measurement. You cannot manage without measurement, the fortune cookie goes, and so salaried practice has been accompanied by a range of measures of outcome or quality from all sources. Some of this measurement is aimed at those who, having been promised a paycheck no matter what, might slack off at work – but all physicians must be punished to avoid this. The idea that there is to be external evaluation of how well you do your job when you feel you are satisfied with your performance also rankles professionals – teachers evaluated by students (get new ties!) or physicians who lack empathy or have an imperious manner that reduces their patient satisfaction scores. Managers can pass the buck by noting that these metrics are often imposed outside the health system (insurers award stars, websites list complaints), but there is still a need for attention.

[13] Pauly, M. V., & Burns, L. R. (2024). Equity investment in physician practices: What's all this brouhaha? *Journal of Health Politics, Policy and Law*, *49*(4), 631–664. https://doi.org/10.1215/03616878-11186103.

Bureaucracy. In the olden golden days, it was kumbaya, as many physicians remember. Professionals gave orders, they were usually followed, everyone was treated as a partner, and people talked things out. Now, salaried physicians in hospitals have rules they have to follow; have permissions they need to take the time to seek, either from the patient's insurer's 800 number or from the system managers; and always have to go through and try to manage channels of higher authority. The primary reason for all this, physicians know, is to keep costs down – a reasonability formerly delegated to lesser authorities in the back room who stayed out of the doctor's way but who now make their presence known. It almost goes without saying that a skillful manager will try to keep rules inside a velvet glove, cater to professional judgment and pride, and try to keep things running smoothly. What is also important to say is that, apparently, the formula for doing this consistently is unknown. Some managers have grace but so far have not been able to bottle it and ship it elsewhere even in their own hospital much less nationwide. Coase's theory of the firm did not get into personalities, management models of organizational behavior tell you much more about structure than process, and we are still not sure how things will work out.

Economics and common sense do offer some advice here. Keep groups as small as possible, because the sense of responsibility per person diminishes as groups grow larger (and remember, economies of scale are fleeting), substitute for professional time (e.g., with scribes) where it is cost-effective to do so, make sure incentives are linked with firm goals and not with what is fashionable, and poach skilled managers wherever you find them. Beyond that, we have the usual invocation of a competitive market to sort it out, whatever it is: Successful firms, however they do it, should be given wide scope to capture more of the market. My personal expectation is that hospital–physician coordination will always show more room for improvement but not be able to improve that much, unless and until someone knows more about the process of care and permits its commodification – which in turn may not be what patients want. Where we are may be as good as it gets.

Conclusion: The Questions That Remain – Who Is in Charge Here? Where Is the Money Going?

The essence of the economic theory of the firm is that bosses give orders and workers follow them. Within a firm, they do not negotiate, and that saves enough time and money to make everyone better off. The essence of an ideal healthcare system is that expert professionals can see that each individual patient is treated in a distinctive way based on patient condition and their technical knowledge. The problem: These two visions clash. Organizational theory, a part of management as a discipline, has explored what firms (as organizations) can or should do when they must delegate key resource-use decisions to workers or other underlings who know more than their managers.

The actual division of authority within a hospital is probably more important than its formal organizational structure. Methods of coordination within the group of staff physicians are as important – if not more important – than coordination of physicians' supplied inputs to the hospital.

What division is best still seems to be in doubt. Who is the recipient of the residual income? Legal limits as noted prevent the hospital or health system management from capturing would-be profits as money income. Economists have postulated many nonfinancial goods that might go into manager utility functions – respect, quality, emoluments, volume of size – the list is both long and unproven. I remain prejudiced toward the idea that the medical staff somehow – perhaps at some remove if they are salaried – have de facto control and see that the hospital is run to serve their interests.

However, there is a puzzle suggested earlier. One way to test alternative models of the hospital would be to see what they would say about an exogenous change that affected market prospects. In Chapter 12, we will review evidence suggesting that horizontal combinations within a given local market among hospitals lead to higher *hospital* prices. What such changes mean (to all participants in the local market, not just the merging firms) is not well known. Do these combinations lead to higher hospital net incomes? Are they associated with higher prices for the complementary physician services? Going further, if hospitals do report higher profits, what do they do with the money? If physician fees rise, do they do so to a greater extent in hospitals with better coordinated and/or salaried medical staff? The market may be the best entity to support the ideal coordination and organization, but the resolution still remains to be seen. There is at present a great gulf between industrial organization evidence on changes in market-level competition and models of the nonprofit hospitals that are doing the combining. Perhaps it is all empire-building by managers. Readers who are on the inside of the industry will know more than I (or other health economists) know. In this case, we are ready for some unexpected insights.

5 How Good Can We Be? How Big Should We Be? Should We Try to Conquer the World?

Introduction

Every manager knows that having revenue greater than cost is a good thing, often something necessary for survival (of both the firm and the manager's job). Obviously, a healthcare system, a hospital, or a physician group has a choice about how much of what kinds of services it wants to produce. "Out there" somewhere are customers who are (one hopes) willing to pay for these services. But even if managers know potential demand, they also need to know potential cost to decide what to do.

Of course, firms have accounting systems which, after the fact, tell them whether the revenues they brought in were enough to cover the payments they laid out for inputs, plus a little extra for a rainy day or stockholder needs. Sometimes those accounting systems try to be prospective and say what will happen to costs if outputs change and revenue comes in. Often the accounting figures on cost are very wrong from an economic perspective (and as a guide to managerial decisions), because they add all kinds of overhead or fixed costs (which are not affected by output change) to the actual increment in real resources used for any output. Health economic research suggests that the accounting systems used in many organizations are misleading guides to what is more or less incrementally profitable. Here I will offer some observations on when accounting data is truthful (or at least useful) versus when it just kids around. I hasten to add that I have never run a hospital (or a railroad) so these are cautionary messages from the more abstract world of economics and should be given whatever credit you think appropriate to their source.

Most economic work on the production of medical care has involved hospital inpatient care (because that is where the money and the good data are). In the US, hospitals historically did not employ physicians but rather granted them admitting privileges, which permitted them to use hospital surgical and procedure suites and to provide their patients room and board with nurse attendance but to bill separately for their services. This meant that hospital net income compared the cost of those inputs it supplied with revenues paid for that purpose, and that hospital data and analysis in the US leaves out both physician costs, physician inputs, and physician revenues. Physicians were paid separately for services provided in the hospital with the only explicit costs for them sometimes being for follow-up care later in physician offices. Studies of hospital costs and production thus typically leave out any variation in physician input, even though it is obvious that physician effort can substitute for hospital labor and capital. This omission calls for caution in interpretation of research results.

Given this setting, economic studies of hospital production have generally addressed two issues: (1) did hospitals choose the cost-minimizing mix of labor of various types and physical capital and (2) are there economies of scale in the production of hospital procedures, admissions, and days of stay?

Input Combinations, Production Functions, and Cost of Production

The methods of empirical analysis used by economists are cross-sectional or time period comparisons of the relationship between bundles of inputs and measures of outputs. In contrast, a manager of a specific health system is likely to rely on the average cost per admission and use it as a proxy for the change in cost per admission, along with perhaps a small amount of unstable data on how things have changed in the last few years. While often opaque prepackaged accounting cost analysis programs are common, at base the change in cost a manager should expect to use, and to compare with revenue coming in, according to economists, is just sum of changes in inputs used weighted by their prices. The challenge is how to know what this change is – you will know current cost at current output and quality, not how will it change (or how will you have to change it) to produce a change in output. You know that one more inpatient admission will require more of some inputs for sure – like meals and linen. But what about staff (nursing and other)? What about the marketing department?

It is confusing. A small increase in volume probably would not trigger hiring of new clinical staff in most instances; workers would just have to work a little harder. However, in a few cases, where staff were already extra-busy, the increased load would lead to a new hire. Suppose that 19 times out of 20 hiring a new worker at labor cost of $70,000 would not happen when a particular output is increased, but in 5% of cases it would. One could say that the additional cost of one more unit of output per time period would average (0.05)*(70,000), or $3,500 – and managers could expect this additional cost on average over a multitude of cases.

One way to think about this issue – which will come in handy later on in the chapter to explain some puzzles – is that hospitals often buy inputs that embody a stock or inventory of productive activities – a new piece of lab equipment can run tests up to its capacity, a new salaried nurse is a stock of hours and effort that can be drawn upon, again up to a point. When either input use reaches capacity, the hospital has to buy another one.

Although many types of labor, operating rooms, and patient capacity might fit this "stochastic marginal cost" story,[1] there would be also some fixed costs that need to be incurred to get a hospital started but then do not increase (or do not increase much) with additional volume. Costs to incorporate and organize the activity, the CEO's salary, and the purchase of needed equipment that has lots of capacity would fall into this category. The hospital is better off financially the larger the number of units of output over which it can spread these fixed costs. After a point, the truly fixed cost per unit of output becomes vanishingly small, so overall long-run average and marginal costs are more or less constant over larger volumes – which means there is no longer an advantage to greater size beyond that point. Studies of hospital costs suggest that this point of "leveling out" occurs at about the level of inpatient care associated with 250–300 beds.[2] This clean theoretical point gets fuzzy in practice. It may look like the cost of the C-suite, or the marketing department, should not vary with hospital output – but these types of cost are almost always larger in larger volume hospitals. Somehow, when output grows and things get busy, managers of almost all departments hire more staff.

Hospitals can be larger than 300 beds – and many are – but they no longer have serious cost advantages over their medium-sized competitors. Even worse for the "size matters" hypothesis, there is some research that shows that, at very large sizes, average cost starts to increase because of the need to hire more people to coordinate a large organization. The punchline is that, for inpatient care, the cost-minimizing size of hospitals in general is not one number but includes the range of 300 to perhaps 600 beds. Perhaps not

[1] Friedman, B., & Pauly, M. (1981). Cost functions for a service firm with variable quality and stochastic demand: The case of hospitals. *The Review of Economics and Statistics*, *63*(4), 620–624.

[2] Gaynor, M. S., Kleiner, S. A., & Vogt, W. B. (2015). Analysis of hospital production: An output index approach. *Journal of Applied Econometrics*, *30*(3), 398–421.

surprisingly, hospitals in the US in large cities have clustered in this range, as behemoth county hospitals closed and private hospitals decentralized. It appears that there was a kind of Darwinian process in which huge hospitals (often the public or county hospital in a large city) went the way of the dinosaurs – too large to be nimble in the modern era.

Of course, these conclusions are only helpful to the managers of the average hospital – and no manager thinks of their hospital as average. Still the range is wide enough to suggest that, above a minimum level, getting a bigger physical plant to reduce costs should not be a management objective. In fact, most large health systems are collections of individual hospital plants or campuses of about the size indicated. Adding more copies of the same optimal sized model also does not seem to affect the average cost of care but it does raise the wages of the C-suite: Their costs are not really fixed after all but, as with almost all firms, management wages are higher the bigger they are. Extra pay for empire-building may not convey the ideal incentives to managers but, as we shall see, external discipline on such ambitions is sometimes lacking.

The idea that inputs are stocks of productive activities also helps to explain a paradox in the analysis of hospital costs. Analysts find that when a hospital experiences a sudden surge in demand, its nursing costs do not rise much, while a temporary fall will not be associated with a large reduction in cost. One might then conclude that "short-run" additional nursing costs are small. But if demand increases and stays high for a long period, nurses get tired, so you need more of them, and costs increase by more. Then a puzzle: How can it be more costly to respond to a change in output when the manager has time to adjust compared to when the increase must be met with what is on hand? The answer is that the "real" labor cost borne by nurses is actually higher for the unexpected increase requiring all to work harder, and controlling costs (and maintaining staff morale) requires more employment if that increase becomes permanent. This is an example of how accounting costs can be misleading; "true" short-run marginal costs are actually higher than longer-run costs, but the accounting data says the opposite.

What messages for managers are provided by economic (rather than accounting) analyses of hospital production and cost? Many hospital economic studies are studies of "production functions" in which primarily physical measures of hospital inputs (labor hours of various types, square feet of capital, equipment expense) are related to some type of composite index of output. These studies do not assume that all managers chose the cost-minimizing mix of inputs, given their prices. In fact, one dividend of this research can be a discovery that some input is relatively underused or overused. There are several punchlines from this research:

(1) Some hospitals get a lot more output out of given mixes of inputs than others. This is circumstantial evidence for production inefficiency, although it can often also be due to imperfect measurement of inputs and outputs – especially of the quality of both.
(2) Physician time substitutes for other hospital inputs, even when the hospital does not employ the physicians (but also when it does). So medical staff ordering overuse of other inputs, especially nursing, to reduce their time commitment is something to watch out for.
(3) Physical capital often has a zero or negative marginal product – bricks and mortar just get in the way, and the "edifice complex" is not helpful to efficiency.
(4) Some inputs have higher marginal products (the amount of output one more unit of them will produce) relative to their price than others, indicating that the mix of inputs at a given level of output is not cost-minimizing.

A disclaimer: I will discuss results of some of these economic studies of production and cost functions presently, and I will argue that they told managers some things that they did not already know. However, an individual manager's ability to produce journal-quality estimates is obviously limited by the data available. The economic approach needs many (like hundreds, for best results) of observations on different output and input or cost levels – and even within a large health system that kind of luxury is going to be hard to find. The conceptual insights from the studies to be discussed are still going to be useful, and an informed manager should be a consumer of such analyses. If you have enough data, it still makes sense to try some of these methods (or hire an itinerant economist to do them for you) because what a smaller sample sacrifices in precision it gains in relevance to a particular firm or market. And managers may have a hands-on knowledge of what are the unmeasured peculiarities of each site or time period. These economic insights are most useful as a check on accounting data or as a resource when you need a general or directional result. The insights can still help.

Economies and Diseconomies of Scope

A hospital or health system does not look at its output as a single physical measure (even if we analysts sometime use patient days or adjusted admissions as output metrics). Managers know that their systems produce a mix of different services using different amounts and kinds of inputs, sometimes dictated by the mix of patients they attract, but often a choice for the health system. Some of what we might call "intermediate outputs," like room and board, can be used for a variety of different final outputs, but some are more specialized. Most health systems aspire to and do offer a full range of services that might be needed by a heterogeneous mix of patients, although there are some hospitals that specialize (e.g., in orthopedic or eye surgery, maternity care, or psychiatric and behavioral healthcare). They do so either because their geographic area has a mixed patient population or because their medical staff prefers to specialize in one set of outputs. But generally, there are, up to a point, "economies of scope" in production (costs are lower for a mix of outputs if they are produced in one place rather than in multiple separate specialized sites).

However, a health system often has to decide whether or not to add another line of business or to expand an existing service. For new "centers" (for burns, for sleep, for behavioral health), the economic calculus is the usual one – how much more revenue will they bring in, and how does that compare with the cost they add? A pertinent point sometimes ignored is whether the answer to the latter question is higher than the cost incurred in a freestanding new entity. If it would be higher when added to the existing physical or organizational structure, the competitive future of your new center would be in doubt – because it could not compete with a new entity.

This issue has most frequently been discussed in the context of ambulatory surgery centers, which I will discuss in more detail later in the chapter. But it applies to ambulatory or outpatient care more broadly. The evidence so far is that hospital organized outpatient care is definitely not less costly and is probably more costly than freestanding output care – even "semi emergency" care in instant care clinics. One reason why cost can be higher in the hospital is that, in the health system, costly inputs used for sick inpatients are also more easily available for outpatient care – so tests and consultations can proliferate. More intensive and costly but low-value care may be too convenient to patients and doctors in the health system setting – which is why many outpatient clinics run by health systems are physically separated from the inpatient services. The spread of health-system branded but physically separate outpatient facilities in suburban office parks is consistent with this hypothesis. If special Medicare additional payments for hospital-associated facilities disappear as site-neutral systems are introduced, any diseconomies of scope from hospital linkages will be a liability. Darwin seems not to have arrived here yet. There will be economies of scope if a new line of output is able to use any long-run scale economies of some activity that was already needed for older inputs; the linen from the new treatment may be more cheaply washed in the existing laundry. Diseconomies of scope often involve bad behavior rather than bad engineering: Because the laundry is so close, workers use more linen than they otherwise would – or some more elevated version of this story.

The Hospital at Home: An Untapped Source of Free Inputs?

Another issue in the analysis of hospital costs deals with programs in which patients or their families voluntarily provide inputs without pay in the care of the patient. One example are children's hospital programs that allow parents to stay overnight in their child's room after a procedure. Not only does this reassure the child but the parents can also handle minor episodes of distress that would otherwise require nurse time. Or consider the "hospital at home" model, in which a patient is quickly transferred to home, and the health system then only has to provide periodic visits from staff and be on call for emergencies.[3] This has a lower health system cost than an inpatient stay, because the patient's household provides free room and board, and family members or friends are available to provide some services that nurses or aides furnish in the hospital. Of course, neither parent nor family member time is really free (though we probably would not rent out grandma's bedroom if she were hospitalized for a week), so the lower health system costs to some extent understate the true opportunity cost of the procedure and recovery.

What can make these programs attractive is that some patients may actually prefer care from family members rather than from strangers, so that if participation is truly voluntary (rather than a response to social pressure) that gain in family well-being more than offsets the cost of donated services. Different values different households place on the ability to provide care themselves will limit the generalizability of these programs as a cost-containment device – and managers will need to take that into account. Permanent Medicare approval for such programs is still pending, but private insurers can cover them as they wish and at potentially lower prices.

[3] Adams, D., Wolfe, A. J., Warren, J., Laberge, A., Richards, A. C., Herzer, K., & Fleisher, L. A. (2023). Initial findings from an acute hospital care at home waiver initiative. *JAMA Health Forum* 4(11), e233667.

How to Detect Waste

I noted in Chapter 1 that it is commonplace to claim that there is substantial waste in the US medical care system, challenging managers to defend what they do, but that it is much less common to offer practical advice on what to do to improve matters in ways likely to do more good than harm. In this chapter, I will outline some economic techniques that can be used to measure inefficiency and point to solutions. (Of course, that is not the end of the story because some managers will actually have to follow our advice.)

Inefficiency in economics can arise either on the production (supply) side or on the use (demand) side. An example of demand-side inefficiency (and what to do about it) will be discussed in the context of moral hazard – if insurance for middle-class people has too low a level of cost-sharing, patients will use care worth less than its cost without adequate reward in terms of risk protection. In this chapter, we deal with the two components of efficient production: technical waste and input combination inefficiency.

The overarching objective for efficient production, both in a firm and in the market in which it operates, is to minimize the real opportunity cost of whatever output is produced, at a given level of quality. Getting the volume of output for a given population right, given efficient production, is a demand-side problem that I will assume here has been solved. But a manager who wants to produce some predetermined output must choose inputs that will be able to produce that output.

Hitting your quota is a necessary step, but it is not enough; you are supposed to do so with efficient use of resources, given their relative prices. What does that mean? It means two things: (1) whatever set of resources (different kinds of worker hours, building space, machinery, and everything else) you use to produce output, it should be managed so as to produce the maximum output. Or, to flip it around, you should minimize resources for whatever output you do produce. This is called technical efficiency; (2) to make more sense out of the last restatement, you should minimize the cost of the resources you use (equivalent to saying you should minimize a weighted sum of the total resources you use, where the weights are the costs, prices, or wages per unit of each resource). This is called input efficiency.

The production functions can detect technical inefficiencies, in ways I will now describe. They can also detect input inefficiencies if you have data on the cost or price of an additional input and some inputs display a level of productivity relative to their costs which is different than average.

Economists have developed statistical tools to estimate production functions, the relationship between inputs and outputs. They come in two flavors, tailored to the two aspects of efficiency. Let us take the second one first. How are inputs related to outputs, and are they combined in the cost-minimizing combination? Imagine you have data from a large number of firms or "plants" producing a single kind of output (of a given quality) with a mix of inputs; your data tells you how much output and how many of each kind of input. Then you can ask the computer to tell you what the relationship is between various mixes of inputs and volumes of output. Imagine something that was done in reality – that you have data on the number of patient visits to a set of physician practices, along with measures of doctor time, nurse time, non-nurse aide time, office space, and a dollar measure of other practice costs. You can ask a computer to look at all of these combinations and then ask it to tell you, for your favorite input (say, nurse time), on average how many more patients a practice sees when it adds one more full-time nurse holding constant doctor time, aide time, office square feet, and other practice expense.

The computer will spit out a number which describes how many more visits are associated with more nurses, what economists call the "marginal productivity of that (nurse) input." It is "marginal" because it tells you about one more input – it does not answer the question of what would happen to output if all the nurses quit; it only deals with one more or one less. You could do the same things for doctor time, other aide time, and so on.

These results are only the beginning, but they can already tell you something. For instance, if an additional doctor hour contributes twice as much to the volume of visits as a nurse hour, you could say (with poetic license) that a doctor is equivalent to two nurses. Put on your flak jacket, because nurses and doctors (and all the people in a firm) usually think they are important. But the good news you can give to doctors is that they can do more in a given amount of time than nurses (hence, med school paid off). The good news you can give to nurses is that they can substitute for doctors; they can contribute to output in the same way as doctors can.

What is actually going on behind the numbers in the doctor–nurse firm is, in some ways, the more fundamental management issue. I would not be brave enough to outline which tasks physicians perform (if they have to) that nurses could also perform as well but will only say "there are some." That is all we need to support the statistical method – but clearly how each practice itself manages task allocation internally is going to matter.

How does this econometric process differ from what a manager could generate from internal cost accounting data? The econometric approach looks to see which costs (of whatever input) did in fact change when the output changed, and to what extent. The downside, of course, is that this approach yields only the "average marginal" cost across the different hospitals that supplied the data points – it is not necessarily your system's marginal cost today. Rather it will be an average (although with measurable characteristics controlled for) or average across your hospital back into the past. So, it probably is best used along with your accounting data. If the two concur, congratulations! If they differ by a lot, more investigation is needed. What about the next question – cost minimization in terms of input combinations? Here you need more information – what is the cost, price, or wage per unit of each of the inputs. Should it happen that nurses are half as productive but are paid just half as much per hour than doctors, that would tell you that (on average) practices in your dataset were indeed using the cost-minimizing combination. If in contrast, nurse wages per hour were less than half of doctor wages, the practice could lower cost by using more nurse time (cheap relative to its marginal product) and less doctor time (expensive even given its larger marginal product). As we will soon discuss, this analysis is exactly what Uwe Reinhardt used for his doctoral thesis, which then caused controversy because it said the best way to get more visits to patients was to train more nurses rather than found more medical schools.

How to Use Econometric Production and Cost Functions

If you as a manager were trying to make invidious comparisons among different physician practices or outpatient clinics in your health system, you could use this analysis to predict what inputs and input costs would be incurred by the average practice for a given number of patient visits, and then pick on any of your practices or clinics that had higher costs than that predicted amount, while awarding gold stars (figuratively and literally) to the practices with much lower costs. You could even deal with practices in different geographic areas where (say) nurse wages were unusually high – by determining whether the practices had reduced the nurse–doctor ratio appropriately. More to the point, this comparison could tell you about technical efficiency – since the practices with higher-than-average cost given some output and set of input prices must not have been getting the maximum number of office visits from their inputs. You could see if the higher cost comes from more paid worker time wasted on breaks, on tasks that did not contribute to output, or on renting more space than was needed. You can look at input efficiency to see if the mixes of inputs are such that all inputs have the same ratio of marginal product to input prices (see Box 5.1).[4]

Box 5.1 Evidence: Economic magic

Here is an example, using the techniques described, of how managers could be helped by economics. A long-standing controversy in healthcare concerns the production of what are labeled "physician services." These services are usually defined as ones typically produced in a physician's office and/or involving physician interaction (time and effort) with a patient. (As we have seen, whatever bright line there was between these services and hospital – or other – services has become dim over time.) The controversy was over the role of nonphysicians in the production of these services. The issue was whether nonphysicians contributed to the production of this kind of care; the bomb-throwing issue was whether at least some of the care could be produced by nonphysicians alone. The economic fuse was whether these nonphysicians could be paid directly.

Economists were above the fray. Reared on the production function approach, they imagined that these services were most efficiently produced by combinations of physician time and other inputs – rather than all of one or all of the other. And they philosophically opined that payment to each input should equal its contribution to output, whatever that was.

Others were not so dispassionate. To state legislators that gave or withheld legal licenses to sell medical care to the public, physician organizations lobbied vigorously to keep other kinds of professionals with different credentials out – psychologists, nurses, therapists, and dietitians. To federal funders, the same physician organizations argued that the only way to increase access to these services was to train more doctors partially at taxpayers' expense.

The late and famous health economist Uwe Reinhardt confronted these issues when it was time for him to write his doctoral thesis.[5] His idea was to estimate a production function for services designated as physician services, which he imagined could be measured by either office visits to a physician practice or billings by that practice. He obtained survey data from a large number of practices on these output measures per week along with input metrics per week such as physician hours, medical aide time, nonmedical employee time, square feet of space, and the like. He used this data to determine how much an extra physician hour added to output, an extra nurse hour, an extra receptionist hour, and so forth. (Note that the econometric method does not require you to directly observe how much of each input was applied to each patient; that all comes out in the data.) He then divided each of these increments in output by an estimate of the cost of each kind of hour and discovered that, even

[4] Hollingsworth, B. (2008). The measurement of efficiency and productivity of health care delivery. *Health Economics*, *17*(10), 1107–1128; Heimeshoff, M., Schreyögg, J., & Kwietniewski, L. (2014). Cost and technical efficiency of physician practices: A stochastic frontier approach using panel data. *Health Care Management Science*, *17*, 150–161; Zuckerman, S., Hadley, J., & Iezzoni, L. (1994). Measuring hospital efficiency with frontier cost functions. *Journal of Health Economics*, *13*(3), 255–280.

[5] Reinhardt, U. E. (1970). An economic analysis of physician's practices. PhD dissertation. Yale University.

though a nurse hour added less to output than a doctor hour, nurses wages were so much lower that the output per dollar of cost was greater for them than for physicians. The implication was that the cheapest way to increase access to physician services was for current physicians to hire more nurses (and receptionists too) rather than have the government pay for more medical schools. Not only that but the physician practices that did increase aide employment would actually yield more income to physician owners because the additional visits aide time made possible brought in enough revenue to more than compensate them.

Box 5.2 Evidence: Examples of results from production and cost functions – the impact of economic magic

The text discusses the techniques economists have developed to extract important messages for management from data on a sample of providers of care that records their inputs (hours of different types of labor) and measures of output (physical measures like office visits or inpatient medical admissions, or financial measures like total billings).

Reinhardt used these measures to estimate a production function for physician office care for his doctoral thesis in 1972 and obtained results using data from the late 1960s that indicated that the contribution of aides to output and billings (defined broadly to include registered nurses [RNs] and licensed practical nurses [LPNs], and other office staff) was definitely positive (though smaller than the contribution of physicians) but was large enough relative to their low wages at the time that practices could increase profits by hiring more aides – or give overworked doctors more time off with no cut in practice profits by substituting aides for doctors. Douglas Brown undertook a similar study in 1988, using data from about 10 years later.[6] During this interval, the number of aides per physician in practices increased by about one-third – which would have been expected to lower their relative productivity. Brown obtained the results shown when he compared his estimates of productivity of each type of worker with data on their wages. Ideally, if practices were maximizing profits and if these average productivity estimates applied to each practice, the amount of output per dollar of wage cost, shown in column 2 of Exhibit 5.1, should be equal across worker types. Instead, for the LPN hours–physician hours comparison in solo practices, he found the same result as Reinhardt: Relative to physician time, LPN time was still a bargain since it yielded more output per dollar of wage cost. So, incidentally, were LPNs relative to RNs. The same indication of high value shows up for physician assistants in group practices. However, the overall contribution of all types of aides to output relative to wages in Brown's data is now a little above the physician figure; aides as a group are not underused. Perhaps physicians had read Reinhardt's thesis, hired more aides, and overshot a little. Perhaps aide wages had risen relative to LPN and doctor wages. But we do have guidance from these kinds of estimates – always holding enthusiasm in reserve because of variations in data quality and samples.

[6] Brown, D. M. (1988). Do physicians underutilize aides? *Journal of Human Resources*, *23*(3), 342–355.

Economists also estimate cost functions to generate numbers for the marginal costs of different kinds of outputs, given wage rates and other input prices. One study in which I participated had as its primary goal the estimation of the marginal cost of hospital-produced outpatient care. The motivation for the study was a managerial problem: Compared to outpatient care doctors can furnish in their offices or clinics, should hospitals be in the business of producing outpatient care? More precisely, could they do so at the same or lower cost than the alternative? The study used data from about 1,000 short-term general hospitals that reported their total patient care costs, and measures of the volumes of outpatient care and various types of inpatient care – medical, surgical, obstetric, and so on – along with measures of each hospital's wage rate and cost of capital. The most important wrinkle was to allow the marginal cost of outpatient care to depend on the mix of outpatient versus inpatient care the hospital supplied. Large hospitals tended to have lower ratios than smaller ones, but there was considerable variation even when holding a measure of size constant. The main findings of interest are shown in Exhibit 5.2. At the time of the study, the average fee for a routine office visit was about $35. The message was stark: Hospitals oriented toward mostly inpatient care could not compete on cost of outpatient care they did supply with doctors' offices. Unless they could charge more than the competition, they would be losing money the more outpatient care they produced. However, hospitals oriented more toward outpatient care did have marginal costs in the same ballpark as freestanding offices. The latter finding contrasted with accounting estimates of the cost of outpatient care in such hospitals that were much higher than the econometric ones, presumably because accounting systems loaded more costs that were not variable or marginal on these outputs. The punchline was that there are diseconomies of scope in hospital production of outpatient and inpatient care combined. As a curiosity, the study also found that, other things equal, costs were higher when the medical staff was younger – but it did not look at whether outcomes were better.

Of course, none of these estimates are bulletproof. If units with larger outputs have more skilled management who can better handle task allocation to different kinds of workers, numbers like Reinhardt's will overstate the contribution of the average aide in the average firm. Still, they can provide useful information to managers and can be performed in situations where there is a large enough set of observations on different combinations of outputs and inputs – a potential boost for larger health systems.

Since these early days, there have been dozens of published estimates of healthcare cost and production functions, while data analytics packages based on these insights are now available from outside firms and in-house units in health systems charged with finding something useful in the bonanza of data now available. For a manager, careful discernment is important. There is a circle within a circle here, as one looks for research that evaluates whether health systems that rely more heavily on data analytics (or, for that matter, evidence-based care) can be shown to perform better by some metric than those who do not. Such "evidence on evidence," a consumers' report on production and cost data analysis, can be helpful when it is available.

Exhibit 5.1 Marginal products and efficiency of input use

	All physicians		Solo physicians		Group physicians	
Input	MP	MP/P	MP	MP/P	MP	MP/P
H	2.967	0.114	2.686	0.102	2.793	0.110
Sec	0.192	0.043	0.253	0.058	0.105	0.023
RN	0.585	0.104	0.628	0.109	0.625	0.114
PN	0.542	0.129	0.533	0.132	0.485	0.109
Tech	0.320	0.067	0.321	0.069	0.278	0.057
PA	0.231	0.040	−0.014	−0.003	1.082	0.192
L_j	0.295	0.063	0.327	0.071	0.308	0.065

Source: Brown, D. M. (1988). Do physicians underutilize aides? *Journal of Human Resources*, *23*(3), 342–355.
Note: MP (marginal product) and MP/P (marginal product to input price ratio) were computed from the parameters of a production function that included "H = total hours worked per week, Sec = average weekly hours of secretarial, administrative and clerical work in physician i's office, RN = weekly hours of office work by registered nurses, PN = weekly hours of office work by practical nurses, Tech = weekly hours of office work by technicians, PA = weekly hours of office work by physician assistants and extenders, and Lj = all five types of aides potentially employed by the physician (secretary, RN, PN, technician, PA). The factor prices were computed as follows: (a) for H, annual net income was divided by annual hours of work; (b) for L_j, sample average wages paid were employed. L_j is the weighted (by weekly hours worked) average of L_j for both the marginal product and factor price calculations."

Exhibit 5.2 Per visit costs and economies of scale for hospital outpatient care, by levels of output

	Margins cost (dollars)
At means	83
Level of inpatient days	
High	109
Medium	67
Low	33
Level of ED visits	
High	81
Medium	83
Low	181
Level of OPD visits	
High	84
Medium	82
Low	81

Source: Grannemann, T. W., Brown, R. S., & Pauly, M. V. (1986). Estimating hospital costs: A multiple-output analysis. *Journal of Health Economics*, *5*(2), 107–127.

Note: Marginal and average costs are calculated from the estimated cost function parameters with all variables other than inpatient days, emergency department (ED) visits, and outpatient department (OPD) visits set at their sample means. Costs are evaluated with these outputs set at low (approximately 25th percentile), medium (about 50th percentile), and high (75th percentile) levels:

	Low	Medium	High	Means
Inpatient days	18,000	49,000	90,000	63,000
ED visits	7,000	17,000	21,000	21,000
OPD visits	3,000	16,000	48,000	38,000

For these computations, the level of discharges was varied with the level of inpatient days in order to keep the implicit average length of stay per admission constant at seven days.

This kind of analysis may seem (and is) exciting, but it only works well if you trust the output measures. Medical settings produce multiple kinds of outputs – checkups, new patient visits, minor procedures. To deal with this, as well as to confirm the technical efficiency results, you can ask the computer a slightly different question: Given input prices, and a count of the different kinds of output you produce, how much on average does cost increase when output rises by one more of one of those kinds of output per week? This cost function will tell you the marginal cost of each of the outputs you produce. The alternative, using a stopwatch to track the time of each worker for each kind of output, is much more time(!)-consuming and imprecise. You can then compare the price you can get for each kind of output with its marginal cost to see how much profit you are making (or losing) when you supply more of that output.

Not only that, you can use this analysis to predict the total cost for a given set of outputs produced in different production units and see which ones have higher total costs (which will also get at fixed costs that may not vary beyond some point with output). Finally, if you have a measure of quality for each output, and enough data on plants that produce outputs of different quality, you can see how much it adds to cost to produce a higher quality version of a given output. Depending on the difference (if any) in the price you can collect for outputs of different quality, you can see if producing the "highest-quality care" is profitable. This is not the end. See Box 5.2 for the rest of the story.

Economies and Diseconomies of Scope: How to Tell and What to Expect

The cost function approach also allows you to unpack whether there are economies of scope among different types of output that might or might not be produced together in one "plant" (your hospital) or in separate production units. Economies of scope occur when it is cheaper to produce X units of one kind of care and Y units of another kind together in one plant, firm, or organization; diseconomies occur when it is better to keep them separate. To get to the empirical punchline first, you can get an insight into what is going on by having data from different settings (locations of plants/facilities) or the same facilities at different points in time where there are different mixes of outputs being supplied.

Here is an example. One study I performed (with others) was intended to look at the cost of nonemergency outpatient care produced in hospitals compared to that produced in doctors' offices (where they only produce outpatient care).[7] We had an estimate of the cost of office-based outpatient care only (from studies like those of Reinhardt and Brown). We got data on total costs and the mix of inpatient and outpatient care (of various types) from about 1,000 hospitals. We asked the computer to tell us what the addition was to total cost from additional outpatient visits *as a function of the volume of inpatient admissions*. When we looked at the hospitals with a heavy inpatient load relative to outpatient care, the marginal cost of an outpatient visit was about three times that of a doctor's office. But when we looked at other hospitals with a heavy emphasis on outpatient care and fewer inpatient admissions, we found that their marginal cost for an outpatient visit was about the same as in a doctor's office (Exhibit 5.2).

That answered the empirical question, but what is the explanation? An inpatient practice in a large hospital can send people to labs and specialists who are on the hospital grounds, whereas a doctor's office or a hospital with a small number of beds will only have a rudimentary lab and few convenient referrals. However, when we followed up with hospital administrators, they were much less surprised than we were by our results. They conjectured (correctly) that the physicians in the large hospital were used to treating sicker patients than those in the smaller hospital, and that they were therefore more likely to treat anyone with more tests and referrals than doctors with

[7] Grannemann, T. W., Brown, R. S., & Pauly, M. V. (1986). Estimating hospital costs: A multiple-output analysis. *Journal of Health Economics*, 5(2), 107–127.

different experiences. Plus, everything was close so why not refer a patient with a puzzling problem to the office or lab down the hall? Those additional costs all added up in the bigger hospitals. In fact, some administrators said that when they designed new outpatient facilities, they put them in separate buildings far away from the hospital's main campus and staffed them largely with outpatient-only doctors. There could have been economies of scope from the sharing of some facilities with fixed costs, but physician practice patterns turned them into diseconomies.

Diseconomies of Scope in Spades: Hospital Inpatient and Outpatient Surgery

One of the most remarkable trends in medical services provision over the last few decades has been the migration of many procedures, even some serious-sounding ones, from an inpatient setting to an outpatient setting. Hospitals have responded by expanding their own capabilities in outpatient care that attempt to mimic what is done in freestanding facilities owned by physician groups or others, but the question of the best or the equilibrium distribution of volume across different types of sites is still unsettled. In the heyday of hospital bed regulation, limits were put on outpatient substitutes to hold down their output (and also to diminish hospital competition). Both Medicare and private insurers have lately moved to agree to pay for care that does not involve an overnight stay in the hospital, with less agreement on how much they should pay in different sites. Can economic thinking at least pose some insightful questions here and perhaps even provide some answers? Here we focus on surgery as the service whose ultimate ideal location is unknown, but the issues are similar for many other procedures.

We begin as usual with a listing of economic pitfalls to be avoided in thinking about this question. One is not to rely on reimbursement rates as a guide to costs. Up to the present, hospitals have charged and been paid much more for a given surgical procedure provided to an inpatient who stayed overnight, compared to an ambulatory surgery center (ASC) who sent the patient home before the painkillers wore off. The room and wonderful food obviously had a cost, so did the nurses who stayed up all night, and the hospitalized patients were probably sicker. Hospitals even charged more, and Medicare paid more, for outpatient surgery patients they did send home; they got a higher "facility fee" than a freestanding ASC.

The economic point to be made here is that any difference in payments does not necessarily reflect differences in real resource costs – and the latter are what matter for efficiency. Patients who would be candidates for ASC almost surely require less postoperative care than the average surgical inpatient in a hospital. The cost of meals and linen may be the same, but the needs for nursing hours and other inputs are likely to be less in the ASC, and crucially less than the dollar difference in typical reimbursements. The same observation applies, with a twist, to hospital outpatient surgery versus ASCs. For reasons lost in the mists of history, insurers have typically paid higher reimbursement (through a facility fee add-on) for hospital-based outpatient surgery than for ASCs. This is now controversial, with campaigns for site-neutral payments (generally set at the lower level of current average payments) underway. It is then easy to calculate "cost savings" from paying less to hospitals but that is only a cut in their net income, not (necessarily) in their costs. If the actual (and marginal) cost of outpatient surgery is the same in a hospital as in a freestanding ASC, society gains nothing by reducing payments to hospitals – but hospitals lose the profit margin. This is not the place to ask what hospitals do with the extra profit, though that would be interesting.

A second caution is that hospital accounting costs, for both the inpatient and the outpatient version of a surgical procedure, almost surely overstate the hospital's marginal cost of production. Typical accounting systems load those overhead costs discussed earlier across all revenue-generating aspects of a hospital, even on activities that themselves have zero impact on overhead costs. The kind of cost function estimation shown earlier in the chapter would be the path to truth here, in determining what really is the marginal real resource cost of performing a particular surgical procedure in a hospital outpatient setting.

The third caution is a warning not to be deceived by a kind of shell game associated with same-day surgery. Compared to inpatient care, it will load more costs on the household for the patient who comes home early, compared to having hospital staff watch and worry during recovery. Often this cost is offset by patient and family preferences for home-based care, but it is still a cost – and not one that is necessarily negligible, even for families pressured into taking care of a family member a little sooner.

Since we apparently do not have economic cost function estimates of marginal cost in hospital outpatient versus ASC settings, how much credibility should we give to claims that the latter is only half the cost of the former? One set of tea leaves is provided by a bean-counting exercise summarized by

Munnich and Parente.[8] They had a physical measure of the number of minutes of different kinds of care for people ostensibly similar in risk who underwent similar surgical procedures in a relatively large sample of the two types of setting. (The survey data they used has not been collected since 2006 so some of this may be out of date.) They broke down the surgical patient's journey into three parts – preoperative time, when the patient is in the operating room waiting for something to happen; the actual surgical time itself, from scalpel to closure; and postoperative time in recovery. On average all were higher in the hospital outpatient department (OPD), with the longest excess being time in recovery. One caution to using the average is that times were highly variable, and the excess OPD time was concentrated in a small fraction of the patient sample.

So, if we conclude that ASCs work faster than OPDs, it would be reassuring if we could answer the question of why. The pre-op and the post-op times seem compressible, able to be shortened depending on protocols but also of relatively low additional marginal cost for extra minutes – unless there is a bed shortage. The shorter time for the surgery itself is harder to explain if it is the same procedure; the best candidate would be to modify the old saying to "practice makes quicker," if ASCs do have higher volumes.

Where does this leave the manager of a health system or a health insurer? Is it desirable to flog staff to work more quickly, or are there patient flow procedures that could be copied but have not been? Should insurers embark on a search-and-destroy mission for overly costly providers? As usual, we researchers worry that patients were not randomly assigned to sites or surgeons in this comparison – what if the patients or the doctors were different in ways that cannot be observed but also cannot be changed?

What excuses do hospitals offer on the ASC debate? They point out that there can be complications in any surgery, and they have been chosen to provide the backup for those complications – even if they occur in a nearby ASC to a patient who was transferred to the hospital. Whether such backup use by ASCs is substantial can be known, and even the standby cost the hospital incurs can be valued based on the frequency this safety device is used.

Will markets sort this out? The financial incentive to patients should ideally reflect any lower cost at an ASC compared to OPD, and in economic theory, consumers can decide whether any quality differences (e.g., not having to be transferred to a hospital in case of complications) are worth

[8] Munnich, E. L., & Parente, S. T. (2014). Procedures take less time at ambulatory surgery centers, keeping costs down and ability to meet demand up. *Health Affairs*, *33*(5), 764–769.

the additional price. Or they can delegate that task to the managers of a network that contracts with and allocates patients to both types of facilities.

The future of hospital OPD surgery should depend on whether consumers think it is worth its extra cost – if it does have extra cost. Neither the current Medicare policy of paying more for the same procedure at an OPD nor the alternative of paying the same will get it exactly right without taking both patient preferences and relative costs into account. Arrangements to do that would be complicated because insurances will have to give patients the option of paying more for what might be perceived as better care, an option not present in original Medicare and only very indirectly in Medicare Advantage.

Variation and Efficiency

A commonsense way for managers to detect inefficiency in production when they have observations on multiple settings with the same inputs is to measure variation in some metric of output across settings and tag the setting with the highest output as the more efficient. Whether it be calls answered at a call center or widgets produced at a work stand, variations in output or productivity (outputs given inputs) almost always occur, and it is surely logical (even in economics) to say that they indicate the possibility of inefficiency. This idea is commonly used in healthcare, both in day-to-day management (compare visits per day in two similar clinics) and most famously across geographic areas – which healthcare markets have the lowest mortality or highest cost for their Medicare populations? Documentation of this variation largely due to the careful work of the research group at Dartmouth College has been interpreted as evidence for inefficiency in the US healthcare system and has prompted efforts to do something about the variation.[9]

The skeptical economics approach as usual favors curbing enthusiasm until you know more – in particular, whether the sites really are identical and what is the reason (if it can be found) for the differences observed. A homely economics parable from the early nineteenth-century economist David Ricardo (no relation to Ricky) asks us to think about cabbage farming and about how to interpret data on cabbages produced from two plots of land. The more productive cabbage patch is observed to have the same seed,

[9] Alford-Teaster, J., Bronner, K., Bubolz, T. et al. (2024). End of life inpatient care (1994–2019). Dartmouth Dataverse. V1. http://dx.doi.org/10.21989/D9/WX4EHG; Skinner, J., & Fisher, E. (2010). Reflections on geographic variations in US health care. Dartmouth Institute for Health Policy and Clinical Practice. https://data.dartmouthatlas.org/downloads/press/Skinner_Fisher_DA_05_10.pdf.

fertilizer, and weeding hours as the other but is still more bountiful. Ricardo concludes that the reason is probably different fertility of soil in the different sites, presumably as the result of whatever geological and soil flow processes are in play. His main economic point was to conclude that the owner of the more productive plot will be able to collect more rent on the land, even though exerting no more effort than the owner of the other plot – and then to point out that if demand for cabbages increases, that rent will increase. More land will be brought into cabbage production, while average productivity per acre will fall. The paradox is that changes in rent as the cost of the land is determined by changes in demand, not by supply. The econometric frustration is that if rent (or rent-like payment) is a component of cost, changes in costs when demand changes may bear little relationship to changes in efficiency.[10]

So, this exercise in vegetable economics is useful for healthcare because it makes the point that, sometimes, observed variation is not the result of any inefficiency that can be improved but is just a fact of life attributable to the original creation of more fertile land, better locations, or more skillful managers. (I have also used this metaphor in a paper with Kyle Myers to explain why drug productivity fell as rising consumer incomes increased the demand for drug-based cures.) In connection with the Dartmouth variations (discussed in the following paragraphs), the main point is the need both to control for any observables that might have influenced the outcome (mortality or Medicare basket reimbursement per beneficiary) and ideally to have some evidence on what causes any remaining variation.

Here is my take on what we have learned from studying variations but still need to find out. Researchers at Dartmouth studying variation in Medicare costs across cities were careful to adjust for observables such as age but viewed Medicare data as the best available because the populations being treated were of similar age across areas (which they carefully defined as "hospital referral regions") and because Medicare tries to pay the same price after adjustment for local input cost nationwide – hence, variations in spending per person should proxy variation in use of the Medicare base of services (most healthcare but not prevention). As an attempt to control for risk, they compared Medicare spending in the last year of life, under the assumption that all of those who died were equally sick for the previous 12

[10] Pauly, M., & Myers, K. (2019). Endogenous productivity of demand-induced R&D: Evidence from pharmaceuticals. *The RAND Journal of Economics*, *50*(3), 591–614.

months.[11] The headline from their work as usual looked at the extremes: The Medicare payment per expired beneficiary in 2017 was almost two times greater in McAllen, Texas (the highest) than in Grand Junction, Colorado (the lowest).[12] (I have visited both places but mostly observed that McAllen, on the Mexico border, was warmer and flatter than Grand Junction and so is not as good a setting for skiing.) There was evidence for blame and praise: The high costs in McAllen were largely attributable to a few physician groups but not others and the physicians in Grand Junction took great pride in their culture of collegiality and the healthy lifestyles of their patients. Much of the variation in Medicare spending was due to variation in use of post-acute (nursing home and home health) care.

The sensational result from the early Dartmouth studies of variation in Medicare spending was that there was very large variation across cities in spending and use of care that was not associated with differences in measures of health outcomes, either from selected medical procedures or in population of frail elders near death. The message to national policy was stark: The variation from one extreme to the other in this setting was primarily driven by specialist services, leading to the assertion that somehow those specialists, in places where there were more of them, were inducing the use of more of their services as well as the complementary and expensive hospital services. The additional care patients received must be waste, since there were no apparent health benefits from higher volume and spending more. This naturally prompted political calls to curtail the spending in the high-spending areas. The study also documented the cause of this variation: There were more hospitals and medical specialists in the high-cost areas than in the low-cost ones.

From a political viewpoint, these results motivated politicians, especially those from low-cost areas like Iowa, to propose some way to clamp down on the excessive costs in those high-cost areas. From an economic viewpoint, the attention to causation was praiseworthy but the substance tautological: Since the highest-cost Medicare services are inpatient and specialist care, of course areas using above-average amounts of these services needed more hospitals and specialists to supply them. But that left the unanswered question of what

[11] Gottlieb, D. J., Zhou, W., Song, Y., Andrews, K. G., Skinner, J. S., & Sutherland, J. M. (2010). Prices don't drive regional Medicare spending variations. *Health Affairs, 29*(3), 537–543.

[12] Dartmouth Atlas Project. End of life care. Database. www.dartmouthatlas.org/interactive-apps/end-of-life-care/#county; Dartmouth Atlas Project. (1999). *The quality of medical care in the United States: A report on the Medicare Program – the Dartmouth Atlas of health care.* https://data.dartmouthatlas.org/downloads/atlases/99Atlas.pdf.

caused these variations in the first place – did some random process tag certain cities with an oversupply of specialists relative to others, or extra-strong tastes for seeing specialists, and, if so, how did that work to bring about the observed regional variations?

Two serious issues have been raised about what inferences to draw from this data. One was a set of studies by Jack Hadley and colleagues showing that high-cost areas had sicker people.[13] For example, in McAllen Texas, the highest cost city, the large Hispanic population was poor and uninsured before going on Medicare: No wonder a lot was spent on them, but they still ended up less healthy than the average person on Medicare. This "previous poverty" explanation for variation in Medicare spending was elaborated by Richard Cooper – finding, among other things, that in states or cities with high average incomes there were more pockets of poor people in poor health using a lot of care once they went on Medicare.[14] The other was an Institute of Medicine report from a committee chaired by Joe Newhouse that found that there was as much variation in cost per beneficiary associated with individual physicians within high-cost areas as there was across areas: If there was an area of level physician culture, it did not bring about uniformity.[15]

The latter finding put an end to policy proposals to punish high-cost areas by cutting payments to all of their providers and then telling them to be more efficient. (Celebrations in McAllen and Miami.) However, there are still some remaining open questions. Why do some physicians treat middle-class insured patients at the same income levels in more costly ways than others? Is it really the case that poor people attract specialists? Attributing all the variation to physician supply–induced services seems wrong but so does attributing it all to the greater health needs of poor people. There is still a lot of unexplained variation in spending not related to outcomes, potential flags for "inefficiency."

If there were to be incentives for efficiency (such as the value-based price P* model to be discussed in Chapter 10), they should ideally face every overusing physician, regardless of what other physicians in town were doing. Moreover, if we could have a randomized controlled trial comparing

[13] Reschovsky, J. D., Hadley, J., & Romano, P. S. (2013). Geographic variation in fee-for-service Medicare beneficiaries' medical costs is largely explained by disease burden. *Medical Care Research and Review*, *70*(5), 542–563.

[14] Cooper, R. B. (2019). *Poverty and the myths of health care reform*. Johns Hopkins University Press.

[15] Newhouse, J. P., & Garber, A. M. (2013). Geographic variation in health care spending in the United States: Insights from an Institute of Medicine report. *JAMA*, *310*(12), 1227–1228.

physicians paid P* by Medicare with however much they are paid today, any resulting reduction in resource use would (at long last) be a defensible measure of how much waste there is – at least a lower bound but actionable measure.

These are important messages for managers today. They challenge managers to try to do something about the root causes of poor health and poor health habits. They tell them that they should try to incentivize individual providers to be efficient, with redesigned payment systems and high degrees of competition, rather than try to change or chastise physician behavior and culture.

In addition to these specific messages, there are also some more general ones. The most important is a caution: Be slow to attribute differences in measured outcomes, given apparently similar inputs, to inefficiency. Instead look as hard as you can to find causes for those variations other than provider behavior. And then be careful to choose ways to alter provider behavior that have evidence of effectiveness. Both of these tasks are difficult and difficult to get credit for doing, but they are still worth it.

A comment on linkage between this discussion and the production or cost functions described earlier in the chapter: If you estimate a cost function that relates cost in a set of similar organizations to their output levels and input prices, you will be able to find (for a given mix of input prices and outputs) which organization or site it is that has the lowest cost. You could (and economists have) call this observation a point on the "efficiency frontier" and judge all other sites as less efficient. You could even do the arithmetic to estimate how much more output you would have if all sites were as productive as the best. However, as the cabbage patch example shows, this calculation would be useless if the basis for good performance could not be transferred to other organizations; there may be only one farm that will grow the largest number of prizewinning cabbages no matter what farmers do; there may be only one hospital management team that can win the gold star time after time no matter what the boards at other hospitals do. And among a population of managers, there will only be one who is the best, no matter what the incentives. To tell, you need to explore why (and how consistently) a given site is on the frontier: It may be dumb luck, it may be brilliant management, it may be a welcoming consumer and labor market – or it may be changeable if incentives are changed. You need to know before you leap (see Box 5.3 for further discussion).

Box 5.3 Theory: What managers can and cannot do about inefficiency

The kind of data analysis just discussed allows estimation of what costs were, given measures of input prices, quality, and severity, for the average "plant" in a dataset, but it also identifies sites that have the lowest cost (or the highest productivity) for different values of the observed variables. The lowest cost data points can be "enveloped," and one can determine the impact of variations in volume (economies of scale), variations in observed quality, and other influences on these most efficient sites as well as on the average ones; sometimes the relationships are different. But the most common use of data envelopment analysis (DEA) is to compare the efficiency of different sites and decide if managerial action is warranted.[16]

One of the boldest steps would be for insurance managers to limit payment to all sites (controlling for observables) to a little above the cost level of the most efficient frontier sites. (This was what Senator Grassley of Iowa had in mind for Medicare.) After all, if one site (or one Hospital Referral Region) can achieve a given low cost level, won't all the other sites decide to do so if they only are paid enough to cover their costs when they are ideally efficient? At a minimum, the managers of the interior sites should have some explaining to do. However, this drastic interpretation is good management only if one can be sure that all the measured characteristics of sites, wages, and outputs capture everything that could legitimately affect cost. (What "legitimately" means is part of the issue.) If costs at your site are higher than the lowest, you may have several explanations (not an exhaustive list):

(1) Our patients are sicker and therefore require more care.
(2) Our quality is higher in unmeasured ways.
(3) We were not as lucky.
(4) Our management was not as skilled.

The easiest answer to the first two reasons is to get better measures – or to challenge managers to prove that their patients are sicker or their quality higher. The third explanation takes into account that there are random events in life that can cause different outcomes from the same apparent process, thought, and effort – there might be errors in measurement, or there might be things that happened from unknown causes. The last explanation does not sound like a good excuse for a manager but maybe it is the most realistic of all.

Data analysts have tried to separate out these identifiable sources of error by increasingly complex statistical techniques, based on assumptions about the underlying process and the distribution of exogenous errors in measurement or performance. Or the analyst might get lucky. For example, if the analyst somehow knows that quality is constant at a given site over time, looking at how cost varies with output over time will not be contaminated by variations in unobserved quality (or anything else that is site-specific but not time-varying). Sometimes the data can trace out trends over time in site-specific but unmeasured factors and somehow control for it. You can never prove for sure that you are comparing apples with apples, but you can beat the data into exhaustion as best you can.

[16] Bowlin, W. F. (1998). Measuring performance: An introduction to data envelopment analysis (DEA). *The Journal of Cost Analysis*, *15*(2), 3–27.

Would a manager or a payer have the nerve to go ahead with treating all sites as if they were or could be as good as the most efficient? Maybe, but it would be wise to be cautious. If managerial skill (or leadership or culture or some other soft influence people can feel but not measure) is the reason for higher-than-average cost, the system may just have to accept it. Not every hospital CEO can be the best manager in town. Even if people pull up their socks, they may not be able to emulate the best. In principle, detectable differences in managerial skill should be offset by lower or higher salaries, but you may run out of effective bonuses before you can equalize total costs. There is some evidence that less skilled managers can sustain quality or volume by hiring more of other inputs,[17] but in the iron triangle unit cost will have to give.

In fact, if you punish high-cost units by paying them less you may just force them to cut quality or to exit entirely; they may be doing as well as they can – so cost variation is not inefficiency that they (or anyone else) can correct. Likewise rewarding the stars may not get them to do any better; they may be at their limits. All of these "maybes" in theory need to be known by skilled central management – either that or the market will sort it out.

Here is how the market is supposed to work. We would usually draw the supply curve for hospital care in a local market as upward sloping even in the long run. There can be many reasons for costs to rise as desired output expands but they all must be related to some input that itself has diminishing returns. Maybe there are only so many really good nurses, or hospitalists, or CEOs. The P* diagram in the discussion of value-based pricing in Chapter 10 (Figure 10.1) shows that, given demand, there will be an equilibrium where, in effect, the suppliers with the lowest cost or the most skills are willing to accept that market price, while those potential suppliers with costs they just cannot get down will exit (or never exist in the first place). The best and most productive managers will collect "rent" (just like the most fertile cabbage patch), payment in excess of the minimum amount they would require to do this job. So, some managers, nurses, and hospitalists at some hospitals will be happier than those at other less productive sites, but all will stay where they are since there is nothing better in prospect.

As far as I know, none of the voluminous literature on variations in cost have tried to bridge the gap to a market equilibrium. In part, that is because DEA is a favorite tool in countries with fully regulated and government paid systems, where policy managers have to decide on rewards and punishments and need to pick out the bad apples. In markets, the invisible hand does this – given a demand curve and buyers who want to pay as little as possible. Part of the confusion arises because hospitals are mostly not-for-profit, so the "rent" from good management or good luck cannot be fully captured by nonowners or legally paid out as bonuses tied directly to profitability. Hospital CEO compensation, the data shows, is strongly related to firm size, and not so strongly related to measured profitability. Still, the need to cover costs imposes discipline no matter who gets paid what. More generally, those high-cost hospitals in US studies that are inside the frontier and survive year after year must be facilitated by payment systems that allow them to do so. That observation brings us full circle to the discussion of how to pay efficiently – but hopefully the P* model keeps us from running around in circles.

[17] Doyle, J. J., Jr., Ewer, S. M., & Wagner, T. H. (2010). Returns to physician human capital: Evidence from patients randomized to physician teams. *Journal of Health Economics*, *29*(6), 866–882.

Conclusion

The Dartmouth variations work, now more than 20 years old, is still the primary source for the contention that 30%–50% of US medical spending is wasteful – based on the cost differences between Grand Junction and McAllen. Reaction to the variations evidence illustrates a somewhat subtle but important distinction between theoretical inefficiency and practical or applied inefficiency that is relevant to management. Theoretical inefficiency means that there are changes that could be made to make everyone better off, while practical inefficiency means that there are changes that can be made to do so. The jump from "could" to "can" depends on evidence that actions were actually done that resulted in the desired change. One problem with the Dartmouth story was that, if one accepts the hypothesis that physician culture is a main determinant of efficiency, no one has figured out the production function for that culture – ways that actually work to change it. In a set of studies led by Mark McClellan intended to answer the question of "how did they do it?,"[18] the most the analysts could come up with was that leadership affects culture, and culture affects the intensity of care and therefore cost. They could not find how to produce different leadership. That study did rule out other plausible causes (such as high reimbursement, a surplus of surgeons, and other physician-related suggestions that turned out not to be related to Medicare cost), but it did not rule in any organizational or economic factor proven to be both changeable and effective.

The same comments apply to frontier production approaches. However, that work did show that feasible changes, such as adding more nurses or separating ambulatory care from hospital inpatient care, were effective in lowering cost, without evidence of offsetting harm to patient health or consumer satisfaction – so all is not lost. Some things can work to improve efficiency in the sense of doing more good than harm (with the former compensating the latter) as will be shown in the chapters later in this book on insurance (Chapter 7), social determinants of health (Chapter 15), and other management issues. See Box 5.4 for a discussion on CEO's compensation.

[18] McClellan, M. (2011). Reforming payments to healthcare providers: The key to slowing healthcare cost growth while improving quality? *Journal of Economic Perspectives*, *25*(2), 69–92; McClellan, M., & Rivlin, A. (2014). Improving health while reducing cost growth: What is possible? Health Policy Issue Brief, Brookings.

Box 5.4 Theory: Hospital management – CEO compensation is a controversial topic

The majority of consumers feel that CEO compensation for large firms in any industry is excessive. It is high relative to wages per worker and grows more rapidly than do wages per worker. In healthcare and in other industries, the single most important determinant of CEO compensation or its change over time is size, measured either by beds (for hospitals) or by revenues (for any industry). In studies of hospital CEOs in particular, both beds and an index of technology (both highly correlated with revenues) are associated with higher compensation.[19] Direct measures of financial performance are not associated with CEO compensation overall, although very low margins and high proportions of poor patients are associated with lower compensation. Across hospitals, better clinical outcomes, higher quality, or greater contribution to community health (other than the presumably larger contribution from running a larger hospital) are not related to CEO compensation, though there is a small effect of lower consumer satisfaction scores.

Is there an economic explanation for this pattern? Could it be changed in ways that would improve efficiency? The most important economic insight is that in theory payment to someone in a given executive job is not related to how hard they work but is related to two important factors: how much they add to the firm's goals and what they would be paid in other jobs in the economy. For CEO pay, things can go awry. If boards setting CEO compensation for some reason generally overpay relative to the value furnished, the second factor will cause that pattern to spread to all firms: We need to pay you a lot because otherwise you will leave for a firm that pays you even more. The other peculiarity has to do with (as discussed in chapter 4) ambiguity about the goals of nonprofit hospitals – if it is not maximization of profit or the value of the firm, then what? And if there are opportunities at for-profit firms that do pay based on such factors, that pattern will spill over into payment for nonprofit executives, whether university, hospital, or museum CEOs. It is likely that the existence of for-profit hospitals provides a kind of anchor that keeps nonprofit hospital CEO compensation higher than if there were no such alternative.[20]

There is an extensive literature on the economics of CEO compensation for profit-seeking firms that may furnish some insights for nonprofit hospitals and health systems. That literature has three major conclusions:

(1) Some portion of higher CEO compensation comes from managers' ability to use inside information and daily presences to extract "rent" from pliant and inattentive directors.
(2) But some portion is also payment for actions which increase profits or the value of the firm and reflect managers' responses to board-designed incentives to achieve firm objectives – this is so even though CEO compensation in any form is a tiny fraction of firm revenues or profits.

[19] Joynt, K. E., Le, S. T., Orav, E. J., & Jha, A. K. (2014). Compensation of chief executive officers at nonprofit US hospitals. *JAMA Internal Medicine, 174*(1), 61–67.

[20] Burns, L. R., & Pauly, M. V. (2023). Big Med's spread. *The Milbank Quarterly, 101*(2), 287–324.

(3) Incentive payments have largely taken the form of stock options over the last four decades.[21] Compensation of CEOs has risen in line with an increase in the market value of firms.

The possibility that nonprofit CEOs extract rents from their boards of directors is surely real, even though research suggests that hidden payment as "perks" is much less common. However, the most striking thought is that nonprofits have had to forego use of financial incentives tied to firm revenues, profits, or value because of the rules limiting nonprofit rewards to managers based on such financial indicators. Probably this feature has contributed to lower productivity growth in hospitals as well as to increases in the share of investor-owned hospitals; nonprofits are disadvantaged relative to other forms of ownership.

One final insight from research. It seems rational, and seems to occur on average, that the best CEOs manage the largest firms – either because those firms can pay them the most or because their skill makes their firms grow. An optimist would imagine that there is a place to match every manager's skill with the compensation fitted to it – although the matching does not always occur (and, if not, may lead to those observations inside the DEA frontier). It does not take much imagination to recommend that directors pay attention to their duties and not become too unwilling to let a poor-performing CEO go. If nonprofits are truly going to have different objectives in terms of quality or equity, there needs to be more direct linkage of pay with these goals than there is now. The ideal match would be with a humble person who is a skilled manager and whose personal preferences link to quality or community service.

[21] Frydman, C., & Jenter, D. (2010). CEO compensation. *Annual Review of Financial Economics*, *2*(1), 75–102.

6 Dancing in the Dark

Managing with Moral Hazard, Adverse Selection, and Other Information Imperfections

Introduction: Insurance Markets Fail When Customers Know More Than Insurers

Insurance is one of mankind's greatest inventions. While consuming almost no real resources, it produces an agreement or contract among agents in a risky world that allows risk to be eliminated. If people prefer less risk than nature provides, they can bring about that result almost for free; all they need to do is to make an agreement that, after the fact, the winners will compensate the losers. This agreement is concluded before it is known who among a set of people at risk will suffer a loss; the result of the agreement is that those who do suffer losses get claims payments that exceed any premiums they paid; those who did not suffer losses are happy even if they had to pay premiums. It allows people, before the fact, to convert settings in which they might suffer very large losses into much smaller certain payments.[1] Insurance companies are the usual vehicle to put this agreement in place, although there are insurance organizations in health and other insurance lines set up as mutual firms, owned by their policyholders, or as special nonprofit organizations.

Insurance to cover the cost of healthcare is one version of such an agreement. Most people most of the time are not sick and have little need for medical care. But sometimes illness strikes, and sometimes there are medical treatments that can reduce the harm to a person's health. The problem is that, even if the medical treatment can make you as good as new, without insurance you will have the unexpected burden of paying for it. So, you would prefer an arrangement where you pay into a fund beforehand and in return can claim much more than you paid under the (hopefully) uncommon and unexpected case in which you are very sick and the cure very costly. The reason why people voluntarily buy health insurance, in the

[1] Eisen, R., & Eckles, D. L. (2011). *Insurance economics.* Springer.

general economic theory of insurance, is to protect their wealth (and ability to spend on other types of consumption) from being depleted by high healthcare costs. It is an arrangement in which those who become sick unexpectedly are compensated by those who are lucky enough to stay well.

Health insurance would work perfectly for this purpose but for a potentially crucial flaw: asymmetric information. Insurance consumers may know more about how sick they are, either when buying coverage or when making claims, than whoever administers the insurance plan for them, and take advantage.

Knowing more than the insurer knows about your illness level or benefit from care is not a necessary feature of health insurance design; the earliest forms of it prespecified dollar amounts conditional on something anyone could observe, like the loss of a finger. But whether or not you have back pain, and whether or not it is mild or severe, only you (and sometimes your doctor) can tell – which means that if you claim worse illness than you actually are experiencing, the insurance must still pay up for whatever care you get. This would be fine if you were the only person engaging in this scam – but if everybody does it, the insurance will have to carry a higher premium, and everyone could be worse off. The cost-inflating behavior is called "moral hazard," and it arises because health insurance attenuates the incentive for people with insurance to use the correct or ideal amount of spending and care for their personal situation, taking account of both costs and benefits of care.[2]

Because of moral hazard, health insurance is (in my opinion) the economic source of almost all good and bad in any healthcare system. Cost-sharing and managed care, both regarded as mixed blessings, only exist because they are thought to control moral hazard. Low prices paid to physicians, or waiting lists and crowded hospitals, are there to control moral hazard; they are used abroad as well as in the US. People with generous insurance have little incentive to gravitate toward lower-priced providers, and so private insurance reimbursements are higher and more arbitrary than they would otherwise be. In the US system, with a mix of private and public insurances covering patients who seek care, the challenge to managers is to control moral hazard as best they can, and that task is doubly challenging because people have different kinds of insurance plans which use different kinds of controls in often different ways.[3] I elaborate on moral hazard in Part 1 of this chapter.

[2] Pauly, M. V. (1968). The economics of moral hazard: Comment. *The American Economic Review*, *58*(3), 531–537.

[3] Finkelstein, A. (2014). *Moral hazard in health insurance*. Columbia University Press.

In addition to knowing more about how sick they are once insurance is bought and illness strikes, insurance customers may also know more than insurance sellers about their prospective risk level for the next period of coverage before they buy. That means that they will be eager to buy coverage if they are high-risk and tempted to avoid it if they are low-risk if the premium does not depend on risk. This kind of buyer behavior can lead to "adverse selection" (which can be made worse if insurers are not allowed to vary premiums with risks they do know), causing underinsurance for low-risk individuals and high premiums for high-risk. Part 2 of this chapter deals with adverse selection.

Consumers of health insurance, and policymakers who care about them, frequently view themselves as victims of insurance companies who overcharge for coverage and underprovide benefits. It is therefore ironic that the key sources of market failure happen when better informed individual consumers are able to take advantage of well-meaning but ignorant insurance sellers. The upshot of such behavior, however, is that consumers as a whole are made worse off than if information were less asymmetric.

To sum up: If insurance buyers know more about their future risk than insurers know (or are allowed to know), adverse selection ensues. Forbidding insurers to look for preexisting conditions among applicants can disrupt the market. Even if all risks are believed to be the same before insurance is bought but, after illness strikes, some insurance buyers know more about how sick they are or how much they would benefit from care than insurers do, then moral hazard will happen, and there will also be issues in how markets function. So, if insurance buyers know more than sellers, either before purchase or after purchase, their efforts to use their informational advantage can wreak havoc on the insurance markets they need to use.

Part 1: The Simple Economics of Moral Hazard and the Complexity of Solution

If an insurance plan could accurately observe how sick each person was when illness struck, it could propose various payment amounts conditional on the occurrence of each type of illness. More precisely, if it knew all the details of a person's illness, it could make claims payment amounts conditional on the marginal benefit from healthcare. Then if the payment was above cost, the treatment would be supplied, but if the marginal benefit amount was less than cost, there would (and should) be no treatment. Probably the best practical design would pay more for more care the sicker you are, as long as the marginal benefit from care rises with illness severity. This arrangement would in either case be *indemnity insurance*, the payment of a specific and fixed dollar benefit conditional on the event that has happened, and it is the usual form insurance takes in covering other kinds of perils. If you buy a million dollars of life insurance, that insurance will pay your heirs a million dollars if and only if you die. While there are a number of 1940s movies premised on someone faking the death of a person to collect insurance, in real life insurers can usually and easily identify if death happened. If you insure your house for a million dollars if it burns to the ground, the insurer will send an adjuster to make sure that the damage happened, and then (eventually) you will be paid the million dollars. In both cases, the insurer needs to and can determine the size and dollar amount of the loss, and how that relates to coverage in the policy. You will get your money according to the prespecified terms and dollar amounts of your insurance policy.

Even with these kinds of insurance, nothing is quite perfect: The fender bender that pays for your smashed taillight may also cover the dent that was already there from the time you backed into the garden gate, and the water damage to your hardwood floors might really have come from a flood rather than windblown rain and technically be uncovered (unless you bought flood insurance along with homeowners' insurance). There are always challenges in determining the true economic damages or loss as there are disputes about the insurance contract and its language.

Determining exactly what loss has occurred is much worse for health insurance – and that difficulty motivates even noble human beings to behave differently when they have health insurance compared to when they do not. The usual historical note says that the first forms of health insurance tried to avoid this problem by paying prespecified fixed dollar amounts (or indemnities), but consumers wanted insurance that covered more types of illnesses and care, and yet did not depend on an arbitrary decision on how bad your back pain or cancer or pain that drove you to the emergency room really was. So, the response of insurers and providers was to create insurance that made the monetary payment depend on the cost of care used, something (usually) observable, correlated with how sick you were and how much it would cost to make you better – but not perfectly correlated, and so potentially changeable depending on whether or not there was insurance that would pay.

Imperfect information for insurers therefore motivates even good people to incur more medical costs when they are insured than when they are not.

Solid middle-class households that could have stretched to afford to pay for treatment of most illnesses – but would rather have insurance pay – will do this. (Insurers felt that this was immoral behavior, hence the term "moral hazard," but economists viewed it as the expected result from insurance setting user prices lower than the true cost of care.)

Note that a necessary condition for moral hazard is that, after illness strikes, some customers have estimates of value of the benefit from additional care lower than its cost – and some higher. How much benefit the consumer would get (often proxied by illness severity) is what the patient knows but the insurer may not. The insurer may know the average benefit from a particular treatment (compared to no treatment) for the whole population of people sick with a given illness, but for ideal insurance functioning, it must also know which individuals are sicker or less sick than average.

The empirical hypothesis that insurance is associated with higher use and cost of care than without it (or with less of it) has been tested over and over by health economists. The numbers on the size of the impact bounce around a bit from study to study (and recently they have been bouncing higher), but a positive effect is always there. The conclusion, implausible to some (even to some health economists), is that ordinary people incur more medical expenses when they are insured than when they are not – and that the increase in spending is both substantial and higher than could be explained by financial benefit alone (see Box 6.1 for more about moral hazard's theory).[4]

Box 6.1 Theory: Moral hazard in pictures

While I have tried to explain how moral hazard needs to be controlled in designing efficient health insurance plans, in this box I provide a diagrammatic treatment of the subject. I do so for those who might be interested but also because it is the substance of my first published paper on health insurance (as a young assistant professor in 1970)[5] and generated a kind and supportive response from Kenneth Arrow, Nobel prizewinner and author of the first real economics paper on healthcare.

My paper largely consisted of a diagrammatic numerical example. One of the most important historical propositions in the theory of insurance, attributed to Bernoulli, says

[4] Newhouse, J. P. (1993). *Free for all? Lessons from the RAND health insurance experiment.* Harvard University Press; Aron-Dine, A., Einav, L., & Finkelstein, A. (2013). The RAND health insurance experiment, three decades later. *Journal of Economic Perspectives*, 27(1), 197–222; Card, D., Dobkin, C., & Maestas, N. (2009). Does Medicare save lives? *The Quarterly Journal of Economics*, *124*(2), 597–636.

[5] Pauly, M. V. (1970). The welfare economics of community rating. *The Journal of Risk and Insurance*, *37* (3), 407–418. https://doi.org/10.2307/250907.

that risk-averse people will prefer full coverage of an uncertain loss if insurance is priced at actuarially fair premiums. ("Fair" here means no administrative cost and a premium just high enough to cover a large number of independent losses.) Arrow noted (in 1963) that US insurance markets did not match this pattern, with the proportion out of pocket then more than 50% (compared to 10% now).[6] My goal was to show how the presence of moral hazard would make incomplete coverage the best that a market could do (if it could not prevent moral hazard) – and so to use this phenomenon as a way to explain the type of coverage people chose.

Here is the numerical example, slightly modified. Suppose a person faces the possibility of either a mild illness (M) or a severe illness (S), along with no illness. Suppose also that the use of medical care by a person once insured does respond to out-of-pocket payment – a hazard that has nothing to do with morality but everything to do with the economic theory of demand. Suppose the demand curves in both cases are as shown in Figure 6.1 and care is available at a (competitive) price equal to its marginal cost MC, which we set equal to 1. Finally suppose the severe and mild illnesses have equal probabilities conditional on the occurrence of the illness to be treated, so if you have an illness, the probability of mild or severe forms is 1/2.

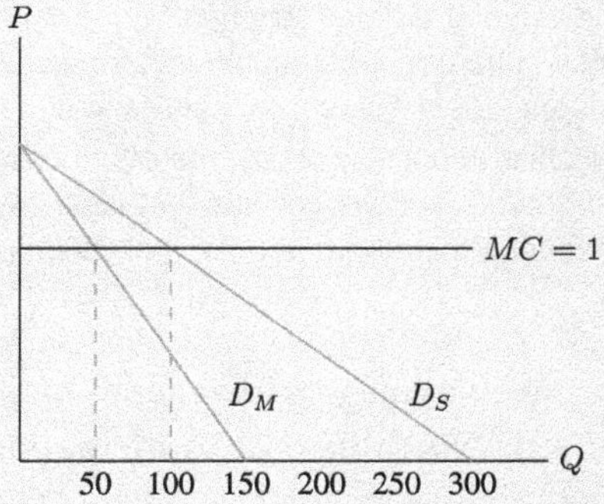

Figure 6.1 Example of demand for two different sick levels.

For a population without insurance, the demand curves say that each person would demand 50 units of care if a minor illness struck, 100 units if a serious illness struck, and (not in the picture) 0 if no illness occurred. Bernoulli's theorem, the basis of the academic theory of insurance demand, would say that the person would prefer to pay the actuarially fair premium for full coverage of both events rather than face the prospect of the three uncertain outcomes just described. (That premium would be 75 times the probability of any illness – equally weighting 50 and 100 at 1/2.) But now imagine full-coverage insurance was offered, and use increased to 150 and 300, respectively. Now the actuarially fair premium for full coverage would be higher (at 225 times the probability of any illness) – and even a risk-averse person might prefer to be uninsured and face the uncertain prospect (with its lower

[6] Arrow, K. J. (1963). Uncertainty and the welfare economics of medical care. *The American Economic Review*, *53*(5), 941–973.

expected spending of 75 times the probability of any illness) than to pay that much higher of a premium.

There is more. One might observe that even if the premium were higher with moral hazard, the person would be getting more medical care and more health. However, the demand curves show that the value of units of care beyond 50 and 100 are not worth what they cost; the demander's marginal value for care corresponds to the point on the demand curve at each quantity. In fact, an approximation of the value of the additional care induced by full coverage is provided by the triangles to the right of 50 and 100. (They would have an expected value of 75 times the probability of any illness.) So, it is easy to see (if you have your economist glasses on) that the expected value of or benefit from the additional care associated with insurance coverage (75) is less than its additional premium cost (225 – 75 = 150), which must include the full cost of the extra care used when fully insured – presto! Inefficiency. Of course, if instead the demand curves had been vertical – use is totally unresponsive to coverage – then there would be no moral hazard, and full coverage would be ideal for the insurance buyer.

There is still more, as a denouement. This welfare loss from moral hazard must be traded off against the value of a lower financial risk to risk-averse buyers. However, we know (starting at full coverage) that the value of a little reduction from full financial risk protection (and zero out-of-pocket cost) will be tiny, whereas the difference between the value of care (also tiny) and MC will be large (low-value units of service) – so full coverage cannot be ideal. Without knowing the specifics about how people feel about risk, we cannot be specific about the ideal level of cost-sharing, but we can say that ideal coverage that insurance buyers will prefer must be less than full coverage (take that, Bernoulli).

It is easy then to state the challenge to managers in general: Make sure that people with insurance get care that is worth its cost to them, but only that care, and no more – or at least get as close to this outcome as you can. The trick is to find a graceful way to stop them and potentially their doctors from having insurance to pay for care they would not have bought if they confronted its cost – effective but not cost-effective care. Of course, and as usual, what is ideal may not be in the interest of all managers – for example, those from health delivery firms will make money the more care is used, and those from health insurer firms will make more money the less care is used. The consumer as patient and insurance buyer is going to be caught in the middle; it will be an exquisite balancing act to get the best feasible set of incentives all around.

There are three broad classes of economic tools for dealing with this problem. One approach is to back up insurance coverage with out-of-pocket payments that make consumers bear at least some of the cost of care. The problem: You are exposed to financial risk when your insurance has demand-side cost-sharing. Your wealth will fall if you have to pay something for care – though not by as much as if you had no insurance. The second is to reduce payments to providers to levels at which they will only want to supply cost-effective care, and so will ignore patient demands for more, even though insurance will cover it. Setting payment to hit ideal rates of use on average is discussed in Chapter 9. Such supply-side cost-sharing poses the risk that the patient may actually be sicker than they look (even to physicians, much less to insurers) and so run the risk of getting zero care when they really could get high benefit from it – a different kind of risk than in the first case – health risk rather than financial risk – but still something people will dislike. The third strategy dispenses with financial incentives but instead uses rules or protocols – in our health plan, or in our care network, this is what we will do for you if you claim back pain. This issue is treated in detail in Chapter 7. Here again there is a risk that the rules are wrong for your specific case (even if they are generally right) and you do not get care (unless you are willing to go out of plan or network and pay for it yourself). Or these three methods can be combined in a single plan.

Obviously design and specification of these methods is the task of insurance plan management – who then have the further tasks of setting the insurance premium that covers the cost associated with the premium revision triggered by plan design and then persuading consumers to buy the plan. Next is the turn of health system managers – you have to figure out how to supply (and get your physicians to supply) the amount and type of care consistent with what your customers with different types of insurance want, based on what insurance policy and limits they chose when they chose their insurance policy – and based on what you or your providers are willing to supply, given what you are paid by insurers. Box 6.2 shows the economic analysis that determines whether cost-sharing for a given service should be large or small.

The Value of Improved Access: Economic Interpretations

A manager with single-minded devotion to controlling moral hazard is likely to be challenged on two different but related grounds. Isn't one of the purposes of health insurance, people will ask, to improve access to care for everyone? Why then go along with or even encourage cost-sharing or managed care rules that are intended to cut down on use? What about people who are not middle income, possibly members of a disadvantaged group, but who are not on Medicaid? Isn't any increase in the use of effective care that improves their health a good thing that no one should want to deter?

Box 6.2 Theory: Will buyers of insurance prefer cost-sharing to be high or low?

Suppose there is a population of potential insurance buyers facing a set of risks of treatable illnesses. Insurance can cover the costs of different kinds of treatments. For some illnesses, the level of treatment that balances benefits and costs is very similar across patients once the condition occurs; there is one good treatment that will be best for all. For another illness, with similar financial risk without insurance, the value of care will vary depending on how severe the person's illness is.

In the first case, regardless of the level of cost-sharing, patients with this condition will all use about the same amount of care. Demand is not responsive to out-of-pocket price – which means there is not much moral hazard. In the second case, demand may vary substantially with out-of-pocket price: If the cost-sharing is zero, everyone with the illness, even if mild, will seek care, so choosing a plan in which you have to pay something will deter use to a greater extent. Demand is responsive to price; there is moral hazard.

The message from insurance theory is that coverage can and should be close to 100% in the first case but not in the second. Cover care for a stroke with no charge but impose cost-sharing for back pain treatment. Sometimes the messages are not popular or politic; demand for outpatient psychiatrist visits appears to be highly price-responsive, but higher cost-sharing for them can violate goals of parity between coverage of mental and physical health services. Of course, no provider of any medical service wants to see their service with high cost-sharing, but sometimes insurance buyers will (before the fact) want incentives for hard choices. The better those choices can discern where moral hazard is great or small, other things equal, the better. There is evidence that, despite the complexity, actual patterns of coverage chosen in private insurance mimic this ideal pattern.[7]

The first issue of improving access to care (sometimes imprecisely labeled "affordability") goes back to the point about indemnity insurance. If a person who suffers a large loss does not have insurance, that person may not be able to afford to repair the damage – whereas with an insurance payment, the resulting improvement in income may be enough to change the choice to use the insurance process to make up at least some of the damage. Would you give up on rebuilding your house after a fire without insurance but call the contractor if you got an insurance check? This kind of income or wealth effect in healthcare, much discussed by the economist John Nyman,[8] may be especially strong for serious illnesses with expensive treatments that might

[7] Einav, L., Finkelstein, A., & Polyakova, M. (2018). Private provision of social insurance: Drug-specific price elasticities and cost sharing in Medicare Part D. *American Economic Journal: Economic Policy, 10*(3), 122–153.

[8] Nyman, J. A. (2003). *The theory of demand for health insurance.* Stanford University Press.

affect a person with moderate wealth, like an organ transplant or gene therapy. Without insurance, there is no hope of paying for such care even for a middle-class person, but the extra spending power provided by insurance may make all the difference. So, people will use more care with insurance than without; it will look like moral hazard, but it is not, because it is not due to distorted incentives. This effect should, one might note, be generally confined to really expensive treatments and compared to no insurance; catastrophic coverage would make this problem go away.

The income effect may be minimal for typical cost-sharing variation for acute treatments in private coverage (which averages about 10% – i.e., a few hundred dollars of deductible) compared (say) to free care; income effects matter little in relevant policy discussions of higher or lower cost-sharing for middle-class people. It should also mean that lower-middle-income people should have the strongest demand for at least some health insurance, since they will suffer most from lack of affordability – a pattern not shown in the data on insurance coverage related to income. I conclude that income effects, while present in theory, may not be important for evaluating variations in types of insurance coverage among the already insured. They are important for evaluating effects of programs that get more people, especially the middle class and above, to carry some insurance rather than risk a catastrophic expense but not for discussing the consequences of more or less generous coverage, given that you have some insurance.

However, managers of health systems must be able to deliver the kind of care that insured people will demand because of income effects. That care should be cost-effective, and without extras that push up cost, but it should be supplied. Researchers trying to design efficient insurance policies should also be careful to subtract out any increases in use attributable to higher income in the "really sick" state when they are trying to estimate the size of any moral hazard. The market for insurance should endorse the level of cost-sharing that controls moral hazard due to imperfect insurer information but not be concerned with deterring any increase in spending that comes from income effects and the demand for access. Direct and unqualified estimates of the difference cost-sharing makes can get you into the right neighborhood, but then some trial and error, seeing how insurance buyers respond, will be the best way to fine-tune coverage.

People with incomes a little above the level at which they become eligible for Medicaid often do fall through the cracks, although recent increases in subsidies to Affordable Care Act (ACA) Exchange plans greatly reduced this problem. When near-poor people have no or minimal coverage, the interpretation of moral hazard may reverse – it may change from being a source of inefficiency to a vehicle helping to achieve desired social outcomes. Put carefully, there may be social value in fostering insurance coverage for people who would otherwise underuse effective care, care effective enough that it would be cost-effective if their health were valued closer to the same level as middle-class people value their own health. That social value is not, in economics, an amorphous warm glow but rather it is tied to altruistic taxpayer willingness to pay to help lower-income community members afford effective care.[9] Of course, someone will have to cover the cost of insurance or the cost of safety net care for this population, and taxpayer willingness to pay is not unlimited (as evidenced by constrained Medicaid programs). However, health system managers will need to be concerned about such potential underuse. The best solution would be to get decent insurance to everyone, even mandating that all have it and pay what is regarded as affordable premiums.[10] People who lack coverage adequate for their income (a subjective judgment but still one felt strongly by many) will pose a problem for health system managers.

The Evidence on Price Responsiveness

Do patients really respond to higher cost-sharing by using less care? Most people would believe that high cost-sharing would affect use by lower-income people because payment of deductibles or coinsurance could be unaffordable, but what about the middle-class majority? It is one of the most definitive contributions of empirical health economics to demonstrate that what is predicted by theory works out in practice: Higher cost-sharing for the middle class does reduce total spending and use, as well as insurance premiums (see Boxes 6.3 and 6.4).[11]

Of course, most people do not go to the hospital or take pills for the fun of it, but for the middle-class person with symptoms that might go away (but might not), the promise of free care will stimulate contact with doctors, and the rest can be an expensive history. Some studies even show that quite

[9] Pauly, M. V. (1971). *Medical care at public expense: A study in applied welfare economics*. Praeger Publishers.

[10] Einav, L., & Finkelstein, A. (2023). *We've got you covered: Rebooting American health care*. Penguin.

[11] Newhouse, J. P. (1993). *Free for all? Lessons from the RAND health insurance experiment*. Harvard University Press.

Box 6.3 Evidence: The effect of cost-sharing on use for the middle class

The most definitive evidence that middle-class healthcare demand curves slope downward and to the right comes from the famous (among health economists, anyway) RAND health insurance experiment (HIE) begun in the early 1980s.[12] In an effort to nail down the answer to the question of whether free care caused more cost pressure from greater use (a fear associated with the US adoption of a UK-style national health service), a social experiment was undertaken which randomly assigned populations to insurance plans with levels of cost-sharing ranging from 0% to as high as 15% of income.

Since the results of this study are often misrepresented to managers and the general public, I will take some time to dwell on them here. I should add that subsequent empirical studies have very much confirmed the HIE results, and found even larger quantitative impacts – so just because these results are old, they still are some of the best evidence we have that spending was higher under free care than under cost-sharing, to the tune of up to 43%.[13] That increase was a little higher for drugs and ambulatory care, but even inpatient spending rose by about a third. The second is that, for the 86% of the random sample that were not poor and sick to begin with, there were no detectable adverse impacts on health even after five years. There was no differential effect of free care on poor health practices (like smoking), on self-reported health, or on clinical measures of health that should have responded to care. There was a detectable effect only for blood pressure control for the 14% of subjects with low income and initial high blood pressure risk.

How people who experienced substantial reductions in use of care managed to sustain their measured health levels was puzzling enough, but the experiment raised even more questions when it used clinical expertise to characterize the types of reduced care as clinically necessary and effective versus not. It found that cost-sharing reduced use of both types by the same proportion. Critics of cost-sharing cite the finding that cost-sharing reduced clinician-designated needed care as a serious flaw. Apparently, patients with cost-sharing cut their use of care despite their doctors' advice that it would add a lot to their health.

That finding is indeed worrisome, but the challenge is to explain why there was then no effect from foregoing needed care on outcome measures. The nonclinician cynic might say that the labeling was in error – after all, even types of care that are effective on average can be overused to the point where their marginal benefit is minimal. The experiment's

[12] Newhouse, J. P. (1993). *Free for all? Lessons from the RAND health insurance experiment.* Harvard University Press.

[13] Eichner, M. J. (1998). The demand for medical care: What people pay does matter. *The American Economic Review*, *88*(2), 117–121; Eichner, M. J. (1997). Medical expenditures and major risk health insurance. PhD dissertation. MIT. (2015). Estimating the tradeoff between risk protection and moral hazard with a nonlinear budget set model of health insurance. *International Journal of Industrial Organization*, *43*, 122–135; Kowalski, A. (2016). Censored quantile instrumental variable estimates of the price elasticity of expenditure on medical care. *Journal of Business & Economic Statistics*, *34*(1), 107–117.

researchers preferred instead to hypothesize that what must have happened is that additional use of some of the care by the free care group – either demanded by patients or recommended by doctors – harmed health enough to offset benefits from the effective care. Either story is chilling.

The plot thickens even further when we note two other results: There was no effect of cost-sharing on cost per episode of care for patients once they decided to enter the medical system, but there was a clinically rational set of choices patients made about use of the emergency room. That is, before seeking professional advice, cost-sharing kept people with upset stomachs from the ER but not if they were coughing up blood. After getting into the system, patient cost-sharing no longer mattered; doctors treated them all the same way.

The experiment did not include fly-on-the-wall information on what patients said and what doctors said to them about the benefits from care compared to whatever level of cost they faced that might have clarified matters. Still, it does seem fair to conclude both that there probably were some adverse health effects from cost-sharing and that they were too small to be detected in the main population – which benefited from lower spending overall but at the expense of exposure to greater financial risk.

As a treatment for high levels of cost, increased patient financial responsibility works but has some adverse fiscal side effects and a small risk of health impacts. Based on the results from the experiment, reasonable middle-class consumers might go either way in terms of the coverage–moral hazard trade-off; moderate cost-sharing (no one in the experiment was assigned to zero insurance coverage) might be best for some but not necessarily all; some might prefer more expensive insurance with less financial worry. This looks exactly like the kind of case where markets will be the best policy. Some frugal consumers might choose coverage which in the opinion of others represents "underinsurance." Let middle-class people choose whether they want the kind of insurance that rewards but does not compel economizing; they can then reap the benefits of low premiums and lower overall medical care cost.

Box 6.4 Evidence: How large is the effect of cost-sharing on medical care spending?

The RAND experiment already described provides a definitive estimate of the difference cost-sharing (versus free care) made to spending and use of medical care in the 1980s. The bottom line is that, comparing care free of any cost-sharing with the highest cost-sharing plans, the average costs of those randomly assigned to free care were 43% greater than those assigned to the high deductible plans. All plans had an upper limit on cost-sharing relative to income. The difference in spending was spread across the use of all types of care: physician care fell, drug use dropped, and preventive care fell. Even the rate of use of hospitals as an inpatient grew by a third when hospitalization was free compared to when there was cost-sharing. As already noted, this fall in the use of care did not affect measured health outcomes for the bulk of the sample population (86%) who were not low-income or high-risk. Are these results believable?

Not to everyone. The journalist and author Malcolm Gladwell is certain that "we only go to the doctor when we are sick" and do not treat medical services like other goods where we pay attention to price, a view he feels is "plainly absurd."[14] And yet empirical study after empirical study show that use and spending fall when people have to pay and do so for approximately equal percentage amounts for the middle class as for those with low income.[15] This is the data, though no one as far as I know has admitted to being a person who wants to make a choice based on price, except to complain. Probably we are not talking about people who would prefer checking in to the hospital than playing golf but rather those in situations we have all been in – I am not feeling well or am having worrying symptoms; I could wait, but maybe I had better play it safe and go to the emergency room or call my doctor. The second option is more attractive if it is free. After that, according to the experiment, once you are in the healthcare system, it is reluctant to let you go unless you or your insurer spends some money. We have all been in the throes of indecision where what we ask for or what we agree to could go either way, and a copayment may be the thumb on the scale that leads to watchful waiting rather than a full-court press.

Whatever the psychology of decision-making and how it is affected by having to pay something versus having the insurance pay, the empirical evidence since the RAND experiment has only confirmed the idea that there is an impact of cost-sharing. Not only that, but the magnitude of that impact in more recent work has generally been larger than what RAND found.[16] Economists usually describe the price responsiveness of the quantity of some good or service by "elasticity," the percentage change in quantity for a given percentage change in price. The RAND experiment generated varying elasticities depending on the plan and the size of the potential bill, but the central tendency was about 0.2. That smallish number can translate into big bucks, however, when you start with a user price of 0. If you go from there to 25% coinsurance, over that range the percentage change in use would be 0.2[25%/ 0.125], using the midway point between 0 and 0.25 as the average price – or 0.2(200%) = 40%, about what the experiment found.

No one has (and probably no one could) replicate the RAND experiment today – after all, it bribed some subjects to take less insurance coverage than they already had. Many other studies therefore looked at actual experience in households that had already exceeded the deductible compared to those who did not. If your family member already had a skiing accident that blew through the deductible all the way to a cap on out-of-pocket spending, you used a lot more care for free if you got sick around the holidays. Point elasticity estimates were usually in the 0.4 to 0.7 range, though some were as high as 2.0.

14 Gladwell, M. (2005). The moral-hazard myth. *The New Yorker*, August 21. www.newyorker.com/magazine/2005/08/29/the-moral-hazard-myth.

15 Wong, M. D., Andersen, R., Sherbourne, C. D., Hays, R. D., & Shapiro, M. F. (2001). Effects of cost sharing on care seeking and health status: Results from the Medical Outcomes Study. *American Journal of Public Health*, *91*(11), 1889–1894. https://doi.org/10.2105/ajph.91.11.1889.

16 Duarte, F. (2012). Price elasticity of expenditure across health care services. *Journal of Health Economics*, *31*(6), 824–841.

Concretely, observational studies found that even small amounts of increased copayment (say from $2 to $10 for a prescription) were associated with large percentage decreases in use, both because more people stayed away from filling prescriptions altogether and because those who did fill some prescriptions used fewer.[17]

The other more recent research that finds a larger effect than RAND is a study by Amy Finkelstein of the effect of increased coverage from Medicare, back in 1965, on spending of the elderly.[18] That policy change was followed by accelerated growth in spending for this population to a much larger extent than would have been expected based on the classic RAND elasticity of 0.2. Her explanation, relevant to managers, has to do with the economics of product variety discussed earlier. For a number of reasons, some economic and some ethical, some physician practices (like other firms) would find it costly to offer a custom-tailored product to each patient who presents with the same condition – even if some had more insurance than others.

Now suppose (as in the experiment) a patient shows up and tells the doctor she has free care from the experiment, so cost is no concern. Even so, the individual physician or practice is likely to treat that patient about the same as all others; the same would be true of the person with the high-deductible insurance. The result of this behavior is that the difference in cost between the two extremes is likely to be small, compared to what would happen if almost all patients had free care, or almost all had a deductible-based incentive to economize. In effect, the consequences of a change in coverage for a large share of a practice's patients will have spillover effects on the other patients; this phenomenon is termed the "norms hypothesis," and there is evidence that the qualitative features of care a person gets depend not only on their insurance but also on that of everyone else in town using the same provider.[19] Medicare did significantly increase the coverage of the high-using elderly population, which led, Finkelstein found, to a larger change in the style and intensity of practice than if only one person had gone on Medicare. (The same sort of spillover effect has been documented for large levels of health maintenance organization [HMO] or high-deductible health plan [HDHP] shares.)

The conclusion is that a market-wide change in cost-sharing (up or down) will affect use and cost of the persons subject to it more than one that affects only a few – and will also affect others. For managers, this means that paying attention to shifts in coverage at the market level is important, while small experimental changes (say, a few patients with new value-based insurance) is not going to be worth bothering much about. Of course, good healthcare systems all try to render personalized care, but there are economic influences that make differences in outcomes larger when changes are widespread compared to when they are limited to a few customers.

17 Hillman, A. L., Pauly, M. V., Escarce, J. J., Ripley, K., Gaynor, M., Clouse, J., & Ross, R. (1999). Financial incentives and drug spending in managed care: Incentives for both physicians and patients can interact to help curb spending in this increasingly costly sector. *Health Affairs*, *18*(2), 189–200.

18 Finkelstein, A. (2007). The aggregate effects of health insurance: Evidence from the introduction of Medicare. *The Quarterly Journal of Economics*, *122*(1), 1–37.

19 Pauly, M. V., & Pagán, J. A. (2007). Spillovers and vulnerability: The case of community uninsurance. *Health Affairs*, *26*(5), 1304–1314.

modest charges for drug prescriptions that are surely affordable (say, $10) can have large effects in reducing the use of drugs.[20]

The Managerial Challenges

Insurance plan managers are going to be challenged to get the extent and form of cost-sharing right to balance the premiums and the cost and value of care consumed by their middle-class customers. This is not a job for the faint of heart since, after the fact, patients will always want to complain about cost-sharing and may easily forget about the sizeable premium reduction that accompanied their choice of a plan with high cost-sharing. Not only that, different types of illness and different types of care vary in their susceptibility to moral hazard; sometimes things are cut and dried – you need only this care for your condition, and you wouldn't want any more (or less). The big open empirical question is when or whether a given kind of high-cost care is financially discretionary.

Empirical evidence says that often it is. In the classic RAND health insurance experiment, as already noted (Box 6.3), middle-class people even used one-third more hospital care when it was free compared to when they had to pay for it. Those who had to pay and went without did not have lower health levels than those who went all out for inpatient care. People with cost-sharing did avoid those emergency room visits for stomach distress and other minor complaints, again with no long-term ill effects (see Box 6.5 about patients' perceptions of cost-sharing effects on their spending).

In principle, cost-sharing should be titrated by type of care, by the degree to which consumers need a push toward or a pull back from care depending on its cost-effectiveness, and by any variation in consumer values about the trade-off between money and health risk. In practice, because consumers have a hard time remembering the details of their coverage (until it is too late) and physicians would just as soon assume every patient gets free care, there have to be limits to the complexity of insurance plan design.

The same problem of how to deal with variation presents itself to health system managers and physicians. In any business, it will cost money to add more versions of the business' main product; custom tailoring costs more. If consumers attach high value to getting exactly what they want, it may pay to differentiate. But doing so would pose an obvious problem for physicians treating patients with a wide variety of cost-sharing and insurance coverages;

[20] Hillman, A. L., Pauly, M. V., Escarce, J. J., Ripley, K., Gaynor, M., Clouse, J., & Ross, R. (1999). Financial incentives and drug spending in managed care: Incentives for both physicians and patients can interact to help curb spending in this increasingly costly sector. *Health Affairs*, *18*(2), 189–200.

Box 6.5 Evidence: How people feel about the effects of insurance cost-sharing, and how best to deal with it

In addition to the empirical studies which compare levels of medical spending and use under insurance plans with different levels of patient cost-sharing, there are many opinion surveys which ask consumers if they chose not to use care (that they would otherwise have used) because of cost or if they were worried that they might not use care because of cost.[21] (There are many fewer that ask them if they will tolerate cost-sharing to hold down premiums or keep wages high.)

The results vary by type of care, but the general finding is that, in a year, 25% of middle-class survey respondents said they did not use care because of cost – whether medical care, prescription drugs, or mental health services. The proportion "worried" can rise as high as 50%. The usual implication is that these results indicate a problem with the US insurance system. In an uncertain world, anything can be problematic, but do these results necessarily flag something important?

As usual, economists are going to have a different take than public health officials or politicians. That is because the economic theory of moral hazard says that consumers should and will choose insurance with cost-sharing that will discourage them from using care of low but positive value. To the extent that this kind of reduction happens – which, as shown in the discussion of moral hazard evidence on whether discriminating choices are made is ambiguous – it would presumably show up in an opinion survey as a response that care was (reasonably) not used because of cost compared to the benefit from that care. However, because that foregone use would have been of low value, not worth the full cost (much less the cost-sharing in insurance), the unpopular conclusion is that cost-sharing is working in a potentially efficient way. That is, according to economics, consumers are *supposed* to choose insurance that will cause them to avoid some effective care because of cost. The issue is not whether use was cut back but whether the foregone use was of high value. The term "needed care" does not tell us.

From this perspective, the fraction discouraged appears low relative to estimates of what moderate cost-sharing does in comparative studies like RAND. However, the opinion surveys tap people with all types of insurance, some with very low cost-sharing (such as Medicaid or Medicare supplemented by Medigap). The results from the opinion surveys also show that cost is more discouraging for people with chronic conditions (compared to those without) and for people with low incomes. The former result reflects the fact that healthy people less often seek medical care; the latter result shows that when insurance coverage is less comprehensive for lower-income people, presumably because of politically chosen gaps in the Medicaid and Exchange programs, it may harm health.

For managers of care delivery or insurance, the main message from economics is that any response to the kind of opinion survey data just cited should be nuanced. Whether beneficial change in cost-sharing is possible depends on the cost-effectiveness of the care

21 Lopes, L., Montero, A., Presiado, M., & Hamel, L. (2024). Americans' challenges with health care costs. Kaiser Family Foundation. www.kff.org/health-costs/issue-brief/americans-challenges-with-health-care-costs/.

discouraged, not simply on the fact that quantity demanded was reduced by cost. These results reinforce the view that cost-sharing needs to be targeted rather than abolished.

The case would need to be made that the incremental health and financial protection benefits from better coverage for those with difficulty paying for care they want are large enough to make that additional care cost-effective – and, if so, determine who should get the bill.

To be specific, people with chronic conditions in an ideal setting probably would not choose high-deductible insurance. The thought experiment is to imagine a middle-class person with diabetes able to lower cost-sharing from a high-deductible policy by paying a higher premium based on that person's risk – the person might still well opt for more expensive insurance with a lower deductible if only to protect against financial risk. The consumers in the opinion surveys who had high deductibles and coinsurance probably got their coverage in the employment-based market where they had to take whatever was on offer. For those with low incomes (but not on Medicaid), things are more ambiguous; they may not have been willing to pay for generous health insurance coverage given their other needs, and the issue is whether taxpayers might have been willing in principle to help. However, if there was no opportunity for a lower-income person to get generous coverage at a premium the person could afford, the social evaluation of the benefit from reducing cost-sharing to increase in use of medical care is unknown.

This economic analysis, hard-hearted as it is, could provide a rationale for insurance managers to avoid criticism of the adverse impact of cost-sharing. They could ask who would be willing to pay to reduce cost-sharing for those challenged by it – if you pay them, insurers will do whatever you want.

they would probably prefer to treat everyone with the same clinical presentation the same, thus holding true to medical ethics and avoiding the need to ask the patient about their insurance (or to find out about it if the patient does not know). The empirical evidence is quite strong for the hypothesis that the kind of insurance coverage most prevalent in a community affects the amount and cost of care everyone gets, regardless of their specific insurance.[22] Some differentiation is made; Medicaid patients are discriminated against because of their low payment rates, and physicians and hospitals prefer to organize in networks that deal with patients with roughly the same insurance.[23] In the case of admired plans like Kaiser, all patients are supposed to have the same insurance or at least the same insurance company which makes life a lot easier for their doctors and hospitals.

[22] Pauly, M. (1980). *Doctors and their workshops*. University of Chicago Press.

[23] Decker, S. L. (2012). In 2011 nearly one-third of physicians said they would not accept new Medicaid patients, but rising fees may help. *Health Affairs*, *31*(8), 1673–1679; Alexander, D., & Schnell, M. (2024). The impacts of physician payments on patient access, use, and health. *American Economic Journal: Applied Economics*, *16*(3), 142–177.

At present, I think it is fair to say that physicians and health system managers do not have good ways of dealing with patients with high cost-sharing; there are no health system billboards for "we are HDHP specialists." And yet as deductibles increase over time, there should be scope and need for more targeted forms of care management (just as there are for the varieties of HMO and preferred provider organization [PPO] rules).

Messages for Managers on Cost-Sharing

For managers of medical care delivery systems, there is as usual a fork in the road that you will have to take. You could configure your delivery system to fit with one of the moral hazard control models: capitated managed care (with low cost-sharing), high-deductible health plans, or plans with nuanced cost-sharing. There has been some evolution of delivery systems of the first type (though many got in trouble over the decades by overpredicting the triumph of managed care). In contrast, I know of no specific healthcare provider with a goal of offering the best possible care for a middle-class population with high deductibles, or with subtle patient (and provider) pushes based on value and patient perception of value.

There is potential for improvement, especially in the information and options, that might be provided by health systems and by physicians who work in (and for) them. When patients are responsible for relatively large upfront cost-sharing for treatment of a given condition, that is supposed to change the kind of care they get and where they get it. Picking up on the last point, it does appear that some providers of commodity-type services (like MRI scans of the back) have configured both their production and their marketing to offer lower prices to those patients who will gain from searching out lower-priced suppliers. At a minimum, they advertise that they are lower priced (rather than wait for searching consumers, if there are any, to discover them). They may also find it helpful to change the style of care to fit better with an economizing model for consumers with insurance that offers them incentives to economize.[24] I am not sure if the MRI version of "plain pipe racks at Robert Hall Clothes" will be the best marketing approach, but emphasis on conservative and less intensive care communicated to the public

[24] Pauly M.V., Rao K., & Futoran, D. (2021). Light under a bushel: Medical price transparency regulation and low-priced seller behavior. *Health Management, Policy and Innovation (HMPI.org)*, *6*(1). https://hmpi.org/2021/01/12/light-under-a-bushel-medical-price-transparency-regulation-and-low-priced-seller-behavior/.

and to referring physicians, coupled with information on financial benefits, can enhance market share.

On the kind of care more generally, consumers with high-deductible plans will be pleased to know about lower-priced alternative types of treatments – even ones that are less convenient or slower. They may not choose to trade off money for mild discomfort, but they will appreciate the option to move to a more economical version at the cost of some bells and (you guessed it) whistles. Another kind of system response is for a system or a health plan to search out physicians whose own preferred style of practice is lower cost than average – there must be some. Consumers with high deductibles will gravitate toward providers who are active (rather than reluctant) to provide information about price transparency and what different therapies will cost. There may be a network that enlists such physicians (thus saving the consumer the bother of searching and asking) that can be packaged and marketed to patients with insurance in which they bear greater financial responsibility.

To be sure, this trade-off-based model – which is the original Harvard Business School model of creative destruction – has not been typical in medical care. The idea of an offering which lacks some dimensions of quality but is much less costly – the original fable about Canon versus Xerox in the copier market – is not what medical care suppliers are used to thinking about.[25] This model abjures "the highest possible quality" in return for reasonably good quality at a much lower price. It may be a while before acceptable language for talking about US healthcare in this way develops, though such differences are well known in other countries where less costly public options compete with private but higher-cost providers for those able and willing to pay for the hope of something a little bit extra. Even though less costly HMO insurances with more pointed financial constraints for doctors have existed for a while, they have experienced bad publicity and backlash (and recently market stagnation) when it turned out that consumers decided they could afford to pay more for that little bit extra – and told their employers to favor that kind of coverage. If medical spending takes a bigger bite out of wages and budgets, the scene may transform.

Managers looking over their shoulders at politicians who feel compelled to meddle in insurance design – either favoring cost-sharing if they are intrusive Republicans or trying to keep out short-term low-coverage plans if they are

[25] Bower, J. L., & Christensen, C. M. (1995). Disruptive technologies: Catching the wave. *Harvard Business Review*. https://hbr.org/1995/01/disruptive-technologies-catching-the-wave.

Democrats – should be prepared. Insurance managers should be prepared to defend offering a large menu of choices regarding cost-sharing and managed care while staying at arm's length from the silver bullet du jour. Managers of medical delivery should already have planned to cope with a variety of designs and try as best they can to forecast what type will gain market share (either for economic or for political reasons). Having in place service delivery models that fit well with whatever comes down the pike in terms of insurance design is the best preparation.

Advice for Managers: How to Aim Cost-Sharing

There is no longer any question that moral hazard is important in health insurance. Across the board, from low- to high-income, young to old, healthy to sick, people use less medical care the less of its cost is covered by insurance and the more they have to pay out of pocket. Precisely because the instrument of cost-sharing is so potent, it needs to be handled with care. Slogans like "skin in the game" or "no barriers to access" do not help. Exposing skin hurts, and more access costs money. We know that the goal is to use insurance design to encourage the use of cost-effective care and discourage the use of effective care that is not worth its cost, but the problem is that "we" outside experts (working as researchers or for the insurance company) cannot accurately tell which situation is which, precisely because there is a considerable gray area in medicine where effectiveness varies based on things that might be known by the patient (like how bad they feel) but which cannot be known by an insurance manager. We can invoke "medical necessity," but we cannot fashion it into an effective tool for settling the close calls where cost-sharing matters. This means that "we" do know that there needs to be self-rationing, but titrating the incentives to do so is not a job for the timid, nor for those with beliefs rather than evidence.

We can begin by clearing the underbrush with two comments, one theoretical and one empirical. The theoretical comment is that if there are some treatments where we are pretty sure everyone who uses them will expect the same benefit ("homogeneous" to use the 75-cent word), and if we have good cost-effectiveness evidence at current prices, we can be doctrinaire: If a treatment is cost-effective for everyone with an illness, it should be covered 100%, and if it is not cost-effective for anyone, it should not be covered at all. Period.

The empirical observation is that, in responding to differences in cost-sharing, and despite their necessarily imperfect clinical knowledge, consumers using their own judgment (about initiating care) appear to make more reasonable judgments about what to drop and what to retain than when they are advised by physicians (about what care to use once they have contacted the system). However, even here they did not always make the high-value visit and avoid the useless one. The RAND experiment showed this. The three-cornered interaction among patient, physician, and insurer still remains a puzzle – it does not always seem to work out well for the patient. There must be insurance designs that combine incentives to patients, incentives to doctors, and managed care rules that work out better than others – but no one yet knows what they are.

If instead we consider services where the expected benefit from the same service is known to vary across patients (say, with illness severity) and patients and their physicians know more about severity than insurers can know, we have reasonably crisp advice from economic theory: other things equal, have lower cost-sharing for illnesses or treatments where there is less variation in clinical benefit, and higher for treatments with more variable effectiveness. Target for high cost-sharing those situations in which patients are sick, but treatment can display wide variation in cost and comfort. In economics, this variation can be measured by demand responsiveness or elasticity for informed patients. The greater the elasticity, other things equal, the higher should be cost-sharing – precisely because there will be a larger share of potentially effective treatments to discourage because they are not effective enough to justify their full cost that consumers will eventually pay in insurance premiums.

These results are the ones where you can hang your hat as a manager. There is at least one other case which is much more troubling, however. This is the case in which patients incorrectly estimate the health benefits of a treatment. The classic example here is taking statins after a heart attack. The clinical evidence shows a great deal of benefit in avoiding future myocardial infarction. But 40% or more of middle-class well-educated patients do not comply. When statins cost $2 a pill (now they are less than 20 cents), it turned out in a well-designed experiment that lowering cost-sharing to zero bumped up the percentage taking from 35.9% to 49%.[26] Not a big deal, but a step in the right direction, and one that led to improved health outcomes

[26] Choudhry, N. K., Avorn, J., Glynn, R. J., Antman, E. M., Schneeweiss, S., Toscano, M., . . . & Shrank, W. H. (2011). Full coverage for preventive medications after myocardial infarction. *New England Journal of Medicine*, *365*(22), 2088–2097.

with little or no additional spending. There have been almost no similar experiments in increasing cost-sharing for services that are thought to be overused, beyond products like Viagra or older weight-loss drugs, but presumably one could expect the same effect in the opposite direction there. We do know that Medicare Part D insurers charge higher copayments for costly drugs whose use seems more responsive to coverage, but we do not know if they get it right when they do so. And then Congress gets into the act requiring zero coinsurance for some treatments that seem like a good idea, such as immunizations, or lowering copays for insulin (more on this in Box 6.6). Because cost-sharing means causing someone to avoid care that would have improved their health, the potentially correct default is always free care. But then more is spent, and more is wasted. The sellers of care almost always want their services to be free, so managers face a tough choice.

Box 6.6 Evidence: Behavioral economics and healthcare mistakes

The analysis of the impact of changes in cost-sharing on patient use of statins after a heart attack provides a good example of the role of behavioral economics in healthcare. Since Penn is one of the centers of this kind of research through its Center for Health Incentives and Behavioral Economics, and since it sometimes develops empirical findings inconsistent with the basic economic models of rational demander and producer behavior that we teach freshman econ majors, its messages for healthcare managers are important to consider. The best summary of economists' research on this subject (as opposed to psychologists') in is the review essay by Chandra, Handel, and Schwartzstein.[27]

We must be humble enough to note that conventional economic theory and its positive conclusions about human behavior are not intended to be universally true without exceptions. The prediction that higher prices reduce quantity demanded does not imply that every person will cut back; they are intended to describe market-based tendencies. Your Uncle Joe may buy more of a beer that increased its price because he thinks it means it is a better or more prestigious brew, and most people have better things to do than pay attention to every wrinkle in prices or probabilities. But you can bet that Molson Coors will sell more if it drastically cuts the price of Miller Lite.

More to the point, rationality has multiple dimensions. Those apparently irrational patients who did not take their recommended statins were nevertheless rational enough to be somewhat more adherent when cost-sharing disappeared than when they had to pay; they responded rationally to prices even if irrationally to physician advice. At a deeper level, as noted, this kind of behavioral observation does not necessarily lead to good management

[27] Chandra, A., Handel, B., & Schwartzstein, J. (2019). Behavioral economics and health-care markets. In B. D. Bernheim, S. DellaVigna, & D. Laibson (eds.), *Handbook of behavioral economics: Applications and foundations 1* (Vol. 2, pp. 459–502). North-Holland.

policy; insurers may not be able to sell the more expensive coverage that tricks patients into doing what is best for their own good. Journalists love behavioral economics because, in addition to making Milton Friedman disciples look foolish, it often implies that someone else (a policymaker who comes from somewhere) should pass judgment on the choices consumers make – at least a nudge and maybe a push – so they do what is really best for them. The absence of an anointed authority in the US to tell the plebes what to do – even in justifiable cases like pandemics – has irritated some writers and European commentators on our health policy but is not likely to change anytime soon.

One set of behavioral studies shows that not all consumers buy the insurance that carries the lowest loading given their situations – that is, the insurance that will provide the largest financial benefits relative to its premiums. They cite the behavioral phenomenon of "choice overload" obscuring rational cost-benefit analysis, which is often time-consuming. Most of this work deals with Medicare drug coverage (and not with employer choices); it shows that people taking some set of drugs often do not choose the plan that would lead to the lowest out-of-pocket payment for them,[28] although they appear to learn to do better over time.[29]

There are also inertia and bad choices when workers face group insurance options. Invoking costs of information and attention would usually be enough to explain this behavior, though other models of how people choose in risky situations might help. The "healthcare markets" the authors invoke should supply decision aids to reduce the chances that buyers will leave money on the table, and there are brokers, consultants, and navigators to help. But any setting in which there is an opportunity for choice is an opportunity to make a mistake, so there is a trade-off here. Selection also matters; no one has worked out what would happen in Medicare Part D if people who got the most benefit from a given plan's formulary and cost-sharing all flocked to that plan, and no one else. If people were rational, it might not be pretty.

Of course, not all nudges work. Removing deductibles for diabetics did not increase compliance with care,[30] and paying physicians more to get them to do something experts think is better does not always matter. The correct but not especially useful punchline is that managers need to consider the possibility that even things that sound like a good idea to economists may not work because of behavioral responses. Such a finding is red meat for researchers – find out why not. In the meantime, we come back to emphasizing evidence as well as theory as important in managerial decision-making: not a revolution or a reason to throw away your Econ 1 notes, but the usual advice for caution.

In the setting where cost-sharing can vary by employer, if value-based insurance that tries to counteract underuse of highly cost-effective care by lower cost-sharing carries a higher premium or is more complex than blunt instrument coverage, will an employer that offers it (and lower wages) reduce the firm's compensation cost? The usual rule for informed patients that cost-sharing should be higher for types of care that are more responsive to demand

[28] Abaluck, J., & Gruber, J. (2011). Choice inconsistencies among the elderly: Evidence from plan choice in the Medicare Part D program. *American Economic Review, 101*(4), 1180–1210.

[29] Ketcham, J. D., Lucarelli, C., & Powers, C. A. (2015). Paying attention or paying too much in Medicare Part D. *American Economic Review, 105*(1), 204–233.

[30] Huang, C. X., Turk, N., Ettner, S. L., Mangione, C. M., Moin, T., O'Shea, D., . . . & Duru, O. K. (2022). Does the diabetes health plan have a differential impact on medication adherence among beneficiaries with fewer financial resources? *Journal of Managed Care & Specialty Pharmacy, 28*(9), 948–957.

might be incorrect; cost-sharing should be low both for highly demand-elastic but seriously underused care and for less elastically demanded care. The first case is to incentivize more beneficial use, and the second case is to protect against financial risk. However, according to economists, the employer would have to convince potential workers that its benefit package will leave them a little poorer but so much healthier that they will choose the job at lower wages. "Even though our wages are a little less, our company's workers have better health outcomes after heart attacks." Making that a persuasive message might be close to mission impossible. Perhaps "building a benefits package that demonstrates to potential employees that their health matters"[31] will make it possible to lower compensation costs, but the evidence is not there yet.

The premise of behavioral economics is that there is some repository of wisdom that can judge when consumers make mistakes and force or nudge corrections, but the demand and supply curve for such wisdom in competitive insurance or labor markets has not been established. So here again there may be some useful messages, but they need to be curated carefully.

Advice for Policymakers: Policy Choices about Cost-Sharing

Several different groups of policy advocates have, with almost religious zeal, suggested different alternative cost-sharing designs that employers or governments should (in their view) implement. One camp has for decades argued that HDHPs, usually coupled with some kind of earmarked and tax-advantaged spending account, should be spread over the land. Cost-sharing in these plans is the opposite of targeted: Other than zero copayment for a few preventive services, they have required that all spending be subject to the same high deductible. This movement has gradually resulted in a sizeable minority of workers having such high-deductible coverage. An opposite approach imagines that cost-sharing should be based on the value of care, known as value-based insurance design (VBID). The definition of value (beyond the obvious of no coverage for things thought to be worthless and good coverage for care for people bleeding to death) is somewhat soft, but some version of this approach has been embodied in some Medicare Advantage plans in recent years. With trepidation, here I offer advice on how to decide which religion is the best, and for whom.

Let us begin with the product that has roots at Penn. The idea of VBID has been embraced by Dr. Mark Fendrick, who was an undergraduate student

[31] Curative. (2022). How to attract and retain talent with better health benefits. Curative blog. https://curative.com/blog/attract-and-retain-talent-with-better-health-benefits.

and research assistant in the Leonard Davis Institute of Health Economics at Penn. There is an unsophisticated version of this idea intended to appeal to physicians: cover most generously those therapies that physicians think are most important or most effective for health. The doctor knows best. As expected, economists raise an eyebrow and say that cost (which doctors usually do not know) as well as effectiveness should be considered, and that the size of any impact of changing cost-sharing on use as well as the cost of any additional use matters. The best VBID change would be one that seriously boosted use of cost-effective care.

We will consider the general idea of using cost-effectiveness analysis to design insurance coverage in Chapter 8. Here we note that treatments that are firmly believed by consumers to be cost-effective will, according to economics, be sought even if there is very high cost-sharing – because their benefits are worth their full cost. The case for low or zero cost-sharing in VBID is strongest when a treatment is cost-effective for almost everyone with the condition but when almost everyone with the condition does not believe it is worth that much. The example of statins for heart attack patients fits this model perfectly.

If a social planner were designing cost-sharing for society's benefit, low cost-sharing would be the advice to follow. However, a glitch appears if insurance choice by imperfectly informed consumers is voluntary. The problem is that such VBID coverage is intended to trick patients into using effective care they think ineffective – and then asks them to pay higher premiums for insurance that does this. Some people may go for this, but for workers that have the courage of their incorrect convictions, it may not pay for employers to foster such more costly coverage, as discussed in Chapter 11. The larger the cost offsets (which do reduce benefits' costs), the more sense VBID will make – but most treatments, even most effective treatments, do not pay for themselves in a short period of time. Preaching the virtues of VBID still goes on, but so far it is not close to beating HDHPs in terms of private insurance market share.

High-Deductible Health Plans

From the theory already discussed, we know that there is no intrinsic merit to cost-sharing being high or low – it all depends on the marginal cost-effectiveness of treatments and the insurance buyer's attitude toward financial risk. However, the tax exclusion discussed in Chapter 11 provides a biased incentive toward plans with low cost-sharing. The policy of a tax-shielded spending account combined with insurance required to be high-deductible is intended to offset this bias. It does so in two ways – it requires higher cost-sharing for a consumer who wants to take advantage of tax benefits for saving and it offers those additional tax benefits as a way of roughly equalizing the net cost to an insurance buyer of choosing either an aggressive managed care plan (with limits on low-value care from plan rules) or a high-deductible plan (with limits on low-value care from beneficiary choices). There is also an objective of encouraging savings by Americans which are low by international standards (could the reason be that more is spent on healthcare here?).

There are two broad policy questions: (1) Do HDHPs curtail spending and the growth in spending? (2) Assuming they do lower spending, is the gain from doing so offset by worse health outcomes? The evidence so far on these questions is somewhat nuanced, so fasten your seatbelts.

There are two ways to address the question of effectiveness: One is to compare the level of spending of people who switched (or were switched) to HDHPs to their spending levels before the switch. The most common finding is that exogenously switching consumers from low- to high-deductible plans is associated with a permanent fall in their level of spending following the time of switching. The general result here echoes the HIE; spending levels fell, usually by 10%–20% as people were phased into these new plan designs.[32] These results primarily come from before and after studies of employers who, buoyed by exuberant enthusiasm for HDHPs, compelled all of their workers to move to such plans from more generous ones. These are thus studies with subjects that are largely the same in both periods (though some people might have quit because of poorer coverage and others may have taken a job to get access to tax-subsidized savings accounts). Virtually all such studies show a reduction in spending over the next few years following a switch.[33] However, that comparison does not address the longer-term growth in spending. To do that, we must compare people after a switch who stayed in high-deductible plans for many years with people who continued in low-deductible plans. In this case there is no evidence of lower overall spending growth, though lower growth was exhibited in drug

32 Waters, T. M., Chang, C. F., Cecil, W. T., Kasteridis, P., & Mirvis, D. (2011). Impact of high-deductible health plans on health care utilization and costs. *Health Services Research*, *46*(1pt.1), 155–172; Rabideau, B., Eisenberg, M. D., Reid, R., & Sood, N. (2021). Effects of employer-offered high-deductible plans on low-value spending in the privately insured population. *Journal of Health Economics*, *76*, 102424.

33 Brot-Goldberg, Z. C., Chandra, A., Handel, B. R., & Kolstad, J. T. (2017). What does a deductible do? The impact of cost-sharing on health care prices, quantities, and spending dynamics. *The Quarterly Journal of Economics*, *132*(3), 1261–1318.

spending, offset in part by higher growth in other kinds of spending (as one might have expected).[34]

The other way is to compare local markets in which workers have had higher than average deductibles for many years with markets in which the market-level average deductible is lower. Here there is evidence that market-wide exposure to higher cost-sharing lowers spending growth moderately. (Not surprisingly, market-level deductibles were lower in areas with more unions and more Democrats, since HDHP is a tenet of Republican health reform.)[35]

Here is where the nuance reaches a fever pitch (sorry for the mixed metaphor). One explanation for the difference is that within a market or within a physician's practice, the physician does not pay much attention to differences in insurance cost-sharing provisions in deciding whether or not to recommend a costly new treatment; there are good reasons to treat all patients more or less the same. But when many of all doctors' patients start complaining about higher out-of-pocket payments, all physicians are motivated to be more thoughtful about net benefit, especially since the doctors in the office down the hall are doing the same. As noted earlier in the chapter, Amy Finkelstein found this kind of story to be an explanation of why Medicare led to a market-level spike in spending much greater than occurred in the RAND experiment when only a few patients got the free care insurance, and the same kind of market-wide effect of cost-sharing may be going on here.[36]

What about the impacts on health of high-deductible plans compared to ones with less cost-sharing? One of the unpopular messages from health economics is that theory implies that financial incentives to cut patient use of care should harm health, at least a little. The empirical evidence also indicates that people do not shop around for lower-priced versions of the same health-care but rather cut back on overall care.[37] So far, the evidence on harms to health from HDHPs is similar to that from the RAND experiment: Harm is

[34] Lucarelli, C., Frean, M., Gordon, A. S., Hua, L. M., & Pauly, M. (2020). How does cost-sharing impact spending growth and cost-effective treatments? Evidence from deductibles. National Bureau of Economic Research Working Paper No. w28155.

[35] Frean, M., & Pauly, M. V. (2023). Do higher deductibles slow health spending growth? *International Journal of the Economics of Business*, *30*(1), 31–49.

[36] Finkelstein, A., & McKnight, R. (2008). What did Medicare do? The initial impact of Medicare on mortality and out of pocket medical spending. *Journal of Public Economics*, *92*(7), 1644–1668.

[37] Baicker, K., & Goldman, D. (2011). Patient cost-sharing and healthcare spending growth. *Journal of Economic Perspectives*, *25*(2), 47–68; Bundorf, M. K. (2016). Consumer-directed health plans: A review of the evidence. *Journal of Risk and Insurance*, *83*(1), 9–41; Bundorf, M. K., Levin, J., & Mahoney, N. (2012). Pricing and welfare in health plan choice. *American Economic Review*, *102*(7), 3214–3248; Fronstin, P. (2010). What do we really know about consumer-driven health plans? EBRI Issue Brief No. 345.

most pronounced for subjects with lower income and high initial risk.[38] Of course, people with heart conditions or diabetes should not be choosing plans with high cost-sharing; that is just asking for trouble. But sometimes they have no choice or no ability to afford generous coverage.

Overall, it seems that HDHPs do have a moderately large impact on lowering spending as people switch into them from more generous plans. Future impacts on spending growth, if they are to occur, require wider spread within a market (and benefit all insurers including Medicare from lower market-level spending growth). Impacts on health are limited to a small minority of the population, and those most at risk of harm to health tend not to choose such plans unless their employers force them to do so.

As far as I know, there has been no comprehensive study comparing HDHPs, which are a blunt instrument for patient cost-sharing, with more selective plan designs. (There have been some studies showing that exempting some cost-effective preventive care from deductibles protects it.)[39] Of course, administrative costs (and mistakes) will be greater if a plan has all sorts of different levels of cost-sharing for different treatments – patients and physicians can hardly be expected to remember which provision goes with which treatment (though this seems like a golden opportunity for a real-time app that will spit out your cost-sharing for any treatment recommendation your doctor makes). I believe that at present evidence is insufficient to crown or condemn either approach; this seems like the ideal setting for an informed marketplace to handle things, and it will probably find some division of the population into both camps will prevail after things settle down.

Will High Cost-Sharing Get You into Heaven?

The moral hazard story has a sharp edge, and economists are often blamed for mentioning it (though they are not responsible for it). As noted in the theory discussion at the beginning of this chapter, efficiency in economics as applied to healthcare implies that, in order to save money, everyone should

[38] Jiang, D. H., Herrin, J., Van Houten, H. K., & McCoy, R. G. (2023). Evaluation of high-deductible health plans and acute glycemic complications among adults with diabetes. *JAMA Network Open*, *6*(1), e2250602; Kozhimannil, K. B., Law, M. R., Blauer-Peterson, C., Zhang, F., & Wharam, J. F. (2013). The impact of high-deductible health plans on men and women: An analysis of emergency department care. *Medical Care*, *51*(8), 639–645.

[39] Norris, H. C., Richardson, H. M., Benoit, M. A. C., Shrosbree, B., Smith, J. E., & Fendrick, A. M. (2022). Utilization impact of cost-sharing elimination for preventive care services: A rapid review. *Medical Care Research and Review*, *79*(2), 175–197.

forego some care that would improve health in some dimension. Everyone, it is said, wants to get to heaven but no one wants to die. Similarly, everyone wants less costly medical care but no one wants to risk bad health. The criticism leveled against health plans with cost-sharing (as opposed to free care) is that they may lead people to underuse care that could be beneficial to their health. A solution to this concern as discussed is to target cost-sharing, rather than offer poorly designed blunt instrument plans, in ways that account for consumers' ability (or inability) to make choices about benefits versus costs that are as good as what external care managers could offer (as reviewed in Box 6.2).

However, the economic explanation does not predict that only irrational, useless, or harmful care will fall but that the reduction in total cost (premium plus average cost-sharing) will be more valuable than the lost health benefits. So, is it ethical to have plans that do so? If it is, as a matter of public policy, should all consumers be allowed to choose plans with higher levels of cost-sharing or should some be forbidden or directed away?

I do not yet know of a way to discuss this logical inevitability without discomfort. It may help to think of a setting (which exists sometimes somewhere) in which all potential patients have approximately equal incomes and wealth. The theory of moral hazard says that many will prefer insurance with cost-sharing (at a low price) to insurance with free care at a high price. They will have traded off access for money.

If we consider instead the setting in the US in which there is substantial variation in income, we are then confronted with what is usually framed as an ethical dilemma: Is cost-sharing for lower-income families ethically justified? (We will assume that ethicists will have no concerns about young MBAs choosing high-deductible health plans.) If not, one policy option would be to modify the current option for such plans in the US (along with tax-shielded spending accounts) so that lower-income families would be forbidden to use them. But then either those families would have to pay a lot for the more costly free or near-free care plans or someone else would have to pay for them. Making billionaires pay their fair share in taxes will not necessarily or even plausibly lead to funding of free care insurance for the lower middle class. Other taxpayers may wish to fund subsidies to coverage that will yield health benefits to low-income people because those taxpayers value the health of their fellow citizens, but that case needs to be made, not assumed. At least not yet.

The discussion in Chapter 8 on cost-effectiveness about community concern for the health of all members is relevant here. It makes the commonsense point that having Medicaid programs pay providers high prices, even on a fee-for-service (FFS) basis, for services known to be highly cost-effective but underused is desirable. Establishing the evidence on what really works – not all preventive care should be included – remains a challenge but a worthy one.

A final word on cost-sharing. It is one of the ways that patients can pre-commit to limiting their use of beneficial but low-value care. It puts a heavy decision burden on the patient-consumer (who is after all not a specialist in epidemiology) and on the physician offering advice. Some experts believe that this task is hopeless, that consumers cannot be relied upon to understand marginal health benefits of different treatments, even with help. But then the hardest question – what is the alternative way to curtail the use of low-value care? You could alternatively sign on to HMO insurance with low cost-sharing but lots of rules, some of which make mistakes – but would the same consumers know what they are giving up? Or you could be a real optimist and imagine some medical association or government regulator could figure out what is of value to you and design a plan to supply that care (and only that care) to you. For the present, it seems like cost-sharing is here to stay – but we should always be on the lookout for a gift from the gods that might allow moral hazard to be less of a problem. In the meantime, we do the best we can with the tools at hand.

Part 2: Adverse Selection

Everyone agrees that insurance markets of any type would work well if all potential purchasers of insurance were known to have the same risk – the same expected value of future claims given some policy design. Since this risk uniformity is not the case in health insurance, there is controversy about what to do. If you and your twin brother both built the same frame house but yours is across the street from the firehouse and your twin's is in the inflammable piney woods 30 miles from town, neither of you would be surprised that your fire insurance premium would be lower than your twin's, though discussing this at Thanksgiving might lead to sibling conflict. But what if your twin has diabetes and you do not? Or if it is not your twin but your older brother? Would you both agree that your health insurance premium deserves to be lower and his higher, because of the older age or the preexisting condition? You could be generous and agree to help your brother lobby the insurance company for the same premium as yours, but the company would argue that, if it were forced to charge the same premium, it would have to raise yours to fund the lower premium for your brother. After all, on average, the owner of the house in the woods or the sibling with a chronic condition is going to collect more money from a given insurance policy. If insurers know risk, the iron fist of insurer competition will force every person's premium to align with the average or expected cost of the benefits they will collect.

As hinted, the problem of how to deal with variations in health risk has bothered policymakers and people of good will for decades. No one wants to add the insult of higher premiums to the injury of coming down with a costly chronic condition. However, the main conclusion of insurance theory is that efficient premiums should vary "as much as possible" with risk level variations, especially those that buyers know about.[40] If the insurer knows or can know everything the buyer knows about risk, this will be the competitive outcome, and then people will buy whatever coverage they choose at those different premiums. There will still be protection from risk because even high-risk individuals might or might not suffer large losses, but there will also be variation in premiums known for sure beforehand. (If insurers can tell who is a higher risk but buyers cannot, competitive insurers will try to do the low-risk buyers a special favor by offering them lower premiums, so it works out the same as if buyers were informed.)

The higher-risk buyer, even one faced with a higher premium for additional coverage compared to lower-risk individuals, might choose to buy about the same coverage as a lower-risk individual – since the higher premium would be offset by higher expected benefits.[41] If there are income effects and the higher premium bites deeply into the high-risk buyer's wealth, that person might buy less or no coverage. In reality, an individual with high health risk might buy even more coverage if the buyer is older, wiser, or more risk-averse.[42] Technically, a higher premium for high-risk individuals will still be affordable in the sense that the high-risk buyer will prefer to pay that premium than risk the higher expense, as long as the buyer has a decent income. After all, the alternative to paying the higher premium with insurance is facing a more likely big bill without insurance, and the former will usually be preferable.

[40] Arrow, K. J. (1978). Uncertainty and the welfare economics of medical care. In P. Diamond & M. Rothschild (eds.), *Uncertainty in economics* (pp. 345–375). Academic Press.

[41] Ehrlich, I., & Becker, G. S. (1972). Market insurance, self-insurance, and self-protection. *Journal of Political Economy*, *80*(4), 623–648.

[42] Pauly, M. V., & Nichols, L. M. (2003). The nongroup health insurance market: Short on facts, long on opinions and policy disputes. *Health Affairs*, 21(suppl.1). https://doi.org/10.1377/hlthaff.w2.325.

However, it may be one thing to accept higher premiums if you choose to build your house in the woods or on the seashore but another thing if you are sick (or older) through no fault of your own. Economists will be happy with risk-rated insurance markets, but many normal people will not. Women should not pay more for retirement insurance or less for life insurance (because they live longer), and people who happen to have houses near the beach should not pay more for hurricane insurance than those who live much further inland. Or so the arguments go. The economic purpose of insurance is to deal with losses that have yet to happen, not with risks that have already occurred. Risk rating may be efficient but it seems unfair.

How markets will work in practice thus depends on whether insurers know about the risk of different potential customers and are able to use their knowledge to charge premiums that vary with risk. In one of the most famous papers in insurance economics, Michael Rothschild and Joseph Stiglitz showed that, if insurers are not as well informed about individual risk as buyers are, then adverse selection can cause the market to be inefficient if an equilibrium exists at all (see Box 6.7).[43]

Even when insurers can get information of different risk levels, "risk rating" health insurance premiums – and the collection of underwriting information needed to do it well – thus seem to kick a person when they are down, and so policymakers have often passed rules that require, to a greater or lesser degree, some form of premium averaging as a way of helping out higher-risk individuals. They try to compel insurers to ignore information on preexisting conditions and supply insurance to higher-risk buyers for premiums that will not cover their losses. This is a very imperfect economic solution if consumers at different risk levels can still choose to buy different amounts of insurance (or no insurance at all) at the same premium per unit – what are called "community rated" premiums. I argued some time ago that, whatever its merits in terms of perceived fairness and political favor, community rating was inefficient if adverse selection did not destroy the market – because it led low-risk buyers to buy too little insurance even as high-risk ones were incentivized to buy too much.[44] What is more, when insurers are forced to charge premiums that ignore differences in risk, exactly the same kind of consternation discussed by Rothschild and Stiglitz will

[43] Rothschild, M., & Stiglitz, J. (1978). Equilibrium in competitive insurance markets: An essay on the economics of imperfect information. In P. Diamond & M. Rothschild (eds.), *Uncertainty in economics* (pp. 257–280). Academic Press.

[44] Pauly, M. V. (1970). The welfare economics of community rating. *The Journal of Risk and Insurance, 37* (3), 407–418. https://doi.org/10.2307/250907.

Box 6.7 Evidence: Ivy League universities dump generous worker health insurance – should they?

One aspect of selection that economists love to talk about is the possibility that adverse selection may kill off a generous employment-based health insurance policy that would have survived if only workers had not switched out based on their low risk levels. The reason for this fascination is that the semi-complex Rothschild and Stiglitz theory suggests this could happen even if insurance markets are competitive; has such market failure ever materialized? There are two competing anecdotes, both at nonprofit universities (the antithesis, in more ways than one, of an unfettered competitive market but still subject to labor market discipline), where the generous plan died. In one case, at Harvard, the university moved from subsidizing premiums for the high-coverage option to an arrangement in which the same contribution was made toward each plan. So, the additional premium for the high-coverage option then increased to reflect the difference in claims for those who chose it compared to the claims for those who chose the lower-coverage option. At the other, an unnamed east coast university (which, it can now be revealed, was Penn), the sequence was the reverse.

Cutler and Reber tell the Harvard story.[45] Beginning from a policy in which a generous PPO with a large network was offered at a subsidized incremental premium, the Harvard benefits department decided for some reason to move to one in which the incremental premium reflected the difference in average claims – the uniform contribution approach – resulting in nearly tripling the incremental high-option premium. After this happened, there was movement of lower-risk persons away from the PPO and toward a more restrictive HMO that had already attracted most lower-risk individuals. The erosion of enrollment in the high-coverage plan led to even further premium increases and its eventual demise. This experience is usually interpreted as a "death spiral." That in turn is viewed as a "misadventure in insurance design" and a "mess of good intentions."[46] However, it is important to note that Cutler and Reber estimated only a modest welfare loss from movement toward the uniform lump sum contribution policy, as low as 2% of premiums.

A few years later, the University of Pennsylvania also changed the design of its insurance offerings. However, in this case it was the reverse of the Harvard pattern. Penn had been using the uniform contribution model, with high premiums for the more generous plan chosen by high-risks buyers, but then was advised by benefits consultants that it should lower the explicit worker premium for the high-option FFS PPO. The extra premium would now be set at an estimate of what the difference in claims would have been had both plans been chosen by an average slice of workers. The proposal naturally received strong support in the faculty senate, representing well-off tenured but older professors. But the impact in this case was not the reverse of the Harvard experience: Instead of the high option being saved, it continued to lose enrollment at about the same pace as before. Eventually a new set

[45] Cutler, D. M., & Reber, S. J. (1998). Paying for health insurance: The trade-off between competition and adverse selection. *The Quarterly Journal of Economics, 113*(2), 433–466.

[46] Einav, L., Finkelstein, A., & Fisman, R. (2023). *Risky business: Why insurance markets fail and what to do about it.* Yale University Press.

of consultants came to campus, advised a return to the uniform contribution model, and canceled the high-option plan.

There could be any number of reasons for these differences in responses. Sometimes things just do not reverse, or the workforces of the two universities might have been different. But another possibility is that rising health costs meant that the era of low cost-sharing, highly permissive coverage had come to end (as it eventually did almost everywhere in the US, including in settings where selection was not an issue); perhaps what looked like adverse selection at Harvard was just a coincidence between a change in benefits policy and an inexorable trend. That Harvard made its original misadventure to save on benefits cost (which it did, though why it wanted to change its compensation mix is not known) may have meant that old-fashioned FFS coverage would have been dropped anyway.

happen even if there is no information asymmetry – because insurers are forbidden to use information they do or could have.

In such a case, the low-risk individuals may prefer to buy little insurance because it is overpriced for them, while the high-risk ones purchase as much coverage as they can lay their hands on because it is a great deal. Markets are affected, Rothschild and Stiglitz argue, because insurers can then profitably offer skimpy coverage at low premiums to pick off the low-risk individuals – even if the insurer does not know who is who. The market for insurance may still unravel, with only the highest of high-risk buyers still willing to buy the insurance plan. This may lead to a "death spiral" in which the market may nearly disappear (although, zombie-like, it will come back later). It is perhaps ironic that, if the insurance market does survive, the resulting economic inefficiency suggests sympathy not for the high-risk individuals but rather the low-risk ones who buy too little coverage – because its price is inflated over its true cost by the enforced transfer to high risk buyers.

So, requiring insurers to ignore a risk that everybody knows about in setting premiums can be a bad way to deal with a serious problem; it will cause adverse selection where it did not need to exist. One troubling regulation then begets another: To keep the market from melting down, governments are urged to step in, forbid low-coverage ("junk") policies, and try to mandate that those low-risk individuals keep buying coverage even though it is a terrible deal for them. So, we have a trade-off between a messed-up insurance market (because of premium regulation) or one with many miserable lower-risk buyers – who then lobby their legislators to remove the mandate – as Congress did with the ACA. Better news in a moment.

In a totally unregulated and competitive insurance market, insurers would use whatever information on the risk of prospective purchasers they could obtain at reasonable cost in order to sell insurance at lower premiums to those lucky enough to be measurable lower risks. Adverse selection will then only happen if there is other information buyers have but sellers cannot get. In the case of health insurance, I think that such adverse selection as we observe is primarily caused by regulations or policies that forbid insurers from using information about risk they can easily obtain.[47] Not perfectly, your insurer may not know that this is the year you plan to welcome a baby. However, there is almost always pre-purchase objective evidence of the presence of a chronic condition, either a physician diagnosis or the use of medical care specialized to a condition. Insurers may be willing to bear the cost of looking for this information as part of the underwriting process – though they will ignore it if it is too inconsequential or too hard to find.

If prospective health insurance buyers had to tell insurers the truth about their health conditions before they bought coverage, and if insurers could verify what they were told, there would be very little adverse selection in health insurance. (Not the same for auto insurance, where almost all truly believe they are better than average drivers.) The adverse selection horror stories about unraveling of competitive health insurance markets are about situations where the market is forbidden to vary premiums with knowable risk, *not* when there is failure of an unregulated market.

Now for the good news. This conclusion does not mean that nothing should be done to help people who happen to become high-risk. If it is felt (as I feel) that it is unfair for non-rich high-risk individuals to have to pay much higher than average insurance premiums for decent basic coverage, the best public sector solution would be to use fair taxes (such as the progressive income tax) to raise money to provide them with a premium subsidy, ideally one independent of how much insurance they buy, that brings their payment down to a fair level. The key goal here is to allow low-risk buyers to continue to pay low premiums so they will continue to buy the same decent coverage.

Under the ACA that is not what was done. The program required modified community rating and prohibition on underwriting; some unraveling then ensued. After the Biden administration Covid-era extensions (technically only temporary) furnished premium subsidies to almost everyone who used the Exchanges, even low-risk buyers found insurance a reasonable deal. That solved the selection problem for the present but meant higher tax burdens to pay for money that flowed to a small and nonpoor segment of the population.

[47] Pauly, 221, 296 M. V., McGuire, T. G., & Barros, P. P. (eds.). (2012). *Handbook of health economics* (Vol. 2). Elsevier.

Yet another example of government action begetting more government action – in this case, at a higher cost to taxpayers than subsidies targeted at deserving high-risk individuals. Tape and wire now hold the system together, not the market.

Another potential solution is a market-based one: When most people reach adulthood, they are about the same (low) level of health risk; the problem of risk variation becomes serious as chronic conditions hit some and not others over the life cycle. Young adults could be encouraged to buy an insurance policy for, say, the year from 29 to 30 that not only pays for claims during that year but also promises to cover any future higher premium if that is the year in which they are diagnosed with a high-risk condition. And this could be repeated year after year; the "extra" premium will fall with age as people get closer to Medicare. This feature – "guaranteed renewability at level premiums" – is actually easy for insurers to administer because it means they do not have to seek information to find out which people became higher risks last year; they only need to estimate how many and how costly. Even with disincentives from subsidized Exchange insurance, this feature does now exist in some private health insurance policies.[48] So, there is hope.

The two factors that currently prohibit insurers from charging lower premiums to lower-risk individuals are (1) the ACA prohibition on preexisting condition exclusions in individual and Exchange insurance and (2) the rules (from the Health Insurance Portability and Accountability Act [HIPAA] law) that prohibit employers from varying any explicit employee premiums for the same group insurance policy with a given worker's health risk. (There is no similar prohibition on varying the implicit premiums paid from lower monetary wages with health risk or age, but that would not affect worker insurance choice.[49])

Group insurance managers are thus challenged to avoid their products being adversely selected against by low-risk buyers eager for a lower premium. They could run afoul of rules and regulations by permitting risk segmentation to occur. This is important: Benefits managers are under no obligation to let into their firm's insurance mix a low-premium skimpy plan

48 Pauly, M. V., Kunreuther, H., & Hirth, R. (1995). Guaranteed renewability in insurance. *Journal of Risk and Uncertainty*, *10*, 143–156; Cochrane, J. H. (1995). Time-consistent health insurance. *Journal of Political Economy*, *103*(3), 445–473.

49 Pauly, M. V., & Herring, B. (1999). The effect of risk on insurance purchasing and wages. In Pauly, M. V., & Herring, B. (eds.), *Pooling health insurance risks* (pp. 54–70). American Enterprise Institute.

that could make money by picking off low-risk individuals. Unless they are biased toward raising compensation for low-risk workers, they will choose to avoid confusion and the potential havoc of Rothschild and Stiglitz by keeping the interloper out. Voters too are conflicted; they oppose exclusions for high-risk individuals but want lower premiums if they maintain their health enough to keep themselves low-risk.

Insurer profitability is not much affected by adverse selection if insurers can anticipate such selection and price their products accordingly. Of course, rules which limit overall price adjustments may lead to periods of temporary low profits if an insurer disproportionately attracts high-risk buyers.

What about employers? Should adverse selection among their group insurance plans matter to them? Most workers are covered under self-insured plans, and so the premiums are not affected by state community rating regulations. Employers cannot discriminate among individual employees based on risk, but they have full control over any employee premium share and so can in principle reward low-risk individuals if they choose low-coverage plans. The employer's profit from offering health insurance as a benefit is probably not much affected by the presence of adverse selection. Should it happen, younger or lower-risk workers might gain relative to workers with conditions, but that should not appreciably affect the total cost of insurance for the employee group, which is what determines employer total labor cost.

Health system managers may see a market in which healthier people choose less generous coverage. They will have to manage that care when those people do get sick – and likewise for care for those with chronic conditions. If a health system accepts risk for a population, it will have the same problem as insurers.

There has been some consideration among economists about what happens when there is variation in consumer responsiveness to cost-sharing.[50] You know if you are a stoic and will try to use as little care as possible while your colleague is a hypochondriac who will seize on any insurance coverage to pay for care that just might work. It turns out that, in one firm studied, the stoics chose less insurance coverage than average, flocking to a high-deductible health plan option.[51] This selection distorted the price signal

[50] Einav, L., Finkelstein, A., & Polyakova, M. (2018). Private provision of social insurance: Drug-specific price elasticities and cost sharing in Medicare Part D. *American Economic Journal: Economic Policy, 10* (3), 122–153; Einav, L., & Finkelstein, A. (2018). Moral hazard in health insurance: What we know and how we know it. *Journal of the European Economic Association, 16*(4), 957–982.

[51] Einav, L., Finkelstein, A., Ryan, S. P., Schrimpf, P., & Cullen, M. R. (2013). Selection on moral hazard in health insurance. *American Economic Review, 103*(1), 178–219.

conveyed by the lower premium for the HDHP and may have led more workers to choose it than was ideal. However, as far as we know, the total health benefits cost of the studied firm did not balloon out of control, and employees did not complain – so life went on pretty much as usual.

So, if selection does not matter that much to managers, why do economists make such a big deal about adverse selection? If it happens, it can cause some inefficiency – it can incentivize low-risk individuals to choose less generous coverage, not to control moral hazard but rather to separate themselves into a plan with a lower premium. Perhaps the fascination arises because adverse selection is a market failure which if present makes a prima facie case for a wise government to intervene and correct the possible inefficiency. Because this conclusion comes from a cool but counterintuitive model, economists will need to be hired to guide policy.

However, although there have been some examples of turmoil in early versions of Exchange plans and among workers in firms that offer multiple plans, and although there is a suggestion of selection in unregulated supplementary insurance in the UK,[52] it has not generally prevented stable settings with multiple choices. Adverse selection is thus one problem in the theory of insurance that is usually much more of an issue in theory than in practice. Its theoretical fascination coefficient may well exceed its relevance coefficient, especially in American group insurance.

Cream Skimming, Once and for All

Cream skimming is just another name for adverse selection in a setting where individual consumers can choose among a variety of health plans or health delivery systems. It is usually lamented in the Medicare Advantage program.[53] In that program, beneficiaries can choose either original (FFS) Medicare or a Medicare Advantage plan (usually a managed care plan) (see Box 6.8). The contribution to whatever plan the person chooses is supposed to be an estimate of what that person would have been expected to cost for original Medicare in the person's geographic area, but once that contribution is set (via bidding and collection of data on past risk levels) the plan can make more money if it attracts lower users of care who are not detected by the risk

[52] Olivella, P., & Vera-Hernández, M. (2013). Testing for asymmetric information in private health insurance. *The Economic Journal, 123*(567), 96–130.

[53] Meyers, D. J., Belanger, E., Joyce, N., McHugh, J., Rahman, M., & Mor, V. (2019). Analysis of drivers of disenrollment and plan switching among Medicare Advantage beneficiaries. *JAMA Internal Medicine, 179*(4), 524–532.

Box 6.8 Theory: Risk selection through managed care

In the theoretical economic models of adverse selection, the device used by competitive insurers trying to attract lower-risk buyers is to offer plans with less generous coverage in terms of cost-sharing. Under community rating, lower-risk individuals are tempted to cut back on insurance coverage and that causes adverse selection. However, in practical US insurance markets, often the plan that skims off the healthier insureds is an HMO with little cost-sharing but which offers a style of care that emphasizes benefits attractive to those who already are and try to remain healthy. Not only does marketing feature subjects who are young and healthy (and even going skiing), the benefits package puts heavy weight on preventive care, which obviously is more attractive to those not yet ill, or requires new members to change doctors, which patients with chronic conditions are reluctant to do. For example, plans may offer free preventive services that are not cost-effective, such as wellness programs or prostate-specific antigen tests, which use real resources and so add to cost, but whose costs are offset by the premium reductions associated with a healthier risk pool.[54] So while increasing cost-sharing only moves costs around, these other strategies can actually lead to inefficient use of resources.

This kind of costly adverse selection by policy design obviously is caused by community rating, and so not surprisingly is more common in Medicare Advantage plans and Exchange plans than in most employment-based settings. Group insurance managers, noting that permitting an HMO with this approach to be an option for workers will on balance waste money and disadvantage higher-risk workers, are likely to refuse entry. An important exception is the set of plans offered to federal government employees, where politics makes it prudent to allow in many plans, and where this kind of resource-using adverse selection appears to be more common.

adjustment system. With those proceeds, plus potentially some additional premiums on top of Medicare's income-based Parts B and D premiums, the plans offer different packages of benefits, cost-sharing, managed care prompts or restrictions, and selections of providers in the area. They have captured more than half of the market.

Cream skimming in Medicare requires both competition among plans (the opportunity to choose) and imperfect risk adjustment in determining the size of the Medicare plan contribution (or voucher, which is what it really is). If beneficiaries know more about their next period risk than is built into the Medicare risk adjustment mechanism, if plans are not allowed to tailor their premiums to risk (as they are not), and if there are some

[54] Lieberman, S. M., Ginsburg, P., & Valdez, S. (2023). Medicare Advantage enrolls lower-spending people, leading to large overpayments. USC Leonard D. Schaeffer Center for Health Policy & Economics: White Paper Series. June 2023; Hellinger, F. J., & Wong, H. S. (2002). Selection bias in HMOs: A review of the evidence. *Medical Care Research and Review*, *57*(4), 405–439.

services that appeal more to lower-risk individuals than higher-risk ones, plans can attract those lower-risk buyers by offering more coverage for those services and less coverage for other services – just as in adverse selection models. Conversely, if Medicare's management did a good job of risk adjustment, the incentive to attract low-risk individuals would go away – because they would come with smaller vouchers. There is an important point here: The extent of cream skimming, if it can be observed, is a good indicator of how accurate risk adjustment is. Limits within the Medicare Advantage program on how much cost-sharing can vary may limit this kind of adverse selection compared to what we have seen for some private group insurance settings – and indeed, any limits on plan variation can limit adverse selection.

How should Medicare's managers feel about cream skimming? It can lead to higher costs (mostly for nonelderly taxpayers) if Medicare Advantage plans pick off lower than average cost persons and risk adjustment fails to adjust. Of course, to attract low-risk buyers, Medicare Advantage plans will have to spend on additional benefits (e.g., dental), and so some of the loss to taxpayers is offset by gains to those beneficiaries who opt for Medicare Advantage (and then defend that option vigorously). The overall program could hit any annual budget target it wanted by adjusting the FFS payment downward, but that would harm those beneficiaries as well as those on Medicare Advantage. Overall profits for Medicare Advantage at present seem to be fairly high, so the option does lead to some transfer to owners of those plans. How much of that margin comes from cream skimming (versus greater efficiency or more effective marketing) is not definitively known.

Who is to blame here? The failure so far of Medicare to develop a cheat-proof risk adjustment system, tempting profit-seeking health plans and low-risk beneficiaries to pick up the money that has been left on the table, would be a prime candidate. If we take the defeatist (but probably realistic) view that no ideal method by which external observers can know what low-risk beneficiaries know about their health and preferences can ever be developed, we must conclude that cream skimming will always be with us, at least to some extent.

Designers of a system then face several options. They can at least try to find the indicators that plans know to select lower-risk buyers and offset them with risk penalties: If a plan can lure the Centrum Silver crowd with free gym memberships, have Medicare pay less to Medicare Advantage plans that offer free gym memberships. If researchers can know what new features attract what levels of risk, that information can be built into risk adjustment. If your firm sets up a wellness site, Medicare can find out your risk score (if you trust the government) and build that into its voucher amount for a Medicare Advantage plan you choose. There is a challenge to making markets more competitive and beneficiaries better informed: A large number of choices offered to a population with less inertia and more information about what will be best for them – the apparent goal of some Medicare policies such as the Plan Tracker – is a gold-plated invitation to adverse selection. More competition will transfer more of the benefits from Medicare's mistakes in risk adjustment to the low-risk individuals rather than the insurance firms, which is a public policy goal of somewhat dubious merit.

A little ignorance by insurance buyers, as the work of Ben Handel shows,[55] can actually go a long way toward stabilizing markets and improving efficiency – so there is something to be said for convincing seniors that there is more to life than scoring the best Medicare Advantage and Part D plan for your needs. This is a topic which, at the policy level, needs more adult discussion. At the level of health plan managers, at least understanding the economics of the situation may help them participate more effectively in that discussion.

Does Selection in Health Insurance Matter Anymore?

In contrast to the general theme of this book, I conclude that economics has not helped managers of insurance firms, benefits departments, or healthcare systems in dealing with selection when there is a choice of insurance plans (see Box 6.9 on who cares about selection); it has probably made them more anxious than they need to be. Economists have been concerned with the question of whether an unregulated insurance market would lead to a good outcome when choice is possible, or whether some government intervention is sure to make things better. That is not now or never really has been the realistic world in which managers work. If that question ever was relevant to management or policy in the US, it is now moot because there is no market for health insurance free of government intervention. Choice does not matter for the poor on Medicaid, who must take what they are offered, but for the other segments of the population, there is already substantial tampering with markets. That is obviously true for Medicare and Medicare Advantage (about

[55] Handel, B. R. (2013). Adverse selection and inertia in health insurance markets: When nudging hurts. *American Economic Review, 103*(7), 2643–2682.

Box 6.9 Theory: Who cares about selection in health insurance, one more time?

As already noted, economists have been fascinated by (and won Nobel prizes for) the question of how people choose among different products in risky situations. Whether you are trying to decide on a used car that might turn out to be a high-risk "lemon" or an insurance policy that you expect will pay you more because you are sicker than average, the information gap between buyer and seller causes really interesting problems for markets, a kind of "lemons" problem.[56] Some economists think that these kinds of issues are so important that they deserve a whole book.[57] But how important is this issue for health insurance in the US, with its mixture of private job-related coverage and public programs, most of which offer choices of different plans to those who obtain insurance? Many workers have a choice among different group plans, and seniors have a variety of private Medicare Advantage plan options as well as original Medicare. Do these opportunities for choice create adverse selection as a negative side effect?

Given the peculiar markets for both kinds of insurance, let us begin with managers (of insurance benefits or insurance companies, obviously, but even of health systems). Should they worry? I am going to take a contrarian position here and argue "not so much." As usual, things can be combined to make outcomes undesirable and inefficient, and nothing will ever be perfect – but my conclusion is that selection does not have to be a high priority for either managers or policymakers, unless they choose to make it so.

I think there is strong evidence that, in both markets and politics, Americans want choice in their health insurance – they do not want a single collectively chosen policy that must be the same for all, as (ostensibly at least) many other countries have done. Politically, they may favor "Medicare for those who want it," rather than a single uniform government plan even for those over 65; multiple private Medicare Advantage plans are sweeping the field. In group insurance, most workers have some choice of different health insurance plans, although the extent of variety varies greatly from dozens of options (for federal government workers, ironically) to a small firm that offers only one plan if you want to work for them. Economics actually does quite a good job of explaining what can happen under different assumed sets of circumstances but not so good a job of agreeing on what to do about what happens.

The Best Case for Selection: Identical Risks and Different Tastes

Let us begin with a simple case in which individuals have the same valid and accurate estimates of their health risks. For insurance purposes, this translates into accurate estimates of the claims they would make (given the risk of illness) under some particular health insurance plan (with some level of cost-sharing and managed care rules). With positive insurance administrative costs, they will in theory choose less than full coverage depending on the degree of risk aversion. (We will add moral hazard later.) If they all have the same

[56] Akerlof, G. A. (1970). The market for "lemons": Quality uncertainty and the market mechanism. *The Quarterly Journal of Economics*, *84*(3), 488–500. https://doi.org/10.2307/1879431.

[57] Einav, L., Finkelstein, A., & Fisman, R. (2023). *Risky business: Why insurance markets fail and what to do about it.* Yale University Press.

preferences about financial risk, they will all choose the same plan and there will be no selection problem.

But people do not all have the same willingness to pay to reduce financial risk. Suppose we assume some people have "high" risk aversion and others "low." Still, with an ideal outcome and a competitive market, equilibrium would be one in which the "highs" choose insurance with more generous coverage, but higher premiums based on higher expected benefits, compared to the "lows." The premium differential across plans will be determined by the difference in expected claims or benefits for a high-coverage option compared to a lower-coverage (e.g., larger deductible) option. People with different preferences will then choose what they want, insurers will collect premiums that cover the cost of benefits for different plans, and all will be well.

So far so good. Now let us flip the script and assume we have people with the same risk preferences but different known future risk levels. Those differences most likely will come from preexisting health conditions and age but might also be related to tastes for medical care given illness (some being more hypochondriacal than others). Suppose insurers can tell who is who. If there were two risk groups "high" and "low," they would charge higher premiums to the former than the latter because they would be paying more benefits to the high-risk individuals than to the low-risk; that would be the only fair thing to do. Given risk-based premiums for a menu of different plans, it is likely (though not at all certain) that the "highs" would choose more generous coverage than the "lows," so the premium for the plan they choose would be higher because of both greater generosity and higher risk. Faced with this add-on for the generous coverage, the low-risk buyers would be happy to choose less generous coverage and pay (much) lower premiums. Of course, the high-risk buyers would not be happy to be high-risk, but given that was the hand they were dealt, they would also be as pleased as they could be with the coverage they have. Again, a decent outcome courtesy of competitive markets.

If we get more realistic and assume there is variation in both preferences and risk, the story gets more complicated but still works out with a good market solution. What will blow this up, however, is if we assume that buyers of insurance know more about their future risk than sellers do. This leads to a nightmare scenario that has fascinated economists opining on efficiency and insurers trying to guess (and explain) what premiums they charge.[58]

Before we descend into that netherworld, however, let us ask how important this kind of information differential is likely to be for health insurance. It surely can happen. But in my view, the great bulk of variation in the risk of future health claims can be known by insurers if they try (probably more accurately than insurance buyers can know). The reason is that risk next year is largely dependent on chronic conditions today – and the emergence and discovery of a health condition almost always leave a trail of evidence available to insurers. You usually cannot diagnose your illness by yourself. There will be records of a diagnosis of diabetes, a positive screen for cancer, or treatment of symptoms of heart disease that an insurer can ask about (and refuse coverage if not supplied). There will be some cost to this underwriting (as it is called), but that cost is nominal.

[58] Einav, L., Finkelstein, A., Ryan, S. P., Schrimpf, P., & Cullen, M. R. (2013). Selection on moral hazard in health insurance. *American Economic Review*, *103*(1), 178–219.

Indeed, the primary reason for public concern about selection is not because insurers cannot charge high-risk people higher premiums but because they can – or can refuse coverage if they cannot charge more. The text explains why this concern is about more than politics and how it might be dealt with – but it is not necessarily adverse selection.

18% of the total US population) just discussed. Medicare from the start was a collectively chosen and managed program, so there is no sense in which some other government administration can be called in to deal with whatever issues there are – they are the result of what government has done (or has not done) so far.

For people with private group insurance (about 60% of the population), the HIPAA regulation forbidding risk rating within groups means that benefits managers may be challenged to deal with selection as best they can – or call for government to replace them if they cannot. For those nonpoor who buy individual health insurance, many rules have been put in place (and some repealed) that deal with selection.

The proposition that unregulated health insurance markets would have been ruined by adverse selection is still an obsession among health economists. Any empirical evidence on such a market is now more than a decade old, antedating Obamacare. My conclusion is that, as a matter of historical record, the individual market before substantial subsidies and regulation had problems;[59] the most serious indicator is that about a quarter of the nonpoor under-65 population without access to group coverage was uninsured. Contrary to the predictions of the economic models, the risk levels among those who did buy individual coverage and those who did not for this population were fairly similar; although underwriting based on evidence insurers could collect did limit coverage of some high-risk individuals, and although some low-risk buyers, especially in the younger population, apparently were not willing to buy individual insurance even when they could afford it,[60] things were not ideal. However, health insurance markets appeared to perform as well as other insurance markets that sell to individuals rather than groups; the coverage for term life insurance and homeowners' insurance was similar to that for health insurance; and the

[59] Pauly, M. V. (2013). *Health reform without side effects: Making markets work for individual health insurance*. Hoover Press.

[60] Bundorf, M. K., Herring, B., & Pauly, M. V. (2010). Health risk, income, and employment-based health insurance. *Forum for Health Economics & Policy*, *13*(2). https://doi.org/10.2202/1558-9544.1159.

administrative cost loading for health insurance was actually much lower than for auto or property damage insurance.

A tiny remnant of the unregulated individual market still exists, especially in short-term health insurance settings, expanded under Trump but then reined in under Biden and in blue states, but it is too small to matter to managers. Guaranteed renewability (at class average rates), where the insurer you buy from when you are a low risk promises not to jump your premium if you become a higher risk as long as you stick with the company you first selected, is present to some extent even in the short-term market, so there are examples of market-based efforts to deal with adverse selection. As an empirical matter, however, the US health insurance market seems to have found a way to muddle through issues of selection – so that managers can target their energies to much more important aspects of healthcare like rising spending for all risk levels and trying to squeeze out incentives for low-value care.

Selection in Private Health Insurance: Wrap Up

As noted earlier, the health insurance topic that has captured the greatest interest of health economists is almost surely that of adverse selection: how insurance markets function (or malfunction) when purchasers of insurance differ in their expected losses under a given insurance plan and when insurers cannot charge more to those they expect to collect more benefits. The classic economic argument is that this issue arises from information imperfection: when insurers do not have as much information to predict a buyer's expected loss as the buyer does. In US health insurance markets, it also arises importantly even if insurers can easily tell risk levels of potential buyers but are forbidden to use that information to charge different premiums or deny coverage. So, what is the complete picture on the role of selection in health insurance markets in the US?

For adverse selection to arise, at least four things must be true:

(1) Buyers must both believe and be able to forecast their insurance claims over the time horizon of an insurance policy.

(2) Insurers must not be able to charge higher premiums to higher-risk individuals.

(3) Insurance buyers must have choices of different plans.

(4) Insurance buyers must be responsive to premium differences in their choice of plan.

In the commercial insurance market in the US, as already noted, less than 10% of coverage is chosen by individual buyers from offerings of multiple insurers; most people get group insurance through their job. I believe that, for some reasons I will present, the problem of adverse selection in the group market is not very serious, despite economists' concerns – by which I mean that employers who determine what plans will be offered to their workers and what differences in premiums there are as a function of what plan the worker gets do not usually find adverse selection to be a threat to profitability, labor costs, or overall employee satisfaction with the compensation package. The selection issue is one of much ado about very little.

To go through the four things just noted, workers do choose among jobs based on the benefits offered along with many other job attributes. In the vast majority of cases, a worker will not change their job just because their health status or that of a dependent has changed – because changes in health are often temporary and unpredictable and because changing jobs is not a trivial matter.[61] There surely are cases in which workers choose a job to get coverage for a family member with a chronic condition, or in which they stay in a job with good coverage for fear if they moved to another job the coverage might not be as good. But as a spot market, getting insurance along with a job is not an example of easy switching.

Most group insurance has a cost that varies with the risk level (or expected expenses) of the group, either because coverage is self-insured or because it is experience-rated. There is some limitation on risk rating of coverage for small groups in some states. Within the set of workers in a firm, older workers will generally sacrifice more wages for coverage than younger workers.[62] It is true, however, that those workers with chronic conditions in their families are not charged higher explicit premiums (if there are any). Wages are lower for obese workers, but not for workers with dependents with health conditions.

However, in many firms there is no choice of coverage as long as the worker stays with the firm. For about half of workers, there is some plan choice, but employers can both choose the options to be offered and (most importantly) the difference in any explicit premiums across options. How these choices are affected (if at all) by expectations about how many workers

[61] Madrian, B. C. (1994). Employment-based health insurance and job mobility: Is there evidence of job-lock? *The Quarterly Journal of Economics*, *109*(1), 27–54. https://doi.org/10.2307/2118427.

[62] Pauly, M. V., & Herring, B. (1999). The effect of risk on insurance purchasing and wages. In Pauly, M. V., & Herring, B. (eds.), *Pooling health insurance risks* (pp. 54–70). American Enterprise Institute.

at different risk levels might choose more or less generous plans is not well understood, to say the least.

Conclusion

What is the bottom line on moral hazard, adverse selection, cost-sharing, and premium regulation? Gross and Notowidigdo (in a subsection titled "the bottom line") give us anodyne advice: They say that cost-sharing saves a lot of money but "on the other hand, [it does] hurt those at high risk for health problems [and creates] a barrier that leads many people to delay important care."[63]

I have already argued that careful attention is needed in designing cost-sharing to deal with moral hazard (though I am less worried about adverse selection). But I think this conventional wisdom is not economically correct. Take the second half of the statement: An economic interpretation of "important" care would be care that is cost-beneficial if rendered without delay. However, if that were the case, and patients were well informed by their doctors, they would not delay just because they had to pay a fraction of the cost as cost-sharing; they would have been willing to pay the full cost. If they are not well informed or well motivated and underestimate health benefits of more care, there might be a case for value-based cost-sharing to avoid inefficient delay – but either way, there is a solution in careful patterns of insurance design.

The first part of the bottom-line comment actually brings in adverse selection alongside moral hazard: The pure economic theory of insurance would say that high-risk people should not choose coverage with high cost-sharing that hurts them more than they save on premiums and costs. Diabetic individuals should not be in health plans with high deductibles. If high-risk individuals would have preferred more generous coverage but are stuck in a generally lower-risk employee group when a generous option would be unraveled by adverse selection, we know the cause, but it will be up to benefits managers to decide what to do about it. Cross-subsidize a high-coverage option for high-risk buyers so they are not so harmed by cost-sharing, or urge high-risk or high-demand workers to choose a different job with better coverage? Or something else?

[63] Gross, T., & Notowidigdo, M. J. (2024). *Better health economics: An introduction for everyone.* University of Chicago Press.

The conclusion is that equilibrium in US private insurance markets is the semi-toxic mix of subsidies, rules, and imperfect information – nothing is ever perfect. The optimistic follow-up is that there may be opportunities for insurance managers who are clever in plan design and pricing to offer products that are superior to the current menu, and opportunities for benefit managers to assemble them in a sustainable way. That has not happened yet – although the health plan "Oscar," marketed as a smart and modern take on coverage, has given a good shot at change, and may be starting to make profits.

The bottom line for this book is that private managers have a choice to do something about selection in employment-based group insurance, and there the amount of difference it makes to subsidize incremental premiums for more generous coverage (especially in a setting where all kinds of other cross-subsidies are flying around) is small and may not be worth much managerial attention. If you are a benefits manager or an insurer offering coverage to employers, you can experiment with titrating the premium differences across plans and see what sells (either to employers or to employees), and maybe there is a niche of low-risk but risk-averse workers you want to target. Compared to other serious issues in insurance – like getting value-based payment to work – dealing with selection is more likely to be a hobby rather than a top priority.

7 Managing Insurance and Managing with Insurance

Introduction

It is an everyday fact of life for healthcare managers delivering care to patients that there is another presence in the room – the insurer (private or public) that pays the bulk of the bill for whatever services the patient receives. In another part of town, it is an everyday fact for managers of insurance plans that they have more to do than just cut checks for the benefits their insurance customers receive; they will need to review claims for consistency with the terms of the insurance contract, make decisions on gray areas, and more broadly decide on policies for payments to suppliers of medical services. They will need to be mindful that, whatever they do in the payment and processing area, the fiscal consequences and the consumer satisfaction consequences will rebound on premiums and affect whether they can retain these consumers as customers.

At the level of the obvious, the relationship between insurers as proxy demanders and payers for medical services and the firms providing those services looks like a miasma of arm-wrestling: Providers would rather get more payment, quickly and without hassle, while insurers would rather pay less, stretch it out over weeks, and request documentation of the necessity of doling out every dime. Insured persons just want payment to be settled but with low cost to them and delays avoided. From the viewpoint of economic efficiency, these interactions should result in an outcome in which all the parties – workers and consumers buying insurance, providers of medical services, the organizations which insure those services, employers (in the case of private coverage), and taxpayers (in the case of public coverage) – receive mutual benefit. But do they? In this chapter we ask what could possibly go wrong with this process.

How It Would Work under Competition, and Why Competition Might Not Work

Since the ultimate purpose of any market, according to economists, is to make consumers as well-off as they can be, given limits on scarce resources, we need to start this complicated story with the consumer. The simplest economic story about insurance is one in which consumers seeking to avoid financial risk associated with unpredictable medical expenses choose to buy insurance because they want to cover part of the financial risk of those expenses. They do not want an insurer who cares; they want one who pays. If they are informed and buy coverage from competitive insurers, their premiums will reflect the average claims costs of many people like them, with a modest addition for insurer profit and administrative costs. They will choose the generosity of coverage based in part on the need to control those administrative costs and moral hazard (discussed in Chapter 6). They will rely on managers of the insurer to arrange reasonable payment to competitive medical care suppliers for those services which is sufficient to incentivize those suppliers to render all those services that are cost-effective and none that are not.

Sounds easy, right? But there are many potential slips for consumers and challenges for managers that arise in practice, so much so that it is close to correct to say that the source of all problems in the US health system for the middle class and above ultimately is the fault of insurance (though not necessarily of insurance managers). (The problem for poor people is that they are poor.) The general private insurance market problem comes in two flavors. One is ubiquitous in all markets – sellers may have imperfect information about what consumers want and buyers may have only imperfect information about what they are going to get. The other is that, with considerable variation across geography, neither provider markets nor insurance markets (private and public) are always competitive. I will tackle the latter issue first and then come back to the former. There is always the possibility that insurers (or providers of care) with market power will earn exorbitant profits by means other than pleasing buyers.

When Elephants Fight, You Can Get Squashed

In many (though not all) local markets in the US, sellers of care, sellers of insurance, or both, are not perfect competitors – at least by measures of number of firms, their market share, and that Herfindahl–Hirschman index discussed in Chapter 12. In some markets there is now and always has been a dominant private insurer (usually a Blue Cross plan) interacting with small-fry suppliers of hospital and physician care. (Large insurer dominance is less common in very large metropolitan areas such as New York and Los Angeles but is typical in smaller cities and rural states.) In some other markets, there is a dominant health system or two dealing with many insurers, some small and local and others larger and nationwide but with a small presence in that market. And then there is the third case in which a giant insurer faces off against a monster health system. Even for people on Medicare, the extent of local private Medicare Advantage and Medigap options span the spectrum from numerous to few.

Some of the evidence we have is voluminous and obvious: When the insurer is big relative to providers, payments to providers are low.[1] In the reverse case with a big health system and diffuse insurers, the price is high. We do not know which bad scene is worse for consumers, but we know that neither is as good as with many suppliers of both care and insurance. Economic theory says that two wrongs do not make a right but make a wrong worse. That is, if you as a consumer are at the mercy of a big health system, the arrival of a big insurer is likely to make matters worse for you (even if worse for the health system, too). Practically, the two giants may find it easy to collude to keep both profits of care providers and insurers high. Even when they deal at arm's length, the "dual monopoly" models in theory lead to even less use of beneficial care and worse outcomes for consumers than either threat alone.[2] If neither market is competitive, insurer and health system profits each will be lower than if there was only one monopoly, but consumers will be worse off if there are two. This conclusion is explained further a little later in this chapter.

Why does all this misery happen, and how common is it? Individuals generally do not buy and pay for their health insurance like they buy other insurances (home, auto, life). In fact, about 90% of private insurance in the

[1] Ho, K., & Lee, R. S. (2017). Insurer competition in health care markets. *Econometrica*, *85*(2), 379–417; Dafny, L., Ho, K., & Lee, R. S. (2019). The price effects of cross-market mergers: Theory and evidence from the hospital industry. *The RAND Journal of Economics*, *50*(2), 286–325; Shepard, M. (2022). Hospital network competition and adverse selection: Evidence from the Massachusetts health insurance exchange. *American Economic Review*, *112*(2), 578–615.

[2] Pauly, M. V. (1988). Market power, monopsony, and health insurance markets. *Journal of Health Economics*, *7*(2), 111–128.

US is obtained by consumers not as direct purchase in a market of any kind but rather as part of the compensation for their labor through their employer. Very small firms are less likely to try to pick out and manage insurance for their workers, but larger firms (not very large, say, more than 50 workers) arrange one or more insurance plans for their workers and make payment for the bulk of the premium as part of their total compensation costs. The workers explicitly and voluntarily pay about a fifth of the premium. No surprise, with your cost only 20 cents on the dollar, you are likely to buy into your employer plan – and fewer than 5% of eligible workers turn down this offer that is hard to refuse. As noted in Chapter 11, some of the reason why things have worked out this way has to do with tax policy, but some of the reason also is that the administrative costs per person insured are much lower with group insurance than with à la carte individual coverage. In the latter you only pay for what you get (as the slogan goes), but you will pay more for the privilege. (Automobile insurance, which puts much marketing emphasis on a person's ability to get the coverage they want, typically has administrative costs as a fraction of premiums that are several multiples of that in group health insurance; here again, you only pay for what you need but you only get what you paid for.)

This rather unusual link of this kind of insurance to employment has a rather unusual but ignored implication for many workers – when their "insurer" refuses to pay for a claim for a service, the entity that would benefit from the money saved is not the insurer but their employer. That is because most employment-based insurance is self-insured, with the employer ultimately making a payment equal to claims. "Large corporate insurers" may administer the coverage, but they do not gain from stinting on payments or bothering insureds; employers do. The worker may see the name and even the products of the insurance company that is administering the process, but their boss ultimately will pay. You should fight your employer, not the insurer, who is just a go-between.

The use of this DIY self-insurance option puts tough limits on the profits group health insurers can make. Employers as managers of health benefit plans presumably do not want to make their workers angry, but they do want to avoid paying low-value or questionable claims. Perhaps it is best if workers vent their fury on the insurer administrator, but some self-insured employers have chosen to put in place mechanisms to assist workers who have problems with the administrator and (presumably) ultimately override some claims denials.

The Worst of Both Worlds

Even now, many workers, especially those in smaller firms or unionized firms (or public employees), deal with a "full coverage" insurer that makes more money the less it pays out. So, John Q. Worker is threatened from both sides, from the health system and (in many states) from a grasping dominant insurer. Here is the economic story (with an unhappy ending) to explain how it will work out. Suppose initially there are many insurers but one large health system in the local market. As discussed in Chapter 12 on antirust, that can mean that the healthcare price is higher than competitive, that is, higher than marginal cost, with the excess of revenues over cost used either to gladden owners of the hospital or pay for activities that hospital management favors. The process is a little murky, but the consumer will probably end up with less care and a higher premium than if the provider market were competitive and provider prices were lower. (Either higher cost-sharing or more aggressive managed care will hold down quantity.) Now let insurers consolidate into one large entity and start bargaining with the health system over a lower price. Here is the key issue: If the system is forced to face a lower price, will it also choose to supply a lower quantity? Economics usually says yes. If so, the insurer will note that pushing price down will increase its profits even as it reduces the quantity its insureds get even farther below the profit-maximizing level. The premium may then fall a little (compared to weak insurers), but consumers will be worse off because the fall in use will harm them even more. They may get the worst of both worlds.

Now let's change the fable in a brighter direction and assume that the dominant insurer behaves as if it was owned by the consumers whose care it covers. (This is actually possible, and in theory prevails for those Blue plans which are still organized as mutual insurance owned by their policyholders; it certainly should be the case for a large, self-insured employer who competes for workers.) This "buyers' cartel" will, however, still want to push the quantity down, even at the cost of less usage. The difference is that, in this case, any price savings will go to consumers in the form of lower premiums rather than to insurance company stockholders as higher profits.

It is important to note that this tale of inefficiency is premised on the assumption that lower prices will cause the health system to supply a lower volume of care. If we start at the monopoly price as in Figure 7.1, for some initial reductions in price, that might not happen. Even if a lower price might still leave

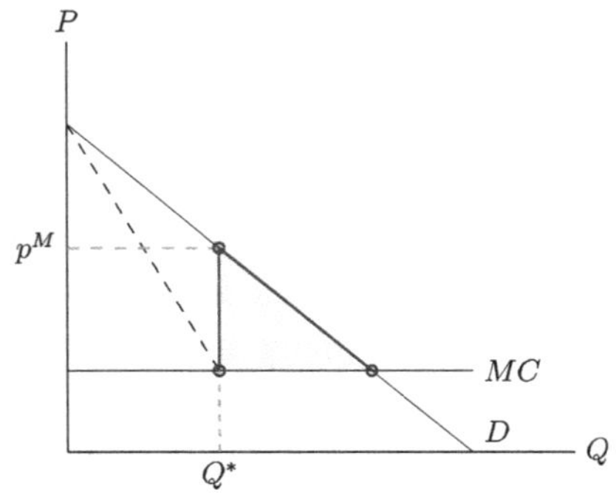

Figure 7.1 Monopoly.

units of care as profitable, just not as profitable as before, the insurers' cartel should blow through these price reductions and get to a low enough price level that some high marginal cost output does becomes less profitable for providers. So, we would still get the bad news–less care equilibrium. But how bad it will be will depend on both health system behavior and the technical issue of whether the health system has increasing marginal costs (even if falling average costs) beyond some point.

In practice, insurer-health system bargaining is not pretty. Typically, a healthcare provider that wants to hold out for more money will be threatened by an insurer with expulsion from the set of contracted providers. For insured persons, that will mean that they will have to pay more out of pocket to a nonpreferred provider, and the provider, freed from insurer restrictions, may balance bill. As with most bargaining arrangements, economists have no good theory about how it will turn out – and beyond case studies there is little aggregated empirical evidence. Often just the threat to make insureds have to pay more and jump through hoops is enough to pressure employers to pressure insurers to cave, especially if the reluctant provider is popular. We know that, on average, commercial insurance payments to providers end up high (relative to Medicare or Medicaid payments), but they are not infinite. Somehow agreement is reached, and life goes on.[3]

[3] Ho, K., & Lee, R. S. (2017). Insurer competition in health care markets. *Econometrica*, *85*(2), 379–417; Ho, K., & Lee, R. S. (2019). Equilibrium provider networks: Bargaining and exclusion in health care markets. *American Economic Review*, *109*(2), 473–522; Roberts, E. T., Chernew, M. E., & McWilliams, J. M. (2017). Market share matters: Evidence of insurer and provider bargaining over prices. *Health Affairs*, *36*(1), 141–148; Gowrisankaran, G., Nevo, A., & Town, R. (2015). Mergers when prices are negotiated: Evidence from the hospital industry. *American Economic Review*, *105*(1), 172–203.

Managing Managed Care

Health insurance in most of the US began as a vehicle for financing care and assuring income for hospitals and doctors. Those were the goals of the "Blue" plans which historically were created by providers and dominated the insurance market (and still do in many states). Because of their close organizational links to hospital and physician associations, these insurers did not originally plan to interfere with patient-provider interactions; their main function was to pay bills. The protective shield was not perfect; plans did negotiate prices and Blue Shield (doctor services in hospitals) did discriminate in what they paid in favor of lower-income insureds (when they could identify them).[4] But the only instrument to affect quantity was the extent of patient cost-sharing, usually offered as a choice between a low-option and a high-option plan.[5]

The Pacific Coast is different from the rest of the US (in many ways, but health insurance is one). There Blue plans had less dominance, and other plans that integrated physician and hospital payment and insurance supply by what were originally called "prepaid group practices," such as Kaiser in California and Group Health in Seattle, were typical. They were also fiercely resisted by local fee-for-service (FFS) physicians and hospitals. More importantly, they integrated salaried physicians with plan-owned hospitals, a separate but parallel system to the one used by patients with other insurances.

Most people in healthcare know the ups and downs of the rest of the story as it unfolded 30 years ago. Physician-led legal resistance ended, there was a managed care boom as almost all private insurers converted from old-style "indemnity" no-interference coverage to something labeled "managed care." Politicians, especially the Clinton administration, embraced the idea of "HMOs [health maintenance organizations] for All" as a way to fulfill the promise of better care at lower cost. Consumers switched into HMOs. Medical spending as a share of GDP fell for the first time in years. Then things turned sour. The Clinton HMOs for All proposal failed to get voter

4 Bodenheimer, T. (1997). The Oregon health plan: Lessons for the nation. *New England Journal of Medicine*, *337*(9), 651–655.

5 Thomasson, M. A. (2002). From sickness to health: The twentieth-century development of US health insurance. *Explorations in Economic History*, *39*(3), 233–253; Stevens, R., Rosenberg, C. E., & Burns, L. R. (eds.). (2006). *History and health policy in the United States: Putting the past back in*. Rutgers University Press.

traction and disappeared. Medical spending growth resumed its usual trajectory once the market completed its transition into (slightly) managed care.

Hollywood decided that HMO limits on care made them good villains. Moreover, in their heyday, HMOs often put the physician at substantial downside risk for referred services; if a doctor accounted for more prescriptions than average, the insurer cut their bonus. And when they had choices, the largest share of consumers opted for the softer preferred provider organization (PPO) model rather than the HMO, since the former had kinder rules, paid something even if you used out-of-network care, and generally did not penalize providers for spending in excess of some target. That high spending equilibrium in private markets has generally been maintained up to the present day. The only development of note is that private Medicare Advantage plans, 20 years later than the HMO revolution, are repeating the managed care takeover for the Medicare population, and many state Medicaid programs have contracted out their coverage to private managed care entities. The Centers for Medicare and Medicaid Services (CMS) is now moving gingerly to restore downside risk to Medicare accountable care organizations (ACOs) (also known as HMOs for progressives).

What does economics have to say about all this? After the fact, and despite the fact that some economists were (and still are) cheerleaders for California-type managed care, we were not surprised that change fizzled. Being able to offer a plan with affordable premiums and little cost-sharing (HMO marketing made "deductible" sound like a multisyllable dirty word) required some other way to control moral hazard (more about this later). Rules were the substitute, but rules impose time and bother costs on insureds and their sympathetic doctors – people got mad, professing surprise at rejected care plans and delays for approval. Consumers for the most part eventually compromised for kinder and gentler managed care, and premiums returned to growing at the same old rate, helped along by a burst of macroeconomic prosperity. And then inertia took over.

Economists figured out that the main way HMOs lowered spending was by discouraging the high rates of inpatient care that prevailed under FFS – but they could only do so up to a point.[6] The changed financing incentives under capitation were transmitted to some provider groups, but they were not pleased to have their incomes docked if they won the prize for most hospitalizations or most prescription drug spending this month. Rules have to be

[6] Dudley, R. A., Miller, R. H., Korenbrot, T. Y., & Luft, H. S. (1998). The impact of financial incentives on quality of health care. *The Milbank Quarterly*, *76*(4), 649–686; Glied, S. (2000). Managed care. In A. J. Culyer & J. P. Newhouse (eds.), *Handbook of health economics* (Vol. 1, pp. 707–753). Elsevier.

the same for everybody; no matter how hard managers tried, they could not put limits on total use of care that hit it just right for every patient. Those who were sicker than they looked necessarily got cut short.[7] Much of the initial criticism was because managed care was overhyped, but eventually private insurance muddled through to a tolerable if not ideal situation, one that has barely changed by three decades of subsequent recessions, Obamacare for the individual market, and industry self-criticism about errors, quality, and cost.

Down in the Details

It seems clear that there will be no revolutionary change that will affect private managed care anytime soon. Value-based care and insurance has had a trivial impact on cost despite a lot of backing and filling in payment arrangements and outcome metrics. There are some suggestions from economics about how to improve individual components of managed care that may help. Some economists believe that the most we can hope for is an accretion of small improvements rather than any giant steps. So, what are those small forward movements? In this chapter I will omit the gorilla of virtual care and (now) artificial intelligence in part because there is not yet enough evidence on these methods and in part because so far economists have not had much useful to say about them. I will stick my neck out and make some observations about them in the concluding chapter.

A General Model of Managed Care Insurance

I will assume that the goal of managed care is to control moral hazard in health insurance. Sometimes it may be preferable to rely on mixes of rules and limits, as well as discouraging provider incentives, to limit the use of low-value care rather than confront insureds with a return to the financial risk of out-of-pocket payment that they bought insurance to avoid.

How might this work? The economist James Baumgardner has suggested a theoretical interpretation,[8] which still is the only economic theory to explain what managed care can and cannot do. Remember the numerical example

[7] Morgan, R. O., Virnig, B. A., DeVito, C. A., & Persily, N. A. (1997). The Medicare-HMO revolving door: The healthy go in and the sick go out. *New England Journal of Medicine*, *337*(3), 169–175.

[8] Baumgardner, J. R. (1991). The interaction between forms of insurance contract and types of technical change in medical care. *The Rand Journal of Economics*, *22*(1), 36–53.

from the discussion of moral hazard in chapter 6? It showed that if care were made free (no deductibles or coinsurance), use of care would expand in both mild and moderate illnesses in ways that are not cost-beneficial. One strategy would be for the insurance plan to place a limit of 100 units (the efficient level for severe illness) on all patients with the hypothesized condition. This is how Baumgardner imagined managed care works – it sets upper limits on volume. With that rule, the plan would hit the efficiency nail on the head for those with severe illness, but it would still allow those with mild illness to increase use (up to 100 units from the ideal 50 if they wanted to). Still, compared to more expensive free and unmanaged care, consumers might like this better.

The trade-offs in managed care are more general. Given the variation in illness severity and patient preferences and given that the insurer cannot observe everything the patient and physician know (the root cause of moral hazard), rules will necessarily be blunt instruments, potentially hitting some low-value use but also harming some high-value cases in the process. Before the fact, the managed care insurance buyer has to pick the plan–rules–premium combination that comes closest to what the buyer likes best, but this is a bet that will never be perfect (even if you can look that far ahead).

However, that need not be the end of the story, as Scott Ramsey and I pointed out.[9] Suppose some coinsurance was also introduced. It could cut the overuse in the moderate illness case at the cost of some exposure to risk. But up to a point this might be yet more attractive (though more complicated and probably harder to market and manage) than managed care rules alone. We further showed that cost-sharing might lead to some relaxation of managed care limits compared to free care. It is interesting that many PPO plans now have cost-sharing along with (mild) managed care rules, just as economists suggested (but correlation is not causation).

Step Therapy and Precision Medicine

Step therapy is often required by managed care plans as a way of controlling cost and managing care. Suppose a patient has a condition that can be treated by either of two therapies. If either treatment "works," it will be equally effective, but one therapy has a lower probability of success but also a lower price than the other. Depending on the probabilities, plans may require

[9] Pauly, M. V., & Ramsey, S. D. (1999). Would you like suspenders to go with that belt? An analysis of optimal combinations of cost sharing and managed care. *Journal of Health Economics*, *18*(4), 443–458.

physicians and patients to try the less costly treatment first before allowing access to the more costly option. This process and associated delay can be frustrating to patients and doctors. The economic analysis of this case first notes that it is all a matter of money – if the second treatment were lower cost (or more universally effective) the ideal therapy would just be an empiric approach using only the second treatment (assuming there are no cases where the second treatment would fail while the first would succeed).

If the health plan cannot negotiate a lower enough price for the second therapy to dispense with the steps, it should let potential enrollees know that it uses this approach and that doing so is in part responsible for its low premium. Then buyers can choose, before they know their medical needs, the plan with the set of rules to which they will be bound. Once they opt for a plan with step therapy, they have no right to complain if it applies to them. Of course, hiding rules or making their existence obscure will cause problems, and in any case the choice of plan will now be more complex – a plan may need to characterize its overall approach to step therapy in providing information to prospective buyers. If you choose the plan with the rules, and you are unlucky enough to have the medical condition where they bind, you should not write your senator, but avoiding bad feelings may be hard. Note that if the managed care plan is chosen by your self-insuring employer, it is your employer who saves money by causing you and your doctor trouble. So far regulatory limitations on step therapy, as exemplified by the recent Massachusetts law, have not banned the practice but rather tried to make processes more transparent and more expeditious (such as limiting the time to respond to a request for exemption) – doubtless more costly, but perhaps what consumers would have wanted from health plans that ignored them.

Precision medicine has similar characteristics. Now the expensive treatment is one that may not be effective for everyone, but there is a prior test that can indicate the probability it will work. Should the test be covered, even made mandatory, while the plan announces that it has entered the era of precision medicine? After the fact, the reduced use of the expensive treatment that can be avoided by a cheap test (not to mention any side effects of treatment) is a benefit.[10] Things are trickier if the test is not perfect, so it only changes the odds – if you get a bad test result, the economic question is whether the expensive treatment will still be cost-effective, and the fully insured patient may still want to go ahead. It all depends on the numbers,

[10] Parikh, R. B., Schwartz, J. S., & Navathe, A. S. (2017). Beyond genes and molecules: A precision delivery initiative for precision medicine. *New England Journal of Medicine, 376*(17), 1609–1612.

but copayments may also help avoid low-value progression to an expensive treatment. From insurance plan manager perspective, honesty before the fact is still the best policy.[11]

Payment in Small Bundles

Given the challenge to moving toward universal two-sided capitation, both public and private plans have introduced small slices of managed care in the form of bundled payments for subsets of services for subsets of patients. Medicare has taken the lead here, with mixed results on cost: no impact (even if mandated) for chronic conditions such as heart failure,[12] but modest (less than 5%) savings for joint replacement.[13] The primary source of claims reductions was moving post-acute care from a facility (which was paid) to the patient's household (which was not paid). Overall, it has become fashionable to move care to home (as it has moved from inpatient to outpatient to freestanding), which can reduce insurance paid costs and premiums but whose overall value depends on household valuations of family member time and household inputs. The market solution – differentiate plans on whether they do or do not try to use the home as a substitute for a hospital – seems the best step here. The offsetting premium reductions for home-produced care for a loved one can easily be built into private insurance, but this is more difficult for Medicare and Medicare Advantage.

Wellness Programs

It seems like a good idea. Pay for programs that cause people to be healthier, capture the cost savings from lower use of care by the well, and use some of that money to fund the bonus. However, the "wellness" programs that embody this idea have had a rough time and at present seem to be in

11 Pauly, M. V. (2018). Cost sharing in insurance coverage for precision medicine. In E. R. Berndt, D. P. Goldman, & J. Rowe (eds.), *Economic dimensions of personalized and precision medicine* (pp. 159–184). University of Chicago Press.

12 Joynt Maddox, K. E., Orav, E. J., Zheng, J., & Epstein, A. M. (2018). Evaluation of Medicare's bundled payments initiative for medical conditions. *New England Journal of Medicine, 379*(3), 260–269. https://doi.org/10.1056/NEJMsa1801569.

13 Navathe, A. S., Emanuel, E. J., Venkataramani, A. S., Huang, Q., Gupta, A., Dinh, C. T., . . . & Liao, J. M. (2020). Spending and quality after three years of Medicare's voluntary bundled payment for joint replacement surgery. *Health Affairs, 39*(1), 58–66. https://doi.org/10.1377/hlthaff.2019.00466.

a market doghouse. The reasons are common sense. For one thing, many of the programs did not work to make people change their behavior; paying for a gym only attracted people who used gyms anyway, not those who needed to use them. For another thing, employers and insurers oversold the idea – for employee benefits departments, putting in a wellness program was something to do that would not irritate anyone and show that you were trying to achieve the triple aim; for insurers, at best, you would seem genuinely interested in health and, at worst, it might select lower-risk individuals. The problem: The enormous literature on wellness program fails to provide evidence that they work for health much less that they reduce spending – and nothing at all on the growth of spending. It has been rare to observe interventions that moved the needle – even medical preventive care or patient compliance initiatives. Moreover, wellness plans' apparent benign character was challenged by employees when they were made mandatory or tied to insurance premiums: the unfit revolted. The message: buyer beware and demand either evidence or upfront premium reductions before trying.

Cost-Effectiveness Measures and Managed Care

Cost-effectiveness analysis can do more than just comment on selected innovative treatments. It can be the criterion for describing and managing an insurance plan. The idea is simple: select and announce some dollar value for a quality-adjusted life year (QALY), and then manage all details of coverage and rules in an insurance plan to make sure that all and only care covered is cost-effective by that measure. Buyers of insurance will choose your plan if their own personal trade-offs between health outcomes and money fit the specified threshold you announce. Since there is surely variation across households in how much they value improved health relative to improvements in other kinds of consumption, they can easily decide what plan they should select – the "$100,000 Plan," the "$150,000 Plan," or the "$200,000 Plan." This measure is more relevant than the actuarial value standards in Obamacare that characterize the metal tiers on exchanges, since any plan should choose the level of cost-sharing for specific medical services that meets the QALY threshold: full coverage for treatments that are always above the threshold, and partial coverage for treatments with varying benefits. I know a platinum plan should make me healthier than a bronze plan, but I cannot yet know how much healthier or whether the extra health is worth it. Some of the variation in value of health will depend on household income or wealth, but some will also depend on preferences given income.

Within each "value tier," plans will in theory compete to do the best job of adhering to the cost-effectiveness threshold chosen and of minimizing cost to achieve that level. Premiums will be lower within a value tier for the more efficient plans, and premiums will vary across value tiers depending on the threshold.

Is this kind of measure and set of markets just an economist's fever dream? Perhaps, but there is evidence of its practicality. Several years ago, CVS/Aetna offered a group insurance option that did use cost-effectiveness ratios to determine formularies within its prescription drug benefits. This filter only applied to drugs with substitutes, and the less cost-effective drugs were still available but with cost-sharing (being placed on higher tiers), but the idea was there. Take-up by employers of this option has so far been slow, however.

Most of the rest of the world outside of the US uses some form of cost-effectiveness analysis to make decisions about insurance coverage, payment, and management. There are always exceptions when the rule says "no" but there is a strong constituency for a treatment. There have been some tweaks to the core QALYs-based model, but it still remains by far the international market leader. In the US, given concerns about death panels imposing QALY-based limits, a work-around would be a market in plans that did or did not use this planning tool – and what threshold they used when they did. It could be great.

Conclusion: Choice with Forethought

This chapter could be relatively short because managed care has turned out to do what economics could have reasonably expected of it and no more. If an insurance plan refuses to pay for out-of-network care, volumes of treatment in excess of some limit, or treatments that might or might not work, doing so will hold down costs but (compared to insurance that always pays no matter what) will irritate patients. Now that we have had 30 years of experience, I think that even the average American consumer (as well as the average American economist) sees managed care insurance as a mixed blessing, fine for people who like that sort of thing (lower premiums but more challenges for you to be demanding) compared to the old-fashioned insurance we dimly remember, with about the same overall satisfaction quotient as other insurances that try to hold down cost, like plans with high cost-sharing. Both mixtures had their moments of popularity (HMOs before high-deductible health plans) but now they are regarded as unavoidable evidence that this is not a perfect world – but we have to live in it.

Everyone knows that once you buy insurance and pay your premium, the insurer will make more money the less it pays out. Sensible buyers of insurance know that, rather than be at the mercy of a greedy insurer, they need to find out before they pay the premium what a given insurer's practices are in terms of payout. A "Good Hands" or "We Care" slogan helps but may not do the trick; you need evidence. For conventional insurance that pays cash benefits when documented covered losses occur, the information buyers need is simple: What percentage of the premium does this insurer typically pay out? Any shortfall from 100% makes a given purchase a worse deal.

The loading percentage (is also relevant to conventional insurance. But it is not the only thing that buyers need to forecast; they also need to know whether any managed care features are present, and whether an insurer will deliver paid benefits with little hassle.[14] Too many hoops to jump through is not a good thing. Here economists invoke the usual slogan of trade-offs. We believe that insurers are not intrinsically nasty, grasping, or slick; it all depends on what you are paying in premiums and whether you are paying attention. A high premium for a given set of stated benefits is necessary (even if not sufficient) for an insurer to be nice – and a low insurance premium means you are more likely to have to struggle when you try to use it.

This choice is pretty much the story on managed care insurance. Consumers did not like the original Rambo-esque HMOs even though they had low premiums, and so the market has largely moved to more expensive but more permissive PPOs. The punchline for policy is that consumers need to be wary but need to choose the mix of payment and permission they find most attractive – and insurers will do best if they can find the sweet spot that most people most prefer. There will still be hard feelings in this business – either you wasted your premium money because you were not lucky enough to get sick or you did claim benefits but with strings attached. That is the nature of any contract where you pay upfront and wait for promised goods to be delivered. Adults are aware of this reality and deal with it as best they can. The search for a new and improved version of managed care goes on. The

[14] Chernew, M. E., & Frick, K. D. (1999). The impact of managed care on the existence of equilibrium in health insurance markets. *Journal of Health Economics*, *18*(5), 573–592.

Medicare Innovation Center tries to get ACOs to make a difference.[15] The Purchaser Business Group on Health rolls out new models emphasizing primary care for California.[16] Consumers wait and see.

For the future, the most important consideration is not whether these plans maintain health or discourage low-value care but what impact if any they have on the rate of access to and diffusion of new health-benefiting technology. On this score, we do have the post-1990s circumstantial evidence that HMO (and even Kaiser) premiums grew at the same rate as other kinds of insurance, having produced a one-time (but not inconsiderable) 15% saving. As noted in Chapter 13, there is as yet no intervention in healthcare that gives a positive answer to the question of what you have done for me lately. Small steps and constant vigilance may be called for.

15 NORC at the University of Chicago. (2024). *Evaluation of the next generation accountable care organization (NGACO) model: Final report.* www.cms.gov/priorities/innovation/data-and-reports/2024/nextgenaco-sixthevalrpt; L&M Policy Research. (2016). *Evaluation of CMMI accountable care organization initiatives: Pioneer ACO final report.* www.cms.gov/priorities/innovation/files/reports/pioneeraco-finalevalrpt.pdf.

16 Purchaser Business Group on Health California Quality Collaborative. (2023). *Measuring advanced primary care in California pilot results and the path forward.* www.calquality.org/wp-content/uploads/2023/12/APC_California_IssueBrief_PilotResults_Dec2023.pdf.

8 Cost-Effectiveness and Insurance Coverage

Messages for True Believers

Introduction

The economically ideal healthcare system should supply all treatments whose benefits are greater than their cost. It should supply no other treatments, even if they are beneficial. This ideal is, like most goals, not perfectly achievable, but there are methods to develop rough-and-ready approximations of measures of benefits and costs (some of them rougher or less ready than others). In many countries, attempts to compare the money value of health benefits and costs are central to decisions on insurance coverage and pricing. In the US, despite some concerns, the ivory tower theory has the potential to be practical (when handled with care) if we can determine the costs and benefits from a given treatment offered to a given individual. So far, no economically correct alternative to giving this decision measure a try has emerged. There is a cottage industry that measures benefits and costs which operates under the general label of "cost-effectiveness analysis." In this chapter, I provide a short summary of the techniques currently used in that analysis and a longer discussion which addresses for US insurers and insureds the question: "Treatment X furnished to population Y has an average cost per unit of outcome of $180,000. Now what?"

The question of how to use cost-effectiveness information is, I will assume, most immediately relevant to managers of private insurance plans trying to decide how to cover (or whether to cover) some "effective" new treatment, that is, one for which the health benefits are likely to outweigh the health risks in real-world use. The decisions they make then filter down to managers of health systems considering the supply of that treatment. The economic touchstone for insurance managers contemplating a change in coverage that is associated with a change in premiums is whether coverage (to whatever degree) of the novel treatment will please their plan members or subscribers. Put in a little more jargony terms – whether the additional willingness to pay for an insurance plan that adds that specific coverage of that specific treatment with that specific amount of health benefit is larger than any additional premium needed to cover any increase in claims associated with it. That is, are the health benefits (even if positive) large enough to have value greater than their additional premium cost?

Generally, the additional premium that can be charged for coverage of a new technology should in theory be strongly related to its cost-effectiveness as defined by the average improvement in health (valued somehow) per dollar spent. Consumers should be willing to pay a little higher premium for a treatment of low cost and high value – because there is in theory no fixed budget for private insurance in the US. There is no regulatory limit on their claims or premiums, and any budget that insurance management may set is self-imposed and therefore changeable if circumstances require. However, risk-averse consumers may also value any reduction in health risk associated with a new technology (perfect prevention avoids the risk of getting sick), as well as considerations of financial risk associated with the new treatment. So, cost-effectiveness estimates do not furnish a perfect guide to coverage, but they can help flag which effective but costly treatments should not be covered.

A Primer on Cost-Effectiveness Analysis and Its Problems

There is a movement, in the US and abroad, devoted to producing and discussing this type of measurement of health interventions. It is often termed "Pharmacoeconomics" or "Outcomes Research," because it most often piggybacks on clinical trials of new drugs, using the trial outcomes to project health and economic impacts. But it is also applied to all other kinds of interventions. As indicated earlier, in economics (and I believe in ideal life), we would like all decisions about going ahead with some costly new activity to come with measures of benefits and costs, so that we would only get the things where benefits exceed costs, and none of them where they do not. In that sense, cost-effectiveness analysis embodies economics' ideal concept of efficiency – so it can be very important. It is much less clear whether this kind of analysis is necessary in all situations – after all, as noted earlier in this book, a competitive market operates as a kind of collective cost-benefit calculator and produces efficient results on its own. So, formal analysis of the type to be described can best help you check whether competition in markets for innovations is working or forecast what should happen or if adjustments are needed. This kind of analysis can help even more if there is some impediment to competition. So, the value of this information, like all information, depends on the context and on what else is operating in terms of buyer and seller information about prices and product characteristics as well as incentives for making cost-conscious choices.

The core measures for trying to assemble this kind of information in healthcare are the two parts of the value ratio to be discussed in Chapter 9: the dollar value of health benefits on top and the resource costs on the bottom, with the decision rule that if the ratio is greater than one, go for it. This approach is used directly or indirectly in almost all other developed countries for some kind of collective choice or regulation of medical investment, access to services, and prices. For the US, such data is still assembled,[1] but its use occurs behind a screen hidden from explicit public scrutiny – for reasons to be discussed.

A kind of liturgical ritual has developed associated with cost-effectiveness analysis, a set of assumptions or assertions about how things are usually measured, not necessarily based on rigorous normative economic theory but because it is common, or easier, to do them this way. That necessarily means for economic purists a certain disdain and for economic practitioners a certain humility – we all admit this is not ideal, but it is the best game in town until something better comes along, and there are no promising alternative candidates waiting in the wings.

Cost-effectiveness analysis is always, always comparative: A treatment is never absolutely cost-effective but should be labeled "cost-effective relative to some alternative," whether that is no treatment, usual care, or some specific alternative. The denominator is a measure of health added (relative to the comparator), usually in terms of "quality-adjusted life years" (QALYs). The numerator is incremental cost of the treatment relative to the comparator, usually measured by incremental spending associated with the treatment (including spending changes or cost-offsets elsewhere in the system). To decide whether or not to go ahead with a treatment in a world where there is no fixed medical budget (since a good treatment can always be financed in a market system), you need to attach a monetary value to a QALY so the parts of the ratio are in the same units. This is a tricky process since the value would clearly differ among individuals. The threshold dollar value per health increment is sometimes based on subjective judgment from somewhere outside the data and sometimes based on a tenuously assumed link to GDP

[1] Cost-Effectiveness Analysis (CEA) Registry. Center for the Evaluation of Value and Risk in Health, Tufts Medical Center. https://cevr.tuftsmedicalcenter.org/databases/cea-registry.

per capita; it is not strictly based on evidence provided either by economists or by physicians but is an asserted value judgment rationalized in a variety of ways.

In practice, if the ratio exceeds one, benefits are greater than costs and the green light goes on for a treatment; there is usually not much fuss. Note that the advice on coverage in such a case does not depend on the size of the net benefit as long as it is greater than the cost – as long as you can be certain about the numbers. Therefore, a ratio of 1.1 is as much of a green light for full coverage as one of 10.0, however more reassuring the latter would be. When a treatment is found to be cost-effective, almost everyone will be happy with the analysis. Only insurers who have to raise premiums to cover the treatment price may fret.

Objections from noneconomists to the use of cost-effectiveness analysis therefore mostly arise when a treatment adds QALYs but at a high cost per QALY, and so is judged not to be cost-effective at the current cost. Those who would be denied the treatment then look for loopholes in the methods (see Box 8.1 about a loophole in Medicare). The hard message that there is an effective treatment but it is not effective enough (relative to other uses of resources) is difficult to hear. If you are the family of the patient with the condition that would have been improved, even at a high cost, you think

Box 8.1 Evidence: Why Medicare cannot use cost-effectiveness analysis

Private insurance plans can walk away from an FDA-approved drug if its price is too high. However, both Medicare and Medicaid are required by law to cover at least some drugs for every class of treatments. If there is only one drug in some class, it must be covered. So, there is even less discipline on high prices. This limit on the most effective bargaining tactic is presumably part of the reason why the Inflation Reduction Act gave Medicare some power to negotiate prices of some older branded drugs directly. Presumably that negotiation includes permission for Medicare to walk away from an effective drug if the price is too high, although the provisions of the law make that unlikely. Medicare does now try to limit use of new expensive drugs by putting in place managed care type rules limiting the sites at which those drugs can be obtained or requiring a plan in which use of a new drug only occurs if evidence is gathered on its clinical effects in the process. Still, managers of drug insurance plans for Medicare Part D and Medicare Advantage plans are limited in the extent to which they can do anything if a new drug firm's current price is above the "fair price" – other than complain. Medicare has started trying to negotiate the price of some drugs, slipping in considerations of effectiveness, but so far not of costs.

there must be something wrong with the benefit measure. And there are some soft spots in the theory and practice of benefit measurement, so there is a case to be made. Patients have an incentive to want everything in the benefit package so long as there is some chance of a positive health benefit and doing so is not thought to raise premiums. Indeed, any single treatment or any single technology usually adds little to premiums, so there is a temptation to think everything should be covered for free. However, the sum total of all such small things arguably adds up to a large total – so premiums would have to increase. Insurance blocks logic: The person who would have refused to pay a higher premium before the fact will demand that a treatment be covered after the fact.

What could be wrong with using cost-effectiveness to constrain acting on these feelings? One issue has to do with measuring quality of life. The core of most cost-effectiveness analyses actually comes down to life years added per dollar of cost, and usually life years (alive and not dead) can easily be defined even if hard to measure. But some illnesses are never fatal yet still harm people: they itch, they feel pain, they look disfigured, they cannot hear well or play tennis. And consumers will pay for treatments that help.

There are several methods to convert these adverse health outcomes into life-year or "healthy" life-year equivalents. The most intuitive one, to my mind, is the time trade-off: You tell someone there is a treatment for an illness that causes a reduction in quality of life (blindness, for example) that will restore sight perfectly but runs the risk of fatal side effects. Would you be indifferent to living 30 years with blindness (without the treatment) versus 15 years with perfect sight because the treatment has a 50% mortality rate? If yes, we will measure one year of life with blindness as equivalent to six months with sight.

These are hard questions to get reliably answered; people do not like to think about such things and different people would make different trade-offs. Moreover, if insurance refuses to cover a treatment which does not much affect survival but does seriously affect some dimensions of quality of life, measurement is worth arguing about. And there are going to be second thoughts. Most obviously, the previous result if interpreted literally would imply that additional life years for blind people or anyone with a disability would be valued as less than an additional year for someone in perfect health. Revulsion at this kind of calculation has led to the use of QALYs being banned in some federal decision-making in the US.[2] The estimation of

[2] Cohen, J. (2024). *Forbes*, February 9. www.forbes.com/sites/joshuacohen/2024/02/09/house-of-representatives-passes-bill-to-ban-use-of-qalys-in-federally-funded-healthcare-programs/.

trade-off between survival and quality of life as well is not robust: Different methods, different people, different ways of asking, and timing before or after disability occurs all have major impacts on the numbers that come out. On the other hand, it's not clear how much this imprecision would actually affect access to care in the US: Our system generally tries to treat hypertension or heart disease regardless of whether a patient is wheelchair-bound or ambulatory. We perform hip replacements in people over age 90. This is probably because, as I will discuss later, most treatment choices are highly cost-effective at current prices, so any small bump in QALYs from some theoretical measurement issue would not matter in practice; it would only be relevant for close calls.

What if we just used life years? We still get problems. Is the life of an older person worth more or less than that of a newborn? Do all people even with the same incomes have the same value of life years? In other countries, they either get agreement on or assume agreement on the answers to these questions and punch ahead; in the US we are holding back (or resist deciding this centrally at the population level).

Economists as charismatic accountants have problems with the denominator; the cost numbers do not always speak for themselves. Even if you have accurate measures of spending, those only translate into resource costs if the prices built into them are equal to cost. Where there is market power – as there surely is for patented drugs but also for many other medical services, the change in spending overstates the change in cost.[3] You should worry about where the profits go and possible benefits from their subsequent use (such as investment in the discovery of new drugs or help for the disadvantaged).

There is another kind of bias in cost-effectiveness analysis that David Meltzer has noted in a much-discussed article.[4] A treatment that extends years of life means that more of what would otherwise have been a bequest to the next generation will be consumed instead – so adding life years costs society more than adding quality of life for people who would have survived and consumed anyway. Avoiding death costs more than avoiding disability.

With all of these objections, what should be done? The response of those who work on pharmacoeconomics is given above: Ask your critics – do you

[3] Garrison, L. P., Jr., Jiao, B., & Dabbous, O. (2021). Gene therapy may not be as expensive as people think: Challenges in assessing the value of single and short-term therapies. *Journal of Managed Care & Specialty Pharmacy*, *27*(5), 674–681.

[4] Meltzer, D. (1997). Accounting for future costs in medical cost-effectiveness analysis. *Journal of Health Economics*, *16*(1), 33–64.

have a better way to judge the value of new programs? Until you do, give our results some respect, but feel free to fudge the decision if it is a close call. Cop out and argue for the need for an informed conversation – also known as a stakeholder-engaged deliberative process – but a realistic one willing to face up to trade-offs.

For the manager of an insurance plan or a health system disengaged from the mechanics of cost-effectiveness analysis, the best practical advice is to pray that your decision will not involve some activity with a ratio of less than one. That failing, read the rest of this chapter and then take your chances with full disclosure. There is, however, a "market test": cover a batch of new treatments that are effective but maybe not cost-effective, raise the premium enough to cover them, and see if this insurance will sell. Or suppose that we are the low-priced health plan or health system that has decided not to cover or furnish some effective but too high-cost treatment; would you want us to raise our premiums so you can get access to it here? It is either that or blame the government.

The Mechanics of Measuring Health Benefits in Money: Pondering the Imponderable

Although the idea of someone's willingness to pay for health improvements seems simple, as you might imagine, measuring it in a defensible way is challenging and complicated. All of us make decisions every day that alter ever so slightly our health risk – drive or fly, Twinkie or kale – and yet we humans resist thinking about our future health state (how well we feel, what we are able to do) even when we do not consider mortality. Adding in the certainty of death at some uncertain date makes thinking deeply about those choices even more upsetting. However, while it is dirty work, someone has to do it, and so economists (and as we will see, noneconomists) have tried to develop ways to come up with rational measures for rational discussions about trade-offs between money (as a proxy for other goods we like) and health. The ultimate goal of these discussions, I will argue, is to improve the decisions managers make, especially (but not only) about new treatments.

That is the point about Michael Porter's value measure for healthcare – the ratio of benefits to cost – and the even better economic concept of net monetary benefits – the money value of improved health minus the money value of the costs incurred to produce it. The ratio version – the so-called cost-effectiveness ratio – is the usual way the evidence needed to decide on this trade-off is formulated, and managers need to understand this basic concept – and its costs and benefits. Here I will try to explain the idea and the challenges to it that a manager needs to know.

Research on the cost-effectiveness ratio usually entails a lot of precise objective measures of clinical outcomes and less precise but still defensible metrics of resource use that are then combined with subjective judgments about the money value of health. A measure that combines objective measures with subjective measures is still subjective. So, if this measure is going to be helpful for decisions, whose subjective judgments should matter? I will argue that *measures of the value of health outcomes of a treatment should depend on the preferences of those who are paying the cost of the treatment.* So for private insurance, you should consult the preferences of consumer buyers (directly or as filtered through their employer proxies), for Medicaid it would be the preferences of taxpayers who are footing the bill, and for Medicare it would be some messy combination of elderly beneficiaries, their grandchildren who will cover much of their cost, and their children who are contemplating both what taxes they are paying now and what provisions they want to be in effect when they go on Medicare. Concerns of ethicists, patient and consumer advocacy groups, and policymakers ideally should not matter (except as ultimate payers pay attention to them). Of course, the board of directors for Medicare are the members of Congress – a thought that reassures some and terrifies others – but even those members should be advised to vote on the preferences of beneficiaries and their children, not their own.

What Does Effectiveness Look Like (to Whom)?

One starting point for the use of cost-effectiveness analysis for any treatment is – in statistician's jargon – the degree of homogeneity of treatment effects: Does the treatment affect everyone with the condition it treats in the same way? Sometimes this happens: A treatment for people with similar skin rashes may cure all of them; then, they all get the same upward bump in their health (or their future healthy days). But often this is not the expected pattern. One possibility is random heterogeneity: We know some people will not benefit, others will benefit a little, and still others by a lot – but no one can tell beforehand who is who. We can determine the *average* benefit for a population even though no person gets exactly that average benefit. The other, more complex case is when there will be different effects but some of the agents (advisors) involved can tell who will benefit more than others. For instance, in many cases, a treatment will provide more benefit to people with more severe cases of the condition it treats, and the treating physician can know severity for a given patient. Of course, if the insurer does not know severity, it cannot know variation in cost-effectiveness.

It is therefore easiest to announce decision rules for insurance managers in the homogeneous uniform benefit case. If a treatment yields more benefit than cost to a subpopulation (in, say, the clinical trial) of people with such a condition, it also yields more benefit than cost to any (premium-paying) member of the health plan. If so, all should get the treatment if medically warranted. So, the insurer that covers the full cost of the treatment at a higher premium reflective of the cost should win the market. If the occurrence of the illness is uncertain, there will still be demand for insurance to reduce risk – but, after that, the treatment should be covered either for all or for none, depending on whether the expected net monetary benefit (health benefit in money terms minus additional cost) is positive or negative.

What about random heterogeneity? Some of the treated will get better; others will not, but no one can predict who. The simple solution then is to use the average health benefit – not because it will be right after the fact but because it is the best bet before the fact. If the treatment reduces the variation in outcome relative to no treatment, that could be another benefit that should be factored in.[5] But, generally speaking, full coverage of cost-effective treatments and no coverage at all for any others that are not cost-effective is still close to the best rule. (Risk aversion may justify treatments that reduce risk even if they just miss the cutoff.)[6]

In the case of known heterogeneity and full insurer knowledge, the coverage rule is an adaptation of the earlier one – full coverage for the subset of patients sick enough to have high marginal benefit, and no coverage for those with mild illness. There still may be pushback from those patients, but they are also consumers who should prefer the hard-hearted but less expensive insurance that makes the right economic decision. Hollywood may not agree about the beneficence of insurers, but the market will.

Cost-sharing comes into play when the final chooser – the patient – knows or can know more about the expected benefit from treatment than the insurer. This is the case of moral hazard discussed in Chapter 6, and the appropriate coverage decisions are the same as there: cover but with cost-sharing with the

[5] Phelps, C. E., & Lakdawalla, D. N. (2024). *Valuing health: The generalized and risk-adjusted cost-effectiveness (GRACE) model*. Oxford University Press.

[6] Lakdawalla, D. N., & Phelps, C. E. (2020). Health technology assessment with risk aversion in health. *Journal of Health Economics, 72*, 102346. https://doi.org/10.1016/j.jhealeco.2020.102346.

size of the sharing dependent on the extent to which some patients have positive benefits that are less than the cost. One important implication for cost-effectiveness analysis of using cost-sharing is that it can convert a treatment that is not cost-effective if rendered to all patients into one which is cost-effective for those patients willing to pay the cost-sharing and thus signal their above-average benefits.[7]

In theory, these rules are all that an insurance manager needs to know about designing coverage based on rigorous cost-effectiveness analysis. Plan managers can expect some subscriber pushback if a treatment is not covered, even though it improves health, but is not cost-effective. How dare an insurer place a dollar value on my loved one's health? The risky response to this rhetorical question invokes the need for good stewardship of the contributions of all health plan members. But it is still uncomfortable.[8] An alternative strategy is to estimate the lower incremental price at which the treatment would be cost-effective and then blame the sellers for not charging that price or achieving that low a level of incremental cost. This is roughly the approach adopted by the Institute for Clinical and Economic Review (ICER) discussed later in the chapter.

Cost-Effectiveness and Supply-Side Management

Suppose you are the manager of an organization which supplies a novel treatment. If the treatment is cost-effective on average and benefits are or are expected to be uniform in the plan population, you will have a happy day (more about the measure of benefits and quality in Box 8.2). Insurance should cover your price in full. Your only challenge is to make sure that you produce the treatment at minimum cost and price it just above cost to yield the profit margin needed to retain your equity capital.

What we can call the "asymmetrically known heterogeneity case" presents more of a dilemma. Let me explain. If you, as the physician provider of the treatment, know when its effectiveness is more likely to be high than low, whom should you tell? Your patient has a right to know as much as you do (and perhaps then some), but should you keep this information about low marginal benefit away from your patient's insurer? If coverage started out as

7 Pauly, M. V., Comanor, W. S., Frech, H. E., III, & Martinez, J. (2021). Cost-effectiveness analysis of branded drugs with market demand and insurance. *Value in Health*, *24*(10), 1476–1483.

8 Ubel, P. A., & Jagsi, R. (2014). Promoting population health through financial stewardship. *New England Journal of Medicine*, *370*(14), 1280–1281.

Box 8.2 Theory: Cost-effectiveness analysis and the highest possible quality – economists cause trouble again

Some characteristics of care labeled "quality" have a revered status in health policy and management; almost everyone is for "quality care" (as opposed to no-quality care) and the level of quality should be high, sometimes said to be as high as possible. Defining and measuring quality has nevertheless proved to be a challenge because it is multidimensional; it is affected by any patient's prior risk level (and behavior), and it depends on patient preferences. Economists too have a notion of quality: It is any characteristic of a good or service that affects consumer welfare other than quantity – the volume of that good or service. The sizzle on the steak, the durability of the dishwasher, the performance at the symphony – all can vary and usually are varied by those who supply the product.

The simplest economic story about how a profit-seeking firm will choose quality assumes that all actions that improve quality and lower cost will already have been taken, so quality is set at the level at which the marginal consumer willingness to pay for improvements in all dimensions of quality is equal to the (positive) marginal cost of doing so. This simple model gets much more complex when different consumers have different preferences for quality; we then enter the netherworld of differentiated products, and it is tricky to set things up so the distribution of quality offerings by firms matches the preferences of consumers, especially because it is more costly to offer all products custom-designed and à la carte. So, some consumers may settle for something cheaper but pretty close to their ideal. Sometimes totally gluten-free can be hard to come by.

It would seem straightforward to adapt this economic model to healthcare. We economists would begin by measuring (or asking somebody to measure) the marginal contribution to health of changes in quality – the durability of an implant, the skill of a board-certified cardiologist, or the deaths avoided by a defibrillator. Then the efficient and competitive level of any one of these dimensions would be determined by comparing that benefit measured in money terms (e.g., QALYs added times the threshold dollar value of a QALY) with the marginal real resource cost of higher quality. It does seem in healthcare, however, that sometimes actions regarded as higher quality turn out to be lower cost (cesarean section versus higher-quality normal births at the population level). These cases should only happen in an efficient profit-seeking firm out of managerial or provider ignorance or misunderstanding of quality.

When higher quality does cost more, what then? Clinicians as a profession have a hard time saying that some actions sure to improve health outcomes should not be done if their cost is too high. For example, a collective statement by cardiologists in *Circulation* started with a platitude, "Value Based Payment should continue to move away from FFS [fee-for-service] toward more flexible spending that allows clinicians to focus resources on the interventions that help patients." Then fear creeps in: "The most crucial challenge of cost consideration is the potential adverse impact on quality of care . . . through decreased use of clinically effective services." Trade-offs are scary: "When [quality and cost considerations] are at odds, clinical benefits should be considered primary." Only a logical error can get the authors out of trouble: "If program benefits are distributed only to high quality performers and quality is adequately measured, higher quality care will be appropriately prioritized . . . VBP [value-based payment] models must be explicit that quality is the dominant concept."[9]

Managers can see what is missing from this exit – the *dollar amount* of those program benefits for higher quality has to be enough to cover the cost – and somebody has to decide when quality costs more than the benefit it provides. The job of being that decider is the job nobody wants, but somebody has to do it, one way or another. Cost-effectiveness analysis builds it in as an assumption about the threshold value of health and hopes nobody gets too upset.

The economic approach to managing quality, based on cost-effectiveness analysis, is different from the quality improvement (QI) approach in much of industry and healthcare management and advice. That approach, whether labeled "Six Sigma" or "Continuous Quality Improvement" or any other of many slogans, often focuses on the hospital or clinic workforce – it imagines that if they worked harder, or differently, quality would improve.[10] There would be fewer mistakes, fewer useless or harmful actions without evidence-based support, and more change to methods with evidence of effectiveness, all to be undertaken by more thoughtful physicians and nurses who work in the healthcare system. Much of the evidence here deals not with an organization's decision to increase quality but rather with the success of implementing program already in place – and the results on effectiveness have not been reassuring.

The Institute of Medicine (IOM) (now National Academy of Medicine) definition of quality in healthcare – "the *degree to which* health services increase individual and population health" – starts in the right direction.[11] In economics, the "degree" of improvement would be represented by added QALYs and monetized in some fashion. What is most prominently missing from this noneconomic approach is equal consideration of the cost of changing quality. Even an internal program to whip up worker enthusiasm for doing better will have a cost, and, more generally, real resources will have to be added. This cost of resources aspect is often treated as less important (an "indirect" influence) on implementation because costs are often not known to stakeholders.[12] However, in economics, there is supposed to be a crucial and unavoidable comparison: Is the degree to which a change improves health outcomes (as perceived by patients, presumably) large enough to justify those costs? Finally, in business, there is the bottom-line question: To what extent will higher quality chosen by a provider foster larger market shares or higher prices, or have cost-offsets – again all compared to the cost of any change?

[9] Sandhu, A. T., Heidenreich, P. A., Borden, W., Farmer, S. A., Ho, P. M., Hammond, G., . . . American Heart Association Advocacy Coordinating Committee. (2023). Value-based payment for clinicians treating cardiovascular disease: A policy statement from the American Heart Association. *Circulation, 148*(6): 543–563. https://doi.org/10.1161/CIR.0000000000001143.

[10] Burns, L. R., Bradley, E., & Weiner, B. (eds.). (2019). *Shortell & Kaluzny's Health care management: Organization design and behavior* (7th ed.). Delmar Cengage Learning.

[11] Committee on Quality of Health Care in America. (2001). *Crossing the quality chasm: A new health system for the 21st century*. National Academies Press.

[12] Damschroder, L. J., Aron, D. C., Keith, R. E., Kirsh, S. R., Alexander, J. A., & Lowery, J. C. (2009). Fostering implementation of health services research findings into practice: A consolidated framework for advancing implementation science. *Implementation Science*, *4*, 1–15.

full coverage, keeping any indicators of variation in benefit secret would allow all your patients, even ones with low benefit relative to cost, to collect from the insurer and receive the treatment. But if you and your fellow providers present a united front of sealed lips, premiums will rise and cost-sharing will kick in. That may be the best that is possible, but isn't there some other better deal all around?

There is no painless solution to this question. The best that economics (or social intelligence) can offer is to make clear beforehand what a health plan expects of the providers its insureds will use: If you join a Kaiser health plan – or other plans that require "prior authorization" for selected services – you know that your doctor will follow rules designed to reduce low-value use by you, should you be in a situation where such care is the only option.

Managing Noncompetitive Prices and Managing with Noncompetitive Prices

So far, we have usually been assuming that any novel treatment is supplied at a competitive market price, one that just covers marginal cost. If only because of novelty, and for other reasons, prices (at least at first) for new treatments can in reality exceed the competitive level. The most common situation in which this happens is with novel patented drugs or devices, where the government forbids competitors from copying the new idea for the term of patent protection. There is never going to be a free or competitive market in such products as long as they are on patent. It also happens in local markets where the first entrant to offer a new type of procedure or program has market power while competitors try to keep up, or in local markets where the health system already has market power for current services and is able to extend that control to new treatments.

How should insurers manage access when confronted with a seller of a novel treatment that is able to set its price above marginal cost? In an ivory tower setting where a single insurer tries to maximize society's welfare, the "cost" in cost-effectiveness analysis should not be the price but rather the marginal resource cost to society. Using this measure (e.g., a near-zero cost for an expensive drug) can result in the endorsement of very high use rates and high profits for sellers and low welfare for consumers, so it is usually not undertaken: Analysts use price rather than true societal marginal cost. If the cost is used to recommend quantity but users pay the high price, consumers will be worse off even if the outcome is efficient. One scenario using the price instead imagines that multiple insurers just passively take the price set by the firms with market power as given. Then another considers active bargaining over price and quantity between an insurer and a seller with market power.

We consider the passive case first. This may apply where there is a dominant seller and many competitive insurers (as in some large cities) or where the treatment makes up too small a fraction of claims to make the bargaining effort worthwhile.

Assume that demand is based on the patient-known heterogeneity case (the one that leads to moral hazard). Before insurance covers the treatment, there is a consumer demand curve for it based on the distribution of expected benefits among patients. In the usual Economics 101 model, the seller would set the profit-maximizing price where marginal revenue (based on the number of new users attracted by lower prices) equals marginal cost. However, as in the moral hazard story, if consumers are risk-averse and the illness that prompts the need for the treatment is uncertain, they may prefer to insure it. Suppose they demand (before they know illness incidence or severity) insurance with the most efficient level of coinsurance that balances financial protection with stimulus to low-value use from moral hazard. This is not the end of the story. If insurance is present (so coinsurance is less than 100%), that will make consumers less price-sensitive once they get sick because they are no longer paying the full price. So, then the seller can raise the price. At this new higher price, depending on the circumstances, consumers might want lower coinsurance so as to have more financial protection. If they added more generous coverage that would kick off another round of price increases. And so on and so forth.[13]

If the price of the service and the premium for insurance to cover it rises high enough, this cycle will eventually stop. At a minimum, this discussion makes the point that insurance coverage when added to seller market power can trigger an "inflationary" spiral in prices. If that increase is large enough, buyers of insurance may find themselves paying so much for coverage of the treatment that they decide they are better off forgetting the whole thing – no insurance, no treatment, back to the starting point – even if the treatment would have improved health a lot.

To avoid this nightmare scenario, if possible, it might be better for insurers to become more active and negotiate with sellers of treatments for a better

[13] Pauly, M., Comanor, W., & Frech, H. E. (2023). Drug pricing in the United States: Theory and evidence. *Health Management, Policy and Innovation (HMPI.org)*, *8*(1), special issue.

deal. How might they do so? One answer (though I will argue a very incomplete one) is provided by the Institute for Clinical and Economic Review (ICER) which studies and publicizes the likely effectiveness and cost-effectiveness of new drugs and devices – arguably, a kind of privately supplied regulation. The other is for even a small insurer to offer the seller an arrangement in which, in return for a lower prespecified unit price, the insurer agrees to make the treatment available to more of its insureds than it would have done had it accepted the initial monopoly price. For drugs with very low marginal costs, this volume discount deal can take the form of a predetermined payment to the seller for coverage of a given population in return for the seller agreeing to make the drug available to all insureds who need it or want it; this is sometimes called the subscription or Netflix model of pricing. We now will look at each of these from the insurance manager (and insurance buyer) perspective – later we will see what role the sellers of medical services might play.

The ICER Model

The ICER has come to play an outsize role in the US in assembling information on new drugs and other medical innovations for use by insurers, consumers, and external commentators. Its work is usually used to comment on prices of innovations, although it can be used to guide coverage or use of innovations given some (or any) price. Should (or when should) managers pay attention to what ICER has to say?

The fundamental ICER model relies on what is usually very careful clinical analysis of the likely effect of an innovation on QALYs added (along with footnotes about the degree of precision of measures of health benefit). This estimate of QALYs added per treatment is then multiplied by an assumed dollar value of a QALY (or a range of values). From the product of this multiplication, any cost added or offset for needed tests or other medical services is then added or subtracted. The final step then solves for the unit price of the intervention that will make the sum of monetized net health benefits equal to the intervention's price per treatment; this price is called the "fair price."

If this verbalization of arithmetic has not lost you, you will see that the ICER ultimate fair price measure generates a measure of willingness to pay for the treatment that equates incremental benefits to incremental cost – the most a buyer could pay and still be better off (even if ever so slightly) from using the innovation compared to not. There are also some subjective secondary considerations for payers bound by fixed healthcare budgets (not total budget) to see if paying for an intervention priced to yield positive net benefits fits that budget. Since neither private insurers nor Medicare have such budgets, I will ignore this aspect of their evaluation. Moreover, if the alternative care is only partially covered by insurance, it is the plan payment rather than the full amount of cost saving that is a correct measure of the value of the cost offset.[14]

What use can one make of an ICER statement about the fair price for an innovation? The main product is usually a publication of the analysis, indicating the fair price and whether the current or proposed price is above the fair price. Journalists sometimes use this comparison to conclude that, if the seller is going to charge more than the fair price, that shows that the seller is being unfair. The ICER itself is less aggressive; it argues that the fair price (according to it) can somehow serve as a "benchmark for bargaining," largely bargaining between insurers and drug firms, but also between hospitals and drug and implant makers, or between the Veterans Affairs (VA) and everyone.

How this bargaining is supposed to work is left to your imagination. The concept of a "fair" price is not one based on economics, which limits itself to dealing with efficiency not justice. So, is the ICER target price an efficient price? Economists would argue that if the price actually charged is higher than the "fair" price, and if the value of QALYs used to calculate that price truly reflects the buyer's value, the buyer can credibly say it will not buy the intervention at a price higher than the fair price. The seller charging more then has to decide whether to forego this sale – or perhaps all sales – or cut the price. Maybe buyer and seller can agree on splitting the difference between the original price and the ICER fair price if the latter is still above the marginal cost (the key criterion for economic efficiency) – or maybe not. There is no business value in charging a high price if no one will pay it. Hence, economics would not judge whether a fair price was efficient or not but would make the commonsense statement that, if ICER is right, it would be inefficient for a buyer to demand the product at a price higher than the buyer's value.

However, if the buyer would be willing to pay more than the fair price and still buy the product, there is no reason for the seller to charge less. What is

[14] Glazer, J., & McGuire, T. G. (2012). A welfare measure of "offset effects" in health insurance. *Journal of Public Economics*, *96*(5–6), 520–523.

key here is the relationship between the fair price and the maximum price the buyer is willing to pay – it is only the latter that matters in economics.

To an economist, this repackaging of cost-benefit analysis (on which we economists have at least a historical copyright) is unexceptionable in concept, although the subjective judgments buried in ICER's fair price (about the money value of improved health) might be made more apparent before buyers try to use it. ICER is, however, conflicted in advising users of its information on what to do. The easiest case is when the treatment is both effective and with a price equal to or below the "fair price." Then buyers (whether consumers or especially insurers) should seek to use the treatment as long as the number of people doing so would not yield too large an increment in the budget; insurers should cover it with whatever their usual cost-sharing is.

But what if the price the seller charges or proposes to charge is above the "fair" price? The first step for insurers, patients, and policymakers is often to try to shame the seller into lowering its price using the ICER report as a weapon to do so. If that does not work, and the seller sticks with a higher price for an effective treatment, conflict emerges. In a masterpiece of double negatives, one ICER comment is, "it would not always be inappropriate for payers to place an unreasonably priced drug on a high tier, albeit within levels of cost sharing that will not serve as a major barrier to access."[15] Economists would have a hard time specifying when it would be appropriate to have insurance-assisted access to an unreasonably priced drug – or even cover it at all. An insurer may also impose some restrictions on direct use (such as requirements for prior authorization or step therapy) to divert patients (by wearing out their and their physician's patience) to alternative treatments of somewhat similar effectiveness. But what if the treatment is such a breakthrough that there are no comparable treatments? This happened with a drug for cystic fibrosis, and there ICER took great pains to emphasize that it was not calling for it to be excluded from coverage; the alternative was to talk with the seller who (ICER assumed) wanted to make its drug affordable.[16]

Economists, not surprisingly, would be less sentimental. If ICER's assumption about the monetary value of a QALY was correct for a population of

[15] Institute for Clinical and Economic Review (ICER). (2020). *Cornerstones of "fair" drug coverage: Appropriate cost-sharing and utilization management policies for pharmaceuticals.* https://icer.org/wp-content/uploads/2020/11/Cornerstones-of-Fair-Drug-Coverage-_-September-28-2020.pdf.

[16] Institute for Clinical and Economic Review (ICER). (2020). *Modulator treatments for cystic fibrosis: Response to public comments on draft evidence report.* https://icer.org/wp-content/uploads/2020/08/ICER_CF_Response-to-Comments_042720.pdf.

insureds, covering the drug would do more harm (with a high premium that reduced buyers' consumption of other goods) than good (by improving health). Even if it is a good product, if the price is too high, do not buy.

The logical problem with the ICER approach is most apparent if the seller sets a price much higher than the fair price and yet sells a high volume of the product. If there turns out to be a good market for a product whose ratio is $180,000 per QALY and that is higher than ICER's assumed threshold, something must be wrong: Buyers and insurers should not be willing to pay such a high price. If they are, that must mean either that buyers have values for incremental QALYs higher than ICER assumed or that they overestimate the benefits from the treatment. Perhaps diffusion of ICER's report will cut sales to zero, but it is also possible that at least some buyers may have dollar values for incremental QALYs higher than ICER's assumed threshold – and a distribution of such values (high for some buyers, lower for others) would be enough to yield a demand curve and a profit-maximizing price above the fair price. It all depends. The challenge to the health system or insurance manager is to determine whether the values their customers attach to the product coincide with what ICER has assumed. There is no magic to draw on here; eliciting true buyer willingness to pay (or, harder yet, the distribution of willingnesses to pay) is the worst task in cost-effectiveness analysis. One must be brave and consider the approach in the next paragraph.

Should insurance managers refuse to cover drugs whose price according to ICER is unfair? They might well get backlash from their insureds with the condition the innovation treats, who might also write to their senator. But if they raise the premium to cover the innovation, an insurance competitor who holds down the premium but does not cover a drug priced higher than the fair price may well get the buyers' insurance business. The invisible hand can be an iron fist when it comes to offering the wrong mix of price and quality in any product, including healthcare and insurance. An explanation should be prepared. It might seem that a safety valve would be offering to cover the price up to the "fair" level and then having the patient pay the rest. There is no harm in offering this but, if ICER was right about value, no informed buyer would take the path of paying – so why bother?

How about protesting or picketing the seller as "unfair"? Again, no harm in trying, but the seller can counter with the argument that even if ICER's price is fair to the buyer, it does not guarantee that the seller will make money, or as much money as it wants to. For reasons we will discuss, this is not a very persuasive argument for branded prescription drugs which typically carry high markups over marginal cost (and even over attributed research and development costs, too), but it may be valid for programs offered by suppliers of medical services that typically have relatively low fixed costs and high marginal costs. Chapter 14 on drugs will explain this further. But if buyers, after knowing ICER's position, are still willing to buy, either ICER must be wrong or buyers must be disbelievers.

Cost-Effectiveness Analysis and the Medical Services Manager

As already noted, many published cost-effectiveness analyses have looked at novel drugs. Clearly, a manager of a health system that uses such drugs needs to worry about their cost-effectiveness. If insurers follow the unalloyed ICER model, they will not pay the manager to dispense drugs that are not cost-effective. But the concept of cost-effectiveness or value is not limited to drugs. A new care delivery program will also have health benefits and additional costs. If some insurers who cover your patients use cost-effectiveness analysis, you will have to deal with these concepts, too. The best defense as usual is a good offense. If you can, assemble and offer evidence that your new program is worth what you are going to charge for it.

ICER and Cost-Sharing: Can We Change the Subject?

I have already discussed the ideal role of cost-sharing in insurance in the context of heterogeneous benefits and moral hazard. What does ICER have to say about cost-sharing? It rarely confronts the issue directly, in part because the detailed clinical data that is its source of competitive advantage is almost always taken from trials with zero cost-sharing. When it does talk about cost-sharing, its advice is that it should (also) be fair but without guidance to determining what would be unfair cost-sharing for insurance for middle-class consumers. ICER does not consider that cost-sharing might winnow out low value uses of a drug and thus improve average cost-effectiveness, a sensible if optimistic position in view of the imprecision of evidence from the RAND experiment onward. (See Chapter 6 for a discussion of the impact of cost-sharing on use.) But ICER also does not try to look for evidence for the drug it is analyzing about what cost-sharing would do to either total use (and cost) or cost-effectiveness. Thus, it has nothing to say about changes in marginal benefit or the cost-effectiveness ratio if there were positive cost-sharing. An insurer that proposes positive cost-sharing for a new high-priced drug may contemplate a bittersweet win-win – either the seller cuts the price or, if not, the buyers will self-select to be ones with higher-than-average marginal benefit.

As noted, ICER does sometimes mention that insurers might want to put drugs with prices higher than fair on a higher tier of cost-sharing but offers no discussion of how this might affect the use of the drug. Should it be expected to go to zero (the economically efficient level)? Or should it still be positive just smaller than without cost-sharing? There is not much help for insurance design here.

What Could Possibly Go Wrong? The Seller's Viewpoint

If the theory behind the ICER model is correct, the price that it asserts to be the maximum fair price should be regarded as a convincing measure of the value of any innovation. Of course, with competition among suppliers, the actual price would be bid down below the maximum, and that should happen without the need for this kind of analysis. It might even be bid down to equal marginal cost – and then would qualify as the economically efficient price. (There is little credit ICER offers to a firm that prices below the fair price.) As already suggested, the main situation in which ICER (and cost-effectiveness) analysis comes into play is if the price the seller sets is not only above marginal cost (because the seller has market power) but also above the value of the benefits from the innovation. However, one might then reasonably ask – why would a seller charge such a high price? Remember that a firm with monopoly power can set any price it wants, but (especially with the insurer reactions mentioned previously) it cannot sell any quantity it wants. So, what are we to make of a case in which the price charged is above the fair price?

There could be seller mistakes. Sellers of innovative products often fall in love with their own inventions and think them to be much better than they really are; they price according to their inflated estimate of value. This sometimes happens: The most notable case was the drug Aduhelm to treat Alzheimer's disease. This drug was barely an advance over previous treatments, but it was priced at $56,000 per year.[17] Medicare officials thought the

[17] Kaiser Family Foundation. (2021). FDA's approval of Biogen's new Alzheimer's drug has huge cost implications for Medicare and beneficiaries. www.kff.org/medicare/issue-brief/fdas-approval-of-biogens-new-alzheimers-drug-has-huge-cost-implications-for-medicare-and-beneficiaries/.

price would stick: They estimated that a large number of beneficiaries would use it and, since Medicare could not negotiate prices directly, that they would have to raise premiums by 14% to cover the extra cost. However, doctors did not use it, and private insurers paid for it only in limited circumstances, so the price fell. (The increase in beneficiary premiums stayed.)

Or ICER might be wrong about its dollar valuation of benefits or even about the clinical value of an intervention, while the innovation's seller knew better. Then demanders should ask for their money back from ICER, not from the drug seller. However, what if everyone has the same accurate information? How would the ICER fair price, correctly estimated, compare with the profit-maximizing drug firm price, correctly estimated?

If the deviation of a drug's marginal benefit from the average based on the distribution of illness severities or other influences was linear, the profit-maximizing price would be identical to the ICER price. A linear demand curve means that, starting from some maximum price that the sickest people might pay, the increase in use associated with a dollar reduction in price is constant all the way to a price of zero – at which 100% of the people who got any benefit from it at all would be buying. ICER still would be wrong, however, if it assumed that all who could benefit would use the drug at that price – only about half would unless insurers could strike a deal with the seller. Compared to this benchmark, to get a profit-maximizing price higher than the ICER price, there would (as noted earlier) need to be a fraction of potential buyers who got much more than average benefit who would pile in and pay a high price but who then would not be followed by many more buyers as the price was reduced below that level.

How Scary Is It Out There?

Managed care limits on the supply side, payment strategies to providers to induce them to make more efficient choices, and patient cost-sharing are all ways to control moral hazard and improve cost-effectiveness. Here we note that they are not mutually exclusive. The trifecta of targeting low-value care for low provider payment, managed care oversight, and high patient cost-sharing may together achieve the MBA holy grail of "aligned incentives."[18] Each effort has some adverse effects: exasperated physicians, complaints

[18] Powers, B. W., Navathe, A. S., Chaguturu, S. K., Ferris, T. G., & Torchiana, D. F. (2017). Aligning incentives for value: The internal performance framework at Partners HealthCare. *Healthcare*, 5(3), 141–149.

about rules, and consumer financial risk – so the choice of the mix is tricky and circumstance-dependent. But for whomever can hit the sweet spot, gains are in prospect as well as a more peaceful life.

When a treatment is cost-effective given some modest consensus value for improvement in health, happiness reigns. Sellers of drugs or care are pleased, patients feel that everything is being done, and doctors are left alone. When the numbers do not work out this way, all are anxious and looking over their shoulders; no one wants to be blamed for saying no. So how common is this case? The answer should please optimists: It is much less common for a treatment that has been studied for cost-effectiveness to be found to fall below the bar than to be placed above. In one analysis, more than 80% of the hundreds of treatments studied (treatment with drugs, screening tests, and novel methods of care) were found to be cost-effective at a cutoff of $100,000 per QALY.[19] If you are a physician, you should only face a challenge with one in five different treatments, on average.

Other studies have come to a similar conclusion.[20] However, one problem is that the set of treatments that have been studied does not necessarily correspond to the set of treatments that insurers pay for; the set of cost-effectiveness studies is not a random sample of all treatments or even of all expensive treatments. The majority of studies are sponsored by drug companies – and they are more likely (though far from guaranteed) to find that the drug studied at its current price is cost-effective. Pharmaceuticals in general are much more likely to be evaluated than other kinds of treatment innovations. However, if we look at the top sellers among branded prescription drugs, many of them have been subject to cost-effectiveness studies, performed by ICER or others in the US or European health technology assessment agencies, if not financed by drug companies.[21]

Here is another piece of evidence that cost-effectiveness need not be the day-to-day bane of existence for physicians or insurers: A review article of cost-effectiveness studies examined how much incremental cost was associated with an additional QALY across studies. The central result was

[19] Glick, H. A., McElligott, S., Pauly, M. V., Willke, R. J., Bergquist, H., Doshi, J., . . . & Schwartz, J. S. (2015). Comparative effectiveness and cost-effectiveness analyses frequently agree on value. *Health Affairs*, *34*(5), 805–811.

[20] Chambers, J. D., Lord, J., Cohen, J. T., Neumann, P. J., & Buxton, M. J. (2013). Illustrating potential efficiency gains from using cost-effectiveness evidence to reallocate Medicare expenditures. *Value in Health*, *16*(4), 629–638; Campbell, J. D., Belozeroff, V., Whittington, M. D., Rubin, R. J., Raggi, P., & Briggs, A. H. (2018). Prices for common cardiovascular drugs in the US are not consistently aligned with value. *Health Affairs*, *37*(8), 1298–1305.

[21] Cost-effectiveness, the QALY and the evLYG. Institute for Clinical and Economic Review (ICER). https://icer.org/our-approach/methods-process/cost-effectiveness-the-qaly-and-the-evlyg/.

encouraging; in the "average" study the incremental cost of an improvement in health was less than $40,000 per QALY – and so prices did roughly track effectiveness. But the "rough" part matters; even in the cases studied, there are a few treatments whose price is very high relative to their effectiveness. The question is why. Some of these low-value treatments are, for that reason, rarely bought – but some others do sell. Moreover, when committees of citizens have been queried about what treatments should be rejected as low value, they have saved some of them, especially low-value treatments for children or those with rare diseases (see Box 8.3 about an alternative cost-effectiveness measure that might explain the demand for these treatments). It appears that there is no Supreme Court of Cost-Effectiveness that can make everyone happy.

Box 8.3 Theory: Dodging some tough decisions – the GRACE model

The use of cost-effectiveness analysis to reduce use of or limit coverage for effective care puts managers in the difficult position of having to say no to people who do not want to take no for an answer. The rough-and-ready character of conventional cost-effectiveness methods, when judged by the standard of welfare economic theory, suggests that there might be some wiggle room in such cases if only inventive economists take a closer look. This has happened with a novel and economically correct approach developed by Darius Lakdawalla and Charles Phelps that takes into account a feature neglected in the usual cost-effectiveness rubric: consumer or patient risk aversion in the health dimension.[22]

The intuition here is simple and persuasive: Risk-averse people would value an intervention that totally prevents or cures a risky but serious disease at more than just the expected number of QALYs added times a fixed threshold dollar value per QALY – because they would be freed of the risk of an uncertain but potentially large shock to their health. Most people are thought to be risk-averse in this way. But if they are, that challenges a key assumption in usual cost-effectiveness analysis – that the dollar value of health units reduced by illness is a constant. If people are thought to be risk-averse, in economics that requires that the marginal value they attach to reductions in harm be increasing – the last QALY I give up is worth more to me than the first – in the spirit of Chapter 7 on insurance. They suffer disproportionately more for each decrement in health from various diseases – so the marginal value of health added is greater the more a disease reduces QALYs, including (especially) the quality of life. The "generalized risk aversion" part of the generalized risk-adjusted cost-effectiveness (GRACE) model captures this idea.

[22] Lakdawalla, D. N., & Phelps, C.E. (2020). Health technology assessment with risk aversion in health. *Journal of Health Economics 72*, 102346; Phelps, C. E., & Lakdawalla, D. N. (2024). *Valuing health: The generalized and risk-adjusted cost-effectiveness (GRACE) model.* Oxford University Press.

What does this mean to managers? Concretely, if there were two treatments of equal cost per QALY added, but one could be expected to cure one person of Alzheimer's while another prevented more milder skin rashes, with the same number of QALYs added at the same additional cost, the former would be preferred. This insight explains and answers all sorts of questions: It explains why treatments for the severely disabled should be worth more, it rationalizes why citizen committees endorsed less cost-effective treatments in childhood than more cost-effective treatments of mild but prevalent conditions in adults; it feels right.

If people are risk-averse in health, this method will lead to better guesses about the values they attach to different treatments than standard cost-effectiveness models. It predicts they will usually be willing to pay more for treatment of more severe conditions (there are exceptions if the treatment adds uncertain effects) and, as noted, pay more for treatment of conditions with more severe quality of life consequences. Markets for insurance plans covering costly treatments of the really sick should do better than those that emphasize patching minor health injuries – as long as adverse selection does not intrude.

For managers, this new theory primarily waves a red flag at close-call decisions on refusing use of or coverage for expensive but highly effective treatments or cures for life-ending or life-altering illnesses – hold off on bringing the hammer down just to save money if the conventional cost-effectiveness measures are just below the threshold and look again at what consumers would be willing to pay. Full resolution will require more information than we have on the money values people attach to QALYs and how they vary across people and over treatments. As noted earlier, this measure is now an informal subjective and soft judgment call in applied cost-effectiveness models. It will also require markets with informed consumers to sort things out.

Ethics and Economics of Cost-Effectiveness Analysis

I was a member of a group of economists who recently studied the foundations and use of cost-effectiveness analysis in healthcare.[23] We recommended that cost per QALY be used in the US as the core method for valuing innovation (and then doing whatever comes from that) but augmented by some additional elements related to reducing uncertainty. This core or traditional method is used in some way in almost all other developed countries: They have advisory or commissioned groups of experts who use cost-effectiveness studies to determine what to cover in their national health systems (which they all have) and how much to pay.

Not so in the US, where there is much less deference to "science" here as elsewhere in public policy. That rejection is active, not passive; an unlikely

[23] Garrison, L. P., Jr., Neumann, P. J., Willke, R. J., Basu, A., Danzon, P. M., Doshi, J. A., . . . & Weinstein, M. C. (2018). A health economics approach to US value assessment frameworks: Summary and recommendations of the ISPOR special task force report [7]. *Value in Health, 21*(2), 161–165.

coalition of patient activists, ethicists, and Republicans have had legislation enacted by the Congress that forbids QALYs to be used in any federal government decision and casts doubt even on measures of comparative clinical effectiveness. Disabled people (with lower quality attached to their life years) and old people (with fewer life years to go) have resisted the use of QALYs as a way of setting priorities on how much to spend on saving a life. The advisory body of economists that backed the measure did so on the grounds that, at present, this method of cost-effectiveness analysis is the only game in town that would permit comparison across diseases with various measures of health outcomes and which was reasonably transparent and inclusive. The doors were left open for an improvement but without much short-term optimism that anything better would come through them.

Here I do not intend to get into a discussion of what are fair measures of outcome or accurate measures of incremental cost. Instead, I would return to the argument made earlier in the chapter – that different competitive insurers could offer products whose coverage was based on different thresholds for the monetary value of health and different metrics for the amount of health, charge the premiums that cover claims made according to different measures, and see which plans buyers prefer. This kind of market test for measurement and the ethics of valuation allows us (including managers) to dodge often unanswerable questions of subjective judgment and still function.

The Right to Healthcare: An Economic Perspective

Economics cannot deal with ethical issues such as rights. Freedom of speech, freedom of religion, and other constraints on what your government can do to your actions are not part of economists' purview. Likewise, though it is not constitutionally guaranteed in the US (though it is in some other countries), economists cannot pronounce on whether there is or is not a right to healthcare for citizens.

They can, however, ask some pertinent questions and propose an interpretation of such a right in a democratic society. The most pertinent question is that of how much and what kinds of healthcare are rightful to whom. This is ultimately an ethical question that ethicists have addressed by offering notions like "full flourishing" or "dignified life." If pushed, an economist could enter into the contest the idea of cost-effectiveness – every person should have a right (with some allowance for complexity of implementation) to the cost-effective amount of each kind of healthcare. This approach obviously brings in the opportunity cost of healthcare in terms of displacing other items of consumption, something often absent for ethical definitions.

This definition does not in itself solve a major problem: What is the monetary value to be attached to improvements in health? I have discussed issues in establishing this threshold earlier in this chapter. In terms of core welfare economic theory, there is a fork in the road. The value of an additional unit of health (think QALYs, with apologies) is supposed to represent someone's willingness to sacrifice other consumption, or willingness to pay (WTP) for that increment in health, which is then compared to its incremental cost. For any person with any level of income or other characteristics, WTP is certainly as large as that person's own informed willingness to sacrifice other consumption. As a rough generalization, this means that higher-income citizens' monetary health values should be their own personal values. Bluntly, the rightful amount of healthcare for the well-off is no more or less than whatever they are willing to buy. The story is quite different for lower-income people. If others in the community would place positive value of additional health produced by effective medical care for one of their less well-off fellow citizens, that (aggregate) WTP should be added to the low-income person's own value (or WTP) to define the rightful amount of healthcare. Medicaid and some aspects of Medicare in the US that subsidize additional use of effective care are consistent with the hypothesis that such concerns exist. Here then the punchline is that the rightful amount of effective healthcare is the level that the person and others in the community are willing to support. This amount will be more than the low-income person would access on their own, but it will be determined by (and limited by) others' altruistic values. Because community support is filtered through a political mechanism in which unanimity is unlikely, that means that there will be differences of opinion, not only among lower-income people and their advocates but even among taxpayers, about what is the rightful amount. The existence of Medicaid and some aspects of Medicare is evidence that there is community concern – but they show variation in the value of health. Particularly if a treatment is effective but costly, like new genetic treatments for sickle cell disease, deciding on the rightful amount is likely to be contentious. Moreover, this economic definition takes as given the initial distribution of income, personal access to care (insurance generosity), and degree of voluntary altruism by those better off, which ethicists and others may question as a proper place to start.

However, this definition is potentially operational and can benefit from data on the effectiveness and costs of treatment. These metrics are necessary but not sufficient for coming to a conclusion because the value of health measure also comes into play. That, economists would say, is what people should be arguing about.

Conclusion

Cost-effectiveness analysis in theory is the holy grail of evaluation of health-care innovation for economists. Cost-effectiveness analysis in practice, however, never reaches this height of unimpeachability. It is sometimes roundly trashed as useless if not harmful. Managers of delivery systems or insurers should not participate in this mob action. The intent of cost-effectiveness analysis is to compare benefits with costs, and that is impeccable economics. Even with its imperfections, current cost-effectiveness analysis practices (yes, including ICER) are the best available and are generally "fit-for-purpose," as they say in the UK. There are some tweaks and patches but usually they will not matter much for a go/no-go decision. Moreover, at least asking what the evidence is that some costly intervention is cost-effective is great discipline on out-of-control healthcare spending.

But both care and caution are needed. The biggest problem was stated in the introduction to this chapter: If an intervention is effective but not cost-effective, then what? In this chapter, I have offered some advice on what policies should follow from different findings. We are still looking for graceful language to excuse cases in which such analysis blocks an effective treatment. Adopting a threshold in advance as a rule of thumb in a system or plan and telling buyers about your rationing rule appeals to economists but probably not (because of use of the "R" word) to others. Maybe "value-based," a term now without content in health management and policy, can be retreaded with the use of a cost-effectiveness model.

9 Value-Based Everything in Healthcare

What Is beyond Slogans?

Introduction

A remedy for the general dissatisfaction with so many things in US healthcare provision and insurance is often embodied in the idea that payment and coverage should change from current arrangements and become "value-based." This change sounds like a good idea to those concerned about current levels of cost and quality of American healthcare and, as we will discuss, it is one that has been embraced by hospitals, physicians, specialty societies, insurers, and politicians. Exactly what it means and what changes it implies are far from clear.

There is a simple logic that says, in healthcare as in anything else, you should specify what you want from a seller and pay for that. Presumably one of the things we want from healthcare is "health," so if we could say clearly what that means and tell when it is furnished, that could be the sole basis for payment. You would pay for the health services you receive if they make you better off and pay nothing if not. (Such arrangements have been proposed for treatments of genetic disease.[1]) Even if (more realistically) you paid beforehand based on expected increments to health, the amount of payment from successful treatment would be linked to the amount of improvement in health and how much you value it.

Such an arrangement seems nearly impossible. Most fundamentally, in this market as in many others, it is practically impossible to say objectively what it is that will yield how much utility – how to specify the satisfaction from a great meal or the enjoyment from a good movie and pay only for that – and refuse to pay if the seller does not deliver. (I still want my money back for those tickets for *Ishtar*.) Instead, we specify some physical

[1] Volpp, K. G., Pauly, M. V., Loewenstein, G., & Bangsberg, D. (2009). P4P4P: An agenda for research on pay-for-performance for patients. *Health Affairs*, *28*(1), 206–214.

commodity or service that embodies what we like, we buy it, and we take our chances. We can, as we will see, try to get some specifics about measurable and non-manipulable health outcome metrics to describe what we want, but there will always be some slippage between what we want and what we can get.[2]

The value-based idea in medical care is usually proposed as an alternative to the historical model of fee-for-service (FFS) payment for à la carte medical services. Instead of FFS-established volume metrics such as hospital discharges or medical procedure codes, the change slogan is "pay for value, not volume." The premise is that FFS always pays more for a larger quantity of specified services, thus offering distorted and inequitable volume-increasing incentives to suppliers of care – because their gross revenues will increase the more services they sell. If you are already convinced that there is an oversupply or mistaken supply of conventionally described services in the US, you are then supposed to find some other basis for insurance coverage and payment that attenuates the bad incentives and substitutes some better ones. Here, however, the discussion stops. While we supposedly know what is wrong – there is so much inefficiency from current reimbursement – the specification in theory and the development of evidence in practice on what is a better method of payment has not been agreed upon.

However, from an economic perspective, this critique is not quite right. While fee-for-service (FFS) can provide the wrong incentives, it does not have to. As described later in this chapter, it can be revised to push things in the right direction, closer to the ideal. There is almost always room for improvement in any system. As I have already noted, conventional health insurance clearly creates distorted incentives for patients about volume in the form of moral hazard. Insurance reimbursement systems for suppliers at a minimum do not offer counterincentives to correct those effects, much less turn supply toward practices that will yield better health outcomes and higher consumer and patient satisfaction with the care they do (or do not) get.

My view begins with the proposition that the meaning of "value" is a tricky issue that, despite its appearance in so many slogans, has not been well explained by the lights of economics to managers of health systems or insurers. Charging off and attaching that label to so many things,

[2] Nicholson, S., Pauly, M. V., Wu, A. Y. J., Murray, J. F., Teutsch, S. M., & Berger, M. L. (2008). Getting real performance out of pay-for-performance. *The Milbank Quarterly*, *86*(3), 435–457.

some good ideas and some not, is premature. Let's start with the first principles of economics – principles which for the most part have already been presented in this book – and go from there.

What Is Value?

Probably few academic discussions have done more harm to healthcare management than Michael Porter's exhortation that decisions should be based on value as he defines it through the "value chain."[3] Coming from outside the healthcare system but with a solid Harvard pedigree and the self-confidence that comes with it, he has been eager to identify problems in healthcare management – and who is not in favor of "value"? The problem is that a useful operational definition of value has proven elusive, and effective programs to achieve it have so far been unattainable. Economics can explain why and what kind of forward progress can be expected.

While there is some license for diversity of opinion here, the usual technical definition of value is in terms of a ratio: the ratio of outcomes achieved per dollar spent.[4] Sometimes the language is a little more poetic: "measured improvement in health outcomes for the cost of achieving that improvement."[5] Is this a correct or useful guide?

This definition leaves some important things to be filled in. Most obviously, what is the metric or measure of health improvement? We have already discussed quality-adjusted life years (QALYs) (with all the criticisms) as one possible measure, but there could be others; we will come back to how the benefits from some healthcare innovation might be defined and measured later in the chapter. To get started, however, we begin by noting that from an economic (or rational investment) perspective, using a ratio can sometimes lead to errors. Ratios are fine if we are comparing alternative programs with the same cost – then the one with the most units of good outcome per dollar is the one to prefer. For example, if either program A or

[3] Porter, M. E. (2008). *Competitive advantage: Creating and sustaining superior performance*. Simon & Schuster.

[4] Porter, M. E. (2010). What is value in health care? *New England Journal of Medicine*, *363*(26), 2477–2481.

[5] Teisberg, E., Wallace, S., & O'Hara, S. (2020). Defining and implementing value-based health care: A strategic framework. *Academic Medicine*, *95*(5), 682–685.

program B cost 10 (thousand dollars, say), program A yielded 20 units of benefit, and program B yielded 18, program A would be preferred. But what if there were two mutually exclusive options – program A and program C that cost 100 but yielded 180 units of benefit? Then C would be the better choice since it would have a net benefit of 80 whereas A would only have a net benefit of 10. Of course, if you could find nine more examples of program A and instead implement them, that would be better than doing program C for a budget of 100.

Equally important, much of the discussion of value dangles before managers an incomplete and usually infeasible aspiration. Managers are told they must "deliver value: higher quality for the same cost, the same quality at lower cost, or higher quality at a lower cost."[6] Not only is this a heavy lift but it also leaves out some other things that might be desirable. Delivering much higher quality at a modest increase in cost could be a good thing, and identifying ways to do so is the burden of most of cost-effectiveness analyses. Economists may also quietly mention that it could be a good thing to deliver a little bit lower quality at a much lower cost.

Cost-effectiveness analysis, discussed in Chapter 8, shows how to get a general rule for delivering value: first convert outcomes to the same unit of measurement as cost (say, dollars) by using a threshold dollar value per unit of output and then choose the set of programs that maximize the excess of benefit over cost. This will usually mean undertaking all programs with positive net benefit. This rule shows how to implement "outcomes for the cost of achieving them."

There are some other clarifications. If the best way to improve health outcomes is to provide more units of some service, then it is perfectly fine for a payment system to reward the volume of those services, up to a point. It is also likely that patients and consumers of health services will care about other things in addition to health outcomes, such as the satisfaction or comfort associated with the services chosen, any reduction in risk, and the dignity of interpersonal relationships with providers of care. There is more to healthcare than health (just as there is more to health than healthcare). The question of value for *whom* is also of importance (Exhibit 9.1 presents elements relevant to the definition of value by Landon and coauthors).[7]

[6] Institute for Healthcare Improvement. (2009). How do they do that? Low-cost high-quality health care in America. www.brookings.edu/events/how-do-they-do-that-low-cost-high-quality-care-in-america/.

[7] Landon, S. N., Padikkala, J., & Horwitz, L. I. (2021). Defining value in health care: A scoping review of the literature. *International Journal for Quality in Health Care*, *33*(4), mzab140.

Exhibit 9.1 Definitions of value

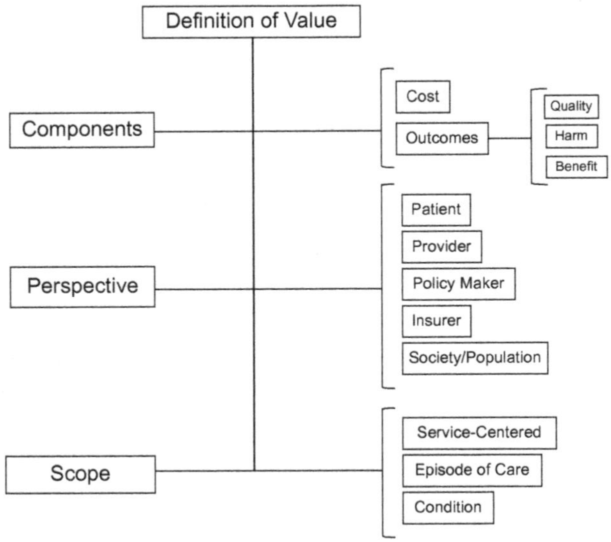

Source: Landon, S. N., Padikkala, J., & Horwitz, L. I. (2021). Defining value in health care: A scoping review of the literature. *International Journal for Quality in Health Care, 33*(4), mzab140. Reproduced by permission of Oxford University Press.

Value-Based Care: What Do People Say about It?

Fortified with these clear-eyed insights, how do we understand (or do we understand) what enthusiasts say about "value-based care," value-based payment, and value-based insurance coverage? In the abstract, the ideal value-based system is simple to describe: It will be one that sets payment to suppliers of care and any cost-sharing for demanders of care at levels to ensure that the set of services patients use are all ones with positive net benefit compared to the alternative of no service or some other service – with incremental value greater than incremental cost. If someone was smart enough to know the costs (both money and time) associated with the use of productive inputs in healthcare, and also to know how much outcomes mattered in money terms to which patients, that smart person could just cover the cost of that set of inputs and be confident that the output (and outcome) would be the one with maximum net value. Put even more simply, define measures of the outcomes you want to pay just enough to get suppliers to supply those outcomes. That is the story from economics; what do friends of value-based payment say?

Some physicians have taken the value-based pledge, and they know what to say to the world: Ask *us experts* what treatments have high value, they say, make sure that all physicians do them, and stop them from doing any treatments which we think are either harmful or wasteful, and thus of low value. You will easily see why economists beg to differ in theory – there is no mention of cost in this advice (mostly because physicians are not experts on it and often do not even know the cost of what they do and what they are criticizing fellow physicians for doing). The biggest sore thumb here is a treatment (often a drug) which adds significantly to health but carries so high a price that it is not cost-effective.

When cost is included in the discussion by consultants and advocates of a value-based approach, what do they say about it? They often blame someone else for being greedy; the cost or price should not be that high. As you might expect, the usual greedy culprits are drug companies charging high prices for branded drugs. Oncologists have been the most outspoken here; they could provide more value-based care if cancer drugs did not cost so much. A skeptical economist might note that very often oncologists treat patients with drugs infused in their facilities – so a higher price for a drug means less for the oncologist if drugs and physician management are bundled. Even if they are not, an insurer looking to assemble a network will look at the bundled price associated with the drug and complementary physician services.

How Do Physicians Deal with High-Priced Drugs?

Ordinarily they do not make cost-effectiveness the decisive factor in what they recommend or use. The Medicare Oncology Care Model (OCM) does pay a bundled payment; it (and its recent successor, the Enhancing Oncology Model) is probably the most discussed value-based payment program that involves physicians. A study in *Cancer* of 12 evaluations of value-based cancer payment of various types found that evaluations did not emphasize quality or health gains but instead focused on before and after effects on cost – and found that a small majority of experiments reported lower costs, though the reduction was often small.[8] A commentary on the OCM in *JAMA*

[8] Aviki, E. M., Schleicher, S. M., Mullangi, S., Matsoukas, K., & Korenstein, D. (2018). Alternative payment and care-delivery models in oncology: A systematic review. *Cancer*, *124*(16), 3293–3306.

Oncology cited the reason why: higher prices for new on patent cancer drugs.[9] The commentators' suggestion: only penalize physicians for using expensive drugs if they use more than the recommended care pathway; no mention of whether they underuse effective or cost-effective drugs. Box 9.6 explores drug payment policy more in depth.

I think it is fair to say that medicine has not yet come to terms with economic models of payment, value-based or otherwise, to be described in the next section. There is still a belief (or perhaps a hope) that proper changes to clinical practice (usually required of the wasteful physicians in the office down the hall) could save money with no harm; trade-offs need not be made. While managers know this is not true, they will be challenged in managing with alternative payment mechanisms probably to a greater extent than with fee-for-service.

In practice, the label "value-based" now applies primarily to payment systems and is often attached to anything other than unqualified fee-for-service. For example, a reimbursement plan largely based on FFS but with some cost or quality targets added would be labeled "value-based." Even more importantly, the idea of "value" is not the quantification of net value you can get from cost-effectiveness analysis. Instead, the term has been largely hijacked by the "triple aim" advocates,[10] who aspire to a system which, compared to the present, has lower cost, better outcomes, and greater access. The core notion of value – even in Porter's version – as a trade-off between cost and health benefits has largely been lost in an excess of exuberance over the hope of doing more for less.

An Economic Interpretation of Value-Based Quantities and Payments

Pricing or reimbursement is a means to an end. The end, already defined, is the use of services and actions whose benefit is greater than their cost. So how much does a simple model of economic incentives help to get there?

Here I outline a model of supplier payment that would lead to maximizing net value. (If you feel the need for supply and demand curves, look at Box 9.1.) Imagine a manager is responsible for the health and spending for a population of persons (either those in an insurance plan or those using

[9] Lyss, A. J., Supalla, S. N., & Schleicher, S. M. (2020). The oncology care model – why it works and why it could work better: Accounting for novel therapies in value-based payment. *JAMA Oncology*, *6*(8), 1161–1162.

[10] Berwick, D. M., Nolan, T. W., & Whittington, J. (2008). The triple aim: Care, health, and cost. *Health Affairs*, *27*(3), 759–769.

Box 9.1 Theory: Value-based pricing in pictures

There are (at least) two versions of the story about the ideal way for a buyer of medical care to set value-based prices that economists have discussed, one simple and two complicated. The simple version, shown in Figure 9.1, looks like the supply and demand curve from your first econ course, but it is not for widgets.

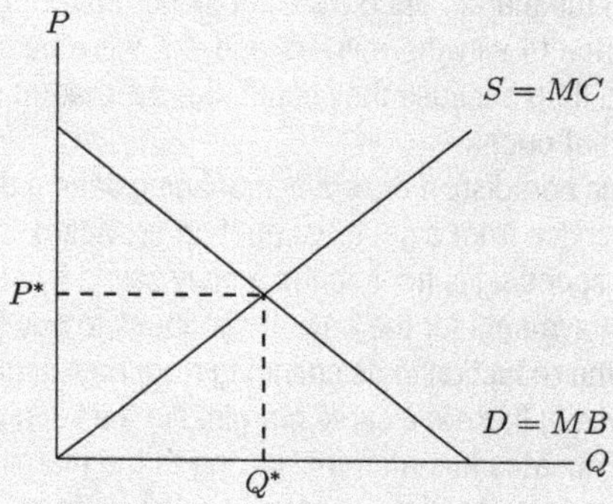

Figure 9.1 Equilibrium in a competitive market.

Health economists have a different interpretation of what is on the axes and where the curves come from. In particular, think of the service being supplied (the "Q") as a physician service, like knee replacement in a population. The supply curve is derived as shown later in Box 9.2. At a low fee, perhaps some larger orthopedic practices with experienced staff and ideal facilities, and enough partners with time on their hands, will be willing to perform this surgery. Raise the price and more practices will come in, and incumbents will be willing to take less time off. Make the payment really lucrative and some general surgeons will start to poach on this territory and Knees-R-Us will advertise on TV.

The "demand" curve here represents more than just consumers maximizing utility (though it does that). In the case of medical care, we can in principle quantify the health benefits from better knee function – fewer days lost from work or with restricted activity for this example. The downward sloping demand curve reflects the assumption that some people will get more benefit from surgery. Their joints may be in worse shape, knee function is more important in their work or play, or they may be better candidates for long-term health improvement. If we attach dollar values to these health improvements (say, as the incremental QALYs discussed in Chapter 8 on cost-effectiveness), at each price reduction the additional buyers brought in have a value of the treatment equal to the price they pay. Of course, the limits on demand at high prices and the incentive to relax them as price falls come proximately from insurance plans, responding to what their premium payers would want them to do. For the population for whom this is the demand curve, it is also the marginal health benefit curve.

The famous intersection of supply and demand at P*Q* then represents the best quantity that doctors and consumers can choose, the quantity per potentially eligible person where marginal benefit equals marginal cost – where the marginal benefit is as usual the value of added health for the last few patients brought in because of a lower price and the marginal cost is the amount needed to cover the cost of the last few doctors attracted by a higher price. All is beautiful.

The ideal, of price set at P*, can be achieved in two ways. The way that is most discussed is for a large insurer (usually Medicare) seeking to set price at the right level, the level that leads to the efficient rate of use of each service by the people it insures. The other is when there is a competitive market in insurance. Suppose that there are 10 identical insurers each with 1/10 of the population. Then each insurer should provide the service to 0.1Q* people. That will happen if insurers compete. If the market price were set higher than P* there would be an incentive for suppliers to cut price to win the market, and if it were below P* there would be an incentive for buyers to bid it up because they could. So, the market equilibrium would be exactly P*, the socially efficient price.

There is, however, potential trouble in paradise. If the entity managing patient demand has market power in buying the medical service from a set of competing providers, it will notice that if it cuts price below P*, the fall in spending is not just the money saved by buying fewer units; it also includes the reduction in payments for the units it continues to buy (and lower-cost suppliers continue to sell). Thus, the reduction in its spending from buying one less unit is larger than the reduction in price times 1; there is a curve marginal to the supply curve that plots its savings from buying less. If it equates this marginal saving to the marginal value of health lost from less care, it will move to a smaller quantity at a lower price. This is the monopsony equilibrium, and it is lower than the efficient quantity. This behavior may correspond to what some Medicaid plans, intent on saving taxpayer money, will choose to do.

Figure 9.2 shows some complications mentioned earlier and much discussed by economists though now slightly out of fashion – but they could come back. Here just for simplicity we make demand fixed at Q* (straight up and down). However, there has been empirical evidence that the supply curve of physician services is not always positively sloped; it might be "backward-bending," as in the figure. The intuition is based on the idea that doctors have a target income – they have an income in mind they think they need (and deserve) to earn (to pay the mortgage, to travel when you can get some time off, to put the kids through an expensive college). If the fee level for knee replacement were to be cut, the way to avoid a (large) cut in income is to do more surgical procedures to make up the gap. That would be shown in the diagram by the increase in quantity if price were reduced from P_1 to P_2.

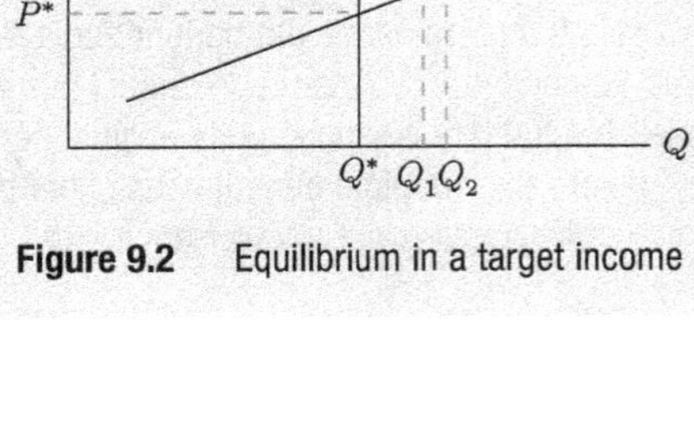

Figure 9.2 Equilibrium in a target income model.

Tom McGuire and I have shown that this behavior by physicians can arise in theory from income effects: As income falls, desired leisure and the value attached to conservative patient management decline, relative to the value of bringing in more money.[11] This apparently happened when Medicare cut what it paid for coronary artery bypass graft (CABG) surgery which made up a large share of the work of cardiac surgeons;[12] there is still a rule of thumb at Centers for Medicare and Medicaid Services (CMS) that about half of expected lower reimbursement from cutting fees will be made up by increases in quantity.

The other issue that can be visualized in the figure is the idea that because physicians can recommend their own services, they can be tempted to do so (with regrets) even if the price falls because of what is sometimes called the "decreasing disutility of discretion" or "supply-induced demand." For example, if by telling white lies to patients, doctors could get them to consume the quantity Q_1 when price was P_2, they might add to demand inducement if price fell to P_2 and they wanted to go to Q_2 – because they are more willing to do so to get their income back up.

There is, however, a solution to all of these problems if the insurer is on the ball: set the price at P*, thus bypassing the range of too-high prices that cause both demand inducement and backward-bending supply. After all, if you as a buyer can get more offered at a lower price, you should keep reducing the price until the supply curve has a positive slope and never pay the price on the backward-bending part. The only challenge would be if the fixed demand were so high that supply would fall short no matter what the price – unlikely to happen if demand is responsive to price because higher prices paid to physicians will eventually staunch demand.

a medical care delivery system) and imagine all physicians and patients with a given symptom agree that there is an ideal volume of services that they would demand, defined by some measurable metric Q*. These services require professional time and other inputs that are going to be supplied by firms.

Paid a price or fee per service, how many services will suppliers be willing to make available to the patient population? The incremental cost of this service starts out low for a few suppliers (say, because they have time on their hands and are initially willing to make a modest effort for little money). This cost rises with total volume (as they give up more leisure and must hire more staff), so price must increase to incentivize larger volumes. We can stop being coy: We assume an upward sloped supply curve, as described in Box 9.2. Then all the manager needs to do is to find the payment or fee level on that

[11] McGuire, T. G., & Pauly, M. V. (1991). Physician response to fee changes with multiple payers. *Journal of Health Economics, 10*(4), 385–410.

[12] Yip, W. C. (1998). Physician response to Medicare fee reductions: Changes in the volume of coronary artery bypass graft (CABG) surgeries in the Medicare and private sectors. *Journal of Health Economics, 17*(6), 675–699.

Box 9.2 Theory: Where do supply curves come from?

I expect that none of us would have trouble imagining that higher prices would somehow call forth a larger production volume of a medical service of a given quality, or that higher payments tied to some metric of quality would mean that suppliers would hit that target more often. Medical services suppliers are like anyone else. But this is a book about health economics, and economists do not take much of anything for granted. So how do they think about the question of why (or when) a higher reimbursement level for some medical service will lead to a greater quantity supplied?

The economic model of competitive equilibrium has a story about why price rises with quantity in the short run with a given number of firms and fixed cost. Marginal cost initially falls but eventually rises with output volume, so the price needed to cover that cost will have to rise too in order to get profit-maximizing firms to expand output. It is the quantity choices of those firms that generate an upward sloping supply curve, a property that need not hold for nonprofit firms.

Things get a little tricky in the longer run where new firms can enter and existing firms can alter capacity. After all, if you can produce a given output at a given average and marginal cost, you should be able to double output and incur the same costs by creating an identical twin. So there needs to be something that is hard to copy. Assume a practice cannot get the physician to add more hours of work. A health system may then find that it must pay higher wages to attract more nurses if it wants to expand. It works the same way in the opposite direction: When you cut output you may not be able to fire enough people fast enough to lower your total cost proportionately. So, in general the assumption of a supply curve with some upward slope seems reasonable. However, the easier it is for firms to replicate or disappear when output varies, the less of a change in price you will need to get those suppliers to want to furnish just the right amount of volume. Dialysis centers are going to be less price-responsive than surgeon practices.

The most plausible model for supply of physician services and for hospital care within a local healthcare market is one that assumes some heterogeneity or variation among potential suppliers. Some have lower marginal costs than others – because of better management, paid-off capital, preferences of workers, or any number of reasons. This implies that, even in the long run, some output will be furnished at low unit prices, but increasing prices paid will call forth more output, as existing firms enter and new firms (slightly disadvantaged, which is why they did not enter before) come in to reap profits. As noted in the preceding paragraph, the steepness of this supply curve depends on how similar new firms can be to old ones – but the key assumption is that they cannot be carbon copies and existing firms cannot perfectly replicate themselves.

How realistic is the assumption of upward sloping supply for medical care? It certainly seems plausible for care provided by profit-seeking firms, either in total or for specific services or procedures. What about physicians? Doctors and doctor practices differ even within a city; indeed, variation in feel for physician practices has been a major research topic by noneconomists at the Dartmouth Institute (and a few economist fellow travelers). They may hold back on supply when price rises because, with a higher income, they feel they do not need the money.[13] However such behavior is not the case for specific services nor in a market as a whole since higher prices attract more doctors.

For care supplied by hospitals, there is probably greater supply response to a given upward bump in prices; even nonprofit hospitals will go where (and if) there is money. A wild card in this story is the elusive concept of quality: Will higher prices lead to higher quality (from existing firms) or bring in lower-quality laggards? The answer in turn depends on heterogeneity – but now in the supply of quality. Some firms are going to be able to increase their quality (say, by hiring more and better nurses) at lower additional cost than others. (See Chapter 5 on production.)

curve that will just bring forth Q* (no more and no less); call this price P*. That is the value-based price that should be reimbursed.

The manager's job is, surprisingly, almost done. All that remains is to determine that, when Q* is made available to the patient population at the price needed to incentivize it, the value (in terms of willingness to sacrifice other consumption) by consumer-patients just equals that price. In this case, we have determined both the value-based volume of care and the value-based payment needed to assure its supply. Life is good. Consumers cannot be made better off at any other quantity, and suppliers are willing to supply that quantity in return for gross revenues P*Q* and profit or net income at whatever is left over after covering marginal real resource cost.

In this model, the outcome is entirely determined by payment to providers and results in supply of the ideal total quantity Q*. To ensure that this quantity is then distributed properly among patients, we might rely on the goodwill of physicians to treat those patients who would benefit most. In addition, cost-sharing in insurance could serve to separate out those patients who would get less benefit from care. Box 9.3 shows how to deal with situations in which physicians cannot or do not behave according to this assumption.

This is, I realize, all quite pedantic, but I have dragged you through it because I think it serves as a protective shield around a decades-long misleading discussion of fee-for-service versus capitation. One common view is that fee-for-service is fatally flawed and needs to be replaced as a payment mechanism because it incentivizes the oversupply of services. It does so, the argument goes, because providers receive more revenue the larger the volume of services they provide. What this view ignores is cost. After all, profit or net income is revenue *minus* cost – so if (marginal) cost is increasing as more care is furnished, there must be a level of output at which the last unit is

[13] McGuire, T. G., & Pauly, M. V. (1991). Physician response to fee changes with multiple payers. *Journal of Health Economics, 10*(4), 385–410.

Box 9.3 Evidence: Sharpening blunt instruments

The approach to value-based payment just discussed can bring about the ideal volume of services rendered by physicians. So can the ideal patient cost-sharing described in Chapter 6. To make things perfect, we only require that physicians distribute the ideal volume to patients who need it the most. Unfortunately, this does not always seem to happen. As Baicker and Obermeyer note, there is considerable evidence that physicians both under-test and over-test at the same time.[14] There are physician errors in judgment, they say, that are due to behavioral biases. Doctors may choose to test low-risk patients who will get little benefit but fail to test high-risk patients who would get substantial potential benefit.

Dealing with the cost of tests is a little tricky because with automated testing equipment the marginal cost of a test can be negligible even if the charge is high as long as capacity is not reached, but let us assume that the price is the cost. Then there are theoretical solutions to the problem (contrary to their paper): make cost-sharing depend on severity or pay more (or only pay something) only for testing of higher-risk patients. Using such high-level high-power financial incentives will, of course, be more complicated and dangerous, so Baicker and Obermeyer discuss alternative organization or behavioral incentives to get physicians to do the right thing. Or it may just not be worth the effort (if tests are not too costly): just go with simple payment combined with exhortations to test when needed and not worry about over-testing; this might be the most cost-effective thing to do.

unprofitable – which is precisely how suppliers determine how much to supply at a given price. We have the empirical evidence from FFS Medicaid and its low payment rates to show that FFS does not necessarily lead to oversupply, so this is more than just theory.[15] The correct conclusion – for an insurance manager deciding how much to pay or a delivery system deciding what contract to accept – is that incentives for quantity depend on the relationship of price to marginal cost. In the end, there must be some finite quantity that a supplier will supply at any price – probably zero at a very low price and then a volume that increases with the price paid. In between zero at a zero price and a very large oversupply at a very high price, there will be an ideal price associated with the ideal quantity. It is just a matter of titrating the price to get close to that point.

[14] Baicker, K., & Obermeyer, Z. (2022). Overuse and underuse of health care: New insights from economics and machine learning. *JAMA Health Forum*, *3*(2), e220428; Mullainathan, S., & Obermeyer, Z. (2022). Diagnosing physician error: A machine learning approach to low-value health care. *The Quarterly Journal of Economics*, *137*(2), 679–727.

[15] Hsiang, W. R., Lukasiewicz, A., Gentry, M., Kim, C. Y., Leslie, M. P., Pelker, R., . . . & Wiznia, D. H. (2019). Medicaid patients have greater difficulty scheduling health care appointments compared with private insurance patients: A meta-analysis. *INQUIRY: The Journal of Health Care Organization, Provision, and Financing*, *56*, 46958019838118.

Another common view is that capitation is intrinsically superior to FFS because it provides no incentive to oversupply and strong incentives to minimize cost and produce efficiently. Both of these statements about incentives are true – but the problem is that the way to minimize cost (and maximize profit) under capitation is to accept the per-person payment and then do as little as possible but do it efficiently. The profit-maximizing supplier's theoretically optimal volume of services is zero, once the capitation payment has been made. Of course, in reality both contract terms and professional ethics mean that some positive volume will be supplied – the minimum amount needed to attract and retain the business of some patients. But there is obviously no reason to think that capitation will lead either the quantity or the quality of care to be at levels where marginal benefit equals cost.

Back to the drawing board. Here is a hint: If volume is too high under generous FFS and too low under full capitation, maybe there is something in between that will get it just right. To get it right, someone first must figure out what P* and Q* are. If the system being replaced is FFS where P has been set above P*, a price cut is the obvious thing to do. But it may be necessary, at least for a time, and for political reasons, to also offer capitation at some level to providers facing a price cut to make up for the lost revenue (at a lower P and Q than where they started). Such a payment can also offset an incentive to health professionals to make up some lost profit at a modestly lower price by increasing volume (up to a point), as it is shown with the backward-bending supply case in Box 9.1; the best deal is close to the original income but with lower productivity incentives (price) and less work effort. Hence this hybrid solution has a reasonably good economic pedigree, though how to determine the level of the fixed payment is challenging (Box 9.4).

The punchline here is this: The ideal payment mechanism combines a fixed payment and a payment that varies with one or more metrics of volume or intensity, a combination of capitation and lower-power fee-for-service. This two-part arrangement will be better than either extreme. However, to turn it into value-based payment, the variable portion needs to be calibrated as well as possible to some understanding of how marginal value is related to volume of use or activity. In the base case discussed at the beginning, the message is clear: If you (the manager) know where Q* is relative to what is currently being supplied, you should increase the marginal payment if you want more of the service and reduce it if you want less. That is, if you know that the marginal value is higher than the current value, pay more to increase value – and vice versa for the other direction.

Box 9.4 Theory: The economics of paying for value, not volume

The technical economics of supply and demand imagines at the outset that we are talking about a specific product of a given quality. In healthcare that is not plausible; many observers (and patients too) have desires about not just the volume of care but also its quality (defined as anything that matters to buyers that is not volume). Unfortunately, the economics of quality determination (when quality is variable) is a mess; there is no simple model, much less simple empirical findings, that can tell us how to get what we want.

All is not lost: The simplest proposition (from Box 8.2 in Chapter 8) – that if there is a marginal cost to adding quality it should be added as long as the marginal benefit to buyers from it is greater than that marginal cost – is still true. There is no problem for economic theory if all buyers want the same quality (whatever it may mean). If cost is a function of quality, and all buyers have the same preferences, then the only task is to establish what the supply function looks like for a service of that quality, determine the volume that is ideal, and pay the price on the supply curve at that volume. If sellers are tempted to cheat on quality but buyers can tell quality when they see it, cheating will not pay in competitive markets, buyers can be held to preset standards, and the outcome will be ideal. I mean economically ideal; the managers in charge would probably face criticism that they have not provided the "highest possible quality," but somebody must pay attention to cost.

There are two problems with how insurers (especially Medicare) have tried to modify FFS payment to assure quality. One problem is that Medicare is not sure how to measure quality or how much it wants. Suppose it wants to reduce infection rates per hospital admission of some type. If Medicare knew the economically ideal level of infection rates (where the marginal benefit of reducing them further just equaled the marginal cost of doing so), it could follow the procedure in the previous paragraph. However, if it knows only that lower infection rates are a good thing but not how much it costs to achieve various rates and/or what rate it would accept at a given price, it has problems. It can implement a search strategy where it proposes a reward or a penalty of a predetermined amount associated with achieving a given rate and then seeing what volume of care hospitals are willing to supply at that amount.[16] Then it must judge whether paying more per unit and settling for whatever volume is offered is what it likes. Or it can flip the script, announce a monetary payment and a volume target and see what level of infection rate is implemented. Experiments of this type are about as far as Medicare has gotten; you can see that with enough trial and error it might get to a good (or at least better) outcome than wherever it started. Not necessarily; its bonus may be too small to cover the cost of any improvement, so the current policy is as good as it gets. Awarding stars to hospitals with low infection rates (or black spots to hospitals with high ones) will help to enlist beneficiaries in offering incentives to hospitals for high quality, but what they will be able to do will be constrained by how much they are paid per admission.

Economic theory adds to complexity if different buyers want different levels of quality (as well as volume). This probably characterizes the private market, though it would be helpful to know how consumers vary in their valuation of quality improvements. For example, they

[16] CMS. (2024). Hospital-Acquired Condition Reduction Program. www.cms.gov/medicare/quality/value-based-programs/hospital-acquired-conditions.

might place different valuations on shorter wait times for treatments for uncomfortable symptoms. Economics sees a core problem here; it is going to be prohibitively costly to produce a different quality of some product for each buyer or each insurance plan. (It is presumably easier, though not costless, to offer different volumes.) Some people will not get exactly what they want; the more so the higher the (fixed) cost of moving to producing a different type or quality of product. Choosing what most people want may leave the minority with more intense preferences unsatisfied, so may not be ideal.

Somehow competitive markets will muddle through, offering some product variety and trying to do the best they can. In this case value will be rewarded without the need for some special redesign of markets or regulation – think of variation in restaurant quality, where value and volume are both rewarded: Do you think there need to be government-imposed incentives to improve the quality of cooking or service? But there will always be some disgruntled people.

There is one other major benefit to getting payment right, at P*. One of the great concerns in the supply of physician services is conflict of interest. You must first ask your physician whether you should have a service that the same physician will supply at a profit. You could get a second opinion, but you would prefer that the first opinion be unbiased. As a consumer you might worry; as a legislator you will pass laws trying to limit conflicts of interest. The best known of such laws are the "Stark Laws," named after Representative Pete Stark, which limit or forbid physicians from referring Medicare patients to facilities in which they have ownership interests.[17]

These laws have a major gap. Physicians can still refer to other physicians in their medical group and then share in the group's total net income. However, there is only a temptation to use a service that is not cost-effective when the price of that service is too high. If the price is at P*, whoever owns the entity that supplies, whether your physician, his brother-in-law, or some private equity investors, will only want to supply the right volume, and only break even on the last unit. Paying correctly eliminates temptation. Put differently, if Medicare could get its FFS payment rates right, it could ditch the Stark Laws and the whole conflict of interest apparatus.

Payment with Imperfect Value Information

Sometimes the slogan "pay for value, not volume" will do the trick. Sometimes it is a little more complicated because both volume and quality

[17] 42 U.S.C. § 1395nn.

are variable. Of course, you may find that the amount you must pay to get some otherwise desirable change in quality or volume is more than the value of that change. Then you should just stay put. The attempt to defend the concept of value-based payment, by arguing that quality has not improved because bonuses offered were too small begs the question of whether it would be worth it to pay bonuses large enough to change provider behavior.[18] Sometimes you must be realistic.

There is another model for payment that does not imagine (or require) that the entity setting payment take a stand on what is ideal. Perhaps not surprisingly, this premise undergirds the current politically sensitive Medicare payment system – but that system has also been copied in one way or another by many other payers (including, especially, Medicare Advantage plans). The original idea here was to jettison the hope of a high-level positive incentive-based system and instead try to build one in which incentives to providers are neutral: They should get the same profit or utility no matter what they do. Then, the argument went, they might as well choose what is best for the patient's health.

This approach was taken in the design of the Medicare physician payment system that based value of relative uses of resources – labeled unimaginatively the resource-based relative value system (RBRVS). Although much tweaked (and maligned), it is the core of the physician payment system still used in original Medicare.[19] For many of those arrangements now flying under the banner of alternative payment systems, the fundamental structure of physician payment is still based on RBRVS and FFS, but with adjustments if outcomes fall short. For example, Medicare's Hospital Readmissions Reduction Program is still based on paying hospital per admission with payment based on resource costs for each diagnosis-related group (DRG); it adds penalties only if a measure of quality (the readmission rate) falls below a target.[20]

In the conceptualization of RBRVS, the setting was a physician trying to decide what set of services to provide to patients with a given condition; there was little role for patient preferences to affect physician reimbursement. If one service used more physician time and effort, as well as other practice inputs, than another, its relative payment rate was to be set proportional to a metric of work and resource use. Once this was done, the financial incentive

[18] Problems with current value-based payment systems: Why "pay for performance" hasn't worked. Center for Healthcare Quality & Payment Reform. https://chqpr.org/VBP_Problems.html.

[19] CMS. (2024). Medicare physician fee schedule. www.cms.gov/medicare/physician-fee-schedule/search/overview.

[20] CMS. (2024). Hospital Readmissions Reduction Program. www.cms.gov/medicare/payment/prospective-payment-systems/acute-inpatient-pps/hospital-readmissions-reduction-program-hrrp.

generated by relative fees would be the same for any set of services – so the physician might as well furnish the set that helps the patient the most. There is an intellectual history in economics; Karl Marx took the viewpoint that the relative prices of goods should be based on the amount of labor or effort embodied in them, termed the "labor theory of value."[21]

One obvious missing part of this Medicare system is that it only determines relative fees; physician income and Medicare reimbursement also require specification of a conversion factor that turns relative values into absolute dollar payments. If this factor is set too high, there will be too much of everything; the only saving grace is that the mix will be right – but the total volume will be wrong. The conversion factor was originally driven by a desire to keep physician payments about the same as before the changeover to the new system. It has over the decades been ratcheted down somewhat based on assumptions about improved productivity and by political decisions on Part B spending targets. [22] But it is still not linked to the value of health benefit it incentivizes.

Moreover, physicians have a legitimate gripe: Medicare payment for their services has not kept up with their practice costs or economy-wide inflation, and commercial payments, though higher, have also lagged. The result obviously is lower net incomes and attenuated incentives to accept new Medicare patients. What appears to be happening politically with the key update factor is that it is not really intended to be neutral regarding total income or total volume but rather to reduce those incentives to supply services to patients – until something bad happens. We know from the Medicaid experience that low payments by an insurer can cause physicians to stop taking new patients covered by that insurer.[23] We do not think that Medicaid-level access will be acceptable in Medicare, given vocal and strong political support. This trial-and-error system is how Medicare FFS now closes the loop on determining physician (and, for that matter, hospital) payment.

The providers' current problem is that, for new Medicare patients, though there has been some erosion in willingness to accept, it has not yet reached

21 Gordon, D. F. (1959). What was the labor theory of value? *The American Economic Review*, *49*(2), 462–472. www.jstor.org/stable/1816138.

22 Wynn, B. O., Burgette, L. F., Mulcahy, A. W., Okeke, E. N., Brantley, I., Iyer, N., . . . & Mehrotra, A. (2015). Development of a model for the validation of work relative value units for the Medicare physician fee schedule. *Rand Health Quarterly*, *5*(1).

23 Hsiang, W. R., Lukasiewicz, A., Gentry, M., Kim, C. Y., Leslie, M. P., Pelker, R., . . . & Wiznia, D. H. (2019). Medicaid patients have greater difficulty scheduling health care appointments compared with private insurance patients: A meta-analysis. *INQUIRY: The Journal of Health Care Organization, Provision, and Financing*, *56*, 46958019838118.

a stage that provokes congressional action. Until there is some major change – for example, widespread physician withdrawing from Medicare or a physicians' strike, as has occurred in many other developed countries – managers should not expect major increases in the conversion factor for the Medicare FFS system. The alternative capitated model – less payment to doctors and hospitals but less work expected from them – will continue to be posed and praised as an alternative.

There has also been another charge of conflict of interest in Medicare FFS, since the physician specialty societies were often consulted in setting the relative value weights. That might have engendered some redistribution among physicians, but it is unclear how it affected total payments. In any case, Medicare is now looking for an alternative value-based method of payment – but so far has not found one. Box 9.5 explores how payment levels affect physician behavior.

Box 9.5 Evidence: Economics of provider payment and moral hazard

One implication of the P* model that was first noticed by the economists Randall Ellis and Thomas McGuire (E&M) is that reimbursement or price can be used by insurance plans to control the volume of a service that will be used by insureds, even when the financial incentives to insureds to care about the cost (of care) are attenuated or absent.[24] If I am a potential insurance buyer and I know beforehand what level of access to some treatment (say, knee replacements) I would want, given their true cost, I just choose the plan that pays P*. That may leave me frustrated if I start to get knee pain and my doctor will not be eager to do the work, but I can be consoled by the thought that at least there is no financial risk if my case is bad enough that I qualify for surgery. Of course, I could also choose a managed care plan with rules or protocols that lead to the same pattern. Here, setting reimbursement at P* will avoid physicians' frustration at being forbidden to do a procedure they would have been eager to do. One implication of the E&M model is that the main role for cost-sharing is not just to put skin in the game for skin's sake but rather to deal with heterogeneity in marginal benefit across patients that is unobservable by the insurer.[25]

Other more recent work on physician and hospital responses to payments has generally found positive supply responses – when they are paid more, they do more, and backward-bending supply seems not to be a problem for the specific procedures for which changes in

[24] Ellis, R. P., & McGuire, T. G. (1988). Insurance principles and the design of prospective payment systems. *Journal of Health Economics*, *7*(3), 215–237.

[25] Ellis, R. P., & McGuire, T. G. (1990). Optimal payment systems for health services. *Journal of Health Economics*, *9*(4), 375–396.

payments have so far been tried. (Maybe they are too small and selective to generate large income effects, or maybe income effects are not that large.) You must get the payments lined up with value; one study showed that paying obstetricians more for cesarean section than normal delivery led to more of the former, suggesting supply-induced demand.[26]

There are three more recent papers on physician responses to payment incentives. To start at one extreme, physicians who are put at risk for the costs of care they recommend seem to change their recommendations. Ho and Pakes found that reducing capitated payments to physicians for the costliness of hospital care associated with their practices (either by including hospital cost in the capitation or by adjusting it downward for above-average costs) caused them to send patients to less costly hospitals further away from patient homes.[27] This parallels an early study by me and colleagues that found that putting physicians at risk for the cost of drugs they prescribe led to lower drug costs.[28] On the FFS supply side, beginning at the bottom of the supply curve, Alexander and Schnell found that Medicaid plans that increased payments to physicians caused fewer beneficiaries to report that physicians refused to treat them.[29] For Medicare, where payments overall are higher, Clemens and Gottlieb nevertheless found that an increase of 2% in physician payments led to a 3% increase in care,[30] contradicting the CMS rule of thumb but raising the possibility of demand inducement (although some physicians do refuse new patients at current payment rates).

The punchline from these more recent studies establishes that physicians are economically responsive in their behavior – so there is hope for an insurer titrating the marginal payments to them to offer incentives to come closer to optimal volume and optimal quality if the insurer can decide what levels of each are its target. Money matters, although it is not the only thing that matters. But it may be the thing that insurance managers can most control; they do not know how to change physician culture. For health system managers, there is a wider array of incentives, but internal payment is certainly one of them.

Varieties of Value-Based Payment

Medicare has adopted a goal of converting its payment under original Medicare to "value-based." (Medicare Advantage plans are free to offer providers whatever system they choose, provided that enough providers in

[26] Gruber, J., Kim, J., & Mayzlin, D. (1999). Physician fees and procedure intensity: The case of cesarean delivery. *Journal of Health Economics, 18*(4), 473–490.

[27] Ho, K., & Pakes, A. (2014). Hospital choices, hospital prices, and financial incentives to physicians. *The American Economic Review, 104*(12), 3841–3884.

[28] Hillman, A. L., Pauly, M. V., Escarce, J. J., Ripley, K., Gaynor, M., Clouse, J., & Ross, R. (1999). Financial incentives and drug spending in managed care: Incentives for both physicians and patients can interact to help curb spending in this increasingly costly sector. *Health Affairs, 18*(2), 189–200.

[29] Alexander, D., & Schnell, M. (2019). The impacts of physician payments on patient access, use, and health. National Bureau of Economic Research. Working Paper No. w26095.

[30] Clemens, J., & Gottlieb, J. D. (2014). Do physicians' financial incentives affect medical treatment and patient health? *The American Economic Review, 104*(4), 1320–1349.

their networks are willing to accept.) It now estimates that about half or a little more of beneficiaries are subject to such payment, but it counts different systems of varying potency (compared to FFS) as value-based. Whether value-based payment in Medicare is flourishing or just window dressing is not known.

What Are the Systems Being Tried, and What Difference (Compared to Unfettered FFS) Do They Appear to Make?

FFS with rewards and penalties. The least intrusive system is one that is voluntary for physicians, pays FFS, but with rewards and punishments based on some selected quality metrics. Such systems are only as good as their metrics and their incentives. I will not provide detail on individual schemes but instead conclude that, even with voluntary participation, these "pay for performance" schemes, at the levels of incentives they offer, have not been consistently shown to affect physician behavior or outcomes; demonstrated effects have been minimal.[31]

Bundled payment. Both the definitions of what set of services over what time periods are to be bundled and how the payment for the bundle is to be set cover a wide range. The most powerful bundled payment systems pay some entity for the complete mix of services used (physician, hospital, drugs, rehabilitation).[32] When applied to defined surgical procedures such as joint replacement surgery they have shown modest but statistically significant savings with no measured negative outcome effects: joint surgery bundles are the poster children here.[33] When applied to patients with medical needs over a calendar time period (such as annual spending for heart failure patients) they appear to have no effect on cost or outcome.[34]

[31] Scott, A., Sivey, P., Ouakrim, D. A., Willenberg, L., Naccarella, L., Furler, J., & Young, D. (2011). The effect of financial incentives on the quality of health care provided by primary care physicians. *Cochrane Database of Systematic Reviews, 2011*(9). https://doi.org/10.1002/14651858.CD008451.pub2; Serumaga, B., Ross-Degnan, D., Avery, A. J., Elliott, R. A., Majumdar, S. R., Zhang, F., & Soumerai, S. B. (2011). Effect of pay for performance on the management and outcomes of hypertension in the United Kingdom: Interrupted time series study. *BMJ, 342.* https://doi.org/10.1136/bmj.d108; Jha, A. K., Joynt, K. E., Orav, E. J., & Epstein, A. M. (2012). The long-term effect of premier pay for performance on patient outcomes. *New England Journal of Medicine, 366*(17), 1606–1615.

[32] CMS. (2024). BPCI Advanced. www.cms.gov/priorities/innovation/innovation-models/bpci-advanced.

[33] Navathe, A. S., Emanuel, E. J., Venkataramani, A. S., Huang, Q., Gupta, A., Dinh, C. T., . . . & Liao, J. M. (2020). Spending and quality after three years of Medicare's voluntary bundled payment for joint replacement surgery: The spending and quality effects of Medicare's bundled payments for care improvement initiative among patients undergoing lower extremity joint-replacement. *Health Affairs, 39*(1), 58–66.

[34] Joynt Maddox, K. E., Orav, E. J., Zheng, J., & Epstein, A. M. (2018). Evaluation of Medicare's bundled payments initiative for medical conditions. *New England Journal of Medicine, 379*(3), 260–269.

The verdict on bundled payment for oncology so far has been mixed but CMS still presses ahead with this approach.[35]

Capitated payments with upside and downside provider risk. The most robust set of alternative incentives is payment of a predetermined fixed dollar amount per person per time period, with the provider willing to participate in this scheme able to collect profit if costs are low and suffer losses if costs are high. This method is still very uncommon in Medicare. The accountable care organization (ACO) model comes closest, because the high-level organization receives an all-inclusive capitation payment. So far there is no evidence of successful transfer of this organization-level incentive down to physicians (putting them at full risk) and also no evidence for major changes in cost or health outcomes.[36]

Voluntary or mandatory. Most Medicare alternative payment models (APMs) so far have been voluntary. Those in the private sector must be voluntary in the sense that providers are free to accept or reject proposed alternatives and move to another insurance plan. The default option could be the loss of contract with a private payer but that rarely occurs. Voluntary payment has two downsides: It will generally result in overly optimistic estimates of the difference a new system makes and therefore underestimates of how much the system would do if extended to all payers. The reason is obvious: Compared to all providers, volunteers will be systems that expect to do better under the new arrangements than under the status quo alternative. If they are rewarded for cost reduction, the volunteers will be systems expecting to be able to reduce costs (or at least appear to do so). Why they needed to wait for a reward to do the right thing is less clear. The holdouts will be less capable of generating similar results if the new system is made mandatory.[37]

Value-Based Insurance Design

The appeal to value has also been used to advocate for particular "value-based" forms of insurance coverage and cost-sharing. This insurance is

[35] Kocher, R. P., & Adashi, E. Y. (2023). A new approach to cancer bundled payments in Medicare: The enhancing oncology model. *JAMA Health Forum*, *4*(1), e224904–e224904.

[36] Kahn, J. G., & Sullivan, K. R. (2022). Promise vs. practice: The actual financial performance of accountable care organizations. *Journal of General Internal Medicine*, *37*(3), 680–681.

[37] Navathe, A. S., Liao, J. M., Polsky, D., Shah, Y., Huang, Q., Zhu, J., . . . & Emanuel, E. J. (2018). Comparison of hospitals participating in Medicare's voluntary and mandatory orthopedic bundle programs. *Health Affairs*, *37*(6), 854–863.

discussed in Chapter 8. For the considerations in this chapter, the most important thing to note is that such insurance very often defines "value" incorrectly by reference only to physician perceptions of clinical benefit without consideration of cost for value-based care. In terms of market choices, it also fails to notice that patients informed by their own efforts or helped by physicians to understand when care is cost-effective should seek that care even if insurance coverage is incomplete. So, the strongest case for lowering cost-sharing is for high-value (net of cost) services that patients undervalue.

The poster children for value-based insurance are reductions in cost-sharing for services with such large cost offsets that total costs fall. The issue is that no insurer should have imposed cost-sharing if there was such an obvious win-win. Because of oversight or for administrative convenience, in reality some cases like this have been found to have existed. But they shouldn't have.[38]

The more serious basis for lowering cost-sharing for highly cost-effective care must come either from patient ignorance – they have not been convinced that the care is worth it (as for example taking statins after a heart attack) or from misperceived cost offsets – patients do not see the claims reductions in other services that some kinds of care can produce. Both of these defects should in principle matter to insurers and should be able to be remedied as part of their efforts to offer the most attractive packages in competitive insurance markets. No lobbyists need apply, but managers do need to guard against patient misperception of health benefits and against insurers that fail to reflect cost offsets in their coverage.

The economic concept of value provides a very different way to look at the problem of value-based insurance targeting. It is (or should be) aimed at services that patients currently underuse because of imperfect information. If insurance was already designed to cover all cost-effective services in full, and only used cost-sharing (if at all) to discourage those users of a service for whom it is not cost-effective, and if patients fully appreciated the health benefits (the QALYs added) by that service, they should be expected to use all cost-beneficial services optimally. They should see that the net value of a drug treatment to them is greater than any cost-sharing or time and inconvenience associated with it; there would be no need for value-based cost-sharing.

[38] Choudhry, N. K., Fischer, M. A., Avorn, J., Schneeweiss, S., Solomon, D. H., Berman, C., . . . & Shrank, W. H. (2010). At Pitney Bowes, value-based insurance design cut copayments and increased drug adherence. *Health Affairs*, *29*(11), 1995–2001.

However, the targets of value-based insurance have been treatments such as taking statins after a heart attack, where noncompliance, nonadherence, and even not filling a prescription are problems. As noted, fewer than half of patients adhered to statin therapy after a myocardial infarction (MI) when the price of a daily statin was about $2 per pill; removal of cost-sharing in a randomized controlled trial bumped up adherence by 4–6 percentage points with modest improvements in outcomes.[39] Another study of high-priced branded specialized medicines for cancer, hepatitis C, and other conditions found a failure-to-fill rate of about 30% with Medicare Part D coverage.[40]

Statins after MI are definitely cost-effective for virtually all candidates; the cost-effectiveness of prescribed high-priced drugs is less certain but is positive for some (e.g., hepatitis C).[41] If patients knew the benefits from taking these treatments whose benefits exceeded their full price, they would take them – even if there was cost-sharing that exposed them to a fraction of the full price. Physicians traditionally (since Hippocrates) have blamed patients for nonadherence (and lying about it). The economic principal-agent view is different: Patients pay physicians to provide accurate advice on the benefits of proposed treatments and then can choose whether to consent to following any recommendation. The key missing link, it seems obvious to us economists, is physician failure to provide convincing information. Why is that, and how can it be changed?

To go straight to the end – would you (or your employees) ever prefer an insurance plan with a given premium that achieved lower rates of "non-initiation" of highly effective drugs or adherence to cost-effective care regimens? Would you pay more for better? Would you regard measures of outcomes affected by patient behavior, like glycemic or cholesterol control, to be better no matter how achieved? Positive answers to all of these questions would support strong appropriate incentives to physicians to assure patient adherence. That would still leave unanswered which physician incentives work best. Pay for more time counseling patients? Financial rewards like positive payments or lottery winnings? Peer pressure and contests (among

[39] Choudhry, N. K., Avorn, J., Glynn, R. J., Antman, E. M., Schneeweiss, S., Toscano, M., . . . & Shrank, W. H. (2011). Full coverage for preventive medications after myocardial infarction. *New England Journal of Medicine*, *365*(22), 2088–2097.

[40] Dusetzina, S. B., Huskamp, H. A., Rothman, R. L., Pinheiro, L. C., Roberts, A. W., Shah, N. D., . . . & Keating, N. L. (2022). Many Medicare beneficiaries do not fill high-price specialty drug prescriptions. *Health Affairs*, *41*(4), 487–496.

[41] Linas, B. P., & Nolen, S. (2018). A guide to the economics of hepatitis C virus cure in 2017. *Infectious Disease Clinics*, *32*(2), 447–459.

patients and physicians)? Economists might be willing to go for cost-effective nudges despite an inherent preference for informed decision-making. The latter would involve the challenges of dealing with probabilities – a challenge perhaps more for physicians than poker-playing patients – as well as emphasis on communication, reminders for the forgetful or distracted, and other decision aids. It could pay off.

Cost-Effectiveness-Based Patient Dialog about Value

There are thousands of articles by and for physicians about how to improve patient adherence. They generally deal with the obvious: use language patients understand, inquire about their individual goals, pay attention to environmental and social factors that might inhibit drug taking, keep it as simple as possible, and so on. So far, I have not found any model that would use the economists' favorite cost-effectiveness formulation. We have written articles on how to explain this approach (especially the hard parts about saying no to effective but high-cost care) to policymakers and patient advocacy groups but do not suggest using it as a framework for counseling patients.[42] At the risk of getting out over my skis, I am going to try to offer some thoughts to physicians and patients. Here goes.

Let us begin with a slam dunk cost-effective treatment (like statins after a heart attack, back in the day when statins cost real money) and think of patients with no cost-sharing. Since a cost-effective treatment must be an effective treatment, let's start with effectiveness. The key fact here is that large-scale well-controlled trials show that statins will avoid future heart attacks and death for a significant fraction of patients who take them (compared to those who do not).[43] That is what ought to matter most to, and most needed to be impressed upon, each patient. The first idea is that you will live longer if you take this drug than if you ignore it – either by not taking it or by not bothering to fill this prescription.

Some (but not all) ordinary people have trouble understanding probabilities. People who did not major in math sometimes think a 1 in 200 chance of

[42] Pauly, M. V. (2013). *Health reform without side effects: Making markets work for individual health insurance*. Hoover Press.

[43] Schwartz, G. G., Olsson, A. G., Ezekowitz, M. D., Ganz, P., Oliver, M. F., Waters, D., . . . & Myocardial Ischemia Reduction with Aggressive Cholesterol Lowering (MIRACL) Study Investigators. (2001). Effects of atorvastatin on early recurrent ischemic events in acute coronary syndromes: The MIRACL study: A randomized controlled trial. *JAMA*, *285*(13), 1711–1718.

something bad happening is worse than a 1 in 100 chance, so information must be presented understandably. Economists and decision theorists have put a lot of work into trying to help. Rather than just present a probability (like 0.01 per year), you could say that, of 100 people with a heart attack, over 10 years, 20 will die if they do not take the drug while if they take it only 10 will die. This kind of talk will make people (who tend to think of death as an option) uncomfortable, but it is important.

Then you can talk about not just quantity of life but quality of life – whether there will be any side effects from the treatment, what the disease would do to quality of life if left untreated, and how analysis of QALYs based on average preferences works out. With no cost-sharing, there is no necessity to get into the dollar value of a QALY, but for some patients it still may be more persuasive if you can tell them that taking the drug (compared to not taking it) will return to them health benefits valued at thousands of dollars. In current practice physicians are strongly advised to probe patients' individual goals and values.[44] From an economic viewpoint, there is no harm in doing this because the values attached to both life years added and dollar values of QALYs added are averages. However, most people are, well, average, so it is important to say that these values are from "people like you," making whatever adjustments are needed.

If there is cost-sharing, we know that it may discourage adherence. The message from economics for a slam dunk cost-effective treatment is that *the benefits are worth more than the total cost* – so they are surely worth more than any fractional cost-sharing. The punchline is that cost-sharing should not matter to people for whom a treatment is cost-effective, even as it is supposed to discourage treatment (if a patient asks for a drug) for those for whom it is not cost-effective. The caveat is that this argument applies to a rational decision-making patient with complete information. Patients may not always behave in this manner, especially when overwhelmed with information during a vulnerable period in their lives.

Obviously, there will be ways to frame the cost-effectiveness argument for adherence that are better than what is represented here. Even a more subtle but persuasive approach may still not work well, but then nothing else does either. Your job as manager/advisor is to do the best you can when it comes to fostering adherence to cost-effective care. In the minority of cases where

[44] Seidman, J., Anderson, M., Masi, D., Atkins, M., & Japha, M. (2017). Measuring value based on what matters to patients: A new value assessment framework. *Health Affairs Forefront*, May 23. www.healthaffairs.org/content/forefront/measuring-value-based-matters-patients-new-value-assessment-framework.

Box 9.6 Evidence: Shortages of generic cancer drugs and payment policy

For several years, people being treated for cancer have been concerned that the hospitals and oncology practices that care for them have been unable to obtain highly effective but low-priced generic cancer chemotherapy drugs. A shortage is usually triggered by an unusual event, such as the shutdown of production at a major manufacturing facility because of deficiencies discovered by the US FDA – even if the plant is outside the US. Physicians, managers, and policymakers have failed to develop solutions to these problems, although there has been a wave of suggestions about what to do.

My own thinking on shortages was motivated by a National Academy of Medicine panel on shortages of vaccines on which I served several decades ago.[45] That panel, which has a sizeable economist contingent, concluded that the reason for then concerning vaccines shortage was that the price was too low – in the sense that it did not furnish enough of a profit margin for makers of vaccines to invest in preventive measures against accidents on the production line, failed external inspections, or inventories of doses. Eventually vaccine prices rose and there have been many fewer shortages.[46]

History repeats itself for generic cancer drugs. Economics suggests, as before, not only that prices are too low but why they have settled to levels insufficient to incentivize protection of supply – at the manufacturer, at the hospital, at the clinic – against unpredictable but common threats. I discuss the economics of market failure leading to shortages in Chapter 14 on prescription drugs markets. My guess is that when there are few or conspiratorial buyers, as in the history of nursing markets, this shortage is a predictable outcome of modern-day monopsony – and can best be dealt with by cutting buyer market power.

In particular, for these generic drugs largely obtained by hospitals or large clinics, the task of finding or negotiating prices and delivering supply has been contracted out to three large independent organizations called group purchasing organizations (GPOs). Those entities are large enough that they do not think they can buy any quantity they want at whatever is the current market price; instead, they negotiate the price and try to make it low – because their mission (and the source of their profits) is to purchase inputs for hospital care at low prices. Like classic monopsonists, they therefore push price below the competitive level, to a level so low that sellers are unwilling to sell more than they currently supply. If the monopsony was perfectly (if illegally) coordinated, it would foresee the potential harm and guard against it. But with several players, an unexpected event can occur that further reduces seller willingness to supply at that price. To avoid the adverse consequences of a shortage, the GPOs could increase the price (a lot), but they are unwilling to conspire to do so unless the pain of shortages is so bad that their erstwhile hospital customers force them or bribe them to do so.

[45] Committee on the Evaluation of Vaccine Purchase Financing in the United States. (2003). *Financing vaccines in the 21st century: Assuring access and availability*. National Academies Press.

[46] Ridley, D. B., Bei, X., & Liebman, E. B. (2016). No shot: US vaccine prices and shortages. *Health Affairs*, *35*(2), 235–241.

In a recent *New York Times* story on shortages, an oncologist said, "Every clinician I know would be thrilled to pay more money for a reliable supply of a quality drug."[47] Not that clinicians do pay (either the hospital or an insurer does), but he meant that the value of an increase in supply enough to offset shortages would be worth a higher price. However, GPOs (and hospital purchasing departments) with market power have bigger fish to fry. They notice that they would need to increase price even if no shortage happened, and they would have to pay the higher price not just for the bump in supply needed to curtail a shortage but for all the units they buy. In the face of this high marginal increment in spending, they might reasonably decide that the lost health benefits from an occasional shortage – not only to them but to patients, their insurers, and their doctors – might not be enough to cover that additional cost. So, they keep prices low and cross their fingers, only uncrossing them to point blame at drug firms, regulators, or insurers when things go wrong.

The textbook economic solution to the problem of underpricing under monopsony is to break up the monopsony – to have more than three GPOs so that they do not dominate in the market. In the *New York Times*' laundry list of solutions, this answer does not appear.[48] Instead, they float cost-increasing schemes like stockpiling, making medicines in the US, and regulation setting a price floor(!). The closest they come to addressing the real cause is discussion of a government- or hospital-run factory that presumably would sell straight to hospitals – rather than imagining that more capitalists searching to offer a reliable supply could do the trick.

Hospital and insurer managers should look to the economists' magic of larger numbers rather than to the *Times* for advice. Hospitals themselves were instrumental in organizing (or at least not resisting GPOs), so they may want to think about diverting business to new entrants, trading off a slight price increase for more assurance of supply. I have also suggested that both drug makers and distributors consider buying insurance that pays off when they get the bad news that there were no accidents and they will be stuck with buffer stocks of drugs about to become outdated.

a treatment is not cost-effective, here individual values may be more relevant, and more personalized discussion will be called for. Explaining to patients why effective but not cost-effective care is not for them is probably even more challenging than fostering adherence.

What Is a Manager to Do?

It will come as no surprise that there is as yet no value-based plan – for care, for reimbursement, or for insurance – that can be regarded as best, or that

[47] Jewett, C. (2023). "I'm scared to death": Behind the shortage keeping cancer patients from chemo. *New York Times*, December 19. www.nytimes.com/2023/12/19/health/cancer-drug-shortage.html.

[48] Jewett, C. (2023). Possible ways to ease drug shortages. *New York Times*, December 19. www.nytimes.com/2023/12/19/health/cancer-drugs-solutions.html.

can even be shown to be superior in some way to the FFS methods we all know and are supposed to disparage. How then is a manager, either of a health system or of an insurance plan, to choose? It may also come as no surprise that the best answer to this question right now – with no winners yet crowned – is to let the market choose – the competitive cure-all discussed earlier. The idea should by now be familiar: let different health systems and different insurance plans offer alternative versions of value-based alternatives, and then see which ones get the biggest market share. One virtue of this approach is that it brings consumers and patients – largely ignored in the technical design of value-based provider payment and the marketing enthusiasm – back into the decision. What managers should do is to watch which versions seem to sell best, whether they are anointed as best practices by experts.

Of course, people are both consumers of insurance (often chosen for them by their employer) and patients with insurance choosing care, so moral hazard puts a more expensive thumb on the scale in the latter case. However, whether we are thinking of Medicare enrollees choosing among Medicare Advantage plans with different value-based approaches or middle-class people with high-deductible health plans, the market equilibrium based on the value consumers perceive them to deliver is probably the best guide to true value (and one that will be read differently by different consumers with different preferences). There is a persuasive logic to value-based plans – the commonsense idea that they should pay more for volume or quality, whichever consumers value – but the implementation of market offerings based on this value will doubtless require much trial and error. Wise managers will observe market signals when they can be detected and avoid irrational exuberance for any specific design unless and until it meets a market test.

Conclusion

Why have value-based care and value-based pricing, the quintessential good-sounding idea, failed to generate robust evidence of effectiveness? Why have so many former advocates soured on the prospect of paying for care based on value rather than volume? One answer is that this idea was described in an incorrect but (usually) overly optimistic way. There has so far been no large-scale success in finding programs that change behavior in such a way that health improves and costs fall. Out of CMS's 55 demonstration projects, 50 have failed to meet their target outcomes. There have been some small-scale examples of success, but they have involved low cost and modest benefits. The value-based idea was oversold by people who should have known better. They should have known that there might not be enough targetable waste in the American healthcare system to produce large spending reductions with no adverse side effects.

A more promising conceptual approach, I think, would be one based on cost-effectiveness as a measure of inefficiency and poor insurance design as a source. This approach may even endorse programs that reduce cost but also reduce health benefits, but by a smaller amount. So far, value-based care has not adopted the cost-effectiveness trade-off-based framework. Until it does it will remain more a slogan than a fact.

Managers should be aware of the stubborn inability of the American health system to offer up widescale opportunities for net benefit from new methods of provider payment and/or outcome measurement. Someday someone will probably come up with ideas that work, and managers should be attentive to this possibility. At present, however, economics does not offer strong conceptual or empirical support for the commonly used concepts behind managerial discussions of value-based care. There is an alternative and more substantive approach based on cost-effectiveness that can be developed and used. The commonsense ideas in that approach are going to be more helpful than using labels and invoking slogans that need refinement if they are to be at all helpful. Progress is possible.

10 Pricing That Violates Economic Law

How to Learn to Love Price Discrimination

One of the core conclusions of economic theory is that in perfectly competitive markets, the Law of One Price should hold. This law says that, in competitive equilibrium, all buyers should and will pay the same unit price for a given product – no matter who the buyers are or how much they need the product, how much they buy, or how smart they are – and no matter who the seller is. The quintessential example of such a market is a commodity exchange: you pay the same for a bushel of Chicago soft red winter wheat, no matter who you are or who you buy it from; there is a single market price.

Medical markets don't always work this way. Different buyers do pay different prices for the same medical good or service. When the law is thus violated, we can immediately conclude that the market is not competitive. In particular, the prices of hospital care, physician services, and prescription drugs often vary depending on whether they are paid by different kinds of insurance or out of pocket. For example, insurance plans with large numbers of members are often able to pay lower prices to hospitals for a given diagnosis and admission than would be billed to someone without insurance, and Medicaid plans will pay even less. Or the prices paid in the US for a branded prescription drug (by any buyer) will often be higher than the price paid for the identical drug in other developed countries in Europe or Asia. Finally, the price charged for a standardized medical treatment, such as MRI of the back, will often be different even within the same city at different hospitals and freestanding sites.

If the same thing is sold at different prices in the same market, buyers presumably should prefer to pay the lowest price at which a transaction could occur and are irritated if they cannot. If they all could get access to the lowest price, average prices would also fall, and the amount of effective care use would increase. So, it looks like something is wrong when the law does not hold. I will show you that economists, surprisingly, do not agree that this is always the case, but there is no doubt that price variation ticks some people off and makes everybody nervous.

As a manager, you will often have to preside over this complicated scene, and perhaps determine what your organization's prices are to be, whether to accept a low-priced offer, and whether to leave some other buyers with the short end of the stick paying higher prices. You may also be called upon to explain what you do or would do – why do you charge more to private insurers than you are paid by Medicare? Why do you charge more to the same private insurer for its insureds under 65 than for its Medicare Advantage enrollees? How can you get away with that? If you are a drug company, would you lower your US price if foreigners paid more? And if you do charge different prices, can you keep those who are paying more from complaining about those who are paying less, or even trying to find ways to join them (like buying drugs in Canada)?

Why is medical care peculiar in this way? Here are some theoretical musings that may explain the obvious. If a medical firm has market power, and we think many medical care and drug firms do, their firm-level demand curve usually slopes downward: If price is low rather than high, a firm expects to have more buyers. However, the new arrivals must have been different from those originally willing to pay more. The only challenge then is to tell who is who. Economics tells us tautologically that those original buyers attached more value to the product than the buyers who required a lower price to entice them.

Monopolists in ordinary goods usually cannot do much with this information. For one thing, they cannot tell which buyers have higher values; the seller of nails has no idea what buyer will use the product to fasten a board or save a kingdom. For another thing, if they charge some buyers less, other buyers will deputize those lucky customers to buy more than they need and resell back. However, medical care buyers who get more benefit from a treatment because they are sicker can often be identified in advance, and because care is a personal service, it cannot be bought by a surrogate or resold. The punchline therefore is that medical price discrimination by sellers with market power is a possibility, the more so if needy buyers can be identified (e.g., by their regular doctors) or if the medical treatment cannot be resold (e.g., a heart transplant versus a bottle of pills). So, what happens? And should you as a manager try to get in on the action?

As usual, economics provides a complicated story to explain this situation, and as usual what economics predicts about what will happen (or what you should do) if things change clashes with what many commonsense people think. Here is an example, drawn from recent discussion.[1] You run

[1] Mulligan, C. B. (2022). The value of pharmacy benefit management. National Bureau of Economic Research Working Paper No. w30231.

a pharmaceutical company that makes and sells a given technologically advanced synthetic insulin in the US. You set a list price that you would ordinarily charge to people who paid entirely out of pocket in a pharmacy, but you also sell to specialized drug-buying plans called pharmaceutical benefit managers (PBMs) as well as to state-run public Medicaid plans. Everybody wants a bargain, but some are better at getting one than others. The PBMs ask for discounts in return for their willingness to buy allegedly larger volumes of your brand (than if you do not give discounts). Medicaid plans tell you how much they will pay and dare you to refuse to provide drugs to poor people. The minority who does not have private insurance that covers the drugs will try to find discount cards or buying clubs to get them a special low price but end up paying close to the list price.

Any one of these deals needs an economic explanation, but let us start with how the profit-maximizing seller of a branded drug would set list price (for list price payers). Suppose there are no generic producers of your type of diabetes drug, and you have FDA approval, so you have some power to set price and still sell the product; competitors to drive your product out of the market do not exist, and some patients need your product to manage their diabetes (while some others could alternatively use diet and lifestyle, or other cheaper forms of insulin, to hold down their need). All of this variation leads to a situation where you face a demand curve; you can sell more at lower prices than at higher prices. You can charge what the market will bear. However, you are constrained if the market will not bear very high prices and still buy large quantities.

We now think of the usual economic model – you ask yourself, at any list price you might think of charging (and associated total revenue), what your revenue would be if you charged a little less. If you would collect more revenue from a larger sales volume by doing so, you compare that marginal revenue with your marginal cost of supplying more product; if it is greater, you cut your list price until doing so no longer brings in enough additional revenue. (If you had found that cutting your price lowered total revenue, you would raise the price until that no longer was true.)[2]

What about the PBM market? As noted, PBMs bargain by dangling the prospect of larger volume gains from price cuts (and more punishment for price increases) than individual consumers can credibly do, so you agree on discounts from list price for them, agreeing to larger discounts for the ones

[2] Pauly, M., Comanor, W., & Frech, H. E. (2023). Drug pricing in the United States: Theory and evidence. *Health Management, Policy and Innovation (HMPI.org)*, *8*(1), special issue.

that control more of your potential customers and are more willing to pull them away unless you cave a little more. For Medicaid you either take or leave their offer, but you probably take it as long as it is above your marginal cost so you do not lose money.

The discount story is simple economics: Because PBM demand is more price-responsive, its marginal revenue will be higher at any given price, so you will cut its price further – as long as marginal cost is the same for all buyers. You charge more for list price–paying buyers because you can; you charge less to people covered by PBMs because you must. The marker for price discrimination is variation in demand elasticity – if it varies across buyers (as it might) or across volume per buyer (as it must), firms can increase profit if they can engage in it.

There is much more that could be said about these situations because they involve bargaining, but there is not much more that can be said about bargaining unless you can measure the elusive concept of bargaining strength – you know it when you see it, but you cannot do much about it with economics; maybe psychology will help.

Cost-Shifting Is Impossible

Let us return to the insulin example and let us suppose that PBMs are able to extract bigger discounts from you the seller than used to be the case. Will you respond by raising your list price for insulin (say) to make up for the lost revenue from negotiating discounts with PBMs? Many people think the answer is yes, a nefarious monopolist forced to give price concessions (by a PBM or by Medicaid and now Medicare) will just turn around and charge the rest of us more. Here is a view from a health policy think tank: "PBMs incentivize drug manufacturers to offer competitively high rebates so their specific products are included on formularies and given preferential placement. Hence competition among manufacturers for top tier allocations of their products have driven ever higher rebates, which naturally lead to higher list prices."[3] There is actually a lot going on in this quotation, but for the moment, focus on the assertion that higher rebates will naturally lead to higher list prices. Economics is highly skeptical of such claims of cost-shifting. Did that sound like common sense to you? Perhaps it did; after all,

[3] O'Neill Hayes, T., & Farmer, J. (2020). Insulin cost and pricing trends. American Action Forum. www.americanactionforum.org/research/insulin-cost-and-pricing-trends/.

you as the drug firm manager strong-armed into giving higher rebates from the current list price to a big PBM would want to cover yourself by raising the list price to offset the lost revenue. However, if we go back to the story about how you set that list price in the first place, you might get cold feet. In fact, you would shoot yourself in the (cold) foot if you raised the list price from its original profit-maximizing level because that would lose business from the list price–paying customers to such an extent that there would be less profit from that market.

Having the price change in the rebate market, in other words, should usually not change anything (either marginal revenue or marginal cost) in the list price–paying market, so it should not change the profit-maximizing price in that market. It would be natural to charge a higher price only if it is natural to settle for lower profits, either at the initial price or at the new higher price. Put more dogmatically: Cost-shifting to another market or set of customers will not occur among profit-maximizing firms if they were originally charging the profit-maximizing price in that market. Put more realistically, if you did raise your list price, you would not expect to see many such customers; you would be abandoning this part of the market.

What is the rest of the story? The quote is not clear on what prompted the empirical observation – it was the claim that PBM discounts for the same product offered by a drug firm are higher in recent periods than in previous periods. It hints at a reason – (more) "competition among manufacturers" – but does not explain why a previously less competitive setting in which you the drug maker could get away with a small discount to be on the top tier has changed. One possible reason that would rescue the conclusion but not the argument – though requiring a tortured set of suppositions – would be one in which more potential customers for the drug were signed up by PBMs *and* those customers were more price-sensitive than those that remained paying list price. That would change the marginal revenue in the list price market and lead to a higher price, but we (and the author of the statement) have no idea whether this is true or not.

An even more important part of the story is what seems to be a technical detail: Is the "discount" the PBM gets measured as a dollar amount regardless of the list price or as a percentage of the list price? For example, if the drug list price is $100, is the discount 20% or $20? Seems the same, right, and PBMs should be rewarded by insurance buyers for the dollar size of their discount, since the net discounted price is what buyers pay. A $20 discount costs the drug firm $20, no matter the list price. However, the drug seller could raise its list price to $125, offer a 20% discount to the PBM, and still collect $100 from sales to PBM customers. Not only that, but the PBM could tell its customers that it saved them \$25. What is clear, however, is that PBM customers are no better off in terms of what they end up paying. But so what? If this fiscal sleight of hand benefits the PBM, then what about the drug company? If \$100 was the profit-maximizing price in the list price–paying market, it will sell less in that market at \$125 and make less profit. Depending on the relative sizes of the two markets, the drug firm might have preferred even to offer a \$25 "cash" discount and keep its list price at \$100.

What about Hospitals?

Hospitals also charge or are paid different prices by different payers. They have a very high list price for uninsured users who are wealthy, but almost no one is in that situation. (Does Elon Musk have health insurance?) Hospitals generally accept whatever Medicare or Medicaid offers. They negotiate with private insurers with the reward for a lower price being inclusion in the insurer's network (or the avoidance of being excluded from the network). The prices paid by such insurers vary across insurers but still are almost always much larger than what the government pays.[4]

Now suppose one of the public insurers lowers what it pays in total for its insureds by some amount \$R. How would we expect the hospital to respond? If the hospital is not able or willing to walk away from the government business, it has two choices: (1) raise the price to private payers to recoup some or all of the lost profit (or increased losses) from public payers or (2) accept that profit will be lost or losses grow as long as it can still stay open. The general view of industry managers is that choice (1) is preferable – you should cost-shift even more to private payers.

This is the cost-shifting story applied to hospitals, and the economic dissent is the same as in the PBM drug case. If the hospital had already set the profit-maximizing private price, the choice of raising price to recover profit will already have been foreclosed. If the hospital is for-profit or if, even though it is nonprofit, it was already charging the price the "traffic will bear" in the private sector, it will lose by cost-shifting. If either of these cases hold, such cost-shifting via price increases will be self-defeating since it would reduce private business profit, hardly a sensible solution to reduced public

[4] Morrisey, M. A. (1994). *Cost shifting in health care: Separating evidence from rhetoric*. American Enterprise Institute.

business profit. Only if the initial price had been set below the profit-maximizing level (say, because the hospital was for public relations or altruistic reasons trying to make its care affordable to its patient community and their insurers) could there be leeway to make more profit by increasing price. If the hospital was run for the benefit of physicians, as we argued earlier, those physicians would veto any attempt by the hospital to raise its price because that would mean they would have to cut their fees for services provided to hospitalized patients. Of course, if the Medicare or Medicaid price cuts were so drastic as to drive some hospitals out of business, that might reduce the number of hospitals in the market and allow private prices to be increased because of greater market power among the survivors.

What evidence do we have on what has happened in the past? What we find is at most a tenuous connection between levels and (especially) changes in public payments and the levels or changes in net private prices. Decades ago, studies did find that Medicaid cuts in particular were associated with increases in hospital list prices for nonprofit hospitals, but this relationship has since disappeared.[5] Such a finding would be consistent with a gradual increase in list price by financially stressed hospitals of all ownership types up to the profit-maximizing level.

What then are managers to do if government continues to cut or constrain the prices it pays to hospitals? For private insurance managers, their main task, paradoxically, would seem to be to instruct hospital managers in the principle of profit-maximizing prices and so avoid attempts to raise prices – or, more realistically, to convince managers that, whatever the excuse, their buyers would not be willing to pay higher prices and still direct the same volume of business a hospital's way. Hospital managers are already acutely conscious of their inability to increase prices (however much power they had to get them to current levels). Nothing good can come to hospitals from lower public reimbursement levels; private insurers might or might not care.

Price Discrimination

What determines the extent to which some buyers pay higher prices than others and some sellers pay lower prices than others? For the first question, the answer (as to so many questions in economics) is "demand elasticity." In

[5] Frakt, A. B. (2011). How much do hospitals cost shift? A review of the evidence. *Milbank Quarterly*, *89* (1), 90–130. https://doi.org/10.1111/j.1468-0009.2011.00621.x.

plain English, a seller can charge you or a group of potential customers like you a higher price if you have little capability to respond by reducing what you buy from that seller. Fortunately for some buyers, this proposition reverses: If you are covered by an insurer that can move large batches of compliant insureds from one seller to another, your insurer is going to be able to extract a lower price and, if you are lucky, charge you a lower premium. Among other things that contribute to low demand elasticity is buyer ignorance, especially about the prices charged by other sellers: If you do not know there is a better deal, you may stick with the devil you know when a drug firm, a physician practice, or a hospital raises its prices. However, if you are insured your insurer will almost surely know what prices are being charged where, so this case should be uncommon. The other determinant special to healthcare is the situation in which you find yourself – are you at one seller, in pain, with no knowledge or ability to move to others? Then you may be stuck with a high price unless your insurer rides to your rescue.

This phenomenon sometimes results in "surprise medical bills" that usually arise in a hospital emergency situation when the hospital and its doctors do not tell you upfront what treatment is going to cost – even if you were able to negotiate, which you probably are not. This is presumably the situation when demand elasticity is low; the buyer is stuck. Congress recently passed laws forbidding such behavior, though the laws leave open to arbitration the question of how much the doctor will get, especially among providers with whom your insurance has not made a previous contract.

You could, a know-it-all critic might tell you, have avoided this awkward situation by making sure before an emergency hits that you have an insurance that will cover everything everywhere you might go, but that is asking a lot of consumers who want to have a life doing other things than reading the fine print in health insurance contracts. It is probably impossible to squeeze out every bit of "caveat emptor" in insured healthcare settings. Ideally, managers of insurers and contracted providers should be on the side of consumers, trying to make prices and policies transparent and avoiding the temptation to pull a fast one every now and then to make more money. But you as a manager have to cover your costs, including what doctors want to charge for coming in for a late-night emergency, so resolving to do the right thing sometimes is challenging. If consumers are willing to pay enough to insurers and providers, they can buy reassurance that nothing will ever go wrong financially speaking, but that may come at too high a price for many.

You do not want to be the manager of a health system that surprises customers with large bills, even if the bills come from doctors who are not employed by you but are contracted to staff the emergency room or the pathology lab. But sometimes you may have little choice – if other physicians who charge less are not available in your town and you have to have somebody, anybody, in the emergency room late on a Saturday evening. You could ask yourself – if your health system guaranteed no surprise bills, would that increase the number of patients you would attract? Probably not directly, since patients do not think this will happen to them. You might be a more attractive partner for a better paying insurer, however, and that opportunity (or the lack of it) would seem to be the key to understanding when this abhorrent behavior might arise out of necessity. "Be careful" is the all-purpose economic advice.

Price Discrimination for Good or Evil

There are two kinds of violations of the Law of One Price in what we just discussed. The one is where a services seller (hospital) with market power can increase its profits by charging different prices to different customers compared to the "simple" uniform monopoly price in your economics textbook. The other is where an insurance company (buyer) with market power pays the hospital seller less than the simple monopoly price charged to customers of other insurers and reduces the seller's profits. Hospitals may argue with United or Blue Cross but not with Medicare. Both sellers and buyers can engineer price discrimination. Either way, some pay more than others, but sometimes some sellers gain (and buyers lose) and sometimes it is just the reverse. Should someone enforce the Law of One Price?

The answer to who gains (how much) and who loses (how much) in economics obviously affects winners and losers, but the economic analysis also has some unexpected conclusions about efficiency and desirability.

The Bad Side of Price Discrimination

Price discrimination can improve economic efficiency for reasons indicated in Box 10.1, and so I am biased to say nice but surprisingly favorable things about it. However, before that, let us give the other side its due and recount possible harms. In simple medical monopoly, almost all of those consumers willing to buy the service at the monopoly price at least get some net benefit

Box 10.1 Theory: How price discrimination can make some people happy and no one sad

Here I use a picture to show how price discrimination can be a good thing. Suppose we have a standard story in which a firm has market power over the price of an effective treatment, and suppose different potential patients who attach different values to the benefit from that treatment (say, based on illness severity or income) each demand one or zero treatments. The shape of this demand curve then depends on the distribution of these values. The firm follows the usual rule for profit maximization and sets a price of P*, selling to Q* of the potential patients. They get the consumer surplus indicated by the shaded triangle since all of them except the last to buy gets more benefit than they have to pay. See Figure 10.1.

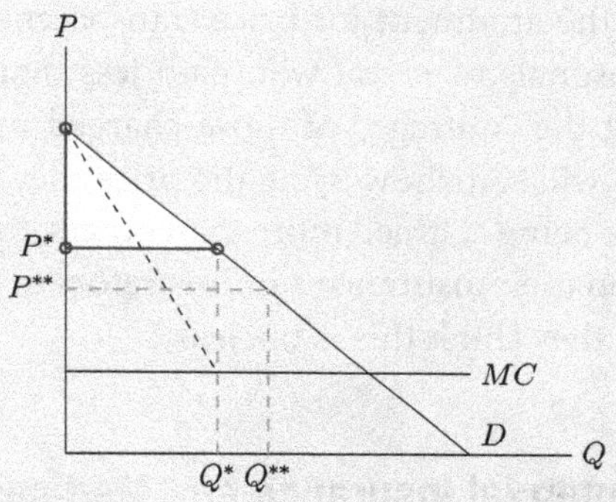

Figure 10.1 Price discrimination.

Now suppose the seller can identify these happy buyers, put them aside, and offer the treatment to the rest of the potential patients at the lower price P**, and more people buy up to Q**. You doubtless have figured out where this is headed: These additional Q**–Q* people are now better off than when they did not get the treatment. The seller is better off because the revenue from this additional sale, P**(Q**–Q*) is greater than cost. Everyone should be pleased – but the original buyers might become envious, wondering why they have to pay a higher price than the latecomers. These malcontents would also note that the seller increased its profit by this gambit. Economists would tell them this new arrangement is more efficient, even if it isn't quite fair. This explanation might not work to keep the peace. It would be even more efficient, but less profitable for the firm, if it cut its price for new customers all the way down to the marginal cost, but such a step would still not change the price or the mood of the high-value buyers.

from it, in the sense that those high up on the demand curve would have been willing to pay more than what they are charged. Of course, those with lower values who are priced out get no benefit from the existence of a good they cannot afford – but at least some people do gain the consumer surplus.

Now suppose the seller can tell which buyers have high and which low values and exactly tailor the price to each person. At a minimum, this new policy will worsen the well-being of those who would have been purchasers without price discrimination but now must pay more; they will be upset if they knew what the simple nondiscriminating monopoly price would have been.

This frustration of those who collected the consumer surplus under uniform pricing has spilled over into regulations and other governmental actions to make price discrimination more difficult. The Robinson–Patman Act makes some price discrimination in selling products (like drugs or devices) a violation of antitrust law, but not services like hospital care or physicians' services. Much of the argument for price transparency for hospital prices – which forces hospitals to reveal who paid less than who – is motivated by the thought that the "outrage" of those charged more (especially self-insuring employers) will somehow bring the price they pay down. Somehow, by knowing they are being charged more than others, they can put pressure on local hospitals or on their insurance administrators to get a lower price from the hospital. (Why they think this is unclear.)

Hospital Price Discrimination: Commercial Insurance and Medicaid

Medicare and Medicaid pay hospitals prices they unilaterally announce, often based on federal or state legislation. Those prices may not be enough to cover the cost of treating their insured patients (if hospitals or some other experts really knew what the cost is) for the average hospital, but many hospitals believe that they lose money (relative to what they think is their marginal or variable cost) on publicly insured patients. Medicaid pays about the same as Medicare, or a little less; a hospital with a patient population nearly all on Medicaid and Medicare would have a difficult time breaking even – at a minimum it would have to hold its costs down below average to survive.

In contrast, commercial insurers pay a multiple of what Medicare and Medicaid pay. The percentage of Medicare payments (on average) paid by commercial insurers is now thought to be about 250%–270%,[6] up from

[6] Bai, G., & Anderson, G. F. (2018). Market power: Price variation among commercial insurers for hospital services. *Health Affairs*, *37*(10), 1615–1622; Kerber, R., Briscombe, B., Kofner, A., Whaley, C. M., & O'Neill, B. (2020). *Nationwide evaluation of health care prices paid by private health plans: Findings from round 3 of an employer-led transparency initiative*. RAND Research Report.

around 140% in the 1990s.[7] It appears that this multiplier has grown by about 5% per year over the last 25 years, though at a somewhat lower rate post 2012.[8] The current ratios are thought to be approaching 300% on average.[9] This price discrimination is not chosen by hospitals to maximize profits (by offering low prices to public insurers in order to attract business); the public price is imposed on them and they are reluctant to refuse to take patients covered by it.

What are the market-level consequences of this arrangement, and how should managers view it? To answer that question, we need evidence currently lacking. We do not have a good model of how commercial reimbursements get determined, nor why they are increasing over time. I will concentrate on the latter phenomenon since it seems most salient. I assume that hospitals set their commercial or private pay price year by year to maximize profits. That implies in turn that any increase must be triggered by a change in one or more of the factors that determines the price. The two candidates in the literature are market power and demand shift.[10] The market power argument is obvious: If competition among hospitals for commercial patients falls in a market, in theory and in practice prices increase because firm-level demand curves become less elastic (see Chapter 12). The problem is that, for market power to account for rising prices, it must increase over time. Concentration has increased across the US, though unevenly, but current estimates of the impact of changes in concentration on market prices are much too low to account for the size of the increase in commercial prices. Kaplan and O'Neill also cite buyer information imperfection as a cause of rising hospital prices, but offer no evidence

[7] Physician Payment Review Commission. (1996). *Annual report to Congress.*

[8] Selden, T. M. (2020). Differences between public and private hospital payment rates narrowed, 2012–16: A data analysis comparing payment rate differences between private insurance and Medicare for inpatient hospital stays, emergency department visits, and outpatient hospital care. *Health Affairs, 39* (1), 94–99.

[9] White, C., & Whaley, C. M. (2021). Prices paid to hospitals by private health plans are high relative to Medicare and vary widely: Findings from an employer-led transparency initiative. *Rand Health Quarterly, 9*(2), 5.

[10] White, C., Reschovsky, J. D., & Bond, A. M. (2019). Understanding differences between high- and low-price hospitals: Implications for efforts to rein in costs. *Health Affairs, 33*(2). https://doi.org/10.1377/hlthaff.2013.0747; Garthwaite, C., Ody, C., & Starc, A. (2022). Endogenous quality investments in the U.S. hospital markets. *Journal of Health Economics, 84*(7), 102636. https://doi.org/10.1016/j.jhealeco.2022.102636; Levinson, Z., Qureshi, N., Liu, J. L, & Whaley, C. (2022). Trends in hospital prices paid by private health plans varied substantially across the US. *Health Affairs, 41*(4), 516–522. https://doi.org/10.1377/hlthaff.2021.01476; White, C., & Whaley, C. M. (2021). Prices paid to hospitals by private health plans are high relative to Medicare and vary widely. *Rand Health Quarterly,* 9(2); Congressional Budget Office. (2022). *The prices that commercial health insurers and Medicare pay for hospitals' and physicians' services.* Congressional Budget Office. www.cbo.gov/publication/57422.

that this has increased over time.[11] The other explanation is that, because of rising incomes and insurance coverage, or just stronger buyer preferences, hospitals face increased demand for aspects of quality that consumers value, such as amenities, shorter wait times, and better demonstrated health outcomes – all the things that various hospital rating systems, including Medicare, compare and measure. Hospitals respond to this increased demand (and willingness to pay) by incurring costs to improve these aspects of quality – but they do so in most cases for all patients, not just for the commercially insured. We have evidence that this demand shift has occurred but no proof of its magnitude, nor an explanation of why some are charged for higher quality but not others. Note that this phenomenon can be interpreted either as hospital managers increasing some aspects of quality to lure commercially insured patients or as those patients demanding that hospitals do what will please them enough to cover its cost.

To the extent that price discrimination has increased because of seller market power increasing, economists would be concerned. However, if commercial prices increased to support improved quality, that would be regarded as a gain both for the commercially insured and for the publicly insured patients who share the same hospital.

For some critics, that is not enough.[12] The mix of payers varies across hospitals, with some hospitals having large commercial shares and others small ones relative to Medicaid and Medicare. That means that improved quality will be distributed unevenly across hospitals – it will be higher in ones with more commercially insured patients (who are usually middle-income white individuals) and lower or nonexistent in hospitals with many Medicaid patients (who are all poor and disproportionately – though not majority – nonwhite). There will be an increase in disparities, not a good thing.

But whose fault is it, and what can be done about it? The obvious economic answer is that this uneven distribution of quality across hospitals happens because Medicaid pays poorly relative to commercial payments and has not kept up with increases in those payments. If the reason for the increase is higher willingness to pay for quality by middle-class privately insured people, the issue is why there has not been a similar increase in willingness to pay for these dimensions of quality by Medicaid and the administrators and taxpayers who deal with Medicaid.

[11] Kaplan, A., & O'Neill, D. (2020). Hospital price discrimination is deepening racial health inequity. *NEJM Catalyst Innovations in Care Delivery*, *1*(6). https://doi.org/10.1056/CAT.20.0593.

[12] Kaplan, A., & O'Neill, D. (2020). Hospital price discrimination is deepening racial health inequity. *NEJM Catalyst Innovations in Care Delivery*, *1*(6). https://doi.org/10.1056/CAT.20.0593.

That conclusion is not the one at which Kaplan and O'Neill arrive. They are similarly concerned about the uneven distribution of quality but propose to alter it by limiting the price commercial insurance can pay. This seems unequivocally inferior (as well as ethically suspect) because it will make commercial customers worse off and leave Medicaid-funded patrons of lower-quality hospitals no better off. Moreover, limiting the prices charged to commercial insurers will lead to lower premiums and higher disposable incomes for their middle-class customers, thus trading one disparity for another. Kaplan and O'Neill dismiss the possibility of much higher Medicaid payment by an assertion that it is "unrealistic and unwise" – but ultimately taxpayers can, if they think the benefit to people on Medicaid from the kinds of quality middle-class white people get is worth their cost, pay enough for Medicaid beneficiaries to be supplied.

There will still be some remaining inequality: Those people on Medicaid who use hospitals with high commercial shares will be better off than those who use hospitals with smaller shares, a phenomenon largely determined by location. The key point, however, is that there is no reason in ethics or economics to prevent hospitals from supplying higher quality to middle-class commercially insured patients as long as doing so is cost-effective – which it should be since those patients pay the full cost but share the benefits. It seems implausible that the tax subsidy to private group insurance is intended to correct the levels of hospital quality, if that subsidy has any welfare rationale.

For managers, this discussion implies that some reasons for higher prices in some hospitals to commercially insured plans have a grounding in consumer choice and willingness to pay, given the uneven distribution of income. Of course, this rationale does not apply to higher prices extracted with yet higher market power or to the deeper question of the need to correct the prevailing uneven distribution of income.

The Good Side of Price Discrimination (in Theory)

From the ivory tower economic theory viewpoint, the good thing about price discrimination compared to simple monopoly is that it can lead to an outcome in which more of the good is sold. Remember that, to economists, the harm from market power is that price in excess of marginal cost means that some consumers who would have been willing to pay more than marginal cost for the good will not get it. Price discrimination cures this flaw when the seller can charge those customers prices closer to marginal cost while still overcharging others. The buyers who get the special discounts – for them only – are made better off than if discounts were nonexistent or illegal.

One example in healthcare – whose heart is in the right place but which has been debated – is the idea suggested by the oncologist (and amateur economist) Peter Bach: that a drug which can treat a variety of different types of cancers might be sold at different prices depending on the indication – if the benefit from the drug is higher for some tumor types than others.[13] Compared to a uniform high price at which a drug would be cost-effective only for one indication, allowing a lower price for another indication might make it cost-effective for that illness as well.

Some economists chastised Dr. Bach for failing to notice that removing any restrictions might lead to higher prices (than initially) for some indications even if they fell for others.[14] They did not mention, however, that even those paying the higher prices would still get to use the treatment – so the overall pattern would be one that leads to more cures. Maybe Dr. Bach is on the right side of the story after all.

A slightly more tattered example deals with the drug Avastin, initially marketed as a treatment for cancer because it reduced the blood supply to tumors. It turns out that this effect also benefits those with retinal bleeding – and so a slightly reformulated version of the same molecule was approved as Lucentis for advanced macular degeneration of the eye and priced at a much higher price per ounce of material. This kind of "gouging" was roundly criticized, and some ophthalmologists turned to buying Avastin and cutting it into smaller doses themselves (a classic way to avoid price discrimination), seeking praise for their actions.

There is a third example of price discrimination for prescription drugs which I will discuss more extensively in Chapter 10, because it is important. The idea here is that an insurer will note that among its population of insureds, a branded drug could benefit many of them – but if it were to be offered at the simple monopoly price it would not be cost-effective to buy it for those with positive but smaller benefits. However, if the marginal cost of the drug were virtually zero, the insurer could offer to buy enough of the drug to treat everyone who could benefit at a total revenue offer to the drug company that would exceed the revenue it would have collected if it charged the monopoly unit price. This deal would make the drug company happy

[13] Bach, P. B. (2014). Indication-specific pricing for cancer drugs. *JAMA*, *312*(16), 1629–1630.

[14] Chandra, A., & Garthwaite, C. (2017). The economics of indication-based drug pricing. *New England Journal of Medicine*, *377*(2), 103–106.

(since it would get more revenue at almost no additional cost), and it would benefit all the insureds who would now have access to an effective drug to a much greater extent.

There is a paradox here. The issue is that price discrimination is more efficient at getting effective treatments to all those who can benefit from them but if uncontrolled can lead in theory to an outcome in which the seller makes much higher profits than without discrimination. Each buyer might be only slightly better off than without the treatment. The holder of the patent collects all the net benefit from the invention – unfair to consumers. An ideal government could just tax away this increased profit and shower the proceeds on patients however it sees fit – but that seems to me to go one step too far toward fables.

What This Means for Managers

It is important for managers to know that price discrimination can be a good thing or something that improves welfare (especially if your job involves doing it), and it is important for policymakers to know there can be virtue in charging more to those most in need of a treatment.

There are thus not one but two different efficient market outcomes for medical goods and services. The obvious one is the competitive equilibrium where everyone who uses the product pays the same competitive prices just equal to marginal cost. The other one is a perfect discriminating monopoly, where everyone pays the same price for the last unit bought but pays higher prices for the more valuable initial units. Both are efficient, but they have very different distributional outcomes. In competitive equilibrium (or something close to it), much of the gain from having the product exist goes to buyers; under price discrimination all the gains go to the seller.[15] Economists are not supposed to play favorites. What they can say, though, is that in dynamic settings where investing and bringing a product to market involves an upfront fixed cost, perfect price discrimination will ensure that everything that should be invented will be invented, while perfect competition may leave some good ideas unfunded. So might simple (nondiscriminating) monopoly. So, we end once more with a trade-off.

[15] Hult, K. J., & Philipson, T. J. (2023). The value of medical innovation versus industry rewards. *Value in Health*, *26*(3), 320–327.

Conclusion

When it comes to price discrimination, managers must grab both ends of the stick. If they manage hospitals or health systems, they are subject to discriminatory payments that insurers propose or impose on them, but they also have the power to set or negotiate different prices for the same thing to different buyers (including those without insurance coverage). If they are insurance managers, they can set the aforementioned discriminatory payments to providers of care, but they need to negotiate with buyers of insurance (especially employers) about what they will be paid as total premiums and what variations in premiums for variations in coverage are acceptable. Buying wheat on the Chicago commodities exchange is, by comparison, a piece of cake.

The main message for sellers of healthcare from the foregoing is probably not much of a surprise: You are going to have to bargain, from positions of more or less strength, so good luck. It is much the same story for insurers, although one message is that you need to be partially humble and not try to collect too much from risk pooling per se; the place where you have real leverage (if you have it at all) is not in market share but in assembling and dealing with provider networks. Large employers can do without you because they can self-insure, yet another reason for humility.

The most surprising message is for policymakers – in economics, price discrimination can be a good thing. It can allow some customers who can get benefit from medical services or drugs to be brought into the market by lower prices just for them, while profits to compensate investors and fund research can be maintained by charging higher prices to buyers who get greater value. Sometimes (though not always) the world can be a better place with price discrimination than if it is forbidden or criticized. But you need economists to help you know what you are doing.

11 Who Is the Buyer of Insured Medical Care?

Introduction

Less than 10% of spending on medical care in the US is made in the usual market way goods and services are bought and sold, in which a buyer hands over money to a seller and the seller hands over the good or provides the service. Instead, the other 90% is covered by a "third party" – an insurer. (There is also a small amount of care that is given away either as charity or as bad debt; that may result in cost, but it does not result in spending.) What is the market for this intervening influence and what do managers need to know about it?

Many medical providers (and policymakers), for obvious reasons, worry a great deal about how insurers will cover and pay for the services they finance; they anxiously ask, "what do insurers want?" Economists think this is the wrong question – our view is that insurers are only messengers carrying letters to providers from those who buy and pay for insurance. So, the right question is: What do buyers of insurance want? The all-purpose answer to that question is: whatever combination of premiums, coverage, and reimbursement that will maximize their utility. But what is that combination, and who decides on it? Who is the buyer who determines how coverage might change when things (like prices, innovations, and risk distributions) change? The answer to this question varies depending on the kind of health insurance Americans have. Insurance casts an important and sometimes dysfunctional veil over the deal between sellers and ultimate buyers, so in this chapter I will talk about who economists think are the players under that veil.

To begin with the obvious: There are different kinds of buyers of insurance in the US. In the private sector, most insurance is arranged as part of *worker compensation*, which covers 54.5% of the US population.[1] Only a small

[1] Census Bureau. (2022). *Health Insurance Coverage in the United States: 2022*. www.census.gov/content/dam/Census/library/publications/2023/demo/p60-281.pdf.

fraction, still less than 10%, is bought by individuals on or off Obamacare exchanges. Then Medicaid, jointly financed by federal and state government taxes, but controlled by each individual's state (subject to some federal rules), furnishes coverage to a growing fraction of low-income households and covers most children. Finally, Medicare, financed by a mix of payroll taxes, extra earmarked income taxes, general revenue taxation, and beneficiary premiums, covers benefits for almost all of the elderly and some of the disabled. There are some choices those with Medicare coverage can make, but many decisions are made by edicts handed down from legislators or government officials.

For the two publicly funded insurances, be forewarned. The operative choices here are collective choices made by taxpayers' representatives, some elected and some not, and there is no good economic theory of collective choice. There is no good theory from other disciplines either.

Pushing off this daunting task until later, I will start with the hopefully more feasible question of private or commercial insurance, which will turn out to be hard enough. The bottom line on all three types of insurance is that there is (or at least there should be) a connection between what those who pay for each type of insurance want and what benefits they get from that insurance, but that connection is complex and unpredictable. We will do the best we can here too.

Does Your Boss Give You Insurance?

In a word, no. Or, in a few more words, not any more than your boss gives you money wages. Economists view health insurance benefits (along with other work-related benefits like childcare, stock options, or free bus passes) as just different parts of the total compensation offered to attract and retain workers. How compensation is split between cash and "kind" is affected, we think, in part by income tax rules and in part by what is less costly and more convenient for workers, but all of these good things you get from working are paid by the same thing – your labor time and what it is worth. Virtually all economists (not just health economists) agree that, in general and in the long run, these parts of total compensation trade off against each other. Charles Phelps makes the definitive statement: "Modern economics tells us that workers really end up paying anyway in the form of lower wages."[2] So, the

2 Phelps, C. E. (2002). *Health Economics* (3rd ed.). Addison Wesley, p. 345.

punchline is that workers pay for their health benefits in the sense that they give up money wages they could have received; benefits are not financed as gifts from your employer out of what would have been profits. That means that, to an employer, benefits costs are different from costs of materials or electricity or other inputs; those costs should be minimized, but lower benefits costs (according to us economists) often mean higher money wages and, more importantly, different numbers and types of workers eager to be hired. Benefits are different.

Box 11.1 describes this wage-benefit trade-off in theory and in evidence in more depth and also flags some modest exceptions. This view of how things work for employment-based insurance will guide what I have to say next.

The proposition that there are trade-offs is valid in competitive labor markets but also (with a vengeance) when unions negotiate for workers. Unions tend to prefer packages heavier on benefits than cash, but their leaders are very aware that higher benefits will result in lower wage increases at settlement. Even professional salaries (for physicians, nurses, and managers) display these offsets.

Although workers pay close to 100% of their healthcare and their healthcare benefits, according to economists, those payments can flow through different channels. In most firms there are explicit worker health insurance premiums, deducted from your paycheck if you opt to take insurance as a benefit, and potentially dependent on which health plan you select if there are options. The explicit premium will also depend on whether you choose self-only or family coverage. Next, the bulk of premiums are "employer paid" out of wages (which means that workers never see them and cannot avoid wage cuts by refusing coverage), sometimes as a fixed dollar wage reduction per worker, sometimes as a percentage of money wages, sometimes arranged in baroque ways. On average, these contributions are about 80% of the total premium of the plan the worker selects, a little higher for self-only coverage and a little lower for family coverage.[3] Finally, in almost all plans, there is some patient cost-sharing in the form of deductibles, coinsurance, copayments, and other strange things that workers pay out of pocket.

One important corollary of the economic view is that it is impossible for employers to shift costs to workers. Increasing worker contributions (to cover the premium) just means you have to pay them more money. So does increasing worker cost-sharing. The bill always shows up at home – so the

[3] Kaiser Family Foundation. (2023). *Employer Health Benefits: 2023 Annual Survey*. https://files.kff.org/attachment/Employer-Health-Benefits-Survey-2023-Annual-Survey.pdf.

Box 11.1 Theory: How profit-maximizing employers deal with selection in group health insurance

The bulk of Americans who are not elderly and not poor get their health insurance as part of their compensation for working. As discussed at length in this chapter, employers who want to maximize profits by minimizing their total compensation costs should choose the health insurance they offer that will most please (be of most net value to) their workers. But for firms hiring workers in a local labor market, how to make this choice is an Excedrin headache problem – and it is a similarly painful problem for economists as well. One problem is that they need to know not only what their current workers want and what their risks are; they also need to know preferences and risks for workers they might attract.

Employers have to choose (at least) four things: (1) whether to offer one or several insurance plans; (2) which plan or plans to offer, differing by extent of coverage, managed care limits, and total premium or expected cost; (3) what money wages to pay; (4) what explicit worker premiums to charge for more generous and less generous plans.

Before you read on, note that, as discussed in Chapter 6 on adverse selection ("Dancing in the Dark"), the estimated theoretical welfare gains from adjusting premium differentials when more than one plan is offered appear to be very modest. Cutler and Reber estimate that the welfare of Harvard employees would increase by 2% of premiums if the best uniform policy were in place,[4] while Bundorf, Levin, and Mahoney find a 2.5% gain in their sample of small employers.[5] (In contrast, they find that breaking the regulation that requires uniform explicit premiums and instituting a smaller incremental premium for lower-risk workers – based on age and previous claims, both of which are potentially known – would yield as much as a 9% gain.) So, as I argue in the following paragraphs, the small gains from fiddling with premiums to deal with the adverse selection that so bothers economists may not be worth a benefit or insurance manager's time. If you want to push on, here goes.

This theoretical problem is incredibly tricky because what a given employer offers will influence how many workers in the local labor market pool will prefer to work for that firm (at what monetary wage) and because different workers in the local pool and probably in the firm's eventual workforce will have different demands for insurance and different risk levels for any given insurance. (The compensation in any one firm has to meet the labor market test; this constraint means that models of group insurance that consider the welfare only of workers currently employed may be neither accurate nor relevant.) We want a model in which, when the music stops, every worker is in the right firm with the right health insurance. But how can an employer, or much less an economist, figure out how to juggle so many different balls and make it end well? We can solve simple models that are unrealistic from the start, but so far, to my knowledge, no economist and no firm has developed a theory of how to do this correctly. (That does not mean that firms and workers and insurers might have

4 Cutler, D. M., & Reber, S. J. (1998). Paying for health insurance: The trade-off between competition and adverse selection. *The Quarterly Journal of Economics, 113*(2), 433–466.

5 Bundorf, M. K., Levin, J., & Mahoney, N. (2012). Pricing and welfare in health plan choice. *American Economic Review, 102*(7), 3214–3248.

muddled through by trial and error, but we just don't know how, and we want to be able to say more than "just see how it turns out.")

To start, assume that insurers sell coverage at premiums that must cover claims and insurer administrative cost ("the loading"). An individual of a given health risk and with a given preference averse to risk will, we know from the economic theory of insurance, then choose a policy with a deductible that will maximize the person's expected utility.[6] The higher the loading, the bigger the deductible. Surprisingly, we cannot say how the level of risk will affect the desired level of coverage since higher-risk buyers would want more coverage at a given premium but the premium for them will be higher – and the two usually offset.[7] If all workers in the labor market had the same risk and the same preferences, all firms would offer just one identical policy across firms, monetary wages per worker would be reduced by the premium for that policy, there would be no explicit worker premiums, and the labor market would be in equilibrium. Getting a little more daring – if workers were the same risk but had different preferences and there were many small firms, there could be an equilibrium in which they "vote with their feet" by sorting themselves across firms into homogeneous workforces in each firm, different firms offer different levels of coverage and different money wages, and workers who are more risk-averse work at firms offering more generous coverage.[8]

It is when there is variation in the labor pool in risk (as well as risk aversion) and when there are not enough different employers in the labor market for perfect segregation that things fall apart. The story starts to become unglued if employers cannot tell who is high-risk; we will get adverse selection. If employers (or the insurers they contract with) can tell who the high-risk individuals are, there might be an equilibrium in which all the high-risk buyers (of a given degree of risk aversion) are forced into homogeneous firms and paid lower money wages, but even this implausible pattern seems unstable. Things get even worse when (as is required by law) employers are not allowed to vary explicit premiums based on risk (even if they can and will vary the money wage with the risk level of all workers with the employer premium contribution).

We want to get to a happy ending in which theory explains what patterns of incremental premiums for more generous coverage set by employers in different firms will maximize profits – but so far, we cannot get there. We can be a little more concrete. Suppose a firm currently offers two plans and follows the "fixed contribution" strategy for setting the additional premium for the high-option plan – the premium is based on the observed differences in claims between those who chose the low option and those who chose the high option. That premium would thus largely reflect the differences in claims for high-risk buyers who are more likely to choose the high option. Inefficiency (compared to perfection) arises because that differential will discourage some more risk-averse lower-risk individuals from choosing the high option when they would have chosen it had the premium differential

[6] Arrow, K. (1963). Uncertainty and the welfare economics of medical care. *American Economic Review*, *55*(1–2), 154–158.

[7] Ehrlich, I., & Becker, G. S. (1972). Market insurance, self-insurance, and self-protection. *Journal of Political Economy*, *80*(4), 623–648.

[8] Goldstein, G. S., & Pauly, M. V. (1976). Group health insurance as a local public good. In R. N. Rosett (ed.), *The role of health insurance in the health services sector* (pp. 73–114). NBER.

only reflected their risk. So, suppose the employer decides to reduce the premium for the high option (as in the study at Harvard we reviewed in Chapter 6) and covers the cost of this subsidy by reducing money wages (which might or might not have happened at Harvard). Would this new compensation package – less salary but lower additional cost for a more generous health benefit – still attract the workers needed at a lower total compensation cost? If so, making the change would increase profits. Could (or when could) the fall in money wages for all workers be larger than the subsidy to premium for those who chose the high option? No one knows how to answer these questions.

One more thought. The previous discussion dealt with adverse selection within the workforce of a firm; a more important effect of group insurance may be to discourage adverse selection among workers across firms. Recall that, according to economists, the main downside of adverse selection is that it discourages insurance purchasing by lower-risk individuals as they try to avoid attracting high-risk ones and the higher average premiums that would make transfers to them. However, in the typical group insurance arrangement, any explicit worker premium is a small fraction of the total premium (about 20%), so even almost all low-risk individuals should regard buying group insurance rather than passing it up as preferred. In effect, any transfer to higher-risk buyers has already been captured in the compulsory wage reduction (if you are going to work for that firm) represented by the employer's premium share. We do not know whether that wage reduction is uniform across all workers or might be higher for some workers (older, higher wage), but regardless of its pattern, the effect of group insurance arrangements is to make taking insurance highly rational for low-risk workers.

boss might as well choose to spend your money on what you would prefer to buy in health benefits to keep you happy.

Not all managers of firms (or other normal people) agree with this economic viewpoint. Some managers think that benefits costs are like any other cost, and so high benefits costs mean they must charge higher prices to make money. Some political scientists are puzzled about why managers have not demonstrated against rising health benefits costs. The occasional journalistic headline that employers are increasingly forcing workers to bear more of the burden of health insurance (as explicit worker premiums or cost-sharing obligations sometimes rise at rapid rates) makes no economic sense in a competitive labor market, since any such increases will be offset by higher (or at least not falling) growth in money wages. Minimum wage laws that put a lower bound on money wages can foreclose the wage adjustment option; rather than causing unemployment, they may force overall premium increases into explicit ones paid by workers (or increase of cost-sharing, deductibles, etc.).

There is no good economic theory about how the cost of a benefit is split between implicit and explicit adjustment – higher explicit premiums can cause some workers to decline coverage entirely, a good thing for an employer if they default to coverage from their spouse's job but maybe not a good thing if they become uninsured. Different firms have different rules on when eligible workers can decline coverage (as well as different rules on who is eligible when).

Managers of Medical Services Systems

These economic propositions about the demand and payment for health insurance tell you some important things if you are the manager of a medical services delivery system. Most obviously, it means that you should look beyond the sensibilities of insurance executives to the preferences of workers at firms where your prospective patients work and get their coverage. Do they seem willing to pay more to get access to the latest technology, or to care supplied free of managed care limits, or to doctors who are paid well to treat them well – or are they more interested in holding medical costs down to keep their yearly raises up? Not an easy temperature to take but one that will eventually govern how insurers respond to what you choose to do (Box 11.2). Sometimes the insurers who cause you problems are not on the same page as the workers they cover, and you may be able to make common cause with insured workers against unreasonable managed care rules. In contrast, trying to figure out the answer to the question "What do insurers want?" is a waste of time; they should and eventually will want whatever those who pay them want. Likewise (according to economics), do not ask employers what they want (or expect a silly answer if you do). Find some consultants who can elicit worker preferences about these trade-offs. Indeed, most privately insured workers are covered by self-insured plans where the employer pays the bills directly, and insurers only function as agents to administer this process. That makes the connection between worker demands and coverage policy even more direct.

Of course, your patient population will not all come from one firm or be covered by one insurer, so you will have to deal with potentially conflicting desires; nothing you do will ever get unanimous approval. This heterogeneous mix may eventually average out, so you need not parse all the individual parts. But you will need to pay attention to them. (The Kaiser system avoids this problem by treating only people with its insurance.)

Another challenge worth noting is that you will manage not only the delivery services but also the health benefits for your own workers. That means you will face the same trade-offs as do the employers who cover your

Box 11.2 Theory: Profit-maximizing insurance coverage choices in detail

To get as close as we can to an answer, we first have to take a tour through the economic research on why firms gain increased profits by offering more than one insurance option. There are two versions of that work. One version just asks if more than one option would (over all workers at the firm) allow each of them to get a plan closer to their personal ideal.[9] A positive answer is a slam dunk, and evidence that something is working is provided by empirical evidence that the matching of plans chosen with demand characteristics of workers is about as good in the group market as in the individual insurance market.[10] The combination of sorting across firms with one option and sorting within firms with multiple options replicates what people choose when they had an unrestricted choice (not the regulated options in today's Obamacare exchanges) – except that workers in unionized firms got more benefits than they wanted.

The other strain relates the offering of more than one choice to heterogeneity in firm workforces – and finds that firms with a distribution of worker characteristics suggesting variation in desired coverage are more likely to have more than one plan to choose from. The literature in the preceding paragraph suggests that more choices than currently are offered might be better, but, speaking of headaches, dealing with many insurance plans and insurers is a cost for employers. What we do know is that preferences across plans (not only relative to cost-sharing but also type of managed care and breadth of networks) seems to vary a lot (an argument against uniform social insurance or even Medicare coverage for all if you ever get involved in that debate).

Back to the main story. An adjustment away from fixed contribution that would improve welfare would be one that attenuates the differences in the uniform explicit premiums that workers pay. Making this change appears to benefit both high-risk workers of average risk aversion and low-risk but risk-averse workers more than it harms low-risk workers of average risk aversion. Will or should that matter to a profit-maximizing employer? Making your generous plan a better deal will draw in high-risk workers from the broader labor market, and their higher costs will force even larger cuts in monetary wages. Since economic theory and current empirical evidence cannot really figure this one out, the best advice to employers is to be careful in trying to fix selection if you are determined to do so. Attention to other aspects of benefits offerings, such as variety and finding the best deal to offer the average worker, may be more productive.

patients. It means that your health system HR department should keep tabs on what other healthcare employers in town are doing with money wage and benefit packages. I comment more on this in Chapter 15.

[9] Dafny, L., Ho, K., & Varela, M. (2013). Let them have choice: Gains from shifting away from employer-sponsored health insurance and toward an individual exchange. *American Economic Journal: Economic Policy*, *5*(1), 32–58.

[10] Pauly, M. V., & Herring, B. (2007). The demand for health insurance in the group setting: Can you always get what you want? *The Journal of Risk and Insurance*, *74*(1), 115–140.

Ideal Large Group Insurance

The economic story already sketched out means that tailoring to worker demands is key to what you should propose as insurance products (or what you advise to self-insuring employers who consult you). Note that it is not just a matter of what you do or do not cover and what happens to the premium the employer will pay; there is also the issue of the relationship of coverage to total premiums – the value problem in another form. In collaboration with each employer, you will need to confront something else – not all workers will have the same values for coverage or want the same thing. As already noted, for small firms with nonspecialized workers, this may not be so much of a problem; workers may sort themselves across firms based on the health benefits they prefer so that each firm ends up with workers who all pretty much like what they are offered. However, even this equilibrium is a moving target from the insurer and employer perspective; you won't know what benefits to offer until you see what workers you hire, but they won't know where to work until they see what you propose to provide.

In larger firms that have to hire different kinds of workers who value different health plans differently, labor compensation cost minimization implies that employers will pay more attention to some employees than to others. Specifically, they will not care about the preferences of workers who are unlikely to leave the firm based on benefits changes or wage changes (probably the older workers though not necessarily the highest paid). Instead, they are supposed to care about the marginal workers (of each type) who might or might not be willing to work for them. If this set of workers comes close to being a random slice of all workers, the best health benefit offering will be the best for all workers. If it leaves some out, the benefits may differ from what those workers would have wanted.

A fundamental issue here is whether there is any correlation between distinguishing characteristics of workers, such as skill set, age, or income, and the value they attach to different levels of health insurance – and whether a firm needs to hire workers with varying levels of those characteristics. Take income. For reasons related to both affordability and taxes, it is likely that higher (family) income workers will want more costly insurance than lower-income workers with more limited resources. They will want their insurance to cover higher-cost treatments, with more generous coverage given the cost of a treatment. More speculatively, they may want higher-cost providers (imagining them, correctly or not, to be higher quality) and fewer hassles from managed care, even those that save money. But lower-income workers in the same firm may prefer bare-bones coverage or tough managed care if they allow wages to be higher. Adding options also raises the possibility of some adverse selection among plans. How the firm sets the premium differentials among plans can affect this behavior, but as described in Chapter 6, employers do not seem especially concerned about selection within the workforce as long as the average total cost of health benefits per worker stays the same. Higher-wage workers tend to go for the more generous plans, but employers do not seem inclined to worry about small differences in total compensation or small deviations from optimal coverage. Compared to economists who worry a lot.

Who Should Know?

Despite the fact that they are paying for insured care, insured employers, unions, and workers often complain that they cannot obtain information on where their own money that pays for insurance is going. (They have gotten politicians to introduce transparency legislation that would give them the details on what their insurance paid to different sellers for different services.) There may be privacy concerns for individuals' use of care, but some self-insured benefits managers imagine that they could use their data to identify problem areas with high costs or high use rates – but cannot. It gets even worse if they use a pharmacy benefit manager (PBM); not only is there another layer to penetrate but PBMs supposedly keep some data secret so that they can entitle themselves to larger bonuses.

From an economic viewpoint, the obvious point to make is that this should not be happening if markets in third-party administrators (TPAs) or PBMs are competitive. If your supplier of administrative services is too tight-lipped, you should find another one who tells you what you need to know. Part of the issue may be that interference by the customer can be costly to the administrator – so transparency will have a price. But the wise firm offering health benefits will know what it is paying (to a PBM, say) and how happy its workers are with the service. Employers do not need to know the machinations of their PBM in detail; all they really need to know is what they are paying – and what some alternative hired hand would charge for the same services. Usually, it works out reasonably well without recourse to legislation or regulation, which are bound to have side effects.

Tax Breaks Get in the Way

One reason for pushing PBM management of coverage somewhat lower on your list of worries is that there is a government policy that has a much larger impact on coverage. This is called the "tax exclusion," and it refers to a provision in the current tax codes (federal and state) under which money compensation of workers is subject to income and payroll taxation but compensation in the form of health benefits (regardless of whether nominally paid by the employer or the employee) is not. This tax break or tax loophole is the virtually universal bugaboo of health economists, who point out that it offers larger tax reductions to higher-income workers, induces workers to choose plans with higher cost (since the cost is tax-free relative to money wages), and encourages more moral hazard than would otherwise be chosen – because the US Treasury bears part of the cost of low-value care. Other than being unfair and inefficient, it is such a great public policy that it has resisted all efforts (including one in original Obamacare) to tamper with it. "Taxing your benefits" seems to produce bipartisan horror among voters and their representatives.

More is involved here than chump change. In fiscal year 2022, the tax exclusion reduced federal tax revenues by \$300 billion.[11] Compared to the federal and state governments taxing the monetary value of benefits at the usual income and payroll tax rates, the gain to those who benefit is estimated to be more than the cost of all Obamacare subsidies and federal Medicaid payments.

One response: Imaginative Republicans have been able to offset some of the bias toward having insurance cover everything medical by putting in place an alternative tax loophole – tax shielded health savings accounts usable only for medical care combined with those high-deductible health plans mentioned earlier. From an economic purist perspective, it would be better to sweep away the whole mass of regulations and subsidies and just add the expected value of health benefits to each worker's income, ideally promising a lower revenue-neutral income tax rate in return. This seems unlikely to happen anytime soon, but correcting the tax treatment of group insurance may be a way to collect more from the better-off while rationalizing their

[11] Urban Institute & Brookings Institution. *How might the tax exclusion for employer-sponsored health insurance be reformed? Key elements of the U.S. tax system*. Tax Policy Center Briefing Book. https://taxpolicycenter.org/briefing-book/key-elements-of-the-u.s./taxes-and-health-care/how-might-the-tax.

private health insurance at the same time – two for the price of one. Economists still hold out hope.

However, from the viewpoint of an insurer selling coverage or a health system providing services, the best thing to do is to go with the enhanced demand generated by this tax subsidy. Buyers will be willing to pay higher premiums for insurance plans that offer better features than if there were no tax advantages, and sellers would be foolish not to satisfy them.

Even though it took a while to get here, this economic policy issue is the main punchline of this whole book. The tax-based subsidy to group insurance is the primary contributor economists can identify to the rat hole discussed in Chapter 1. We dream that it might someday be restricted – in a grand bargain in which the value of health benefits is subject to income taxation but marginal tax rates are then reduced so everyone can gain. The value of the tax break would rise if marginal tax rates (not on just millionaires and billionaires, but them too) were increased, and so (paradoxically) would healthcare demand and spending. The main message here is that the US Treasury should be added to the watch lists of health insurers and health services providers.

Now we turn to Medicaid, the government program for low-income people (that covered 21.2% of the US population in 2023).[12] This program is financed by matching expenditures of the federal government and state government, but its extent and policies are largely chosen by the states. Typically, Medicaid programs have been characterized by restricted budgets which have pushed state officials responsible for administering them to pay low prices to providers (especially physicians), leading to fewer physicians willing to provide access. It does not have to be that way; voters could choose to favor candidates who would raise their taxes to increase access to high-quality providers for poor people, but most voters apparently have not chosen to do so.

There is variation in Medicaid coverage generosity and enrollment by state; the best predictor of generosity is average taxpayer income. The poor are better off in richer states (which are also ones with the most variation in income). The federal matching rates do fall for richer states but not by enough to equalize spending across states. Research shows that states with larger federal matching subsidies or higher incomes are more generous – but rich states are the most generous of all.[13] The current system is not well targeted to help those most in need regardless of state.

[12] Kaiser Family Foundation. (2024). *Health insurance coverage of the total population*. www.kff.org/other/state-indicator/total-population/.

[13] Grannemann, T. W., & Pauly, M. V. (2009). *Equal-burden-for-equal-benefit Medicaid matching rates*. American Enterprise Institute for Public Policy Research.

The public motivation for Medicaid is presumably the "beneficial" moral hazard to be discussed later. Those covered by it pay nothing and so have no direct control, so they are not responsible for low-value care. But Medicaid is the vehicle by which we better-off taxpayers can correct underuse of effective care by our fellow citizens. This is an equally important policy punchline: Inequity in the use of care and financial protection is a result of taxpayer and voter choice; we have the power to change it if we will.

Medicare Demand

The Medicare program, which covers 14.7% of the US population,[14] is said to be the third rail of American politics but its supposed insulation from external influences has not made it a program of outstanding generosity. Despite its live-wire reputation, its political masters have used its large presence for many healthcare providers as a tool for holding down or reducing payments – certainly below the levels private insurers have felt they had to pay, and perhaps below the levels that beneficiaries would truly desire if only they controlled the financing of their coverage.

Beyond this, there is very little evidence on voter demand for more or less Medicare coverage when they are forced to consider the cost; there is strong support for the overall program but much less on specific features when they have a price tag attached. The separation of benefits from payment (by years, in the case of Part A) leads those nearing retirement to assert that they are owed high benefits, while the budget impact makes politicians crusade to cut costs. People on Medicare (and perhaps many others) favor capping out-of-pocket payments for prescription drugs (one of several gaping holes in Medicare coverage) but probably not the higher beneficiary and taxpayer cost to pay for it (though the cost of these items would be blessedly small).

The Supply of Employment-Based Insurance

As noted in Chapter 7, the US private health insurance market is fairly highly concentrated in many (though not all) cities and states.[15] This is not new;

[14] Kaiser Family Foundation. (2024). *Health insurance coverage of the total population*. State Health Facts database. www.kff.org/other/state-indicator/total-population/.

[15] American Medical Association. (2023). *Competition in health insurance: A comprehensive study of U.S. markets*. www.ama-assn.org/system/files/competition-health-insurance-us-markets.pdf.

historically the "Blue" plans were the first arrivals, received special favors from state legislators, and still dominate the market in many states – even when they have changed their names, gone full-bore investor-owned, or spread out of their original geographic territories. This concentration and relative size (compared, say, to medical groups or even hospitals) has meant more to those local providers of care whose customers are covered by these insurers when not covered by Medicare or Medicaid.

In theory, insurer concentration means less to employers as proxy buyers of insurance. As already noted, many firms, and almost all the larger ones, self-insure at least some of their insurance coverage. That means that the supply side of group insurance is divided into two parts. Smaller firms typically buy "complete" or "full insurance" from the well-known insurance companies – the remaining Blues, Aetna/CVS, United, Cigna, and Elevance. By market share measures, this market is moderately concentrated, and both antitrust regulators and economists working for them have been concerned about the extent of competition and have blocked some combinations, horizontal and vertical.[16] Self-insured employers use ASO (administrative services only) or TPA (third-party administrator) firms – but some of them, especially the ASO firms, are children of the same parent insurance companies, issuing the same "membership" cards – but sticking the employer with whatever claims turn out to be at the end of the year. The measures of insurer concentration do not distinguish between workers at small firms with full insurance and those "enrolled" in Blue or commercial plans only by virtue of those firms' management of their coverage (rather than acceptance of risk for illness or claim variation).

Determining the competitiveness of the ASO–TPA market challenges analysts. The mundane task of processing claims and maintaining enrollment records is one that many firms could do – not just the insurance companies who view ASO as a side hustle but also benefit consulting firms with computer capability. There are an estimated 450 TPA firms in this business, with the 10 largest accounting for only 5% of the total market.[17] So, regardless of the current structure, very low entry barriers to this function must limit profits and markup there.

[16] Meyer, H. (2022). *Biden's FTC has blocked 4 hospital mergers and is poised to thwart more consolidation attempts.* Kaiser Family Foundation. https://kffhealthnews.org/news/article/biden-ftc-block-hospital-mergers-antitrust/; Levinson, Z., Godwin, J., Hulver, S., & Neuman, T. (2024). *Ten things to know about consolidation in health care provider markets.* Kaiser Family Foundation. www.kff.org/health-costs/issue-brief/ten-things-to-know-about-consolidation-in-health-care-provider-markets/.

[17] Edgemont. (2021). The growing importance of third-party administrators (TPAs). White Paper, March 12. www.edgemont.com/insights/the-growing-importance-of-tpas/.

When the insurance product also involves a network that leaves out some local providers and negotiates with others, however, there is more possibility that the proprietors of such networks, usually the aforementioned insurers, may have market power; the notion of many overlapping networks especially in smaller markets seems implausible. Is a provider network a natural monopoly? To make things even more complicated, many smaller self-insured firms buy coverage from stop-loss insurance firms that are different from those managing claims and payments; these stop-loss firms are usually not state regulated and have not so far tried to manage care or prices for the high-cost cases they cover.

Empirically, we do not see high profits or markups in the ASO business or in group insurance generally, so that is circumstantial evidence that this market is reasonably competitive. (The big profits come from Medicare Advantage.) However, some self-insured employers have expressed (to Congress) dissatisfaction with their ASO sellers. Most commonly they complain that the ASOs are not transparent in feeding back their own claims data (sometimes binding themselves and others with gag clauses). Also, when ASOs move a level down and contract with PBMs to manage carved-out drug coverage, distrust grows. In principle, an employer worried about the honesty of the administrator can fire it – but are there other better choices to which it can then turn?

Private group insurance plays a disproportionate role in the financing of hospitals and physician practices because the reimbursement levels paid by those plans are much higher than payments for identical services provided to original Medicare or Medicaid plans. For some reasons not well understood, private insurers who run Medicare Advantage plans are also able to pay much lower prices for those insureds than if they were covered by the same insurer in a private plan for people under 65 not on Medicare.

I fear that the current structure of the private insurance market is inherently unstable, not because of traditional causes like adverse selection or moral hazard but because its mismatch with what citizens want it to do makes it vulnerable to political posturing and pressures. The same might be said for the public insurances – Medicare will have to cut Part A benefits or raise more money sometime soon, and Medicaid (I fervently hope) cannot continue to stint on payments for drugs and doctors and still be found acceptable to altruistic voters. The much-forecasted transformation of the delivery system that will solve insurers' price and quality problems has not materialized. At a minimum, employers are going to have to pay more attention to the quality of the coverage they offer and that workers pay for. We may live in interesting times.

12 Competition, Antitrust, and Regulation in Hospital and Healthcare Markets

Introduction

Economists have great reverence for the idea (and expected outcome) of competition. If perfect competition is present in a market, voluntary interactions across firms and buyers will in theory result in a price equal to marginal cost. That outcome will be efficient in the sense of maximizing the sum of consumers' and sellers' surpluses; everyone will be as happy as they can be, without impinging on anyone else's joy. Competition will also result in cost minimization for whatever quantity and quality of output supplied. No external regulation can improve efficiency. From this point, the only way to benefit one group (e.g., insured consumers) would be to harm some other group (e.g., suppliers of care or insurers). Conversely, if prices exceed marginal cost because of seller market power, that will discourage cost-effective consumption; all are worse off than they need to be. Then it is possible (though far from guaranteed) that regulation will help. According to economists, any regulation should first take the form of efforts to reduce market power; if that is impossible, then some wise price limits (if they are feasible) may help.

This general idea of competitive outcomes representing the best that can happen in a market has a long history, first embodied in the medieval scholastic philosophers' idea of a "just price" (the competitive outcome) up to federal antitrust laws enshrining competition as a setting which ensures that welfare is maximized – whatever the price turns out to be, high or low. There are a number of reasons why healthcare markets would often not be expected to be perfectly competitive, ranging from economies of scale in hospital production to the presence of patents for drugs and devices (see Exhibit 12.1). Yet there still remains much of a consensus, among policymakers as well as economists, that the closer a market in medical care or health insurance can come to perfect competition, the better.

Exhibit 12.1 Evidence: Competition in healthcare

Criterion	Economic description	Difficulties in healthcare
Many buyers and sellers	The market consists of a large number of buyers and sellers, ensuring no single entity can influence the price.	Few large dominant health systems; rural disparities in access.
Homogeneous products	All products offered by different sellers are identical, making them perfect substitutes.	Patients benefit differently from identical services, creating different outcomes.
Perfect information	Buyers and sellers have full and equal knowledge about prices, product quality, and market conditions.	Asymmetric information between physician, patient, and payer.
Free entry and exit	Firms can freely enter or exit the market without significant barriers or costs.	Regulatory requirements (e.g., patents for drugs and devices) restrict entry.
Price takers	Firms and buyers accept the prevailing market price, as no single participant can influence it.	Large health systems have significant negotiating power, and so do insurers.
No collusion or market power	There is no cooperation among firms to control prices or restrict competition, and no firm has significant market power.	Increasing consolidation, mergers, and acquisitions.
Profit and utility maximization	Firms are assumed to maximize profits; consumers are assumed to maximize utility.	Other objectives include quality of care and reputation; "nonprofit"?
Short- and long-run equilibrium	In the short run, firms may earn profits or losses, but in the long run, entry and exit ensure zero economic profit.	Changing technologies, evolving protocols, and fluctuating demand.

However, from the viewpoint of firm managers responsible for maximizing the value of a healthcare firm, the optimality of competitive equilibrium is generally beside the point in terms of their goals and rewards. Still, they need to pay attention to it if they are on either end of an antitrust issue – either they say leave us alone because our market is pretty competitive or they say give us a hand because our competitors are exercising market power. The objective of a competitive outcome is enshrined by antitrust law in the legal environment in which managers operate and so must be considered in decision-making.

How should managers think of competition in the markets in which their firms operate? Managers need to know when to call in their lawyers because there can be legal challenges either to their behavior (when they are the defendant) or to that of other firms in their market (when they are the plaintiff). There is an unavoidable short-run conflict here: If you can manage to get your firm to dominate the market – sometimes labeled "sustainable competitive advantage" – you will do better than if there is perfect competition. However, on average and over time you, your firm, and your customers will be better off if competition prevails. For much of this chapter, I will adopt the Machiavellian persona of helping you to be successful in dominating your market. But then I will point out that if every manager follows my advice, the outcome may then be competitive enough to allow me a quiet night's sleep.

One way to reconcile managers' desire for advantage with the notion of competitive equilibrium is to define sustainable competitive advantage as being generated by "value" (versus skullduggery); you need to offer something novel and useful in the market. There are many good ideas that cannot be embodied in a patentable product but which can confer advantage on the firm that offers one of them. To provide incentives, that advantage needs to be sustainable for some time, but not necessarily forever.

The eminent jurist and economist Richard Posner argues that innovation is generally fostered more by competition to be the first and best than by getting a government-enforced patent. A recent *New York Times* story illustrates this process by describing a Bengali immigrant who was the first to open a truck in Brooklyn selling their delicious street food "Fuchka."[1] It wasn't long before other trucks, painted in the same hue and with the same menu, also opened, but the owner of the first truck was pleased because this change identified and so stimulated demand for his innovation that his truck business boomed and he even opened a sit-down restaurant. (The only irritant was when one of the other trucks labeled itself the "Original Fuchka" truck, definitely false unless you interpret original as meaning authentic rather than first.) The same phenomenon can happen in healthcare management – so a rosy view of sustainable competitive advantage is that it can be the vehicle by which innovation is incentivized and diffused. As noted in other chapters, a great prize awaits the first manager able to turn "value" or "care coordination" into processes that actually make consumers better off.

The empirical question of whether there are novel benefits furnished by acquiring or merging firms can actually matter in antitrust cases. Competition may not be right for all kinds of healthcare; even Judge Posner thinks that patents have a role to play for prescription drugs given

[1] Keh, A. (2023). The fuss about Fuchka: A Bengali street food's N.Y. origin story. *New York Times*, October 26. www.nytimes.com/2023/10/26/nyregion/jackson-heights-street-food-fuchka.html.

their long lead time before the investment pays off and the need to invest in research and then establish the effectiveness of discoveries. But for other kinds of medical innovation, and for optimal performance with a given set of services sought by informed buyers, competition is thought by economists to be the best way to get the best outcomes.

The Evidence on the Effects of Hospital Mergers on Prices

It is generally accepted by economists that mergers between hospitals in the same local market that reduce the overall level of competition will lead to higher unit prices for inpatient care, especially in hospitals that are close in distance to the merged ones.[2] The number of mergers in the past decades exceeds thousands. Between 1989 and 2017 there were almost 1,600 mergers in the US, around 450 of them happening after 2012.[3] The positive aspect of these combinations is that they have left us with an extensive and conclusive literature on the effect on prices.

Prices increase after mergers. The magnitude of the increases varies but can reach levels around 20%–30%.[4] The low price elasticity of some health services lets this rise in price be transferred to patients' spending.[5] Interestingly, recent evidence shows that even mergers of hospitals that are not in the same area might drive prices up.[6] Contrary to the theories of scale economies, some merges have been followed by an increase in costs, so that the increase in prices is not necessarily increasing hospitals' profitability for the enlarged systems.[7]

Looking at the other side of the coin, quality of care, the effects do not seem to be better. While there is some evidence of an increase in integration between providers within big health systems, which could improve

[2] Dafny, L. (2009). Estimation and identification of merger effects: An application to hospital mergers. *The Journal of Law and Economics*, *52*(3), 523–550. Merges between 1989 and 1996.

[3] Gaynor, M. (2021). Antitrust applied: Hospital consolidation concerns and solutions. Statement before the US Senate Committee on the Judiciary, Subcommittee on Competition Policy, Antitrust, and Consumer Rights, May 19. US Senate.

[4] Gaynor, M. (2021). Antitrust applied: Hospital consolidation concerns and solutions. Statement before the US Senate Committee on the Judiciary, Subcommittee on Competition Policy, Antitrust, and Consumer Rights, May 19. US Senate.

[5] Cooper, Z., Craig, S. V., Gaynor, M., & Van Reenen, J. (2019). The price ain't right? Hospital prices and health spending on the privately insured. *The Quarterly Journal of Economics*, *134*(1), 51–107.

[6] Dafny, L., Ho, K., & Lee, R. S. (2019). The price effects of cross-market mergers: Theory and evidence from the hospital industry. *The RAND Journal of Economics*, *50*(2), 286–325.

[7] Dranove, D., & Burns, L. R. (2022). *Big med: Megaproviders and the high cost of health care in America*. University of Chicago Press.

outcomes, there is no evidence of such gain – not on health measures such as mortality rates or readmissions, where even negative effects have been found,[8] nor in other quality indicators related to the delivery of care.[9]

But this increase in medical market concentration not only comes from mergers of hospital units. There has also been an increase in acquisitions of physician practices by large health systems. And the effect on prices from these acquisitions follows the same pattern, with price raises of around 14%.[10] Additionally, the effect of this increase in concentration extends to the labor market, negatively affecting health workers' wages, as has been seen in the case of the nursing labor market.[11]

Strong and Weak Economics of Competition

How competitive could healthcare be? Both consolidation and entry have long characterized healthcare. Take hospitals, the sector of most concern. As noted earlier, many hospitals were originally organized by civic or religious groups as places where poor sick people with little residential space could be cared for. The rich had doctors and nurses come to their gilded age mansions; the not rich, often immigrants, could be treated in hospital buildings at lower cost and with better quality and protection from infection than at home. In addition, especially successful physicians often added some overnight beds behind their offices to care for patients who needed a place to be watched while they recuperated; there were many "Doctor Sawbones Hospitals" in the south and west. Over time these facilities often consolidated to get up to efficient scale, and religious orders tending to many hospitals centralized

[8] Capps, C. S. (2005). The quality effects of hospital mergers. US Department of Justice, EAG Discussion Papers (No. 6). Antitrust Division.

[9] Ho, V., & Hamilton, B. H. (2000). Hospital mergers and acquisitions: Does market consolidation harm patients? *Journal of Health Economics*, *19*(5), 767–91; Capps, C. S. (2005). *The quality effects of hospital mergers* (No. 6). US Department of Justice, Antitrust Division; Gaynor, M., Sacarny, A., Sadun, R., Syverson, C., & Venkatesh, S. (2023). The anatomy of a hospital system merger: The patient did not respond well to treatment. *Review of Economics and Statistics*, 1–28. https://doi.org/10.1162/rest_a_01384.

[10] Capps, C., Dranove, D., & Ody, C. (2018). The effect of hospital acquisitions of physician practices on prices and spending. *Journal of Health Economics*, *59*, 139–152; Baker, L., Bundorf, M., & Kessler, D. (2014). Vertical integration: Hospital ownership of physician practices is associated with higher prices and spending. *Health Affairs*, *33*(5), 756–763.

[11] Sullivan, D. (1989). Monopsony power in the market for nurses. *The Journal of Law and Economics*, *32* (2, Pt. 2), S135–S178; Currie, J., Farsi, M., & MacLeod, W. B. (2005). Cut to the bone? Hospital takeovers and nurse employment contracts. *ILR Review*, *58*(3), 471–493; Staiger, D. O., Spetz, J., & Phibbs, C. S. (2010). Is there monopsony in the labor market? Evidence from a natural experiment. *Journal of Labor Economics*, *28*(2), 211–236.

some of the administration and financing. At the same time, new hospitals entered as populations grew and spread to the suburbs. Within the last decades, there has been a pronounced decline in the number of independent hospitals, although there are still thousands of separate hospital "plants" across the country and many in urban areas.

Economists would like to see hospitals along with their medical staffs compete for patients and for insurance network membership. Hospital care is local; distance matters to consumers both in emergencies and for visiting hours. The general hypothesis is that if there is an adequate number of firms within a reasonable distance of most potential users, the market can be declared competitive. Empirical specification of what number of firms is "adequate" obviously is imprecise, but some theory and empirical evidence suggest that the magic number should be at least four.[12] Reasonable distance or time is also subjective, but something like 30 minutes would seem about right. So, a metropolitan area in which there are at least four hospitals affording most consumers access within 30 minutes of their home or work would look pretty competitive.

The quantification of the extent of competitiveness of a defined market is usually an index that represents a weighted average of the market shares of different sellers in a community, termed the Herfindahl–Hirschman Index (HHI). It is the sum of the squares of each seller's percentage market share. For example, if there were four equal-sized hospitals in a market (25% share each), the index would be 4×25^2 or 2,500. The Federal Trade Commission (FTC) would regard a market with this index value to be (moderately) competitive, whereas the index for an area with only one hospital would be 100^2 or 10,000, definitely not competitive. The FTC standards and the labels attached to them change from time to time.

In application, this gets complicated. First, you have to decide on a measure of the market and size (share) of firms. Usually, the size measure is the dollar value of net (of discounts) revenues, but sometimes it might be inpatient beds or admissions. Then, you have to decide which hospitals are in the same market, a hard job because hospitals treat many different kinds of patients who travel different distances, and their shares may vary by patient type. Economists often have to get out their maps to measure distances or plot the ZIP codes from which patients travel. The Dartmouth Atlas has attempted to accomplish this by defining "Hospital Service Areas" and

[12] Henderson, B. (1976). The rule of three and four. BCG. www.bcg.com/publications/1976/business-unit-strategy-growth-rule-three-four.

"Hospital Referral Regions."[13] Both of these measures are not given by nature but depend on what hospitals do, such as what prices they charge and what quality of care in different service lines they provide. For example, hospitals in a given market may be perfectly competitive in the market of orthopedic care but not in the market of obstetric care.

One important point here is that the economic case for greater competition, or for resisting mergers, is by far stronger for combinations of hospitals selling more or less the same types of services in the same (local) market. These are typically deemed "horizontal" mergers and can be of concern when they substantially increase market share or power, as defined by an HHI > 1,500. Other types of combinations, of which there are many, are in a kind of limbo where they may or may not still be guilty of sinning against competition or additionally enhancing the market power of firms that have achieved it locally. These may include "vertical" mergers, in which hospitals acquire primary care practices or post-acute care facilities. These more ambiguous mergers will be discussed later in this chapter.

Hospital Competition and Insurer Competition

One of the things that makes healthcare interesting but confusing is the interposition of insurance between users of healthcare and providers of healthcare. Individual consumers do not usually pay directly for hospital care they get, so they are not concerned about its price. Instead, their insurer faces the price and generally is responsible for paying it. Private markets for health insurance, either the individual markets for Medigap or for Exchange insurance, or the much larger employment-related group insurance, can vary in their extent of competition. At first glance, it seems there is (as usual) a trade-off – if your local insurance market is less than competitive, insurers may use their buyer market power to force provider prices down closer to the competitive level, as well as to reduce consumer out-of-pocket payment, both actions which may offset the inefficient negative effect of provider monopoly on the use of care. On the other hand (as economists almost always say), big insurers may be able to use their seller market power in the insurance market to push premiums above what would have been the competitive level. Unfortunately, because both monopoly hospitals and monopoly insurers set prices based on their marginal

[13] Dartmouth Atlas. "Research methods." www.dartmouthatlas.org/research-methods/.

revenue, this dance with large firms usually is not expected to and empirically does not work out that well for consumers. Gaynor and colleagues show that competitive insurance will not offset the effect of provider monopoly in reducing use, and it is even worse if there is an insurance monopoly.[14] When the dust clears, in those markets that combine insurance and provider monopoly, both the use of care and the extent of insurance risk protection are likely to be too low.

The interposition of insurance means that, especially for hospital care, it is generally one's insurer that will respond to the price charged. If the price is high at your neighborhood hospital, your insurer may seek to find a network that will direct you to a lower-priced hospital; if that fails, your insurer will try harder (mostly through managed care) to constrain your use of this expensive care in order to keep your premiums low. Nevertheless, compared to a setting without insurance, the link between hospital prices and your use of hospital care will be seriously mitigated by insurance, though the link between hospital prices and your insurance premiums will be direct.

It does not have to be so confused. Large employers always have the option (and most of them use it) of self-insuring, so even large insurers cannot charge them excessively high premiums; an employer can always switch to a cheap third-party administrator (TPA). Only if those insurers also have monopolized the "market" for provider networks can they extract high profits as insurance administrators – but they can only charge up to the level of cost that a large employer could achieve on its own by hiring another administrator or paying non-network prices. The point is that even large insurers cannot get away with murder if large employers do not allow it. The Purchasers Business Group on Health is developing and testing some data tools that might help large self-insured employers monitor the insurers,[15] or administrative services only (ASOs) that manage their benefits, though the evidence on impact of use of these tools is not yet in.[16]

To be specific: If a hospital has set charges for small insurers at the level it thinks to be profit-maximizing, and then a large insurer negotiates and threatens and drives down the price it pays, a large self-insured employer can still be assured that its premium cannot be higher than what a plain

[14] Gaynor, M., Haas-Wilson, D., & Vogt, W. B. (2000). Are invisible hands good hands? Moral hazard, competition, and the second-best in health care markets. *Journal of Political Economy*, *108*(5), 992–1005.

[15] Purchasers Business Group. (2023). PBGH health value index. September. www.pbgh.org/wp-content/uploads/2021/01/PBGH-Health-Value-Index_2023.pdf.

[16] Myshko, D. (2021). Business group launches a new PBM. *Managed Healthcare Executive*, November 1. www.managedhealthcareexecutive.com/view/business-group-launches-a-new-pbm.

vanilla insurance administrator would add to the expected claims at the original price plus a competitive margin for administration. There is in theory a limit to the market power of large insurers to overcharge large employers.

Empirical evidence on this issue is scarce. To begin at the end, as far as I am aware, no one has compared the rates of use of care and levels of financial protection among the four corners of combinations: competitive insurers and providers, monopoly insurers and providers, competitive providers and monopoly insurers, and monopoly providers and competitive insurers. There is a study by Dafny and coauthors that looked at cities where a health insurance merger (Aetna and Prudential) had a larger versus smaller effect and found a larger increase in insurer premiums in cities where the merger led to an appreciably larger market share.[17] But they did not take account of self-insurance nor looked for impacts on the use of care and financial protection.

We economists then dispense the usual advice: When in doubt, oppose monopoly wherever it rears its ugly head. But that is based on a theoretical predilection for competition rather than a sledgehammer of facts. Moreover, the highly regulated character and the "Blue" dominance of insurance markets in many states makes it hard to get a clean study of provider market effects alone. So back to the prejudice for competition, something both insurance managers and provider managers will have to worry about if they try to sweep their local market. Moreover, if market power does emerge there is always the option of a mutually beneficial special deal (see Chapter 10 on the Law of One Price) between insurers, providers, and large employers that can avoid the worst outcomes for many consumers. My personal nightmares are much more about provider monopoly than insurer monopoly.

What Is Possible If It Is Not Too Late

Economists prefer market competition to collective choice as a way of allocating resources in a society after the government has performed whatever redistribution that can get consensus. Despite insurance-induced disconnections, they would prefer high hospital competition and associated lower prices to the alternative. In the 10 largest metro areas in the United

[17] Dafny, L., Duggan, M., & Ramanarayanan, S. (2012). Paying a premium on your premium? Consolidation in the US health insurance industry. *American Economic Review*, *102*(2), 1161–1185.

States plus Seattle, Oklahoma City, and San Diego, the extent of hospital competition is strong.[18] Depending on the metric, 30% to 40% of Americans are served by competitive hospitals – but most are not.[19]

As city size shrinks, competition also shrinks, so there is a subset of the population that faces higher than competitive prices and the potential for high hospital profits or excess revenues. As we move closer to rural areas, hospital market power in theory becomes even greater, but paradoxically almost all rural hospitals struggle to make ends meet.

It is the second category of high prices and high profits in medium-sized cities (roughly, not one of the top 10 megacities but large enough to have a big-league sports team) where hospital competition measures are already well below the lower limits that economists think are reasonable. This is the setting where either competition or state government commissions to review and potentially control how much people spend on hospital care are alternatives (see Chapter 13). Truth be told, in these areas it may be too late to play the competitive card with an expectation that it will do more than delay the onset of regulated monopoly, but that is not a foregone conclusion.

What does this mean for managers of care or insurance in these areas that include at least a third of the US population?[20] They may need to plan for dealing with monopoly price and capital regulation once again in the hospital sector, with the concern about political pressure and rent-seeking behavior that implies. Attention will be diverted from offering the best product in the market at a price that attracts buyers.

Might there be an alternative to federal rearguard antitrust actions on competition that can actually do more? After all, those laws mostly say what government should be against when new mergers come to markets, not what it (or the citizenry generally) should be for. The economist and law professor Barak Richman has produced a laundry list of tactics that he thinks might help for such potentially competitive markets. One of them is still defensive – keep as much competition between and among physicians as you can, and do

[18] The Health Care Cost Institute data updated on 2023 shows that New York City (HHI of 775), Los Angeles (HHI of 1,059), and Washington, DC (HHI of 1,156) were some of the least concentrated metropolitan areas in healthcare. https://healthcostinstitute.org/hcci-originals/hmi-interactive#HMI-Concentration-Index.

[19] Kaiser Family Foundation. (2024). Nearly half of metro areas have only one or two hospitals or health systems providing inpatient care. *Health Costs*, October 1. www.kff.org/health-costs/issue-brief/one-or-two-health-systems-controlled-the-entire-market-for-inpatient-hospital-care-in-nearly-half-of-metropolitan-areas-in-2022/.

[20] Council on Health Care Spending and Value. (2023). *A roadmap for action: Recommendations of the Health Affairs Council on Health Care Spending and Value. Executive summary.* Health Affairs. www.healthaffairs.org/pb-assets/documents/CHS_Report/CHS_ExecSummary_2022_R5-1675432669.pdf.

not let hospitals be the instrument for consolidation among physicians who work in them or send patients to them. The other is a strategy which supposes that electronic records and systems, created by digital startups, could be a way of engineering more coordination without necessarily implying more consolidation. The third flies under the banner of innovation in management, hard to argue against but also hard to foster. Richman argues for new business models. He does not expect them to emerge either from large insurers or from large health systems, who often have implicit reciprocal arrangements that lead to higher joint profits, less managerial stress, and higher prices. He has in mind something that might direct patients in need of care to high-quality low-cost centers of excellence located out of the local market area. Let your insureds escape to the big city where competition still prevails and innovation is fostered.

What about that strategy, and are there any others? In economic theory, the alternative to using a monopoly hospital when it raises its price can be some alternative source of care. Buyers turn to this alternative only when prices are high because switching has costs of its own – for example, it may be far away from the patient's home and family. The idea advanced by Richman, and some others such as Tom Emerick,[21] the former benefits chief at Walmart, is that some entity (mostly an employer, or a TPA for a self-insured firm) may be able to organize a more attractive and less costly way to create access to alternatives at some distance. Not necessarily as far away as Thailand or Abu Dhabi but still good and pleasing.

Obviously, if some better way can be found to enlarge the market when a market is initially constrained to one or two major sellers, that will be a good thing. I want to speculate about something different: the possibility that even many existing noncompetitive markets could be made more competitive if entrepreneurial managers seized the task and regulators helped a little. The size of a hospital market (short of cheap and convenient flights to other places) is defined by the population to be served, with a small adjustment for small variations in the prevalence of illness. Some rural geographic areas have small and widely dispersed populations; they can never support more than one hospital of efficient size (see Chapter 5 on efficient production). But much of the US population lives in medium-sized metropolitan areas that could support (and historically have supported) more competitive hospitals than are present today. To go further out on a limb: When

[21] Emerick, T., & Lewis, A. (2013). *Cracking health costs: How to cut your company's health costs and provide employees better care*. John Wiley & Sons.

a hospital merger occurs, the physical plant of the junior partner is either repurposed or used as another campus for the new system. Either way, at least for a time, there is already a facility in town that could serve as the site of a competitor. Is there some way to encourage the emergence or reappearance of more firms competing over price and quality?

We have some history that can be read as reassuring and consistent with Richman's story. The emergence of freestanding ambulatory surgery centers (despite all sorts of hospital efforts to stop them) did create competition by creating a new kind of market. However, after fighting and criticizing same-day surgery as dangerous, hospitals joined the movement with their own versions of ambulatory surgery centers – so now we have a delicate and not especially dynamic truce. The same thing has happened for nurse-led primary care practices in rural areas relative to physician practices. Richman argues that digital technology will create another opportunity attractive to new entrants, and one can only hope that is so.

There are many markets, with populations of around a quarter to a half a million, that suffer from the absence of hospital competition. Pittsburgh is one close to me; its market is dominated by the University of Pittsburgh Medical Center (and health insurance plan), with only mild rivalry with the infamous Allegheny Health Educational Research Foundation (AHERF) system; they divide up the territory not only in the metro region but in most of western Pennsylvania.

We know that a hospital and health system have to achieve a minimum size to be efficient, and that the size that can be expected in a market depends on the population of that market. However, in the Pittsburgh case and in many other similar areas of the country, dividing area population by the minimum population needed to sustain a hospital of efficient size leads to the conclusion that there could be many more competitive hospitals than there currently are.

So why aren't there more, and, more importantly, could something be done to foster more? Entry is not totally blocked in Pennsylvania; the Tower Health system in Reading, Pennsylvania, has entered the western part of the Philadelphia area by acquiring some existing hospitals, and there is a large hospital building up for sale (with some refurbishment needed) in Center City. Widespread advertising has helped to make hospital markets less sluggish. And self-insured large employers are always looking for a better deal, even if local plans have been co-opted by existing systems.

Still, it is apparent that something is needed to generate movement in the right direction. We may still hold out hopes that Walmart or Amazon can be disruptive, but the likelihood of internal reform is not high. There needs to be a set of managers looking for a challenge, but there may also need to be another thumb on another scale under a public policy that gives more than lip service to competition. One strategy would be to exempt new entrants from such limits. There may be other creative ways to foster competition where there is a desire to do so. Managers should be ready to help, and health plans and TPAs should support such efforts.

There is, however, a missing piece of evidence needed to support my pleasant dream of revived competition in Pennsylvania (or anywhere else). While we have good evidence that hospital mergers lead to higher prices, we do not have much to say about where the money goes – or even if there is that much more. This inconsistency is not surprising; in other industries, mergers often are not associated with higher profits for the merged partners much less other sellers in the now less competitive local market. If the shuttered formerly religious hospital with a reasonably modern facility is to become a viable competitor, just accepting lower but still decent profits than existing systems may not be a feasible strategy, and it cannot count on low-wage nuns to give it a cost and managerial advantage. It would have to bring something new and special to the party. Maybe that would be the care coordination and improved electronic systems Richman targets, but evidence is lacking. See Box 12.1 for additional discussion.

Box 12.1 Theory: Expanding the market power of a must-have hospital – Sutter Health story, take one

As already noted, economists are as confident about the consequences of simple monopoly arising from horizontal mergers in medical as in other markets but are much less certain, in theory and in practice, what to say about vertical or conglomerate combinations. The key policy question that will always be asked and managers must be prepared to answer is: Whatever alleged merits such combinations have, can they lead to increases in profits and in financial harm to buyers of healthcare? Here I want to discuss a tactic where economists have reported evidence that suggests concern – the use by a hospital system that includes a large flagship or crown jewel hospital in what amounts to a "tying arrangement," in which any insurer that wants to make the flagship hospital available to its beneficiaries and pay reasonable prices for it is required to pay extra high prices if its beneficiaries include other run-of-the-mill hospitals in the system that operate in competitive markets. (Note that this could not happen if there were two insurers, one for each market.) Such arrangements in healthcare are often labeled "all-or-nothing" deals, since an insurer must accept all hospitals in a system into its network if it wants any of them.

The best known and certainly the most litigated version of this tactic is associated with the Sutter Health System in northern California.[22] That system started in the foothills near Sacramento (hence the name) but has subsequently acquired more than two dozen hospitals including some of the largest and best known in the Bay Area. One of its flagship hospitals is the Alta Bates hospital in Oakland. The tactic under scrutiny is one in which an insurer that wanted to have Alta Bates in its network at a reasonable price must also agree to pay high prices (95% of charges) at other Sutter hospitals and must include them in its network of preferred providers. Two lawsuits have been brought against Sutter for this practice, one of which it won but the other of which it paid to settle.

The plaintiffs' conceptual argument here is simple: Whatever profits Sutter is making from Alta Bates and other highly regarded hospitals in its system, by forcing insurers to allow their insureds to use the other Sutter hospitals at high prices, it can add to those profits by raising charges at the weaker new links (at the expense of insurers, employers who use them, and workers who pay for coverage).

Is this argument economically correct? The answer is "not necessarily." The empirical economic evidence is consistent with the view that this kind of restriction channels patients to those undistinguished but profitable hospitals. Employers and insurers go along with this because both workers and firms view the flagship hospital as a must-have whose absence from their health insurance network would make the insurance second-rate and the jobs it covers undesirable. The question, however, is whether a combination of a flagship hospital with an undistinguished hospital some distance away can add to the market power and profits already associated with the flagship hospital. If yes, the strategy will make sense for managers but is properly at risk for legal scrutiny; if no, there is no basis for concern about threats to competition.

The same soft conceptual argument is sometimes used to explain why some hospital systems have merged with others even in states far away so they can pyramid the attraction of their stars to obtain well-paid roles for their bit players. There have been cases similar to Sutter in North Carolina, in both the Asheville and Charlotte areas, and elsewhere nationwide.

Are these kinds of combinations ones that managers should find attractive as long as they are legal? The continued growth in such conglomerate systems selling in different markets makes it fashionable to get with the trend. But perhaps advantages to the bottom line are overstated. The reason goes back to the simple monopoly diagram presented earlier in Chapter 7 (Figure 7.1): The owner of the flagship hospital stops raising its price not just to be "reasonable" but because doing so will cause some potential patients or their insurers to divert to other options – possibly out-of-hospital care, the use of other hospitals in the flagship hospital town, or perhaps no medical management. Prestige is great, but not at any price. Requiring the use of overpriced members of the network elsewhere will be viewed as the same as price increases at the flagship hospital – so the only way to keep business up there will be to reduce its price. What you gain in Smallville (if anything), you lose in Metropolis.

[22] Waters, R. (2020). *California's Sutter Health settlement.* Milbank Memorial Fund report, September. www.milbank.org/wp-content/uploads/2020/09/Sutter-History-Report_v3.pdf.

Economists believe that if markets can be kept competitive or made competitive, then other kinds of regulation would be unnecessary. Hospital spending might still rise, and medical experts might still worry about waste, but direct regulation of hospital prices or payment by public authorities would add nothing but excess red tape. Given the concern about cost containment in Chapter 13, this view might face political opposition – so the next battle in competition policy might be with the perennial but unattainable wish that expensive things like medical care cost less, and that a way to make that happen is to pass a law.

Of course, large insurers like Medicare and Medicaid (and even some private insurers) still might appropriately adjust what they pay to their views on what they are buying is worth. They might, for example, decide on an "annual update" in payment that is below what would otherwise happen even in a competitive market. Buyers can, according to economics, offer to pay whatever they want, but they cannot dictate what they can get from voluntary suppliers for that payment. Providers may decline new patients with their coverage. Finger-pointing, or worse, is likely to ensue, but reliance on evidence for the competitiveness of markets can avoid political posturing and controversy. We shall see.

It might advance overall social welfare if the public insurers Medicare and Medicaid used some of the taxpayers' money to prop up hospitals in areas where competition is threatened. So far, the political pressure has yielded excess payments to some rural hospitals and hospitals with a disproportionate share of low-income users but not targeted to maintaining competition for privately insured citizens. Right now, this would be potentially efficient but unlikely.

Nonhorizontal Hospital Mergers: Initial Thoughts from Economic Theory

Attention by economists and others has thus turned to other kinds of common mergers – even though the policy importance of them and the case for doing something about them is much less clear than is true for horizontal mergers. Alliances or mergers between hospital systems in one state and those in another, or in dispersed cities in the same state, seem in theory to pose little direct threat to competition – and therefore little opportunity for above-normal profits. Empirically it is true that when a hospital acquires another, the latter almost always raises prices – but that does not mean higher profits especially if the market remains competitive. More than half of the mergers in the last decade were not within but across markets.[23]

So why are these combinations happening, if not to increase profits or otherwise advantage the hospitals making them? There is no consensus explanation. It is an uphill battle in economics to find a theory that would say that cross-market combinations increase market power for combining firms in either market – but I will do my best to find something. Perhaps there can be some gains if the management of one of the partners is stronger than that of the other and has some excess capacity to handle more tasks. Conceivably the merged system might be able to bargain with insurers that cover people in both areas.[24] This would generally not be true of Blue Cross plans which still have geographical territories, and even a nationwide insurer like United is unlikely to yield to a hospital system which must have a tiny share of its national business.[25] Rob Burns and I have argued that the main motive here is managers' desire for a larger empire to rule which usually comes with a higher salary – but not much else.[26] See Box 12.2 for evidence on vertical integration in healthcare.

Combinations have been subject to more scrutiny if one of the partners controls a hospital in one city that has high market power and high prestige, whereas the acquired hospital in another market is run-of-the-mill. The feared gambit is that the merged system will require an insurer that operates in both places (often in the same state) to pay higher prices at the weaker hospital if it wants to maintain access to the must-have alternative elsewhere. This would be beastly behavior and is said to have happened in California with Sutter Health.[27] But does a merger really allow more monopoly gains to be extracted from the flagship hospital? Maybe not – if the firm was successful at extracting profit there, it would already be charging insurers the profit-maximizing price for its crown jewel.

[23] Fulton, B. D., Arnold, D. R., King, J. S., Montague, A. D., Greaney, T. L., & Scheffler, R. M. (2022). The rise of cross-market hospital systems and their market power in the US: Study examines the increase in cross-market hospitals systems and their market power in the US. *Health Affairs*, *41*(11), 1652–1660.

[24] Fulton, B. D., Arnold, D. R., King, J. S., Montague, A. D., Greaney, T. L., & Scheffler, R. M. (2022). The rise of cross-market hospital systems and their market power in the US: Study examines the increase in cross-market hospitals systems and their market power in the US. *Health Affairs*, *41*(11), 1652–1660.

[25] Cooper, Z., Craig, S. V., Gaynor, M., & Van Reenen, J. (2019). The price ain't right? Hospital prices and health spending on the privately insured. *The Quarterly Journal of Economics*, *134*(1), 51–107.

[26] Burns, L. R., & Pauly, M. V. (2023). Big med's spread. *The Milbank Quarterly*, *101*(2), 287–324.

[27] Arnold Ventures. (2020). Sutter Health case sparks growing scrutiny of hospital consolidation, contracting practices. December 17. www.arnoldventures.org/stories/sutter-health-case-sparks-growing-scrutiny-of-hospital-consolidation-contracting-practices.

Box 12.2 Evidence: Geisinger system ups and downs

The Geisinger hospital system is a long-established care provider in the anthracite coal regions of Pennsylvania, especially in the cities of Danville (population 4,200) and Wilkes Barre (440,000). Initially funded by a widow's bequest, the system is atypical in that authority rests primarily with a physician group rather than a separate hospital management. In addition, for many years it has also run a local health insurance plan that covers services at its physician clinics and hospital practices. It is thus a distinctive example of a vertically integrated health system. However, Geisinger recently agreed to be acquired by the Kaiser health plan and hospital system. How has vertical integration worked for this organization, and why has it decided to give up independent operation? (Disclaimer: some years ago, I gave a talk for a modest honorarium to the medical staff of competitor Wilkes Barre hospital.)

Much like its new partner Kaiser, the Geisinger system has provided examples of coordinated and innovative care. Its outcomes are better than average, it was one of the first to move to electronic medical records, its hospitalization rates (compared to others in the same area using other providers) are lower, and it has pioneered things like food as medicine, dispensing nourishing food in response to doctor prescriptions. However, like Kaiser, it has not been able to expand either use of its providers or its insurance outside of its traditional market area. Under the new ownership, Geisinger is to provide a shell for future Kaiser efforts (in an entity christened "Risant") to go beyond the historically integrated model. That shell has moved to North Carolina to acquire a hospital in Greensboro. The hope is that magic will ensue.

Despite the gold star performance on integrated care in Geisinger, it has run into financial difficulties (as has Kaiser) in the post-pandemic period. So, it does not seem that the kind of vertical integration into insurance plans and data banks that both represent has been a recipe for higher net income and market power.[28] Indeed, both types of systems have been challenged by the old-fashioned organizationally fragmented providers in their market areas. While there is some speculation about possible legal issues, this coast-to-coast merger will probably not be challenged by regulators.

What is more questionable, in my view, is whether the Risant model will appeal to managers. Kaiser says it is to be a "platform" that will "expand and accelerate the adoption of value-based care in diverse health care environments."[29] The word salad nature of this statement combines with my skepticism of value-based approaches generally (Chapter 9) to suggest that there is no substantial novel insight behind this effort; it just repackages old ingredients that have not yet jelled. The overall concept of integration beyond the horizontal seems at this point to be neither threatening nor promising. Go slow.

[28] Pearl, R. (2023). What Kaiser's acquisition of Geisinger means for us all. *Forbes*, May 31. www.forbes.com/sites/robertpearl/2023/05/31/what-kaisers-acquisition-of-geisinger-means-for-us-all/?sh=6e34470f5796.

[29] Kaiser Permanente. (2024). Risant Health completes acquisition of Geisinger. Press Release, April 2. https://about.kaiserpermanente.org/news/press-release-archive/risant-health-completes-acquisition-of-geisinger.

There should also be eternal vigilance against acquisitions where service lines of one partner do not overlap all of the activities of the other but there is some horizontal overlap. If a hospital system rounds up all the ambulatory surgery centers or urgent care facilities in a town, that would be reason for concern. These combinations might also allow the hospital system to engage in "raising rivals' costs" by having its subsidiaries charge extra high prices to patients from other hospital systems. Here again, there is not presently a lethal threat from this kind of reorganization of parts but perhaps there could be – and unless there is something helpful to consumers about it, better to discourage.

Durable Treatments and Spillover Benefits: Are Vertical Mergers between Providers and Insurers the Solution?

What about extension of insurer market power? As already noted, many effective treatments have cost offsets – not only do they improve health but because they avoid future illness they also avoid future medical costs. A problem commonly pointed out is that when and if people switch insurers, the plan that paid for the treatment may not benefit from the long-term reduction in spending.[30] There does not seem to be a way around this problem – even if the seller of the treatment asks for payment in installments, there is no way to bind a future insurer to make payments agreed to by the original insurer. All insurers would have to agree beforehand to continue payments for patients who switch into their plan, with the quid pro quo being their relief from payments for their insureds who switch out.

However, the existence of future cost offsets with turnover among insureds need not be a problem. Suppose that the treatment is cost-effective (as it should be if it is to be covered at all). The issue is whether it is still cost-effective even without all future cost-savings taken into account. Consider one of the most important cures of the last decade, Sovaldi for hepatitis C. It originally sold for $82,000, an increase from the approximately $60,000 price of the previous best treatments. But it was a much better drug – it cured with near certainty a disease that later in life would be severe, and it had many fewer side effects. The alternative treatment dropped out of the market.

[30] Gross, T., & Notowidigdo, M. J. (2024). *Better health economics: An introduction for everyone.* University of Chicago Press.

Insurance turnover would mean that the additional premium for your current insurance to cover this cure would need to be higher than if there were no turnover – although with positive interest rates the present value of future cost offsets after a few years would be reduced. Would you still want your insurance to cover it? You definitely would if the value of additional quality-adjusted life years (QALYs) alone exceeded the cost of the drug; cost offsets would just be gravy. Only if the cost offsets would make a difference between cost-effectiveness and cost-ineffectiveness would this spillover be of concern. That was not the case for Sovaldi but could happen for some close calls.[31] In the preferred Sovaldi comparison, future cost offsets were only 24% of additional spending on new drugs and the margin by which Sovaldi was cost-effective at its initial price was large when QALYs were valued at $100,000.

What Economists Can Tell Managers about Vertical Integration in Healthcare

To sum up so far: In contrast with the case of horizontal combinations of hospitals within a given market area, where economists can wheel out the big guns and blow away claims for improved efficiency, for the story for various kinds of vertical and mixed combinations, there is much less we can say with certainty – either in theory or based on what empirical evidence we have.

In theory, there are cases where vertical mergers between insurers and providers can avoid the "holdup problem" in separate firm negotiations, while in theory the possible (though very special) case of bundling allows expansion of market power across geographically separate markets. (See Box 12.3 for a bend-over-backwards example of increasing market power.) Opinions therefore come into play, and they differ among economists.

It seems that after a merger, whether horizontal or vertical or cross-market, whether affecting competition or not, whether made by a for-profit or a nonprofit firm, the acquired firm increases its prices to private insurers. The easiest all-purpose explanation for this would be to assume that prior to the merger managers were asleep or incompetent in making profits, and the new broom swept in new people who noticed and exploited any opportunities for increased profit. Perhaps, even if the price was at the profit-

31 Chhatwal, J., Kanwal, F., Roberts, M. S., & Dunn, M. A. (2015). Cost-effectiveness and budget impact of hepatitis C virus treatment with sofosbuvir and ledipasvir in the United States. *Annals of Internal Medicine, 162*(6), 397–406.

Box 12.3 Theory: Sutter Health story, take two

To begin at the beginning, if the two markets are largely geographically separate in terms of where patients come from, there is no obvious reason why buying a distant hospital whose local market is competitive should allow the now-merged firm to increase its profits by increasing its charges there. As Dranove and Burns note, if the best Ford dealer in Los Angeles buys a dealership in San Francisco, that does not increase its ability to profit by raising prices in either city (if they were already set in both places at the profit-maximizing level).[32] With regard to hospitals, this argument would still hold if there was insurance offered by separate insurance firms to separate employers in each city.

To find something suspicious, we have to go further (as Dafny, Ho, and Lee have done)[33] and find employers who have workers in both towns, and we have to suppose that those employers, to keep down administrative costs, would prefer to deal with one statewide insurer that covers both locations rather than two separate local plans. It is this joint purchasing by employers or insurers that is the linchpin for increased market power from cross-market mergers. To keep administration streamlined, employers may be willing to tolerate higher prices in the smaller site and still use the system hospital there after the merger – but only to the extent that their higher costs for those claims do not offset the administrative costs of breaking the insurance link. How much is it worth to deal with just one insurer being abused by a hospital system? There must be a relatively low limit if there is one at all.

maximizing level, increasing it would show to the outside world that the new management was serious. We do not have strong evidence that these price increases actually improve profit or financial status, so perhaps research documenting them does not tell us anything of consequence. There is no evidence that combinations per se conjure up magic that leads to competitive advantage that would sustain higher prices and profits – unless the combination does affect local market competition.

I would generally be on the side of discouraging any mergers of any type or flavor – both as a matter of public policy and as advice to managers – because they usually do not do anything good, such as lower cost or improve quality, so why take the chance that they may do harm? For the most part, there are no differential improvements compared to a setting in which mergers did not occur – except for a lot of new signage and logo design. As already noted, Rob Burns and I have argued that the reason for these mergers, which do change

[32] Dranove, D., & Burns, L. R. (2022). *Big med: Megaproviders and the high cost of health care in America.* University of Chicago Press.

[33] Dafny, L., Ho, K., & Lee, R. S. (2019). The price effects of cross-market mergers: Theory and evidence from the hospital industry. *The RAND Journal of Economics, 50*(2), 286–325.

the nominal structure of ownership in the industry, is the Napoleon complex in which managers prefer to manage something big rather than something small.[34] On the positive side, if a top-notch management team does have excess capacity, extending its good offices to other hospitals or providers may do a little good. If a health system in Boston buys some hospitals in Boise, it may improve their management, but from an economic perspective this is neither guaranteed nor feared. But for the most part, managers in healthcare appear to do what managers do when they have time on their hands and cannot figure out what else to do to show impact.

So far, we see no big profit gains from such combinations, no big quality improvements or error reductions from such mergers, but no great downsides either – just a waste of managerial energy. We do generally see that the acquired firm raises its prices (but does not make appreciably more money), while the acquiring firm does nothing especially different. Vertical mergers thus appeal to those who like soccer games which end in a tie; they are mildly interesting but not very consequential. So far, the various waves of merger mania, whether activated by nonprofit but charismatic CEOs or private equity investors out for a quick buck, have had a presence in healthcare but not much of a discernible impact. That could change in the future, but our advice to managers at present is to focus not on rearranging who owns what but rather on who does what to avoid low-value care and foster cost-effective innovation. For an additional discussion about combinations, see Box 12.4.

Managing Competition and Managing with Competition

The main message both from economics and from antitrust law to managers of hospitals or health systems is to be especially careful of combinations (mergers or acquisitions) of other hospitals or health systems in the same geographic market – horizontal combinations. Such caution may also reduce the chances of getting a letter from the Department of Justice (DOJ). It may also be warranted if you are concerned about the welfare of consumers in your town. The corollary of this advice is to be concerned about such combinations among your competitors. Practical steps in either case should call for advice from legal counsel, but economic considerations should be at the forefront. Of course, if both you and your potential partner are small fry in a big sea of other hospitals, there is less reason to be concerned. If the HHI

[34] Burns, L. R., & Pauly, M. V. (2023). Big med's spread. *The Milbank Quarterly*, *101*(2), 287–324.

Box 12.4 Theory: Expanding health system profits via bundling

Here is a fable (adapted from Pindyck and Rubinfeld) that describes how it is possible for a health system to increase its profits by requiring employers who include one of its hospitals in their network to also include the other.[35] Suppose a system has a flagship hospital in Metropolis and a smaller hospital in Smallville. It deals with two employers, both of whom have workers at the factory in Metropolis and the branch office in Smallville. We can represent the value to each employer of access to each hospital by the most the employer (on behalf of its workers) would be willing to pay to use that hospital (compared to other less attractive options in town or close by). Exhibit 12.2 indicates the reservation prices for the two firms, BigCo (BC) and Dunder Mifflin (DM).

Exhibit 12.2 Reservation prices of two representative firms

	Hospital	
	Metropolis	Smallville
BC	12 million	3 million
DM	10 million	4 million

To make this story work, it is essential that the *relative* values by each buyer of each option be inversely correlated across firms – both firms attach more value to the flagship hospital, but BC attaches relatively more value to it compared to Smallville than does DM. If the health system has to charge the same price to each customer, the most it could charge to each of two customers for the Metropolis hospital would be $10 million, and the most it could charge for the Smallville hospital would be $3 million. Hence its profits would be $26 million. Now suppose it offered a bundle of access to both hospitals to each employer. DM values the pair at $14 million and BC values it at $15 million – so charging $14 million would bring in both employers. Doing that would raise the firm's profit by $2 million, to $28 million. The health system is better off by bundling; both customers are worse off, and BC loses more than does DM.

However, note that this is a very special case. If relative values were the same for each employer – for example, if DM valued the Smallville hospital at $2.5 million-bundling would not add to profits. If as in the earlier discussion, the hospital market in Smallville were competitive so all buyers paid the same, bundling would not work.

The empirical issue is whether this special case applies to Sutter's situation in California – whether it dealt with employers whose workers had these kinds of values. In most situations so far of multisystem bundling or tying deals, those circumstances have not been established. More generally, the number of studies of the effects of cross-market mergers or combinations is small and mixed. There is suggestive evidence that unit prices (not necessarily profits) are higher after mergers in the acquired hospital but little on what

[35] Pindyck, R. S., & Rubinfeld, D. (1989). *Microeconomics*. Prentice Hall.

happens at the flagship hospital. Such effects as are found seem limited to in-state ("adjacent") mergers, not to ones which cross state lines. Measures are dominated by experiences in California, which is both large and dominated (relative to other states) by statewide insurers and statewide employers. The point estimates of price increases are larger (up to 10% over several years) when they are present.

in your market is already above 2,500, however, you will not be able to hide from scrutiny. This measure is not a precise guide but admits to legal discretion, so be careful if things are close.

The other obvious message is to have a good and evidence-based reason for combining, one that not only appeals to you and your board but you can defend in both courts of law and public opinion. This will be an uphill battle, so be prepared: Evidence on previous combinations has not led to optimism about subsequent lower prices or higher quality – quite the opposite (see Box 12.5).[36] Promises about cost reduction or lower prices are usually not believed, and you definitely do not want to be held to such a promise or be sanctioned if it is broken. Small gestures toward offering bits of community benefit – a health fair or a drop-in clinic – also usually do not serve to offset the threat of higher prices.

The most fundamental issue is not the external excuses you can offer but the internal rationale – exactly how will a combination change the way doctors who treat patients in your hospitals behave, and how will it help you with the room and board services or tools for the doctors' workshop that you provide? Economies from combining the laundry or the kitchen are all very nice but usually not enough to cover the fear of higher markups over whatever costs turn out to be. It seems unlikely that a combination of reasonably large players can lower marginal cost enough to offset expected higher markups over marginal cost.

What about other kinds of combinations? Here they are less of a legal trigger but still are in the crosshairs of the FTC (depending on the administration) or of ambitious attorneys general in some states like California. If I were the czar of hospital competition, I would pay less attention to such prospective vertical combinations and much attention to stopping (cold)

[36] Dafny, L., Duggan, M., & Ramanarayanan, S. (2012). Paying a premium on your premium? Consolidation in the US health insurance industry. *American Economic Review, 102*(2), 1161–1185; Ho, K., & Lee, R. S. (2017). Insurer competition in health care markets. *Econometrica, 85*(2), 379–417; O'Hanlon, C. E., Kranz, A. M., DeYoreo, M., Mahmud, A., Damberg, C. L., & Timbie, J. (2019). Access, quality, and financial performance of rural hospitals following health system affiliation. *Health Affairs, 38*(12), 2095–2104.

Box 12.5 Evidence: Insurer concentration and premiums

There is relatively little empirical evidence on what happens to what consumers ultimately pay and what care they ultimately use if a local insurance market consolidates through merger. There is some evidence that more concentrated health maintenance organization (HMO) markets had higher prices but not the now more common provider preferred organization (PPO) plans.[37] The most definitive study is the one by Dafny and colleagues,[38] which assembled proprietary data on group insurance premiums and related their growth to changes in measures of insurance market concentration. To begin at the end, they found that markets that became more concentrated were associated with lower growth in physician income and in healthcare employment, implying that insurance claims and total medical costs for the privately insured were reduced. (They did not have direct measures of claims.) Another part of their study then found that local markets that became more concentrated in the 2000s (largely through the Aetna–Prudential merger) showed higher growth in premiums; they conjecture that higher insurer profits sopped up any reductions in claims costs and then some.

For smaller employers or state governments who buy full insurance, this is a plausible and distressing story. However, in their data, most workers (55%–80% in different markets) were covered by self-insuring employers. As they note, the "premium" for such insurance that the firm sells to itself is constructed in two parts – an estimate of actual claims paid and the administrative fee charged by a TPA to pay those claims, impose limits, and sometimes negotiate prices with providers in a network. Those TPAs are often insurance firms, and the concentration measures for local insurance markets they used attributed self-insured plans administered by a given insurance firm to that firm; highly concentrated markets were therefore often ones where a few insurers did most of the TPA work. Here is the issue. If those insurers used their large shares to force lower prices and quantities on providers in the market, the only way the "premium" could increase is if the TPA fee took a much bigger jump in markets that consolidated. Surely possible, and some employers might have noticed, but entry into the TPA claims processing business is easy. So, the punchline would have to be that insurer consolidation permitted those firms to increase their charges for their network assembly and management to so great an extent that they kept the profits from lower claims costs and more. Perhaps, but this kind of functioning of the TPA market has not been separately documented, and the reduction in doctor incomes and hospital labor costs should have affected all private users of care administered by all insurers. There is a mystery here – as is true of much of the employer-based self-insured market – which should be relatively resistant to market power of providers, insurers, or their hired surrogates like pharmacy benefit managers (PBMs). Rather than waste their efforts on screening and wellness programs, large employers should be aggressive in managing their self-insurance, and policymakers should be upset if private insurer consolidation reduces access to effective care along with healthcare employment and income; the benefits department should not be a sleepy place. Watch this space.

[37] Wholey, D., Feldman, R., & Christianson, J. B. (1995). The effect of market structure on HMO premiums. *Journal of Health Economics*, *14*(1), 81–105.

[38] Dafny, L., Duggan, M., & Ramanarayanan, S. (2012). Paying a premium on your premium? Consolidation in the US health insurance industry. *American Economic Review*, *102*(2), 1161–1185.

horizontal mergers and local monopolies. In the vertical merger case, the advice to have robust evidence on why you are engineering this combination and what good differences you expect it to make is of even greater importance.

Tax Breaks, Charity Care, and Competition

Most hospitals in the US are private but nonprofit firms. There is also a large though not predominant nonprofit share in nursing homes, hospices, and home health. This legal form of organization usually incurs no taxes on real property at the local level and no taxes on any net income at the federal level. As discussed in Chapter 4, these tax advantages (compared to a for-profit twin) are justified as a way of encouraging and funding the provision of charity care or other activities of community benefit. Rather than trust a statement of good intentions in the hospital's mission statement, however, local governments and even the feds are becoming increasingly concerned about whether these tax advantages turn into actions which both benefit the community and (on net) save money in its fiscal budget.

How much do tax breaks cost your town and how much do you get back from them? This is usually the way the evaluation of tax advantages of nonprofit medical care providers works. At the local level, you calculate what would have been the real estate taxes on land and buildings owned by the hospital and compare that number with a dollar estimate of the value of community benefits. If the latter equals or exceeds the former, you leave the hospital alone. If the benefits fall short of the lost taxes, you ask the hospital to donate a new fire engine or to voluntarily show its civic spirit by making payments in lieu of taxes (PILOTs).

That is accounting, not economics. We need to ask how tax exemptions affect market equilibria, and whether communities are better off with tax-exempt nonprofit hospitals than without them – or with replacement of the local nonprofit hospital by a tax-paying capitalist twin. Doing so will get us even deeper into the swamp that we entered in the chapter on hospital objectives.

Suppose there were many competitive providers of medical services in a city, and all of them were nonprofit firms. Compare that with the same environment but all firms paid property taxes. What differences would economics lead us to expect? The most obvious is that, in the all nonprofit case, either public services would be less generous or taxes on other properties in the city would be higher. Competition among the health providers would bid down their prices to just cover their costs in either setting – so, with all nonprofits, medical costs and prices would be lower than if all paid taxes because these firms would not be facing the cost of taxes. There is not surprisingly a trade-off: lower medical prices against higher taxes. Local consumers get cheaper medical care but higher taxes or less spent on public schools. However, the nonprofit hospitals might instead charge the same prices to paying customers as their for-profit twins and use the would-be profits to pay for community benefits. Then the trade-off for taxpayers is between medical costs for themselves or community benefits. Failure to provide community benefits would not necessarily mean that taxpayers get no benefit from tax exemptions.

Hospitals, not voters, decide on the level of community benefits they will supply. Is this a pretty – or rational – picture? Should boards of private hospitals have the power to decide what care will be rendered to low-income people in your town? More seriously, what if the market allowed health providers to have some market power? Some nonprofit providers might raise prices above the breakeven level to furnish more charity care – becoming God's monopolists. Overcharging for middle-class care is not the best way to fund care for the poor.

In the for-profit twin city, prices of care would be the same, and the profits would go to the owners of those providers – but they would be smaller because there would be higher city tax collections that could themselves fund some charity care if that is how the city fathers wanted to spend the money. This case might be a little more heartwarming for some than the competitive case but an even bigger mess.

Now suppose that for-profit medical services firms emerged. Could they enter Nonprofit City? Probably not – because they would be at a financial disadvantage. The only hope of capitalists would be that nonprofit medical providers either spent all their tax advantages on community benefits or needed equity capital and donors closed their checkbooks – then they could come in and survive.

So much for economic theory. What does this jumbled picture tell us about community benefits and the role of tax breaks? One ignored (but realistic) possibility that we have investigated is that the board of a nonprofit hospital might consider selling out to for-profit owners.[39] Then tax breaks would disappear, but the private board members would now become trustees who

[39] Pauly, M. V. (1996). Health systems ownership: Can regulation preserve community benefits? *Frontiers of Health Services Management*, *12*(3), 3–34.

supervise a foundation with billions of dollars in assets that could be used to fund charity care. Those assets presumably represent the accumulation of retained earnings over the years from the nonprofit that it did not use for contemporaneous community benefits. The annual return from such a fund, given the assets of nonprofit hospitals in major cities in the US, would be much larger than the annual value of local tax breaks, and much larger than current charity care.[40] Perhaps (depending on how the nonprofits had behaved) the prices charged to middle-class patients would rise to cover the profit margins needed by the for-profit investors, so not all would be happy with the results.

Is there a sustainable competitive advantage to for-profit ownership of a medical care provider compared to a nonprofit provider? There are two possibilities. One already mentioned is greater access to equity capital. The other is more hypothetical: Perhaps the for-profit firm could provide better incentives to managers to hold down costs and increase volume. Nonprofits cannot offer stock options; for-profits can. Nonprofit managers can bask in civic virtue; for-profit managers can only get money. Hard to know how it will work out.

The empirical evidence suggests that, tax breaks or not, nonprofit organizations have been able to maintain some dominance in inpatient care markets but not in nursing home or home health markets. Why is this? Home health does not use much real estate, but nursing homes do – suggesting that real estate taxes are not the answer. Rather, the answer may be a function of reimbursement structure. Medicare pays hospice organizations and nursing homes a per diem rate for beneficiaries, enabling these firms to turn a profit more easily by cutting costs and services. Private equity firms are now acquiring hospice agencies at rapidly growing rates.[41]

The Economics of Rural Hospitals

In parts of the country with low population density, hospital care is typically provided by small hospitals with low average occupancy rates. As noted in

40 Nicholson, S., Pauly, M. V., Burns, L. R., Baumritter, A., & Asch, D. A. (2000). Measuring community benefits provided by for-profit and nonprofit hospitals: Nonprofits appear to be falling short of providing the expected level of community benefits, according to this new model. *Health Affairs*, *19*(6), 168–177.

41 Braun, R. T., Stevenson, D. G., & Unruh, M. A. (2021). Acquisitions of hospice agencies by private equity firms and publicly traded corporations. *JAMA Internal Medicine*, *181*(8), 1113–1114.

Chapter 5 on production, there appear to be economies of scale in the production of inpatient care for hospitals of size up to 150 beds or so. These rural hospitals have chronic financial problems even though they are the only source of inpatient care for populations nearby. Apparently whatever market power they have because of no local competition is offset either by low demand or by diseconomies of scale associated with high fixed costs just to stay open and accredited. (Think of your Econ 1 monopoly diagram and move the average cost curve above the entire demand curve.) There is also competition from hospitals in the closest urban areas since many local residents choose to travel to those larger hospitals with better reputations and pass up their local outlet except for emergency care.

It is obvious that the solution to the financial problems of rural hospitals is for all insurers to pay them more than they now do. The policy question, however, is whether additional payment would be cost-effective. That is, compared to the counterfactual in which a local rural hospital closes, would any lost benefits to patient health or consumer satisfaction be greater than the net cost of financial sustainability for that hospital?

Economists have no patience for the typical argument that says that "policymakers are concerned about the financial viability of rural hospitals" when the same policymakers are unwilling to spend the money (or even expand Medicaid) that would solve the problem. Is there a special economic model for rural and/or small hospitals that might help to explain why their financial challenges are more serious than those of nonrural hospitals?

The high fixed cost story seems to be the major distinguishing characteristic: Those high fixed costs (for a similar marginal cost) mean that a smaller hospital will need a higher price to break even. They also probably mean that it will not find it financially attractive to offer a wide range of special services that themselves have additional fixed costs. More speculatively, if small rural hospitals also have low marginal costs (up to capacity), that means that they will accept payment rates from private and public insurers that are lower than the minimum acceptable payment rate for a busy urban hospital.

What about demand? There will be more unpredictable variation in demand which may itself lead to more excess buffer capacity. For non-emergent cases (and even some emergent ones), the availability of better equipped and more prestigious hospitals in urban areas within driving distance may mean that a rural hospital actually has less market power than a hospital in an urban area with a dozen competitors.

The argument about a local hospital being a linchpin for a rural town's economy is probably false. Of course, any subsidized firm is a boon to a local area in terms of employment, but that is not a rationale for make-work projects. Plus, there is supposed to be a shortage of skilled workers rather than a large pool of unemployed who need jobs. It is true that many services subject to economies of scale are lacking in rural areas, but there is nothing special about healthcare.

The Missing Link in the Economics of Healthcare Competition

Both economic theory and US antitrust law agree that seller market power that increases prices above the competitive level is undesirable. As a result, many economists make common cause with antitrust litigators in opposing mergers of hospitals, and the deal is sweetened because economists can be compensated as expert witnesses (on both sides of the argument, actually). The empirical evidence discussed in this chapter that changes in hospital market structure (through mergers or acquisitions that reduce competition) are associated with price increases compared to the alternative of no merger is strong.

However, for completeness, we need to note that there is another piece of evidence that economists should require but that litigators do not. The law only requires (roughly speaking) evidence that a combination reduces consumer welfare for it to be illegal. Economics, in agreement, hypothesizes that this will happen because a price higher than the competitive level will discourage use whose value to consumers is greater than its cost of production (even if equal at the margin to the inflated price). However, how severe this harm will be depends on how responsive the use of the good in question (in this case hospital inpatient care) is to its higher price. The problem for a full-throated economic condemnation is that there is little evidence on the size of this change in quantity demanded from higher hospital prices. If it is near zero, there is still harm to consumer welfare (they pay more for the same thing) but there is no harm to economic welfare, only a transfer from buyers of hospital care to sellers of hospital care.

There is no point in including a lengthy discussion of what we do not know; someone should do a study of challenged but consummated mergers to see if there is evidence of a reduction in volume. In the meantime, we can fuel skepticism by noting that the presence of almost complete insurance probably means that individual insured consumers are buffered against monopoly-associated hospital price increases (except for surprise bills). Instead, the effects, if any, would show up as a reconfiguration of insurance networks that lead to either less volume in total or a change in pattern to less appropriate suppliers (having to travel further).

This missing link would reflect the results of what insurance managers do in response to any hospital price increases. These results could also be used in reverse to address the issue of whether some combination is harmful to efficiency. Remember the ambiguity about the effects of various kinds of vertical and conglomerate combinations? Would Sutter Health's requirement that large employer groups agree to include their smaller and more competitive hospitals in their networks if they wanted good access to Alta Bates hospital, their flagship, really matter for their employees' use of effective healthcare? One answer would be provided if we could observe or forecast whether this plan would reduce the volume of useful care (inpatient or outpatient) at any of its sites. Would volume at Alta Bates go down if some employers walked away? Would total volume in small cities with other Sutter hospitals go up? If the answer is no, or barely, that would imply that the combination did not affect net prices paid by employers and their insurers, as translated to workers. The combination would therefore be irrelevant from an economic perspective, however much it might upset other providers and buyers of healthcare – no need, according to economics, to roll out the antirust armamentarium.

Conclusion

As already noted, the managerial imperative to maximize (or at least stabilize) the value of your firm clashes with the economic nostrum of competition as the salve that binds all wounds. Antitrust law and antitrust policy are largely though not perfectly aligned with welfare economics – so the possibility of being hit with a case provides advice to managers on what to avoid. Avoid anything that looks like price-fixing, either for your hospitals or among your doctors, cool it on efforts to corner the local market, and try (if you can) to have some defensible good things to say about any combination you are contemplating. The same kind of caution applies to insurers, although the safety valve of self-insurance means there is less danger to welfare here – but not necessarily a lower likelihood of DOJ action.

To potential entrants, the economic advice is: Welcome. There are soft spots in large healthcare systems, as the experience of ambulatory surgery centers and urgent care clinics shows. Often those spots are marked with irrational "full cost" pricing by the large system, rather than by strategic pricing, and sometimes by greater convenience and patient service relative to what an empire can deliver. There are few natural or unavoidable impediments to healthcare competition in medium and large local markets, so go for it.

For antitrust policy, I have taken an aggressively old-fashioned view that larger numbers of sellers of the same products in the same market are the best target goals. More baroque combinations usually have little real prospective benefit but (as far as we can tell) are primarily motivated by managerial desire to own and sail a bigger boat for higher wages, not as effective ways to gather either more market power or higher profits. Stories abound, outside investors of various types keep trying to get in on the action, but not much matters for actual benefits and costs.

Finally, competition can be an alternative to regulation. Sometimes state regulation has been wise, so we do not have a basis for being doctrinaire here. However, if we look at the history of health regulation in the US it is not a pretty picture. Plenty of brothers-in-law of regulators or other local political bosses got nursing home franchises for profit, and even well-meaning regulation at best just adds paperwork without making a difference. Maintaining and expanding robust competitive markets is what economists, mistrustful (with good reason) of the political process, would prefer – unless regulators can be sent down from heaven or there are serious physical impediments to competition.

13 Cost Containment

Introduction

There is no good or service that consumers do not wish was cheaper. If they cannot have that happen, their next fondest desire is that things never get more expensive. Once in a while, prices do fall for some things, such as gasoline or bananas. However, as already noted, medical care prices and total spending almost never fall, not just in the US but anywhere else in the developed world. The most you can hope for is slow growth. So, what can we reasonably expect about spending growth, and when can we judge if things can be made better? This is a macro-level question for deep thinkers on healthcare policy and financing, but it also is a day-to-day challenge for managers of medical delivery systems and insurers. What advice can economics offer on what works to slow spending growth and what can reasonably be expected?

Avoiding Confusion

In any discussion of "cost containment," there is one major source of confusion: Are we talking about *levels* of cost (that consumers would like to be lower) or are we talking about *growth* in cost (that consumers would like to be slower)? The second meaning is the one we will use in this chapter. Doing so means ruling out some common stories. For example (as discussed in Chapter 1), US per capita spending on medical goods and services is higher than anywhere else in the world.[1] That is a comparative comment on levels of spending, not about rates of growth in per capita spending. In recent years, the growth rate of US spending has been close to that of comparable

[1] Conover, C. J. (2012). *The American health economy illustrated.* AEI Press.

countries – lower at 3.5% in the US versus 4.1% in comparable countries in the period 2010 to 2015, and higher at 5% versus 3.6% in 2015–2020.[2] The key conceptual point is this: To get the right perspective on the growth in cost (or any other economic variable) from one time period to a later time period, you need to look at influences that are growing or changing over time, not at those that always were suspect or problematic but have not been getting worse.

Here is another example: It is good economics to suppose that the level of prices will be higher where competition is weaker. But to explain "inflation" or growth in prices related to the lack of competition, the market environment needs to be getting less competitive over time. Perhaps there was a big merger that the Federal Trade Commission could not block. That would be expected to increase prices for a while as its impacts diffused. But then there would be no necessary reason why subsequent price or spending growth would be higher in less competitive markets than in more competitive ones. (Spending might happen to grow more slowly in more competitive markets, but we would not know the reason why.) Prescription drugs get government protection of their market power through patents, so their prices can be higher than if there were competition, but if patent protection stays the same, it cannot be a reason for rising drug prices.

This point may be confusing. If you are a monopolist (e.g., if you have a drug patent), can't you just price whatever you want? And can't you increase prices whenever you feel like it? Of course you can, but you cannot sell whatever quantity you want. If you can increase profits by charging more than you did last year, why had you set last year's price low? If you did, you were a poor excuse for a capitalist – unless you have recently increased your market power to sell more at the same price since last year. You can charge what the traffic will bear, but there is always a limit to the traffic – and once you hit it, you cannot go higher.

If a program is found to reduce the level of costs but has a delayed effect, it will reduce the growth of costs as that program is phased in. However, the bending of the cost curve will only be temporary if new technology is the reason for spending growth, and the cost curve will spring back to its former level after a while if discoveries continue to flood in at the same rate. This is thought to be what happened as people moved into managed care in the

[2] Wager, E., McGough, M., Rakshit, S., Amin, K., & Cox, C. (2024). How does health spending in the U.S. compare to other countries? Peterson-KFF Health System Tracker. www.healthsystemtracker.org/chart-collection/health-spending-u-s-compare-countries/.

1990s; cost growth was lowered for a few years, but once almost everyone had switched over, the magic went away.

For managers, this means that if you want to understand why your costs are growing, you should look for what is changing. It probably is not an outbreak of greed among your suppliers but more commonly is a change to higher-cost technology, sometimes obvious but often subtle (Boxes 13.1 and 13.2). It also means that if you want to slow cost growth you need to change something – raise cost-sharing, intensify managed care, search for different suppliers – and not just complain.

Box 13.1 Theory: Varieties of spending growth

The proposition that technological change in healthcare in the US and other developing countries has both improved health outcomes and increased costs and spending is well-established. Furthermore, the proposition that, taken as a whole, the health gains over time from this change have been "worth it" has been supported by the evidence.[3] However, economists have discovered that there are different kinds of innovations that all fall under the flag of "technological change," and that some may have better effects on cost or spending and health than others. Here is a classification based on the literature that managers may find helpful:[4]

(1) *Innovations that lower cost and improve health.* The physician-writer Lewis Thomas called these "decisively effective technologies," in contrast to the "halfway" technologies in the other three classes which do not totally prevent or cure. The polio vaccine is an example since it eliminated the need for (and cost of) care of any other type. These innovations are similar in effect to more common technological changes in other sectors of the economy such as banking and word processing, where computers eliminated many tasks (and jobs), but they have been a relatively small share so far of innovation in healthcare.

(2) *Blockbuster treatments that produce large and homogeneous improvements in health.* Because these treatments are good for everyone with the treatable condition, there is little risk of overuse. Anti-retroviral therapy for HIV is a typical example.

(3) *Treatments that are beneficial on average, but which provide positive but low benefits to some of the population.* These are treatments which provide more benefit to sicker people but some benefit to those mildly ill. In this case, moral hazard can arise.

(4) *Treatments which provide uncertain and small benefits to most users.* There may still be a positive expected benefit, but in many cases the treatment will not help, and when it does, the gains in health are small.

[3] Cutler, D. M., & McClellan, M. (2001). Is technological change in medicine worth it? *Health Affairs, 20*(5), 11–29.

[4] Thomas, L. (1977). On the science and technology of medicine. *Daedalus, 106*(1), 35–46; Chandra, A., & Skinner, J. (2012). Technology growth and expenditure growth in health care. *Journal of Economic Literature, 50*(3), 645–680.

While there is considerable evidence that, at first, adopters of new technology are imperfectly informed on how well the technology will work for them (overconfidence is common), managers should be able to classify emerging technologies into the four cells above. If so, technologies of the first two types are no-brainers; do them. However, prior information on technologies of the other two types is going to be difficult to get – what mix of patients in group 3 will be more or less effective, and for whom, and what candidates in group 4 may ultimately prove to be cost-effective for some?

If providers vary in the skill with which they can use a new technology, we can find the apparently anomalous result that the less skilled use more of it with inferior results compared to the more skilled – greater use and cost will be associated with a smaller improvement in outcome.[5] In effect, the marginal cost of improved health is higher in the less skilled site; the demand elasticity for improvements in health (even if identical in all sites) may lead to more or less spending at a higher price.

While Dr. Thomas viewed technological change in healthcare through a clinical lens, there is an economic interpretation of technical change. We can imagine that discovery of a new effective technology of any type reduces the marginal cost (in money, time, and pain) of increments to health. In the case of a previously untreatable disease, it reduces the cost from infinity, and in other cases it reduces it by a lot. The key issue here to determine effect on spending is how demand for health responds to the fall in price. Buyers might decide to celebrate the lower cost, spend less, but not increase health in this dimension – especially if the new technology makes them as healthy as they can be. The polio vaccine, a decisively effective technology, reduced the risk of infantile paralysis to zero; there was no need for improvement after that. But halfway technologies applied to conditions for which demand is price elastic can have a different effect: Now that it is cheaper and easier to treat a condition, demanders might decide to buy a lot more (as long as they do not bump up against a limit), thus increasing spending. Here an example is laparoscopic gall bladder surgery, which was less costly, less risky, and more effective than open surgery in treating a disease which can cause episodes of intense pain. As a result, people with the disease who put up with their condition rather than go under the knife for major abdominal surgery lined up for the new lower-cost treatment, and spending grew.[6] It is my conjecture that healthcare innovation does not usually lower cost as much as innovation in other industries because demand for health is elastic and the more numerous new technologies have largely been "halfway" in terms of outcome – health is improved but not perfected. This is why healthcare is not like computer chips. These thoughts may help managers understand the impact of new technologies and make them feel better.

[5] Skinner, J. S., Staiger, D. O., & Fisher, E. S. (2006). Is technological change in medicine always worth it? The case of acute myocardial infarction: Waste and inefficiency are not inevitable by-products of technological growth. *Health Affairs*, *25*(Suppl. 1), W34–W47.

[6] Legorreta, A. P., Silber, J. H., Costantino, G. N., Kobylinski, R. W., & Zatz, S. L. (1993). Increased cholecystectomy rate after the introduction of laparoscopic cholecystectomy. *JAMA*, *270*(12), 1429–1432.

Box 13.2 Evidence: Computers, electronic medical records, artificial intelligence, and medical spending growth

Changes in the availability of electronic methods for storing, transmitting, and analyzing data have made major differences in the economy. Convenience has risen and costs (and employment) have fallen in banking, journalism, travel booking, and many other sectors. Over the decades that the power of computers increased (called Moore's law), conventional wisdom has lamented the inertia in healthcare for moving to such methods. There is little rigorous evidence so far, as we shall see, but a lot of boosterism and bright futurism is now directed at artificial intelligence (AI) as the next great hope: what Chaiyachati and Desai call "highly anticipated" changes.[7] What do economic research and theory have to say about the possibility, at last, that the wave will crest?

It is not that electronic methods have not been adopted in US healthcare but rather that the adoption has been selective. Tabulating and paying bills in healthcare, getting the needed information to insurers, and getting the money back to providers has been accomplished. Not only has this mission led to fewer financial errors, less risk to consumers, and more reliable revenue streams for providers but it has changed how care is used. Most obviously, insurance coverage for prescription drugs, and the boost it gives to use (for good or ill), would have been much slower and less complete without the development of systems to process enormous volumes of small-dollar transactions. While this process was developed by profit-seeking insurance firms dealing with revenue-seeking providers, the other major change in healthcare – the electronic medical record (EMR) – has been much more stubborn though subject to much more push from government.

The concept of an easily transmitted and managed EMR is sound. It could in principle improve coordination among providers treating a patient for a given illness. The use by the patient of this record through patient-facing portals may sometimes be helpful but may also generate work if the patient does not understand the terminology or the full plan for care. In practice, the EMR has not had a good reception from physicians. In part, this is because the necessary standardization requires them to gather and record information that may be of low relevance to a particular case – looking at the computer rather than at the patient – and in part because (compared to a physician's own preferred form of documentation) it did not fit as readily with each physician's desire to record the most salient information on a given patient. There is as yet no rigorous evidence on the cost-effectiveness of the EMR.

Virtual visits by necessity surged during the pandemic but as a proportion of the total have largely fallen back to lower levels. Certainly, favorable Medicare reimbursements speeded things up while unfavorable reimbursements by private plans have slowed things down, but insurers have chosen these policies because of a lack of favorable evidence of demand and

[7] Chaiyachati, K. H., & Desai, B. (2022). The unmet and evolving need for evidence-based telehealth. In Pauly, M., Winston, F., Naylor, M. et al., *Seemed like a good idea: Alchemy versus evidence-based approaches to healthcare management innovation* (pp. 301–331). Cambridge University Press.

cost-saving. Here again the greater convenience of virtual contact as opposed to the travel–wait–appointment–drive home model of provider contact may have led to higher costs and spending by stimulating use. This could be a beneficial increase in access, but this could also be inefficient use of care. The primary stimulus to telehealth so far has been a shortage of face-to-face providers. Beyond rural areas where specialists are few, this is not a reliable source of growth nor one associated with cost-reduction.

What about AI? The hope is that AI can help providers find key information about a patient in the sea of data. Continuous monitoring by AI algorithms of some chronically ill patients may help, compared to scheduled visits or patient reports of symptoms. Furthermore, AI could be used to write patient notes or respond to patient portal messages. It may even be able to diagnose patients based on patterns of symptoms, read medical imaging, and devise treatment plans. However, the effectiveness, and especially the cost-effectiveness, of this intervention as with most of the others remains to be proven.

There is no evidence that the spread of computerized billing or EMR has so far lowered the growth of medical spending. The kinds of layoffs and hiring freezes that accompanied the electronic revolution in other sectors have not happened in healthcare and do not seem likely any time soon, nor has there been a surge in improved patient outcomes or satisfaction related to the use of computers in healthcare. Perhaps the personal nature of the key medical encounter between patient and providers cannot be much improved by such means; computers would be no help at the barber shop, and maybe not so much in the examining room, either.

What's So Great about Cost Containment?

The medical care spending that American consumers make is almost all revenue paid out to American providers of healthcare services; there is very little care bought from foreigners or foreign-owned companies. Neither China nor Saudi Arabia, our usual frenemies, are major suppliers. One implication is that cost containment for buyers means income containment for other (American) sellers, to their potential frustration. Economists do not know whom to favor.

Historically, healthcare would be classified as a growth industry with revenues increasing year to year (even in the face of recession) and growing more rapidly than national income or GDP. Usually, we economists interpret growth in revenue and employment in an industry as a sign of something favorable – wealth grows and employment grows. Healthcare revenues – and maybe healthcare employment (of MBAs at least) – are treated as an exception to this favorable view (for reasons noted in Chapter 1). But if higher spending reflects more value, there is no reason to single out this industry for criticism. So, do we think higher medical spending is valueless?

Here I return to the question of spending growth in a specific context. I was one of several dozen experts convened by the journal *Health Affairs* for a three-year study of cost containment in the US as part of the Council on Health Care Spending and Value.[8] This council was chaired by Senator William Frist and former Food and Drug Administration Commissioner Margaret Hamburg. The goal was to discover which (if any) changes somewhere in the system would slow the growth in spending. The council would have been happy if spending fell but that was not a realistic prospect; it was willing to settle for (and endorse) policies that made growth slower than it would have been without those policies. I will summarize the council's deliberations as the best discussion and evidence to date on cost containment.

How Do We Know Something Is Wrong?

The justification the council offers for looking at both levels and growth of cost is fundamentally a feeling – not much more than that – that some (perhaps much) of medical spending in the US does not yield commensurate health benefits – and that this continues to be true of new spending. There are those Scandinavians who spend a little less but are splendidly healthier than us, as the obvious hint of inefficiency. (No one praises the UK model of growing waiting lists and long emergency room lines.) There is also a little less persuasive evidence that the growth in US spending, surely accompanied by improvements in health,[9] should have slowed. Finally, there is the old conclusion that 30% of spending is wasteful because that is the variation in Medicare cost that the Dartmouth study found to be unrelated to Medicare outcomes.[10]

I have argued that these kinds of comparisons do not prove there is waste in our healthcare system that somebody knows something to do about. If they do, somebody should do it. But waste as a cause of the *growth* in spending means something even less well-established – that whatever waste

[8] Council on Health Care Spending and Value. (2023). *A roadmap for action: Recommendations of the Health Affairs Council on Health Care Spending and Value*. Health Affairs. www.healthaffairs.org/pb-assets/documents/CHS_Report/CHS_Report_2022_R5-1675432678.pdf.

[9] Lichtenberg, F. R. (2007). The impact of new drugs on US longevity and medical expenditure, 1990–2003: Evidence from longitudinal, disease-level data. *American Economic Review, 97*(2), 438–443; Almond, D., Doyle, J. J., Jr., Kowalski, A. E., & Williams, H. (2010). Estimating marginal returns to medical care: Evidence from at-risk newborns. *The Quarterly Journal of Economics, 125*(2), 591–634.

[10] Skinner, J., & Fisher, E. (2010). Reflections on geographic variations in US health care. Dartmouth Institute for Health Policy and Clinical Practice, May 12.

there was in the US system last year, it got *worse* over the last 12 months. You would need a story about what determinant changed for the worse to prove this, and until the council convened, no one had.

This negative view of medical cost growth comes despite some fairly persuasive recent evidence that the return on investment in health in the US system is acceptable, even if it might have been yet higher and has been higher in some other countries.[11] To the extent that spending growth is the necessary correlate of more cost-effective treatments – which, by definition, have a positive incremental cost – containing that cost would be a mistake. We can ask the rhetorical question of whether anyone would want the 1960s level of spending if it came with only the 1960s technology. I still miss my Ford Galaxie 500, but it is no comparison to a modern car (even before Tesla). The technical progress that has generated treatment for previously untreatable diseases – whether hepatitis C or psoriatic arthritis – is even more pronounced in healthcare than in other sectors of the economy.

An Alternative Take on Waste as a Cause of Health Spending Growth

Writing in 1977, Lewis Thomas argued that medical spending growth to that point (which President Nixon had claimed was unsustainable) was in large part due to a change in attitudes by consumers and physicians. Thomas thought that "the biggest source of waste results from the general public conviction that contemporary medicine is able to accomplish a great deal more than is in fact possible."[12] This change in expectation is contradicted by the fact that, according to him, "most people are, in real life, abundantly healthy," despite the erroneous perception "that the body is fundamentally flawed, subject to disintegration at any moment, always on the verge of mortal disease, always in need of continual monitoring and support by health care professionals."[13] This hypothesis about hypochondriacal misperception

[11] Dunn, A., Fernando, L., & Liebman, E. (2024). How much are medical innovations worth? A detailed analysis using cost-effectiveness studies. Bureau of Economic Analysis Working Paper No. WP2024-08; Weaver, M. R., Joffe, J., Ciarametaro, M., Dubois, R. W., Dunn, A., Singh, A., . . . & Dieleman, J. L. (2022). Health care spending effectiveness: Estimates suggest that spending improved US health from 1996 to 2016: Study examines health care spending effectiveness, the ratio of an increase in spending per case of illness or injury to an increase in disability-adjusted life-years averted per case. *Health Affairs*, *41*(7), 994–1004; Dunn, A., Whitmire, B., Batch, A., Fernando, L., & Rittmueller, L. (2018). High spending growth rates for key diseases in 2000–14 were driven by technology and demographic factors. *Health Affairs*, *37*(6), 915–924.

[12] Thomas, L. (1977). On the science and technology of medicine. *Daedalus*, *106*(1), 35–46 (at 45).

[13] Thomas, L. (1977). On the science and technology of medicine. *Daedalus*, *106*(1), 35–46 (at 43).

is probably true, and certainly consistent with the current trend toward digital monitoring of patients and retail sales of devices for clinical-quality electrocardiograms for apparently healthy people. Economics cannot provide an explanation of this change in tastes other than to blame continual commercial and public service exhortations about the need for healthcare screening and monitoring of healthy people as part of a public health–based population model. It does, however, suggest that, at a high enough price, consumers might revert to less anxiety about remaining healthy and being satisfied with a much lower rate of buzz about symptoms and treatments. A health maintenance organization (HMO) based on such principles (the no-worries health plan) might even succeed.

It would be bad news for cost containment experts if there is really not that much waste in the US healthcare system – and hence not that much room to cut spending without doing much harm to health outcomes broadly defined. Nevertheless, the Council on Health Care Spending and Value took the view that current levels of spending or growth are both "disproportionate to the health and equity they produce."[14] Needless to say (after everything I have said already), this is not a conclusion supported by bulletproof evidence; there is the hope that there is enough slack as yet to be identified and altered, that there are (in the words of the report) "actions that would reduce the growth rate with little effect on health."

Another concern about spending growth in particular is more forward-looking: There is concern that we may have such a high level of medical spending growth that it "raises concerns about Americans' ability to pay" more than what they are paying. I will discuss this dystopian future more in the section titled "Is Too Much of a Good Thing a Threat to Cost Containment?"

In my summary, the council came up with four specific targets or methods (a little of both) for cost containment, two of which rest on reasonably firm evidence that there is something there (how much is there remaining uncertain) and two of which are speculative but speculation worth having. The four targets are:

(1) Administrative costs, especially those associated with health insurance.
(2) Competition policy in geographic areas where there could be competition.
(3) Politically chosen spending targets by states.
(4) Something about value-based care and payment.

[14] Council on Health Care Spending and Value. (2023). *A roadmap for action: Recommendations of the Health Affairs Council on Health Care Spending and Value.* Health Affairs. www.healthaffairs.org/pb-assets/documents/CHS_Report/CHS_Report_2022_R5-1675432678.pdf.

Here I discuss each of the four, both in the abstract sense of why the council considered them good and promising targets and in the concrete sense of what they would mean for medical system and insurance managers who want to go ahead.

Administrative Costs

Much – how much is in some dispute – of America's medical care delivery system cost is incurred not in providing goods or services but in record-keeping and information transfer associated with providing, coordinating, and paying for those services. Reasonable guesses range from about 15% to 30%. In all countries, there are some nonclinical care costs because care requires recording, storing, and accessing information on patient histories and use of care. This component is not usually regarded as excessive in the US, even if electronic patient record systems are sometimes fiascos, a bane for physicians, and unappreciated by patients. Rather, the costs that might be targeted are those associated with payment – keeping track of what is billable, communicating with multiple insurers who cover the patients at most health systems (Kaiser is the exception), adjudicating the amount of the claim, and then paying it. In addition, there are costs away from the clinic incurred to enroll consumers in insurance plans, collect their premiums, and verify their coverage.

In European countries with multiple sickness funds, there are similar costs and similar arguments between providers and insurers, but those costs are not as large as in the US because there is much less diversity among health plans. Because insurance requires some risk capital, that investment is compensated in the private sector by the part of premiums that goes to profit, although on average this is a small share of total administrative costs. (Public plans also bear risk, and there is an implicit cost to the taxpayers who pay for unpredictable claims in Medicare and Medicaid, but that is never measured.)

The Council on Health Care Spending and Value looked at empirical studies of insurer administrative costs, most especially those done by David Cutler, a member of the council. Their overall conclusion is that all such costs amount to about one-quarter of total health spending, some borne by insurers and some by providers.[15] The percentage of administrative costs

[15] Cutler, D. (2020). *Reducing administrative costs in U.S. healthcare*. The Hamilton Project. Policy Proposal 2020-09. Brookings. www.hamiltonproject.org/assets/files/Cutler_PP_LO.pdf.

for health insurers is actually smaller, at about 15%, than for other kinds of insurances consumers buy, such as homeowners' insurance or auto insurance, where administrative costs can be 50% of premiums or more. Administrative costs are reduced in health insurance by the economies of scale in group insurance and the low explicit administrative costs of Medicare and Medicaid – but they still amount to something. One possible spectacle that would upset observers is an arms race in which providers use expensive computer programs to structure their claims in a way likely to get reimbursed generously, while insurers offer dueling programs to detect and defeat upcoding. In the end, the division of revenues may end up the same but much has been wasted on software and those who run it.

It is much less clear what the growth has been in these costs. The safest conjecture is that their proportion of spending has been fairly constant over time, so their growth must be about the same as that of other healthcare costs.

But now for the hard part: Can managers of insurance plans or medical service delivery systems get these administrative costs down? They could pay every claim that came in, no questions asked, which would lower administrative cost (and delay in payment) but would invite abuse. The council had no surefire solution to offer, and there is no rigorous evidence in the literature of successes in lowering insurer administrative cost. It is probably true that closed panel insurances like Kaiser have lower administrative costs because there is only one integrated insurer, but beyond that little is known.

There is a caution here: US administrative costs are high and higher than in other countries because in the US, in both Medicare and private insurance, consumers have a choice among plans. The Medicare fee-for-service (FFS) plan reports administrative costs as a percentage of claims much lower than the average in the US or in private Medicare Advantage plans, but Medicare bears no explicit costs for selling insurance and collecting premiums, and it makes providers bear the cost of questionable claims. If there was just one big, mandated plan for the whole country, at least there would be no arguing about which insurer should cover the bill, and probably some economies of scale. However, so far Americans seem to prefer having choice among plans and have rejected universal mandates for a single public plan. So, guess what? There is going to be a trade-off between lower administrative costs and less variety of plans. The council explicitly chose to endorse variety and still seek ways to "streamline" (a synonym for "reduce variation in") administrative processes in a way that will reduce spending by $30 billion to $60 billion a year (real money but not a large fraction of total private insurance premiums). Doing both is a heavy lift, to say the least.

Even here there is a bit of an inconsistency. A health plan could spend money on managing managed care, raising its administrative costs but lowering its claims by routing beneficiaries to lower-cost providers and using protocols and prior authorization (and dealing with social determinants of health). Setting issues of satisfaction aside, buyers may prefer a lower premium plan that manages to avoid covering low-value care, even if they have to pay more for nonphysician and electronic gatekeepers – they do not care about the administrative cost percentage per se, only about premiums and benefits. A good example is the private Medicare Advantage plans which have higher administrative costs than original Medicare and yet have a rapidly growing market share.

What advice did the council give to managers? One is a bit of a tangent, involving ways to reduce the administrative burden and attendant frustration of physicians. Here the council suggests streamlined provider directories so consumers can know in real time who is in their insurer network, accepting their payment, and who is not, as well as more uniform credentialling across states to spot poor-performing physicians without imposing heavy burdens on the innocent majority. These changes would save millions but probably not the desired billions.

There is some evidence for larger savings from centralizing and standardizing claims processing, prior authorizations, disputes, and the like. It is likely that no single insurance firm, much less any single insurance manager, could make this happen on their own; the creation of a larger entity to do it would have to be collective in some way.

There are at least two hurdles to doing so. One is that insurers or employers can distinguish themselves by what we might call the strictness of their claims processing. Some are lenient but charge high premiums; others offer low costs but more hassle for patients and doctors. Could this, or should this, be made uniform to save money? And could plans get together and do it free of antitrust scrutiny? The answers to these questions are probably yes, but who takes the first step and who decides on where to go and how is unspecified. Perhaps individual states could take the lead, though they are hobbled by the exemption of self-insured workers from their reach. A federal government compact on these items would be a big deal but worth a try or at least a discussion. Note, however, that in the administrative cost margins of all insurers, public and private, the percentage that goes to claims processing is usually about 3% or 4%, not 20%.

One other hurdle applies to ways to streamline the measurement of medical care or health plan quality. Currently there are dozens of such measures in a measurement market, some required by government (like stars for Medicare Advantage plans) and some technically voluntary but hard to avoid (like US News and World Report rankings). The problem with doing this is obvious: What is that metric? And do consumers care, or care enough to spend more on getting more than one measure? Regulators care, but that is not the same thing. This is another one of those cases where it is worthwhile to see if we can somehow give it a shot. Maybe a failure but alright to try.

The managers most directly responsible for insurer administrative costs are managers of insurance plans. It goes without saying that they should not waste money on useless provisions that bother doctors and patients, but what about investing in an innovative way to limit low-value care? The best medicine for high administrative costs may not be administrative rules but enhancement of competition among insurers which provides a strong incentive to avoid useless care and useless computing.

Competition Policy

The Council on Health Care Spending and Value, especially the economists on it, argued that competition among sellers of medical services is associated with lower levels of prices – and probably spending – than less competition. The argument was based in part on economic theory but also on good evidence – at least for hospitals. They maintained even more strongly that reductions in competition (through mergers within a market) lead to higher and growing spending for a time after such mergers with no improvements in quality however defined.[16] Most of the work on competition refers to competition among hospitals (remember, a third of total spending), and here reality must intrude. There are, as discussed earlier, some economies of scale up to a point in hospitals; little hospitals are costly for what they do and are limited in their ability to do it. The evidence that competition is highest in big cities has a mirror image in the evidence that hospitals in small towns usually have a monopoly. Therefore, the council concluded that regulation rather than competition might be best in these smaller markets.

[16] Dranove, D., & Burns, L. R. (2022). *Big med: Megaproviders and the high cost of health care in America*. University of Chicago Press; Cooper, Z., & Gaynor, M. (2021). Addressing hospital concentration and rising consolidation in the United States. 1% Steps for Health Care Reform. Policy brief. https://onepercentsteps.com/policy-briefs/addressing-hospital-concentration-and-rising-consolidation-in-the-united-states/.

Hospitals in small towns with the structure of monopoly often are financially challenged; they are not the obvious reason for America's high hospital costs. Public policy looks to find subsidies to keep them alive. Even though they are the only game in their town, they often cannot charge high enough prices to stay afloat. This apparent paradox is sometimes explained by lower-than-average incomes in rural towns and sometimes by the greater willingness of residents needing costly care to go to the closest big city with a much better-equipped hospital. While there is a powerful rural hospital lobby, public policy toward them is unclear: Should they be able to be full-service high-quality general hospitals – which, given economies of scale, will make them expensive and require a subsidy – or should they be outposts of larger city-based systems used for very routine services, as a substitute for nursing homes or hospices, and as intake points for patients to be transferred? There probably is a model that matches the local services a small hospital can efficiently provide with complementary structures at larger distant hospitals but so far no one has developed this model. Medicare efforts to bribe smaller hospitals to shrink the number of services they offer in favor of enhanced emergency services have so far failed.[17]

In my view, as already discussed in Chapter 12, the most promising but also daunting area of competition policy (for states as well as the Department of Justice), having succeeded blocking any more horizontal mergers, is to do something about areas with large enough populations to have many efficient-sized hospital competitors but do not. Somewhere between 30% and 40% of the population lives in places like Pittsburgh, Indianapolis, Austin, or Albuquerque where there are only a couple of hospitals of any size. Many times, those hospitals have grown by acquiring or merging with other (financially weak) hospitals in town and they still have separate campuses scattered about. From an economic viewpoint, these combinations could be unwound by public policies intended to try competition before instituting price or cost regulation – as well as by encouraging entry by new hospitals or even new outposts of out-of-town hospital systems. It couldn't hurt. Some states' attorneys general have mutually taken the lead in trying to get more competitive behavior in these cities.

There are now many new combinations of healthcare providers that span geography and provider types. Hospitals buy or offer franchises to medical groups, chains of hospitals span states, and hospital substitutes proliferate. Pharmacies like CVS purchase medical insurers like Aetna, offer Medicare

[17] Gowrisankaran, G., Lucarelli, C., Schmidt-Dengler, P., & Town, R. (2018). Can amputation save the hospital? The impact of the Medicare Rural Flexibility Program on demand and welfare. *Journal of Health Economics*, *58*, 110–122.

Part D plans, operate retail clinics, and dispense medications. Sometimes we economists think that these "nonhorizontal" combinations are problematic but other times they could give a boost to competition. The most glaring concern is associated with changes which combine physicians into larger entities and thus reduce competition among them, so maybe policy should start there.

There the message from economics is that market power leads to higher prices than under competition – but not necessarily to more rapidly increasing prices. One obvious implication is that policy should discourage reductions over time in competition. A less obvious consideration (that the council ignored) is whether empirically the growth in spending (remember, largely as a function of new technology and rising wages) is different in competitive and less competitive markets. This remains an important open question.

One final worry. Although health economists cite lessening of competition as a stock answer to questions about why national spending is increasing, the size of the price or spending increase associated with mergers is only about 15% in the merging market, not nearly enough to account for the kinds of all-market spending increases we are used to seeing (given the percentage of hospitals who merge each year) and not (as far as I know) shown to be correlated with national health expenditure growth. I still maintain the economist's faith that it is better for markets to be competitive, but we need to be humble here (as elsewhere).

It is probably too much to ask of managers of incumbent firms to work toward greater competition and attendant diminution of their own market power. The exhortations about greater competition should go first to federal and especially state attorneys general – but they also present opportunities for potential competitors to hospitals, like freestanding ambulatory surgery or imaging centers. These new entrants should arrive with both lower prices and greater efforts to publicize their lower prices, behaviors that sometimes but not always happen.[18] Insurers should favor greater competition among hospitals and hospitals should favor greater competition among insurers – perhaps these two sentiments can converge.

Government rules requiring price transparency may help, but lower-priced sellers already have strong incentives to let customers know about their prices. If "15 minutes can save you 15% on your car insurance," the potential savings in health insurance costs are much larger.

[18] Pauly, M. V. (2013). *Health reform without side effects: Making markets work for individual health insurance*. Hoover Press.

State-Level Spending Growth Targets

Another tool for cost containment that the Council on Health Care Spending and Value examined is the establishment by individual states of spending growth targets for all or some components of medical spending in that state – not usually for drugs but often for hospitals. The idea is that there would be a collective or political decision on what growth in spending would be desired, usually determined by some existing or new government body charged with this responsibility. That target would then be proclaimed, to anyone who cared to listen, and who wanted to go along with state authorities – for example, state Blue Cross plans and hospital associations. Maryland alone has historically maintained state setting of payments and targets for hospital care, and it serves as the (somewhat imperfect) poster child for this effort. Some other states have now, to a greater or lesser degree, set up ways to determine and promulgate spending growth targets.

The way to determine the target, or to enforce it if it is missed, has so far not been subject to economic analysis, only by political choices in Democratic states like Massachusetts and Washington State. The council agreed that this is an option the citizens of some states might wish to pursue. There was a minority report – of which I was a part – against a policy of "encouraging" state growth target-setting in all states, whatever that might mean, rather than just letting it happen when and if a state's voters choose to make it happen. But there was general acceptance of the desirability of assembling data that might help in such an effort, however that data might be used.

The fundamental concept is that some state entity would express a public preference for a particular aggregate statewide spending growth rate. The next step in the program would then be to compare actual or projected growth with the desired rate – and presumably express alarm or anxiety if the actual rate was or was expected to be above the target, singling out for attention hospitals failing to toe the line. The data collection would be involved with tracking the actual growth – getting accurate information on the revenues of firms in the state in each period to compare with the previous period. Setting the growth target is less dependent on data or evidence and more dependent on the judgment of politicians and regulators, though there would presumably be opportunities for various citizen groups to express preferences. Ideally, the target should depend on data about the causes of future spending growth and the value of health benefits it might offer – a cost-effectiveness calculation – but because such data often does not exist, the target would usually be determined by a consensus of opinion. Often "round numbers" are invoked, such as holding the state GDP share of health spending constant, without attempts to justify or explain the chosen target relative to some other. Sometimes prior state decisions on the growth of insurance premiums or the growth of Medicaid spending are invoked and then generalized to all spending. The reverse may also happen: A state insurance regulator may refuse to approve proposed private insurance premium growth rates that violate the target (but this would not apply to self-insured group insurance). Thus far, beyond moral or political pressure, there has been no enforcement of spending targets beyond their public relations status.

There is an economic rationale for such a procedure. If there is to be regulation of spending growth, we experts typically imagine that evidence on the expected benefits of any new technology that is part of spending growth would be cited, along with evidence on the size and justifiability of other influences on that growth such as malpractice laws or wage increases, accompanied by an assumption about how much waste could be cut over the given time period. Spending growth targets reverse this process. They announce a collectively chosen target, presumably how much more citizens are willing to pay for medical care, and then tell firms supplying that care to do the best they can to stay within that target. They thus avoid tackling the challenging tasks of valuing any potential improvements in health or determining how much waste there is to reduce. Presumably, if firms stay below the target, all is well and good, as long as nothing obviously terrible happens to health outcomes or consumer satisfaction. Should these measures start to go south, presumably the spending targets would be reexamined and adjusted if warranted by a collective comparison of benefits and costs.

There is as yet no evidence on how or if state spending targets would work other than the not-inconsequential evidence that some states are able to choose them. Maryland's "global budget" program eventually slowed hospital spending growth from an initial high level;[19] maybe the cause was not an adept bureaucracy (although it was well managed) but rather regression to the mean. This is where the minority report came in. The members of the council minority (me included) thought there should be more evidence on whether such programs do more good than harm before encouraging them for all states with different capacities for wise regulation and room for

[19] RTI International. (2018). *Evaluation of the Maryland all-payer model: Third annual report*. https://downloads.cms.gov/files/cmmi/md-all-payer-thirdannrpt.pdf.

improvement. It may well be that some state voters, especially in high-spending states (relative to the national average) will want to go this route, while others will not.

One political issue that is likely to arise when private spending growth is driven by private choices (about access to new technologies, for example) is whether the state has a role in forbidding people from spending more of their own money on their own healthcare. Of course, with subsidies to exchange plans and the tax exclusion for group coverage, there is virtually no private buyer of insurance or care who is not now subsidized to some extent.

For managers, it will obviously be better to follow the economic model the state uses and see if you can somehow break even or make reasonable profits by managing costs to stay under the target without doing apparent harm to health or patient satisfaction. In case of bad news – it can't be done this year – managers should have already contributed to a stockpile of evidence showing the unavoidable trade-offs that might be required. Variation across firms is going to make having a united front complicated, so actual supply responses – withdrawing or postponing potentially beneficial but more costly (even if cost-effective) treatments – may be an unavoidable last resort. My own view is that some states should give this a shot. Just not my state.

Continue to Monitor and Hope for Value-Based Care

The Council on Health Care Spending and Value had the same view of value-based care (VBC) as described earlier in this book: enthusiasm about moving away from FFS but disappointment about the small or negligible effects of actual programs to do so up to this point. What is to be encouraged here then is not universal VBC or even large-scale application of the concept to things like cost-sharing in insurance or payment for cancer care but rather encouragement for experimentation to see if someone can get it right. There seems to be no reason to pull the plug on efforts to keep trying, as long as we can avoid the syndrome of declaring success for anything the policymaker thought worthwhile to demonstrate. That is, keep in place the appropriately skeptical and rigorous evaluation of efforts until or if something pulls ahead of the tired pack.

To restate the issue: The theory of optimal incentives in economics says that FFS at the levels currently used in Medicare is not sure to produce the best outcomes. There is plenty of evidence that Medicare outcomes do not match in many cases the ideal of our dreams. The problem is that there is so far no development of an alternative theory of payment that will always produce better outcomes and appreciably lower spending growth, and no evidence at all that any alternative tried so far has done so.[20] Hence my (and the council's) counsel to managers is to watch but be skeptical.

Is Too Much of a Good Thing a Threat to Cost Containment?

There is high-level concern among noneconomist observers of healthcare systems around the world that a flood of effective innovations, along with high prices for them, may drive health spending so high that something bad is bound to happen (despite the good news about effective treatments for currently intractable diseases). A group of physicians writing a forward-looking op-ed in the *New England Journal of Medicine* professed to be worried about "unsustainable cost structures in the developed world" as "future health spending is expected to rise even further as new techniques and therapies become available."[21] Could rising spending turn good news into bad?

Economists would say that this concern is illogical. If "unsustainable" means that buyers will not be willing to pay costs growing above some level, they would refuse or postpone some new technology – they will not spend. Then the sellers of that technology will presumably have to settle for what they can get and so would cut price to a sustainable level (better than selling nothing). If sellers instead exit because lower prices would cause them to lose money, the definition of such an intervention whose costs are greater than buyers' value would be one that is not cost-effective. So, either innovations will be sustainable if they are cost-effective or, if not, they should not be used.

Economics thus provides a negative answer to the question of whether the cost of some innovation is unsustainable. There may need to be a somewhat more sophisticated version of cost-effectiveness analysis, however. Usually, a study of cost-effectiveness analysis of a medical procedure will announce a conclusion like "this new procedure adds QALYs [quality-adjusted life years] at a price of $100,000 per QALY." We are then supposed to compare

[20] Agarwal, R., Liao, J. M., Gupta, A., & Navathe, A. S. (2020). The impact of bundled payment on health care spending, utilization, and quality: A systematic review. *Health Affairs*, *39*(1), 50–57.

[21] Zimlichman, E., Nicklin, W., Aggarwal, R., & Bates, D. W. (2021). Health care 2030: The coming transformation. *NEJM Catalyst Innovations in Care Delivery*, *2*(2). https://catalyst.nejm.org/doi/full/10.1056/CAT.20.0569.

that price with some assumed and fixed threshold maximum dollar value per QALY (like $150,000). However, suppose there was not just one but many cost-effective innovations that arrived all at once, so much so that the cost of paying for them would bite deeply into consumers' purchases of other things they value. (Presumably what the doctors were worried about.) You (as a representative consumer) who followed the simple cost-effectiveness decision rule would say to yourself (and others who cared to listen), "If I or my insurance buys all these treatments, I will be healthier which I like, but will have to pay so much more in premiums that I will have to give up housing, meals away from home, and entertainment, which I like even more." This is the economic idea of diminishing marginal benefit of any specific good – more is better but not that much better, and less is worse but much worse. To translate this into cost-effectiveness language, you would say that the value of other things you would give up to get another QALY has fallen from $150,000, maybe even below $100,000 if you are miserable enough. You could be miserable because your consumption bundle would contain too much health and too little fun – so you will not want all that new health technology.

This aspect of human behavior would then naturally place a voluntary limit on the rate of spread of new beneficial costly technology to the level that people can "afford," if "afford" means they choose to buy it. Of course, if people have different incomes, then low-income people would drop out of the technology-friendly insurance plans first, something fundamentally caused by a maldistribution of income that no one seems poised to change. The punchline is that there cannot be too much of a good thing in voluntary economic markets – if only because the more you get of something the less good it seems to you. Governments may overdo it because they do not have the same kind of consumer constraints, but informed consumers should not.

Does this scholastic (if crystalline-pure) thinking help managers? It at least means that they do not have to prepare for the sky to fall. It also means that, when they put on their analyst hats, they should be prepared to attach somewhat less value to health innovations that would swamp the budget. The problem is not that there is a healthcare budget (as the Institute for Clinical and Economic Review thinks) but rather that people do not want to spend their entire income all on one thing. It probably means that the pace of innovation matters – if there is an admission fee for access to the fountain of youth, payment for permission to visit should be spread over time. A bonanza of new treatments that happen all at once will be more of a problem than if they are spaced out.

How should managers and policymakers prepare for the possibility of a blockbuster health-improving innovation but one with high cost and patent protection? One part of the answer is to take steps in advance to warn and clear the path for premium increases if they are needed to cover the additional payments for treatments that save many QALYs. For employers and their benefit managers, this might mean announcing beforehand that "in our firm we will pay for miracle treatments, even if that means an increase in premiums or a reduction in raises." That might attract high-quality foresighted workers. For Medicare and Medicaid, it means warning that budgets need to be flexible and that the taxpayers as well as the beneficiaries will need to pick up the tab for life-saving innovations, such as genetic treatments for sickle cell disease. In both cases, it is well to announce in advance the criteria used to accept or reject an effective treatment offered at a given price; try once again to put lipstick on cost effectiveness as an acceptable decision criterion.

Looking up the Pipeline: What Might Happen to Spending Growth in the Future?

The easiest and often the most accurate method to predict the future is to imagine it will be like the recent past with maybe a few tweaks. The growth in both national health spending, Medicare costs, and private insurance costs has recently flattened (setting aside the Covid pandemic, which actually reduced spending on healthcare services even as it called forth a flood of federal subsidies to keep healthcare providers afloat). The growth recently has been closer to the growth in real GDP per capita or worker productivity, equal in some years and (except for Covid) less than 1% more. The health spending share of GDP was the same in 2023 as in 2009. Could this continue?

An iron law of arithmetic says that if any component of some aggregate grows faster (by even a small amount) than the aggregate, its share of the total will increase over time. The share cannot go on increasing forever. It is too soon (even after a decade) to declare that we have hit the ceiling; discovery of a cure for Alzheimer's or pancreatic cancer could bump things up – but the hypothesis of never-ending unsustainable growth looks less tenable than it has for years.

As the economist-humorist Herb Stein responded to a similar prediction about another economic measure, "If it cannot go on like this forever, it won't." In the case of the medical care spending share, there is more backing for this aphorism in economic theory. That theory imagines that consumers divide a fixed budget among different categories of spending based in large part on their preferences but also on relative prices. If the price of broccoli rises, it will appear on fewer tables, and the share of spending on cruciferous vegetables will eventually stop growing or fall. Concretely, that elusive number – the dollar value of a QALY (whatever it is) – will eventually fall as people become ever healthier and then, according to economics, attach less value to even more health; this will revolutionize cost-effectiveness analysis but poses no problem for market and consumer adjustment. In addition, as the value of added health falls, so will the prices that innovators can charge for the next great thing. All will (eventually) be well.

Do managers need to anticipate the day when even effective healthcare is less economically lustrous than great meals away from home? The problem is that no one knows the day or the hour when this will happen. We do know some things – for example, that there is a bulging pipeline of potentially expensive but highly effective genetic treatments we may face. However, this prediction has been made for at least a decade without leading to much additional spending (yet) and with market resistance (even when there is political concession) to some very expensive treatments. I personally am not as worried about the payment challenge for good treatments for sickle cell disease or hemophilia as I am about most other things in healthcare – but think that if they appear our health insurance system can handle it – though not without some gnashing of teeth. But that is why we are paid the big bucks.

Conclusion

Managers will not be able to do much about rising health worker wages driving prices and spending growth (nor should they). All hospitals in town, and probably all hospitals nationwide, will be subject to them; the most that can be done is to explain that rising input prices, not increasing inefficiency, explains what is going on. When it comes to costly but beneficial new technology, there may be options both for health system and for insurance managers to control it, if it is the case that consumers have different preferences for paying for early or unlimited access to the latest innovations. The idea then is that providers or insurers can choose a strategy toward the bundles of such technologies (probably not one by one): They can either adopt early and often, with rapidly rising premiums, or hold back and limit, with slower (but still positive) growth.

It will then be up to consumers, or employers as agents for workers, to choose which type of care and cost growth they want – smart but fast or dumb but slow. Transparency and honesty (but also a good advertising slogan) will help here as a way of empowering consumers to choose how they want to spend their gains and income and what potential gains in health they seek. The alternative – a board of wise people evaluating new technology within assumed monetary value for health – has been preferred by other nations and might be chosen by some states. However, there is a market alternative. The competitive markets cure-all can come into play, but it needs public intervention to materialize and persist; that is what antitrust policy is for. The collective decision to keep healthcare markets open to competition is one economists wish for – but politics may dispose.

14 Drugs

Of Golden Eggs, Outrage, and What to Do When You Don't Have a Clue

Introduction

Prescription drug spending gets a lot of attention in discussions of healthcare prices and costs, probably because it is a type of care we almost all use and because we pay for drugs at a pharmacy counter where we see the out-of-pocket price and sometimes the much higher price paid to the drug company – and are shocked. Relatively speaking, as measured by spending, prescription drugs you get at a drug store do not account for nearly as large a share of medical spending as hospital and doctor services – 10% at the prescription counter, somewhat more in the hospital or infusion center, but less than the combined 60% for hospital and doctor care. Still, managers of health systems have to pay attention to drug benefits and prices – and perhaps even more for drugs used in their hospitals, those infused or injected specialty drugs for sicker people that are seeing the most rapid spending growth. Health insurers have also been progressively adding coverage for a range of drugs. They cover generics, very small purchases for pennies that hardly make sense to run through the system but may add up over a year, and they cover the one-time but sometimes very expensive treatments that are the best if not the last resort for dreaded diseases like cancer or heart failure.

The most obvious difference and challenge to managers of health systems here arise because of how far away they are from the decisions that result in drug cost and use. A patient has symptoms, decides to see a doctor who decides to write a prescription (the only way the consumer can get the substance), and then the patient decides whether or not to fill the prescription and take the drug. All of these choices are at a longer arm's length than other medical service choices; how can you control what goes on at a neighborhood Rite Aid? The manager of a health system sits far away from the decisions in the circle around which messages are passed – so it will be hard to keep from things getting garbled.

There is a difference in economics too between medical services and drugs. The most obvious one is that some drugs have patent protection enforced by the government for the purpose of allowing the price and profits to be higher than the competitive level – and there is nothing anyone else can do about it. In contrast, innovative medical services are usually not patented and rarely use patented ingredients or devices.

Another difference that will be important is that drug production is as far away from constant marginal cost as you can get. Instead, to supply a drug the seller must incur a major fixed cost of research and development (R&D) to discover and prove effectiveness before even one pill can be sold. After you get over that hurdle, for most drugs the cost of making additional units beyond the first one is very low, often barely above zero. (This is less true of biologics and untrue for gene therapy.) Once a drug firm knows the recipe for the powerful potion and gets it approved by the FDA, it is usually easy and cheap to cook up a big batch – the only real cost is pressing the material into pills, putting it in bottles, and distributing it to retail outlets. Whatever you think about free market competition in healthcare, the drug market is not going to be it.

Finally, to add to the complexity and the irony, most Americans have prescription drug insurance which reduces what they pay at the point of use (at the drugstore counter). However, often positive cost-sharing is present so they can (and do) decline to fill the prescription that must accompany a drug purchase. We have the odd situation in which consumers buy insurance which contains incentives for them to ignore the recommendations of physicians they have paid to see! Managing this mess is bound to be a challenge.

Making Sense of the Mess

Here is a simplified framework for describing how branded drugs and drug insurance works in the US that will be helpful in what follows. We begin by assuming there are consumer-buyers who seek drugs as part of treatments that they expect to improve their health. These buyers could be individuals, but most of them are represented by employment-based group insurance or in Medicare by competing Part D plans. Insurers (and their hired guns, pharmacy benefit managers [PBMs]) offer products with different levels of patient cost-sharing and with reasonably competitive premiums. Drug firms set list prices (presumably what will be paid by someone without insurance plus any pharmacy dispensing fee) but negotiate varying discounts and rebates that insurers receive directly from the drug seller. Roughly speaking, larger discounts (and therefore lower insurance premiums) are traded off against stricter controls by insurers on which drugs are on their formularies at which cost-sharing tier.

Consumer or employer buyers then choose which insurance package they most prefer, based on the premium, cost-sharing, and access to different drugs on different tiers. Evidence shows that individual consumers often fail to pick the plan that would be the absolute best given the drugs they have been taking, but they do learn – and overall, the market for drug insurance seems to function acceptably.[1] Consumers would prefer lower premiums, and recent laws have given Medicare more power in price negotiation, while lately the net prices paid for branded drugs have increased at slower rates than inflation – a trend that the government forecasts to change to a slightly higher rate.

Different Markets

Most prescriptions dispensed in the US are for generic drugs, drugs whose patent protection has run out. They are very cheap. If all drugs were like most drugs, we would not need a chapter on management of cost, and probably clinicians on their own could usually be trusted to do the right thing without the need for oversight or financial incentives. Some drugs can be dangerous if overused or misused; almost all of them are poison if taken in large amounts, so there is still concern about incentivizing appropriate use. There can also be temporary periods when most manufacturers neglect making some generic drug and then the only firm left can either ration a shortage amount or boost the price a lot, for a while. This upsetting story is still the exception in the drug market, though when it happens it reenforces the commonplace observation that if there is money to be made, someone will try to make it.

More serious and longer-term problems arise with drugs still on patent. They represent a minority of prescriptions but a majority of total spending. Their high profit margins (over marginal cost of production) make their sellers very eager to make sales. Their high prices mean that paying for them

[1] Abaluck, J., & Gruber, J. (2016). Evolving choice inconsistencies in choice of prescription drug insurance. *American Economic Review, 106*(8), 2145–2184; Ketcham, J. D., Lucarelli, C., Miravete, E. J., & Roebuck, M. C. (2012). Sinking, swimming, or learning to swim in Medicare Part D. *American Economic Review, 102*(6), 2639–2673.

even when appropriately used can threaten consumer finances if insurance is absent or incomplete. Patented drug treatments even at high prices often are desirable because they substitute for even more expensive medical services – either as a treatment regimen at a given point in time or because their positive effects on health can help avoid the need for future care. As a sweeping generalization, evidence shows that drugs have cost offsets that are material. We love branded drugs, and we hate them. How do we manage this?

The touchstone of the ideal outcome is still the one specified at the beginning of this book: Use (and cover with insurance) drugs when they are cost-effective and do not use them when they are not. Chapter 8 discusses how to measure cost-effectiveness and what decisions it should trigger. For managers of health systems and of insurance plans, the first question should be cost-effectiveness of a drug at current prices. If it is cost-effective, that sets the level of well-being use of it can be sure to achieve. There may still be some scope for negotiating lower prices or a better deal, and sometimes a lower price can salvage a drug that would not be cost-effective at a higher price.

The incentives both to demanders or managers of drugs and to drug firms themselves differ across three settings in the healthcare system. Some drugs are used for hospitalized inpatients for which a single per admission diagnosis-related group (DRG) is paid; except by special appeal, the use of a new and/or higher-priced drug does not cause any increase in payment to the hospital or to physicians treating the patient. The second case is that of specialized drugs administered by infusion or injection under physician control. Here there are separate insurer payments for the drug material and the services of the infusion site (and often the physician as well if the physician administers an injection). The most obvious example is cancer drugs, but there are others. The third are typical prescription drugs sold in a pharmacy or by mail in response to a physician's prescription and covered by insurance. These drugs are usually oral but sometimes are self-injected. This transaction is often managed by a separate PBM firm.

The first case is the least complicated in economics and the least troublesome in policy. Given some predetermined payment for an inpatient admission and any associated physician services, the health system will (we assume) decide what combinations of inputs are needed to produce output of a given acceptable quality. In this case, drugs as an input are not intrinsically different than labor time, anesthesia, implants, or other services. They are chosen based primarily on their contribution to effective treatment as well as on their relative prices and possibilities for substitution or exclusion (again under a quality constraint). Hospitals typically set up formulary committees to determine which drugs will be used, and if so, to negotiate prices. There is a full incentive to whoever chooses input combinations to minimize cost subject to quality or outcome constraints. Depending on the degree of integration, control may or may not be exercised over physicians' choice of a costly input – of any type.[2]

While this case is one in which hospitals try to pay the lowest prices they can, often assisted by purchasing organizations which bundle the demands of many buyers to seek and find better deals, there is some evidence that things may have gone too far. Hospitals and specialists claim to have been hindered by "shortages" for generic drugs,[3] including clinically important ones used for cancer chemotherapy or antibiotics for syphilis. Usually, such shortages happen when there are few manufacturers and one of the major ones runs into production problems. We are told that "large hospital chains can readily monitor shortage risks and pre-emptively place large orders,"[4] so patients can eventually find care but at a cost of inconvenience for them and lost revenue for the smaller hospital or clinic they would have otherwise used. Here again the arm's-length problem arises; hospital managers may not be bothered by temporary shortages (unless they harm the hospital's reputation and discourage business), even though the patient suffers anxiety and the physician experiences frustration.

The economics of shortages is simple enough; the problem can be cured through higher prices if the problem is bad enough to justify that higher price. If the problem arises because manufacturers compete against each other, cutting costs including the cost of ensuring supply where they can offer the lowest possible prices, the solution is for buyers to pay higher prices to provide incentives for makers to maintain production line quality so breakdowns are less likely – and even include supply assurances in the deals they

[2] American Hospital Association. (2019). *Final report: Recent trends in hospital drug spending and manufacturer shortages.* www.aha.org/system/files/2019-01/aha-drug-pricing-study-report-01152019.pdf.

[3] Hernandez, I., Hershey, T. B., & Donohue, J. M. (2020). Drug shortages in the United States: Are some prices too low? *JAMA*, *323*(9), 819–820. www.iqvia.com/insights/the-iqvia-institute/reports-and-publications/reports/drug-shortages-in-the-us-2023; Jewett, C. (2023). Drug shortages near an all-time high, leading to rationing. *New York Times*, May 17. www.nytimes.com/2023/05/17/health/drug-shortages-cancer.html; Olson, E. (2023). It's not just Adderall: The number of drugs in short supply rose by 30% last year. *NPR*, March 23. www.npr.org/2023/03/23/1165361416/drug-shortages-adderall-flu-medicine-report.

[4] Tucker, E. (2023). America is having yet another drug shortage. Here's why it keeps happening. *New York Times*, December 6. www.nytimes.com/2023/12/06/opinion/drug-shortages-pharmaceuticals.html.

make. Just as a monopoly seller can set any price but not sell any quantity it wants, so a buyer can offer to pay any price but not necessarily get the quantity it wants.

The flaw is that manufacturers and hospital buyers are myopic, not anticipating that things can go wrong that affect supply. Critics argue that legislation is needed to force buyers and sellers to plan ahead without identifying where the mismanagement (because that is what it is) comes from. Buffer stocks would appear to be the best technical solution, but buying additional inventory at a high price in anticipation of a shortage that never materializes will not get the hospital's purchasing agent promoted. There may be ways to insure by having a market in drug futures – contracts that promise to deliver a given quantity at a given price. From a policy perspective, involving legislators with their own agendas may not be the best way to solve a management problem. It seems that some more creative anticipatory market arrangements and establishment of policies to mitigate shortages should be within the reach of healthcare managers when and if the problem of shortages becomes serious enough. Legislators are more likely to pass laws against price increases when shortages happen that will only make shortages more likely.[5]

The case of infused or injected drugs is different because insurers usually have rules about what payment will be made for the drug material. Not only that, in the under-65 market where the total price of a treatment is what matters to buyers, there is necessarily a tension between higher prices for drugs and higher fees for the physicians who treat them and higher charges for the hospitals or other providers of facilities (if separate). It is no accident that oncologists have become most outraged by high drug prices and most eager for some kind of value-based pricing of those drugs they commonly use (though not necessarily of their own services). Insurers thus can and do enlist physicians in the task of channeling patients to lower-cost drugs and monitoring drug prices (in contrast to the case of drugs sold in drug stores). Managers of health systems need to ride herd on this process. Insurers as well (or their PBM agents) must also get down into the details. The metric of cost-effectiveness should be at play here, and sometimes is.

The last case, drugs prescribed by physicians but sold by separate pharmacies, is the most challenging. Obviously, there is still a potential link between prescribing more costly drugs (e.g., dispense as written, no generics) and

[5] Tucker, E. (2023). America is having yet another drug shortage. Here's why it keeps happening. *New York Times*, December 6. www.nytimes.com/2023/12/06/opinion/drug-shortages-pharmaceuticals.html.

physician demand or fee levels, but it is very indirect; most physicians regard pharmacies as a totally separate business and are irritated when either pharmacists with knowledge or patients with references to commercials question their decisions. Moreover, most patients would not know enough to avoid a physician who is an above-average prescriber of expensive drugs. Orders are supposed to be orders, though physicians always recognize that patients may not be adherent, even if they do not recognize high prices as one reason for nonadherence.

Managers of health systems have even less control of (and probably interest in) this process than that for any other healthcare inputs. Insurers, and buyers of insurance, on the other hand, have a lot at stake.

What Economists Know about Prescription Drugs

There are some things economists know, and managers need to know, about prescription drugs:

Insurance increases drug use and drug prices. Drugs were one of the last types of medical care to be covered by insurance. Hospital care and in-hospital physician care took the lead; the public Medicare program did not start coverage of prescription drugs until 40 years after it was first passed. One reason for this was that drugs used to have low prices and so did not represent a threat to either financial security or access. That has changed over time as prices have risen and new drugs have become so effective against so many conditions. The result of course is a demand for drug insurance, but it has some of the usual adverse side effects. One is moral hazard: Although cost-sharing is often decried as something that reduces the use of drugs, insurance in general has had the effect of increasing use, especially of higher-priced drugs. As already discussed, if there are cost-effective but expensive drugs that are underused, this increase is a good thing. But increased use of antibiotics, opioids, and other mind-altering drugs has raised problems.

There is an extra problem with insurance coverage of drugs that are under monopoly control because of patents: When patients are shielded from the full price of drugs by insurance, that opens the door for the patent holder to raise the price.[6] Higher prices then mean more demand for insurance, and in

[6] Besanko, D., Dranove, D., & Garthwaite, C. (2016). Insurance and the high prices of pharmaceuticals. National Bureau of Economic Research, Working Paper No. w22353.

theory, it is even possible for the process to explode; it is possible to have reenforcing cycles of coverage and price increases to drive prices up so far that consumers are worse off using and paying for (through premiums) insured drugs than they were with no insurance.[7]

This insurance-induced drug price "inflation" obviously posed a problem for insurers and their managers, while the need to deal with large numbers of small claims at drugstores challenged their usual claims payment mechanisms. Many insurers and employers (as already noted) responded by subcontracting drug coverage (and also behavioral health coverage) out to specialized firms. Control of the PBMs, often independent of the main insurer and with opaque bargaining with individual drug companies, also generates additional anxiety and blame, though there is plenty to go around. I argue in Box 14.2 that employer demand for drug insurance based on lower premiums (however achieved) limits PBM discretion and harm, but there is no doubt of the need for constant vigilance of drug companies, PBMs, and even physicians who are not always thoughtful in writing prescriptions.

Most drugs, even most branded drugs, are cost-effective at US prices. As noted in Chapter 8 on cost-effectiveness analysis, we have a burgeoning cottage industry in studies of cost-effectiveness, especially of new drugs in the US and abroad. These studies have been collected into a database curated for quality by Tufts University, and researchers have then analyzed the drugs on which there are peer-reviewed studies.

While this set of studies is not a random sample of all drugs, it does include almost all of the big sellers. For once we have some encouraging messages: At prices used in the studies, most branded drugs are cost-effective at typically assumed values for the quality-adjusted life year (QALY) metric. Some are bargains, but most are at least worth what they cost (net of cost offsets), even in the US. Drugs for cancer tend to be the worst deals, and drugs with cost-effective analyses funded with industry support tend to be the better deals – but at least 80% of all drugs studied made the cost-effectiveness cutoff.[8] Another study took a bit of a different tack: It related the additional cost for new drugs to the QALYs they added and found that, again on average, the

[7] Frech, H. E., III, Pauly, M. V., Comanor, W. S., & Martinez, J. R. (2023). Efficiency, consumer welfare, and market equilibrium in private insurance coverage of patented drugs. *Health Management, Policy & Innovation*, 8(2). https://hmpi.org/2023/09/10/efficiency-consumer-welfare-and-market-equilibrium-in-private-insurance-coverage-of-patented-drugs/.

[8] Glick, H. A., McElligott, S., Pauly, M. V., Willke, R. J., Bergquist, H., Doshi, J., . . . & Schwartz, J. S. (2015). Comparative effectiveness and cost-effectiveness analyses frequently agree on value. *Health Affairs*, *34*(5), 805–811.

extra cost of a QALY added by a branded drug was not high – less than $40,000.[9]

Of course, there have to be some drugs that are less cost-effective than average, and we do not know why. We do know that managers should try to avoid use of them. A note of caution: The economically relevant comparator for a new drug is not no treatment (placebo) but rather the incremental benefits and incremental price or cost over the current treatment. A large gain over placebo can be matched with a small improvement over the next best alternative.

Prescription drugs on average are associated with lower physician and hospital costs. It does seem that on balance drugs substitute for medical and hospital care.[10] Although part of the cost associated with a prescription can be the doctor visit you have to make to get it prescribed (unless your doctor will phone it in), taking many drugs so improves health (in a cost-effective way) that it reduces further need for hospital and doctor care. Single-minded devotion to decreasing the use of drugs may backfire, since lower drug use can cause a negative cost offset for other kinds of care. Although preventive care is usually given the gold star as a way of saving money on medical services, some drugs (including but not limited to vaccinations) deserve it even more. This means that managers must be discriminating in holding down drug spending lest they shoot themselves in the financial foot.

What Economists Don't Know about Prescription Drugs (and No One Else Does Either)

How drug prices paid to drug companies ultimately affect usage. As noted earlier, economists, unwilling to play favorites, do not criticize monopoly because it makes sellers rich and consumers poor. They criticize it because it discourages the consumption of goods and services whose marginal value to consumers is greater than their real resource cost. This difference for many drugs is enormous because the marginal cost of making the second and subsequent pills is almost zero once you know the recipe and have it approved, and yet the monopoly price that reflects high average health

[9] Frech, H. E., III, Pauly, M. V., Comanor, W. S., & Martinez, J. R. (2022). Costs and benefits of branded drugs: Insights from cost-effectiveness research. *Journal of Benefit-Cost Analysis, 13*(2), 166–181.

[10] Antos, J., & Spoor, C. (2002). *Issues in designing a prescription drug benefit for Medicare.* Study report. Congress of the United States. Congressional Budget Office.

benefit will discourage marginal lower (but still positive) value use. Even without quantitative evidence, we can conclude that the temporary monopoly that incentivizes R&D for new drugs (more on this later in the chapter) would in itself do harm. But we have no idea how much harm it does because we do not know the extent to which, after the dust clears, lower drug prices would stimulate more use of effective drugs.

One major reason is that drug insurance insulates patients from the total price paid for the drug (even after discounts and rebates), so that what they pay out of pocket may come close to marginal cost. A lower price paid to a drug company does not always translate into a lower user price for the patient; often the effect of lower prices is to lower premiums, valuable in its own right but not relevant to the marginal costs and benefits of drug usage. This dearth of information on how much good lower prices paid to drug companies would do has not stopped politicians in most countries, and now in the US for people on Medicare, from forcing drug firms with patents to charge lower prices than they would have chosen.

We will soon see a natural experiment that will tell us how use will respond to lower prices paid to drug sellers. (We already know a lot about how use responds to out-of-pocket payment, given at total price; it does – but this is a different story.) Consider for example a drug in the crosshairs of Medicare price "negotiation" in the next few years – Eliquis, a high-selling blood thinner. The task for managers of Medicare drug insurance plans and for health system managers will be to see that use increases where it should when this drug becomes more affordable. Patients needing treatment for deep vein thromboses or blood clots after surgery now should be able to have this drug covered at lower cost-sharing; they can move away from currently cheaper but more problematic substitutes like Warfarin to the first-line alternative. This may require a different mindset for managers used to thinking about holding down the use of drugs, but it is what is supposed to happen. Those delivery systems that can get out in front with better ways to use more Eliquis and tell the public about it should gain. We will see.

How drug prices affect R&D and the flow of good new products. The predictable response of drug firms and their lobbyists to proposals to lower prices is to claim that doing so will adversely affect R&D for promising new drugs: There will be an "innovation winter" if prices are forced below the current profit-maximizing levels during periods of patent protection. Critics respond that drugs are overpriced and drug firms are subsidized via National Institutes of Health (NIH) research; they will develop new drugs anyway. Economists think both are wrong.

What is sure to happen is that lower prices which lower expected profits from new drugs will reduce the supply of innovations. What is unsure is how large the reduction will be and, as importantly, how valuable the foregone drugs would have been. That is, we need to know, but do not know, what branded drugs at current market prices just made the cut in terms of proceeding with R&D during the process of development – and what would have happened to those drugs if investors knew their prices could be curtailed if they turned out to be Medicare blockbusters. We know that the failure rate of promising new drug ideas is near 90% at the time of first clinical investigation and is even around 30% when drugs have gone through Phases 1 and 2. We also know that some of the drugs that ended up being treatments of high true value to millions almost died during the process of development – statins, vascular endothelial growth factor (VEGF) drugs for cancer and macular degeneration, and others.[11] Obviously, we do not know the drugs that were canceled but would have been valuable if continued, although there are valuable drugs (e.g., metformin) that were rescued from the discard pile.

Empirical evidence on this crucial question is very incomplete. The supply curve of new ideas – the flash of light that makes everything illuminated – cannot be strongly related to resources or incentives; many discoveries are serendipitous.[12] There are few studies of exogenous price increases and what they do. Instead, economists have studied the effects of arguably random shifts in demand (such as passage of Medicare Part D or recommendations from advisory committees) that might affect R&D. They find that such predictors of increased volume impact not so much the research part of R&D but rather the development part that moves research ideas into new products.[13] How responsive the supply of new drugs is to expected profits from those drugs remains an object of contention.[14] Are there many new

[11] Miller, S., Moos, W., Munk, B., & Munk, S. (2016). *Managing the drug discovery process: How to make it more efficient and cost-effective*. Woodhead Publishing.

[12] Rea, P. A., Pauly, M. V., & Burns, L. R. (2018). *Managing discovery in the life sciences: Harnessing creativity to drive biomedical innovation*. Cambridge University Press.

[13] Finkelstein, A. (2004). Static and dynamic effects of health policy: Evidence from the vaccine industry. *The Quarterly Journal of Economics*, *119*(2), 527–564; Dranove, D., Garthwaite, C., & Hermosilla, M. (2022). Does consumer demand pull scientifically novel drug innovation? *The RAND Journal of Economics*, *53*(3), 590–638; Byrski, D., Gaessler, F., & Higgins, M. J. (2021). Market size and research: Evidence from the pharmaceutical industry. National Bureau of Economic Research, Working Paper No. w28858.

[14] Congressional Budget Office. (2021). *Research and development in the pharmaceutical industry*. Report. www.cbo.gov/publication/57126; Lakdawalla, D., & Philipson, T. (2012). Does intellectual property restrict output? An analysis of pharmaceutical markets. *The Journal of Law and Economics*, *55*(1), 151–187.

ideas parked just above the investment cutoff for drug firms, or are there few? And how valuable are those marginal ideas that will lead to marginal products (literally)? No one knows but many have opinions.

It needs to be emphasized that, from an economic perspective, there is nothing sacrosanct about the flow of profits and incentives for pharmaceutical innovation in current US patent laws and FDA rules on exclusivity. They were not set based on evidence about the trade-offs between the value of new drugs and the reduced use of existing drugs from temporary monopoly. They have been adjusted from time to time by collective choices about periods of price protection, for both orphan drugs and biologics, but not for reasons based on economic theory or evidence. Medicare with new price bargaining powers may act as a monopsonist; if the supply curve of new good drugs is not very price responsive, the marginal benefit from lower prices across the board may offset the loss of new products. It may well be that shortening the period of profit-maximizing prices for Medicare insureds via price bargaining will provide enough benefit in increased access to offset any reduction in the long-term flow of new products, although the connection between lower prices to drug companies and effects on patient use via changes in cost-sharing is neither strong nor well known. No one now knows. We will have to see how this experiment works out, but it will take many years before we even have a chance of seeing if it does more good than harm (no randomized controlled trial).

For managers of health systems, even large ones, the responsibility for paying higher prices to encourage new drugs is probably beyond their remit. Medicare as the country's largest insurance manager and presumably charged with the responsibility for consumer welfare might be encouraged to pay attention to keeping prices high enough to bring forth the cost-effective flow of new products – but practically it would not know how to do so. Moreover, some of the things that it is supposed to pay attention to in its newfound role of price bargainer do not make economic sense. Legislation says it is supposed to take into account R&D spending in years past on a particular drug, even though economics says that those sunk costs should not influence the final price of any one drug. It should consider by law and politics whether the flow of profits from existing drugs is large enough to fund R&D, even though new investors can and do make money available to startups independent of past profits (see Box 14.1). The political process does not after all seem well suited to determining what level of profit or price will offer the right incentives for R&D, so we shall probably have to continue to muddle through as always.

Box 14.1 Evidence: Pharmaceutical industry profit margin

It may be of some interest to managers and policymakers to evaluate realized profit margins for firms investing in innovation and sales of prescription drugs. While expected or before-the-fact long-run returns and short-run profits are what is relevant to drug firm pricing and innovation, we can only know after-the-fact realized returns. These numbers are undoubtedly related to but are not precise measures of those incentives. However, this information may give managers some idea of the average bargaining range over prices for drugs, and it may help policymakers detect barriers to entry or other sources of market power (other than patents and regulatory exclusions, of course) that may affect the flow of new products and the pricing of past discoveries.

As usual we must start with apologies for the imprecision of data and the warning that discovering the profit margins or incentives for individual drug products is infeasible, but we do have some guidance about what happens on average. What is certain is that the long-run average rate of return in this industry has historically not been less than the overall return on investment elsewhere in the economy, and over the past three decades or so has probably averaged somewhat higher than that benchmark. A return on investment in an industry can be higher than the competitive average even if markets are functioning perfectly if demand for or valuation of the products that industry supplies increase and there is a lag in the inflow of new investment into that industry. While this observation is not proof, returns in this industry in about the last decade are about the same as those in other high-tech, high-risk industries (such as computer software and peripherals) but are higher than that from all sectors of the economy. The data also suggest that returns temporarily fell below that benchmark around 2010 or so, when new drug discovery rates plummeted and large pharma companies were returning profits to shareholders as dividends and stock buybacks rather than investing them, only to change course when new science opened new opportunities since about 2014.

Many studies of drug industry returns take the easy route of looking only at large firms whose data are publicly available and find them to be generally profitable (probably part of the reason why they are large). More appropriate investigations which try to take into account the behavior of many small firms which enter, invest, often fail, but sometimes hit a blockbuster discovery find somewhat lower profit rates but still ones that generally suggest healthy rewards for investment in discovery of health-improving substances. Some accounting and tax-related peculiarities (such as limits on depreciation of R&D investment) may also lead measured returns to be biased upward relative to comparator industries.

One issue that has been much discussed is whether patents that award exclusivity for a number of years to the developer of an idea based on being first to apply lead to inefficiency in devoting resources because of the winner-take-all character of patents. Even without this regulation it is likely that the realized returns to drug development would be highly skewed, with a small fraction of products (say, 15%–20%) being blockbusters and the rest having negative realized returns.[15] If one could be certain that a given discovery would be made and

[15] DiMasi, J. A., & Grabowski, H. G. (2012). R&D costs and returns to new drug development: A review of the evidence. In P. Danzon and S. Nicholson (eds.), *The Oxford handbook of the economics of the biopharmaceutical industry* (pp. 21–46). Oxford University Press.

make it to market, the benefit of a slight timing advantage might not justify the resources expended by the losers. However, from a policy perspective there would be no easy way to determine which developer should be given exclusivity in advance of patenting. Moreover, there certainly have been drugs where the seller of the second version ended up sweeping the market – Pfizer's atorvastatin versus Merck's statin being the classic example – and the first entry into the Alzheimer's drug market was a dud. For managers, this feature of drug development only implies that there will be gains to monitoring the market for new products and being prepared for entry when it occurs.

The basic message is that relative to a world in long-run competitive equilibrium, returns to this industry in the long run have been higher than average but not excessively so. Bargaining opportunities will be selective at best.

Patient cost-sharing reduces the use of drugs physicians have prescribed, but we do not know how it affects health. We begin with the RAND results (and those of subsequent studies by economists) that free care stimulated use and spending on everything, including drugs, without affecting health of the average person. This is in contrast to numerous studies of cost-sharing for groups of patients with specific medical conditions, including the classic study of statins after heart attacks but also studies of people with diabetes, cancer, and other diseases. There are also many surveys in which large percentages of respondents (larger than the percentage of low-income persons at high risk) report that drug cost-sharing has caused them to delay or avoid filling prescriptions their doctors gave them. These use-deterring effects appear to happen even when cost-sharing is not large relative to income; people who are shocked at the drugstore by a $50 charge will walk away.

This evidence can be reconciled to some extent if the people have chronic conditions and are poor, but these characteristics are not usually present. The sum of the parts does not add up to the whole, a not uncommon phenomenon when linking evidence on individual behavior to population outcomes. Managers obviously have to be careful in dealing with individual instances of cost-sharing versus managing premiums and care limitations for an insurance plan. There is no substitute for paying attention. The same goes for insurance buyers (in our framework) choosing among insurance plans for groups of consumers who have different health levels and incomes.

How the rate of return on investment in new drugs compares with the competitive rate or normal economic profit margin. In the US there are few explicit barriers to entry into the R&D process. You have to set up a lab, and you have to discover something new before anyone else does, but only then can patents and FDA exclusions allow you to have market power. The empirical evidence on whether investors in drug firms earn above normal rates of return is mixed; the question is complicated because many start-up drug firms fail (just like oil drilling stocks) but sometimes there are block-busters; this is risky business.

Negotiating Drug Prices and Insurance: Can There Still Be an Invisible Hand, and Does It Need Help?

The economic model of an ideal market (for anything) really falls apart when it comes to branded drugs. The production process has high fixed and permanently low marginal costs (MC), so there is no U-shaped long-run average cost (LAC) curve at which P = MC = LAC in equilibrium. The police power of government enforces patents on intellectual property which means that sellers will have market power for years. Insurance distorts the signals to consumers about the selling price of a drug and the marginal cost of a drug. Can this vehicle be rebuilt?

Box 14.2 describes an ideal (though currently speculative) model for private insurer drug price negotiation. At present the more practical approach is less formal but still has as its essence the idea of trading larger volumes of (presumably still profitable) sales for lower prices. Sometimes firms offer such deals; more often they are made by PBMs as part of their management of drug tiering. The basic economic message is that there is an inherent instability in drug pricing because the marginal cost of supplying units of the drug once the cost of discovery and FDA approval have been incurred is so low. There necessarily will be a bargaining range with marginal cost at the bottom end and the dollar value of QALYs added at the top. As long as the drug is cost-effective at whatever price you settle on, you can't lose – but a lower price will always be better. Advice on careful attention to detail and wishes for good luck follow.

A major challenge to management for a drug already deemed cost-effective on average for treating a condition in a given population is to make sure that it is used only for people with that condition for whom it is cost-effective. As in the case of moral hazard, patients may differ in their expected benefit from a drug, but insurers and providers may have challenges in determining when the benefit is high enough to justify the cost. Pretreatment approvals and protocols, despite their potential for patient and physician irritation, may also be a way to discriminate. Cost-sharing can also be employed, but with care, since it may impose out-of-pocket costs on patients who will get high benefit from the drug and may discourage their use.

Box 14.2 Theory: Efficient drug payment and insurance

There is a method in theory, one that might even be working in practice. To illustrate how this works to improve efficiency and the possibility of a mutually beneficial deal (which is the same thing as efficiency), we need to go way back and talk about what is wrong with simple monopoly. The abstract idea is that the price is above marginal cost, but a potentially practical solution is for buyers facing a monopolist to get together, buy out the monopolist for the present discounted value of expected profits, and then price the product at marginal cost. Where I live, our water is supplied by a private firm regulated (to some extent) as a public utility. What we should do is get together, buy out Aqua Pennsylvania, and sell water at marginal cost (which I assume is very low until the reservoirs are dry). That would provide me with the proper incentives to water my garden.

Exactly the same story would work for an effective drug: buy out the patent and sell it at marginal cost (close to zero). This model has worked for the development of some drugs to treat diseases in developing countries when engineered by kindly philanthropies and the World Health Organization (WHO) but runs into problems as a general model. Specifically, how do you get people together and get them to agree on how to split the cost of buying out the drug company?

Darius Lakdawalla and Neeraj Sood have triumphed by suggesting that the vehicle is right in front of us: use insurance.[16] Take the simplest case (and the easiest one) where there is just one (for profit) insurer and one drug to be considered. A solution is for the insurer to negotiate a deal with the drug company: We will pay the value of your profits under simple monopoly and a little more, collect the money as marginal cost, and we in turn will charge that as the unit price to our insured population. This is a perfect deal! Not only in theory, sometimes called the "Netflix" model (get it?), it was actually implemented by Louisiana Medicaid under the supervision of one of my former students to allow that budget-constrained program to cover Sovaldi and other expensive drugs for hepatitis C.[17]

But nothing is ever perfect in real life (though some things are improvements). Lakdawalla and Sood do not explain how this would work in a real market where there are many employers (some large and some small) served by many insurers (some large and some small). Theory will help us here, but this is how the deal might work. Suppose I am the employer or the contracted PBM for a workforce susceptible to a disease for which there is a new patented treatment. Suppose that 100 of my people would benefit from the treatment which has virtually zero marginal cost. Also suppose that if the drug firm charged its simple monopoly price (much above MC), I would want to use cost-sharing to permit 50 of my sickest workers to get the drug (because it is cost-effective at the monopoly price) but not the other 50. I now meet with the drug firm and say,

[16] Lakdawalla, D., & Sood, N. (2009). Innovation and the welfare effects of public drug insurance. *Journal of Public Economics, 93*(3–4), 541–548; Lakdawalla, D., & Sood, N. (2013). Health insurance as a two-part pricing contract. *Journal of Public Economics, 102*, 1–12.

[17] Trusheim, M. R., Cassidy, W. M., & Bach, P. B. (2018). Alternative state-level financing for hepatitis C treatment – the "Netflix model." *JAMA, 320*(19), 1977–1978.

You would make \$X in profit if you sold my people 50 treatments at your monopoly price. Suppose I offer you \$X + \$100 for a deal in which you agree to supply 100 units to us. You will make \$100 more from this deal. As long as the total benefit from my 50 new users is greater than 100, we all are happy too. We could frame this deal as a quantity discount where the price for 50 would be your old monopoly price while the price for 100 would be (X + 100)/100, and I promise to buy 100. Deal?

The good news is that there should be a deal like this that we can strike. We might argue about the excess – should it be 100 or more – but as long as the excess is not greater than the value of the additional use for the lower value users, we can agree. The bad news is that negotiating these deals with every employer or every insurer is going to be a mess. Some big firms may make it work on a face-to-face basis. But that does not sound like a competitive equilibrium or even a feasible overall solution.

So, the next question is whether there is a standard deal, different from the simple monopoly price at which any buyer can buy any quantity, that will work for almost everyone. The answer is yes *if buyers and sellers can agree on and abide by a stipulation about how much in total will be bought.* It is easy to see why this provision is important; it guarantees that the drug seller will collect (X + 100) in total; if less were bought, the seller would lose some of the gain from the price discount. At the level of a group of insureds, demographic and other data would be used to estimate what fraction would have the condition the drug treats, and then the insurer or employer and the drug firm would agree on how many units would be bought per person at a unit price of (X + 100)/100. If there was variation in the prevalence of the condition, that would have to be considered in setting the quantity. And that would be the rub – since the buyer would prefer to buy less at the unit price than the amount needed to treat everyone. But if the quantity demanded at that price were smaller than the maximum amount, the seller would not collect enough to maximize profits.

What about negotiating the alternative Netflix model? Presumably, the "subscription" price would need to be higher for employers or insurance companies with more people who have the condition – just as you cannot buy one Netflix membership and then share it with your neighbor. The same problem of agreeing on or measuring the number of potential users who could benefit as in the quantity discount case would arise. Even so, some standardized procedure of basing the total payment to the seller on the risk-adjusted size of the population eligible for low-priced medicine should be feasible. The result would not be perfect but might be better in many cases than simple monopoly.

Netflix for Ozempic?

A potential application of this model relevant to drug pricing today might involve the drug Ozempic. This drug was originally developed and FDA-approved for people with type 2 diabetes; it appears that, even at its current (high) price, it is a cost-effective treatment for that population. However, as everyone knows, an effect of the drug is weight loss, because it suppresses hunger. Although there are some embarrassing gastrointestinal complications, the drug is being ever more widely prescribed for and used by people who are obese but not diabetic. It is certainly more effective for weight loss than other treatments, some drugs, gastric bypass surgery, and Weight Watchers – although, even with about a 20% cost offset, it may not be cost-effective for obesity alone if the usual QALYs outcome measure is used. A slightly modified version called Wegovy is approved for weight loss for people with other chronic conditions exacerbated by obesity.

The potential cost of this even more potentially profitable treatment has raised concerns. Two economists and a bureaucrat have done the arithmetic, and they have calculated that, at current prices, the cost of such drugs if every obese person used them would eventually be substantial, up to as much as $800 billion if every overweight person used the drug.[18] As discussed in Chapter 13 in the section on "too much of a good thing?," this possibility would not necessarily pose an insolvable problem for private insurance: Would workers want to give up some more money wages to have access to a drug that could slim you down and make you healthier? You could limit payment for yourself if you were diabetic or morbidly obese or you could let everyone who wanted the treatment get one of these drugs.[19] The ultimate question (Chapter 11) is not whether all workers would get benefit from coverage but rather whether adding coverage would be attractive enough to new workers to hold down total compensation costs.

However, the authors note (we assume correctly) that there will be a problem for Medicaid programs – obesity and diabetes are more common among lower income populations, and denying access to low-income individuals with diabetes would "compound existing equity issues surrounding diabetes." Surely true, but Medicaid could cover people with diabetes and not blow the budget. The real issue is treating nondiabetic overweight individuals on Medicaid who want to look and feel better, and lower their cardiovascular and other risks, at taxpayer expense. We can reasonably be expansive here; while the bulk of benefits from losing weight goes to the person who shed the pounds, there can be, as the authors assert, some social benefits – some offsetting reduction in Medicaid spending, some value we would all attach to

[18] Deese, B., Gruber, J., & Cummings, R. (2024). The miracle weight-loss drug is also a major budgetary threat. *New York Times*, March 4. www.nytimes.com/2024/03/04/opinion/ozempic-wegovy-medicare-federal-budget.html.

[19] ICER. (2022). ICER publishes final evidence report and policy recommendations on Tirzepatide for type 2 diabetes. Press release. https://icer.org/news-insights/press-releases/icer-publishes-final-evidence-report-and-policy-recommendations-on-tirzepatide-for-type-2-diabetes/.

better health for our fellow citizens. The issue at the moment is whether those social benefits and private benefits for someone on Medicaid are worth the annual drug cost of $15,000. The authors do not try to prove that the social benefits are as high as the current price; instead, they go for government price regulation to get the price in line with an assumed lower social benefit.

But there is an alternative, and Louisiana has already shown us the way. Rather than nationwide price controls on weight-loss drugs (which sounds scary to me), let state Medicaid programs deal with Novo Nordisk for a "Netflix for pounds" idea. A state could say how much Ozempic or Wegovy it would buy for its Medicaid population at current prices (discounted by 20% if paid by Medicaid). It could propose to limit use by various clinical criteria – certainly pay for those with bad diabetes, maybe for those with prediabetes, require other obese people to try to lose weight in a cheaper way first, and so on – and then offer Novo Nordisk more than what it would have paid under the limited use scheme if the company would make the drug available to its entire obese and overweight Medicaid population. This finesses the unanswerable question of whether the stockholders in the (Danish-headquartered) manufacturer are more or less entitled to their profits than Louisiana taxpayers, puts control at the state level rather than some federal bureau or committee, and challenges taxpayers to think about what value they place on this dimension of population health.

Conclusion

The phenomenon of drug sellers posting unreasonably high unit prices is probably going to continue to give this industry a bad name; Hollywood will never cast a pharma firm CEO as a hero. This is so even though new drugs and vaccines have probably contributed more per dollar of spending to health than any other kind of healthcare. Managers can help channel this net benefit to the people for whom it will do the most good, and they might even be able to foster larger amounts of it if they are creative and levelheaded negotiators with a good knowledge of economics blended with a heavy dose of common sense.

What managers can do is pick out the most cost-effective drugs to encourage, as well as try to avoid negative impacts on the use of those drugs if their prices increase. Insurance can help here, since it can buffer the impact of drug price increases on user prices insureds pay – so that those price increases are absorbed through higher premiums. Still not good news, but possibly better than lower use of drugs that matter to health – until either negotiation or generic entry gets their prices down.

For managers of health systems, the primary task is to manage the use of drugs in a cost-effective way. For inpatients that involves both the protocols for treatments and the decisions made about the system's formulary. An individual provider usually does not have the power to influence the price of a drug but can influence the choice of treatment and the volume of purchases. For a health system with clinical and financial responsibility for a patient population, the challenge is much the same. If in contrast payment for outpatient care is fee-for-service, the system may be able to emphasize its careful attention to drug therapy and lower-priced treatment pathways to attract patients and insurers.

The other group that has a management challenge related to drug treatment is not really insurance managers; they either know what they are doing or farm out their problems to a PBM. The challenge is for employer benefits managers to pick which insurer or PBM to use. The obvious message is to pick the agent that gives you the lowest cost consistent with employee satisfaction – and not the one that makes claims about large cost savings in prices or quantities that somehow never make it to the bottom line. Here, even more so, trust but verify is the best procedure.

15 Social Determinants of Health and Health Spending

Can Healthcare Change the World?

Introduction

In the sea of uncertainties that surrounds medical services delivery and health outcomes, there is one proposition for which there is solid theory and irrefutable evidence: Health outcomes are primarily determined by influences other than the consumption of formal medical care. Illness is usually a random event. Individual choices can affect the odds of illness. They are affected by individual citizen behaviors in many dimensions – what is sometimes called "lifestyle." We all know parts of the lifestyle story as applied to ourselves – my health is affected by my choices about exercise, diet, and risk-taking behavior. Use of or access to formal medical care may help present and future health outcomes, but their effects will be modest. It is easy to blame ourselves, and to blame others, for poor health outcomes – if only their choices had been better and more responsible, outcomes would have been different.

Over time, the realization dawned that, although some individual choices were matters of will, many of them were made in environments adverse to healthy lifestyles. We now know that health outcomes are associated with where we live and work – air quality, chemical pollutants, food access, racism, and the chances of violence or accidents also matter. This choice environment is often determined by social factors, and so it has been labeled the social determinants of health (SDOH). Medical services can repair or avoid some (but not all) of the damage to perfect health caused by some (but not all) of these influences. Estimates suggest that medical care is at most responsible for 10%–20% of the variation in health outcomes.[1] But when social and structural determinants of health are set in the negative zone, some

[1] Hood, C. M., Gennuso, K. P., Swain, G. R., & Catlin, B. B. (2016). County health rankings: Relationships between determinant factors and health outcomes. *American Journal of Preventive Medicine*, *50*(2), 129–135.

of their harmful effects will still come through in final health outcomes, no matter what suppliers of medical services do. Moreover, in addition to the bad health outcomes, the additional use of services associated with them will show up in higher future medical costs.

Defining Social, Environmental, and Structural Determinants of Health

Economists and sociologists before them have hypothesized that this mixed bag of bad influences has two fundamental causes: poverty and racism. Low income and social disadvantage imply that, no matter what patients and doctors do, more collective effort and more societal cost will be needed to achieve a given level of health, if it can be achieved at all. The consequences of poverty and racism manifest in many ways and in many dimensions. The environmental or structural aspects are obviously social or collective – these may include governing processes, economic and social policies, working conditions, housing, and education.[2] Individual lifestyle choices are influenced at a population level by social or collective forces that constrain choice environments.[3] The traditional description of SDOH includes five categories: economic stability, education access and quality, healthcare access and quality, neighborhood and built environment, and social and community context (Exhibit 15.1).

The correlation between SDOH and health outcomes, known as the "health gradient," has been well documented descriptively.[4] Given this correlation, several studies in the economic literature attempt to identify causal effects of SDOH or socioeconomic status (SES) on health. For example, education has been demonstrated to have a causal impact on mortality.[5] Furthermore, maternal health and health behaviors impact infant health, demonstrating an intergenerational effect of SDOH.[6,7] The accumulation of

[2] Illinois Department of Public Health. Understanding social determinants of health. https://dph.illinois.gov/topics-services/life-stages-populations/infant-mortality/toolkit/understanding-sdoh.html.

[3] Rose, G. (2001). Sick individuals and sick populations. *International Journal of Epidemiology*, *30*(3), 427–432.

[4] Chetty, R., Stepner, M., Abraham, S., Lin, S., Scuderi, B., Turner, N., . . . & Cutler, D. (2016). The association between income and life expectancy in the United States, 2001–2014. *JAMA*, *315*(16), 1750–1766.

[5] Lleras-Muney, A. (2005). The relationship between education and adult mortality in the United States. *The Review of Economic Studies*, *72*(1), 189–221.

[6] Aizer, A., & Currie, J. (2014). The intergenerational transmission of inequality: Maternal disadvantage and health at birth. *Science*, *344*(6186), 856–861.

[7] Kennedy-Moulton, K., Miller, S., Persson, P., Rossin-Slater, M., Wherry, L., & Aldana, G. (2022). Maternal and infant health inequality: New evidence from linked administrative data. National Bureau of Economic Research, Working Paper No. w30693.

Exhibit 15.1 Social determinants of health

Economic stability	Education access and quality	Healthcare access and quality	Neighborhood and built environment	Social and community context
• Employment • Food insecurity • Housing instability • Poverty	• Early childhood development and education • Enrollment in higher education • High school graduation • Language and literacy	• Access to health services • Access to primary care • Health literacy	• Access to foods that support healthy dietary patterns • Crime and violence • Environmental conditions • Quality of housing	• Civic participation • Discrimination • Incarceration • Social cohesion

Source: Healthy People 2030. Social determinants of health. Office of Disease Prevention and Health Promotion, US Department of Health and Human Services. https://health.gov/healthypeople/objectives-and-data/social-determinants-health.

adverse effects of SES has been found to begin in childhood and compound over a lifetime.[8] Hypothesized mechanisms for this relationship cover many dimensions, from knowledge and behaviors to ability and opportunity.[9] Some of the difference in health outcomes by SES may be due to health behaviors (the "individual lifestyle" component that we described earlier),[10] while the rest may be due to the environment. It is likely that the two interact (i.e., the environment constrains the choices of the individual). There is a limit to what managers (or anyone) can do: Even in the most egalitarian of egalitarian populations – British civil servants – the original social gradient work found a strong association between rank and health.[11] Which dimensions of SDOH are feasible to manipulate, by health managers or anyone else, is still largely unknown.

[8] Case, A., Lubotsky, D., & Paxson, C. (2002). Economic status and health in childhood: The origins of the gradient. *American Economic Review, 92*(5), 1308–1334.

[9] Cutler, D. M., Lleras-Muney, A., & Vogl, T. (2011). Socioeconomic status and health: Dimensions and mechanisms. In S. Glied & P. C. Smith (eds.), *The Oxford Handbook of Health Economics* (pp. 123–163). Oxford University Press.

[10] Cutler, D. M., & Lleras-Muney, A. (2010). Understanding differences in health behaviors by education. *Journal of Health Economics, 29*(1), 1–28.

[11] Marmot, M. G., Smith, G. D., Stansfeld, S., Patel, C., North, F., Head, J., . . . & Feeney, A. (1991). Health inequalities among British civil servants: The Whitehall II study. *The Lancet, 337*(8), 1387–1393.

Suffice it to say that the scope of the problem has been well defined in the literature – SES and SDOH clearly affect health. Then there is a major gap. What if anything is effective in changing SDOH or its health effects remains a great mystery – even at any cost, much less in a cost-effective way? Lots of opinions, few demonstrable facts.

Why are managers of healthcare systems and health insurance plans among those challenged by SDOH? The ideal society would be one in which collective choice through government resulted in income and wealth distributions that are fair and that are not affected by race or other social categories. However, we are not in this ideal setting; consensus on fair distributions of wealth, employment, and investment opportunities has not been achieved. This decades-long failure (so far) of collective choice in the US to improve the fundamental determinants of SDOH reflects what might be called "government failure." In the face of such a situation, as suggested by Burton Weisbrod (referenced in Chapter 4), the need for and the task of correcting this failure of social choice may then fall on managers of private firms providing goods and services that may alter some of the symptoms of income maldistribution and racism. The private healthcare and insurance system may have to make up for what government has failed to do. But can it, and will it, do so?

To be more concrete, it is not going to be feasible for health system managers, physicians, other health professionals, or insurance executives to redistribute wealth or eliminate racism. There is a set of social goals upon which many agree, but there is (as we shall see in more detail) little evidence and less agreement on sustainable (or costly) actions that might be taken by market players to mitigate the consequences of the failure of collective choice institutions to create a better social environment. However, there are some actions that might help mitigate the consequences of adverse social environments on health. Discovering those actions and then implementing them are both challenges in the current state of evidence, but this chapter will try to categorize potentially effective "points of entry" for managers of health systems to change adverse SDOH.

Managers need to know how and whether the harmful social determinants that affect patients in their health system can be changed by their actions in a cost-effective way. And then, if there are some such actions, they need to know how to pay for them. This chapter will discuss evidence on cost-effective interventions to modify the social and structural determinants of health, and the potential sources of revenue or funding to pay for those programs. Here, above all, modesty should be our watchword. It is natural and human to be outraged by the consequences of adverse SDOH, but such feelings do not necessarily translate into effective actions.

We will talk about using economic methods to identify the potential impact on health outcomes of changing the levels of elements of SDOH; as usual we will be interested in causation not just associations. We will of course also talk about economic models of the behavior of individuals and whatever entities determine the external environment to understand what influences whether their levels are favorable or unfavorable. Then comes the hard work: How do you change these levels, and what will it cost to do so when you can – and are the benefits worth the cost? And finally, the bottom line: What are the sources of funding or payment to reward efforts to change what can be efficiently changed? What are self-financing methods for doing good works? Is there money behind well-meaning words about improving SDOH?

Root Causes and Responsibility

The root causes of adverse SDOH are (1) the unequal distribution of income or wealth and (2) racism (and possibly other social systemic disadvantages). Changing social policies to deal with these causes is a task which economics assigns to government: It is supposed to have a "distribution branch"[12] that will carry out the collective choice on how resources will be distributed, using taxes and transfers if the initial market distribution is regarded as inappropriate or unfair. Likewise, governments have primary responsibility for reducing racism (in large part because their past actions have contributed to it) through laws, regulations, and transfers to disadvantaged groups.

At present, governments in the US (and in many other countries) have not fulfilled these responsibilities. I personally think that wealth should be distributed more evenly in the US than at present and that actions to combat racism should be more robust, but my opinion does not settle the matter; these issues are ones where things should be determined by collective agreement, and it is not up to me (or any one person). Nevertheless, a plausible case can be made that there has so far been "government failure" to perform these core social roles sufficiently well.

In the face of government failure, individual citizens or groups of citizens have two possible reactions. One (as Weisbrod suggested for nonprofit

[12] Musgrave, R. A. (1959). *The theory of public finance: A study in public economy.* McGraw Hill.

hospitals) is to take government failure as given and try to address the symptoms of it by voluntary private actions as much as private resources, ability to induce cooperation, and preferences permit. The other is to work out some kind of cooperative arrangement between private individuals or groups and government entities to share the costs and benefit of moving toward better outcomes.

The implication of this abstract discussion for managers in healthcare is that they alone cannot be expected to cure the problems that government has failed to address; the revolution is unlikely to start with healthcare. Instead, managers need to act on parts of the problem where they can make cost-effective changes. That means both that the intervention is cost-effective and that the benefits the manager gets are greater than the cost. (Of course, if the "cost" is inflated by market power of sellers – of real estate or healthcare – reducing that is another necessary task for government.) They need to watch for ways to support or fund the benefits of the actions they do take. And they need to be open to the possibility of cooperation with the public sector when and if it begins to move on addressing the core problem.

The Manager's Problem

We consider a manager of a program or plan with responsibility for the health outcomes and medical costs of a given population. The manager might be part of an insurance firm or a medical service delivery system that cares for a defined population. What does this manager need to know about SDOH and what should be done with the knowledge?

Present evidence on SDOH is unbalanced. The starting point for researchers is usually evidence that some identifiable group within the population has worse health and/or higher medical services cost than the average for the population as a whole. That group might be defined by income, by race or ethnicity, or by location in a particular neighborhood. The next key question is: What observable factors cause these differences from the average? There is voluminous evidence about the association between various metrics of SDOH and health outcomes. As already suggested, those metrics almost always are affected by poverty and/or racism, but there is no doubt that some of these environmental factors are strongly correlated with health. However, this impressive but discouraging documentation of inequity is rarely matched with evidence on effective ways to change things.

As we already know, just observing associations is not enough to attribute causation – and yet we need to identify causes if we are to target them for change. If we observe that the population lives in a "food desert" neighborhood with few local stores selling healthy foods, or a "food swamp" with fast food and junk food, we need to dig deeper – are there few stores because people prefer processed high sugar diets, because high rents mean that a store can survive only by selling high margin products (Twinkies and chips), or because high crime threats deter supermarket chains who can profit only with low margins and low pilferage? In economic jargon, this is the usual problem of "identifying the exogenous determinants" and observable and potentially correlated explanatory factors that vary for a reason.

Assuming that this treasure hunt is successful in picking up some causes with impacts large enough to matter, the next question for managers is whether they or their organizations can change this environment – and, if they can, at what cost. Sometimes managers can have small influence: The healthcare system is responsible for almost 10% of all US emissions, so asthma-caused air pollution in a given neighborhood might be reduced through "greening" of hospital buildings.[13] However, medical services systems or insurers alone cannot solve the emissions problem; changing the environment requires collective action and political deals. Similarly, moving exposed populations to new locations with better air quality is also not in the remit of these managers; they can build affordable housing for their patients,[14] but they cannot resettle populations. Creativity and good luck might help them find a way, and they might be able to provide housing away from the toxic incinerator, but if the odds are against you, perhaps it is not wise to try. Part of the problem is that housing prices and rents are naturally lower in parts of town with unsafe environments, but low-income people may feel they can only afford such places.

If you can find one or more programs to change SDOH with evidence of effectiveness relative to cost of change, great. Perhaps you will be fortunate enough to find an intervention that lowers total cost such that the reduction in medical costs that results offsets the investment cost of changing the environment. For example, if you can make money developing real estate that will help those with housing needs enough to improve their health, and then make money on the development, that would be a clear win. If you

[13] Ewing, R. (2022). Somewhere that's green. *Penn Medicine Magazine*. www.pennmedicine.org/news/publications-and-special-projects/penn-medicine-magazine/winter-2022/somewhere-thats-green.

[14] Hawryluk, M. (2019). Why hospitals are getting into the housing business. Kaiser Family Foundation. https://kffhealthnews.org/news/why-hospitals-are-getting-into-the-housing-business/.

cannot offset the cost, you need to monetize the benefits – this is often more difficult with populations facing adverse SDOH than with clinical treatments subject to cost-effectiveness analysis because social randomized controlled trials (remember the RAND experiment) are costly and challenging. Still, if an intervention improves the quality of life of lower-income people, there may be some external source that would fund part of it – perhaps altruistic donors or even tax credits for low-income families.

Having made the best case possible for the net value of the intervention you have in mind, you now need to pay for it. A medical service delivery system could seek outside help – donations, grants, or even social impact bonds (but be careful of the last).[15] An insurer could increase premiums and pay for the intervention but would need to convince buyers to pay extra (although it may reduce costs in the long run). Fundamentally, the problem is that "society" should cover the upfront cost of initiating efficient programs to improve SDOH, but often it does not want to pay up.

What Is the Evidence?

So, there is good news and bad news. The good news is that there is firm evidence, growing every day, about the adverse impacts of varying levels of SDOH on populations. The bad news is that there is little evidence on effective ways to produce improvements in SDOH, and even less evidence about the extent to which doing so improves the health of populations.[16]

It is challenging for individual competitive healthcare delivery systems (for-profit or nonprofit) to finance and implement programs to change the SDOH for the populations they serve; the interrelated nature of SDOH elements makes this even worse. They do not have a money pump to provide funding, and they are not paid for neighborhood improvements. There is more scope for large insurers who cover significant fractions of area populations to initiate programs to change SDOH. I discuss these levels of interventions later in the chapter.

There is a good case to be made that the best entry point for changing SDOH is housing, referred to as the "housing first" movement. At one extreme, if vulnerable populations could be moved to better housing and

[15] Pauly, M., & Swanson, A. (2017). Social impact bonds in nonprofit health care: New product or new package? Journal of Law, Economics, and Organization, 33(4), 718–760. https://faculty.wharton.upenn.edu/wp-content/uploads/2016/11/Swanson_CV_wharton-1.pdf.

[16] Gottlieb, L. M., Wing, H., & Adler, N. E. (2017). A systematic review of interventions on patients' social and economic needs. *American Journal of Preventive Medicine*, *53*(5), 719–729.

better neighborhoods, many of the other adverse SDOH issues would go away: Crime would be lower, food more easily accessible, air would be cleaner – add a little more income on top and things would improve a lot. It is well known that geography is often destiny when it comes to health, so changing geography would make sense.

But new neighborhoods will be hard to create for any entity, and probably even harder for medical delivery systems or insurers – at least on a large scale. Where will there be new housing? Should it be in the old neighborhood, and how should it be located relative to the flagship health facilities versus the places where the disadvantaged population lives and works? There have been some small-scale examples of apparent success, but big problems like dealing with the unhoused population are going to require more than a physician's prescription for better housing for the chronically ill. As stated by David Zuckerman, president of the Healthcare Action Network, "[Hospitals are] filling the gap created by the public sectors not providing the necessary subsidy."[17]

While private insurers have not yet done so on a large-scale basis, Medicare and Medicaid programs have paid some attention to the local environments. One of the most important is the Medicare "direct contracting model," an attempt to change primary care provision in ways that improve adverse SDOH and reduce Medicare spending by reducing the volume of avoidable hospital and emergency room use. The program is a value-based program which changes payment for primary care to a capitated or risk-based system and permits providers to alter cost-sharing or pay for social-type services that are thought to improve SDOH. Begun in 2021, the program has affected several thousand physicians and nearly a million beneficiaries.

According to the most recent evaluation of the initial period of the program (October 2023) it did result in changes in how (voluntary) participating providers behaved. They hired more staff for population health management, they added hours for primary care practices, they paid for services (home health and rehabilitation) that Medicare would not usually cover, and they added telehealth. All of these actions were directed at the goal of reducing use of costly care by taking a population health management approach. Unfortunately, the impact of these activities, as with most of the Medicare initiatives, so far has not been cost reduction or consistent quality

[17] Sisson, P. (2024). In hospitals, affordable housing gets the long-term investor it needs. *New York Times*, March 12. www.nytimes.com/2024/03/12/business/affordable-housing-hospitals-investment.html.

improvements. The model distinguished between entities with prior experience with the Center for Medicare and Medicaid Innovation (CMMI) payment reforms and new ones – and in neither case was there a statistically significant reduction in cost per beneficiary, even before incentive payments were taken into account. There was some reduction in inpatient and emergency room use but not enough to offset the cost of higher primary care use. Evaluators speculated that standard participants with prior experience may already have exhausted opportunities to cut avoidable care, while new participants were still learning how to do so. Clearly this innovation combined changes in payment incentives with opportunities to alter SDOH so we cannot separate out potentially mixed effects – but so far hope for improvement from the package has not been fulfilled.

Beyond Medicare, Medicaid programs are also attempting to address health-related social needs. These approaches are often taken through Medicaid managed care organizations or section 1115 waivers.[18] Services include case management; support for housing, employment, transportation, and nutrition; and peer support groups. For example, North Carolina's Medicaid reform demonstration is piloting enhanced case management services that will work with local organizations to deliver tailored support services while linking payment to outcomes.[19] California also launched the "Whole Person Care Pilot" in 2016, which aimed to integrate care for high-utilizing enrollees with services including housing support and benefits assistance. Six years later, enrollees in the program had 45 fewer hospitalizations and 130 fewer emergency department visits per 1,000 beneficiaries per year, and they cost $383 less per year.[20] Project Nurture, a model in Oregon that integrates maternity care, substance use treatment, and social service coordination for Medicaid beneficiaries reduced child maltreatment and increased prenatal visits compared to opioid-dependent women not served by the project.[21]

[18] DeSalvo, K. B., & Leavitt, M. O. (2019). For an option to address social determinants of health, look to Medicaid. *Health Affairs Forefront*, July 8.

[19] Verma, S. (2018). CMS approves North Carolina's innovative Medicaid demonstration to help improve health outcomes. *Health Affairs Forefront*, October 24.

[20] UCLA Center for Health Policy Research. (2023). *Final evaluation of California's Whole Person Care (WPC) program*. Research report. https://healthpolicy.ucla.edu/our-work/publications/final-evaluation-californias-whole-person-care-wpc-program.

[21] McConnell, K. J., Kaufman, M. R., Grunditz, J. I., Bellanca, H., Risser, A., Rodriguez, M. I., & Renfro, S. (2020). Project Nurture integrates care and services to improve outcomes for opioid-dependent mothers and their children: Study assesses Project Nurture, an innovative model that integrates maternity care, substance use treatment, and social service coordination for Medicaid beneficiaries in Portland, Oregon. *Health Affairs*, *39*(4), 595–602.

Evidence outside of Medicare and Medicaid is mounting that programs aimed to address SDOH can have benefits. The Veterans Administration has identified reductions in emergency department visits by embedding social workers in primary care teams.[22] A study randomizing medically complex families to a housing intervention has identified improved family health at six months.[23]

With these semi-practical considerations in mind, what other advice can economics offer to managers? One answer involves a different way to look at SDOH that can suggest both challenges and opportunities.

Adverse SDOH as a Local Public Bad

Despite popular opinion, economic theory and evidence is not limited to private markets in which individuals buy and sell goods and services that only affect them. Instead, there is a well-developed (if incomplete) body of work that deals with what are sometimes called "social goods" but more commonly "public goods." With its usual contrariness, the adjective "public" in economics does not necessarily imply that governments and taxes will have to be involved with these goods; rather it refers to the physical properties of the goods and the impact they have on the public. To begin at the other end, in economics a private good is one that only affects the well-being (or utility) of the person who uses it, while a public good affects everyone in the relevant public – surely the direct user or buyer if one can be defined, but also others. Some goods fall in between ("impure public goods"); they affect some more than others. In many cases, the populations affected are limited by geography or politics – not the entire world population but those who are located in a specific area or within specific political boundaries (nations, states). Goods can be bads – things that make some people worse off – like the smoke from my "Burning of Rome" barbecue that irritates my neighbors and their party guests.

22 Cornell, P. Y., Halladay, C. W., Ader, J., Halaszynski, J., Hogue, M., McClain, C. E., . . . & Rudolph, J. L. (2020). Embedding social workers in Veterans Health Administration primary care teams reduces emergency department visits: An assessment of the Veterans Health Administration program to add social workers to rural primary care teams. *Health Affairs*, *39*(4), 603–612.

23 Bovell-Ammon, A., Mansilla, C., Poblacion, A., Rateau, L., Heeren, T., Cook, J. T., . . . & Sandel, M. T. (2020). Housing intervention for medically complex families associated with improved family health: Pilot randomized trial: Finding an intervention which seeks to improve child health and parental mental health for medically complex families that experienced homelessness and housing instability. *Health Affairs*, *39*(4), 613–621.

Here I want to suggest that we look at many of the SDOH factors or activities in the same way. Government has failed to provide an appropriate program to cause a change in an environmental factor affecting low-income population that would yield more benefit than cost. Air pollution already mentioned is the obvious example: When I drive rather than walk to the grocery the emissions my car exhales add to smog in my metropolitan area (until it hits the mountains or the sea). Similarly, high crime in my neighborhood may benefit the criminals engaged in involuntary redistribution of wealth and health but harms others. Yet another example, public transportation networks benefit both occasional users and nonusers as well as daily commuters.

Enough of examples; you get the idea. What economics says about public goods or bads is what your mother could have told you: Markets, even perfectly competitive ones, will not lead to the right levels – so government or some other source of collective action may need to be called in, imperfect as it is likely to be. The converse of this proposition in that, in these cases, individual consumers or individual firms will not be able to get it right on their own.

That, I would argue, is the challenge with SDOH. As a sometimes noble person, I walk to the store if the weather is nice, but mostly I drive and pollute. On rainy days, I could ask myself what difference it would make to total pollution if I grab the car keys and the answer is "none." The problem, in a nutshell (or wherever you put problems these days), is that what is rational for the individual is not rational for the community – even in a community of identicals, much less in a community of unequals. The "tragedy of the commons" plays out in SDOH.

Would I want my local health system to incur costs in reducing noxious emissions, environmentally correct disposal of biohazards, and dumping things down the drain? Not unless everyone else's hospital in town did. How about avoiding antibiotics that cure but cause resistance? What about efforts to fix up the bad neighborhoods where people who use my hospital live?

Things are not hopeless entirely. If my hospital is a major presence in the community with very severe problems, it may pay for it to pay to mitigate those problems – extra police, renovation of blighted housing, minibuses so people can get around, fix the sidewalks. Economic theory says that the "privately provided public goods" may happen – but they usually will not be carried far enough. So far, they have not been carried far enough when it comes to SDOH.

What to do? Box 15.1 provides the details, but the answer comes down to organizing (if you can) some kind of community effort at both producing and paying for cost-effective programs to reduce SDOH. For health system managers, this means two things: (1) find programs that are cost-effective, not just ones that seem like a good idea or even are most wanted by community activists, and (2) get your partners together and get the show on the road.

Box 15.1 Theory: Hospitals, health, and housing

One of the social determinants that is related to health outcomes is housing. Location may reflect air pollution, crime, education, and social interaction – a whole host of influences on health outcomes. Hospitals and other health institutions may, in the spirit of Weisbrod's model, be called upon to fill the gap created in part by the "financial sector not investing in affordable housing and the public sector not providing the necessary subsidy to make it all work."[24] Add to that social purpose a way to justify your local tax exclusion, provide better housing closer to work for your employees, and a likely ability to circumvent zoning code and shame neighbors who might object to low-rent housing and you can have a strong social and business case for your hospital or health system to get into real estate. If in addition you can combine your affordable housing development assisted by relaxation of zoning rules with some associated housing sold at market levels, you can make money. The business case is buttressed by decades of experience of related programs for the mentally and physically challenged which invested in housing (some new, much existing) associated with group homes and the provision of medical services to their residents (mental health care, physical therapy); those programs have succeeded largely because the housing value boom made their real estate investments profitable even if the medical and care mission was poorly financed.

Evidence on the profitability of housing programs for health systems or health insurers has, however, been stronger than evidence that they improve health outcomes. Nevertheless, investing in housing near the site of medical services delivery that is targeted at unhoused or socially challenged chronically ill patients can be an efficient use of any investible funds a healthcare provider or insurer can raise. The Kaiser plans and the Healthcare Action Network have become big-time real estate investors. Even Medicaid allows for waivers to use its funding for rental support.

There is potential here for a series of modest steps that might cumulate in a major impact. The main issue is whether health systems have the capability to manage as landlords – and whether a focus on healthcare and outcomes can (or should) be maintained. In this case, the real-world economics seem favorable to a sustainable program if it can be run in an effective way.

[24] Sisson, P. (2024). In hospitals, affordable housing gets the long-term investor it needs. *New York Times*, March 12. www.nytimes.com/2024/03/12/business/affordable-housing-hospitals-investment.html.

I suspect that the most important key to success is the advantage healthcare systems are likely to have in getting around zoning, building permitting, and open space requirements imposed by local governments. They may well be able to get approval to build housing that commercial developers cannot. Housing prices are high, and supply is limited by local regulations intended to keep construction out of your and your neighbor's backyard; perhaps health systems can plan an end run around those rules (and any remaining red lines). The resulting increase in the value of property can itself help to finance subsidies to rents for those otherwise unable to afford housing in a given location. Turning higher real estate values into cash may be challenging – adding commercial property or turning part of the housing investment into ordinary housing may be challenged. Or it may be that the medical cost offsets from decent housing for the formerly unhoused can cover the cost of investment.

For insurers, things are potentially different. Suppose that there is one giant insurer that covers almost all of the population in town. It should have an incentive to pay for cost-effective SDOH programs itself. In econo-speak, it can "internalize the externalities," the spillover benefits that flow from better housing or safer streets. However, this insurer will reap most of the financial gains from doing so. Medicare cannot capture all benefits from actions that especially save money on us old folks. Medicaid, with the responsibility to provide for the sick poor, is best positioned but least well organized to alleviate adverse SDOH if it can find a politically feasible way to do so.

However, the best ways to deal with public goods or externality-type SDOH are probably outside the scope of either health systems or health insurers. The causes of the problems have been known for years; bad outcomes follow from poverty and racism. Both of these factors are, in one sense, the quintessential public goods: Government and collective choice are needed to change an unlovely distribution of income and wealth, and to inhibit biased and prejudiced actions by some people against others – whether characterized by race, ethnicity, sexual orientation, or religion. Unless and until major change happens, managers in healthcare cannot and will not take major action.

What they can in principle do is, however, not zero. They can chip away at the symptoms of poverty and racism. Should there emerge a consensus to redistribute income and wealth, even if partially, such as child tax credits or increased Medicaid generosity, managers can be at the ready with programs that will maximize the good effects of such changes. The problem so far is that such actions by managers remain unidentified or unproven. There has been a large inflow of private capital and private start-ups into the SDOH space, and a few of them have achieved modest profitability – though largely through supplying conventional medical private goods, like primary care, rather than impacting the food, air, or housing environment. Medicare's CMMI has poured money into programs that so far have been unsuccessful. With a few exceptions related to childbirth, Medicaid programs have not even tried. We still watch and wait for good news.

Insurance Externalities and SDOH

In addition to the technical externalities just discussed, insurance without risk rating can affect others than the individual. Suppose, for example, that a moderately more costly but more nutritious diet can improve a person's health and reduce claims to such an extent that the lower claims more than offset the cost of the diet. If insurance were perfectly risk-rated, this phenomenon would lead to a premium reduction for those using the diet because the health benefit from the diet would more than offset the cost of the diet. Hence diet as a determinant of health would be privately captured in insurance premiums – and there would be financial incentives to get people to follow it.

However, suppose that premiums cannot or do not vary with diet or other health-related behaviors. Then the person would be disincentivized to pay for the healthier diet because any cost savings would all go to the insurance plan, not to the person paying the full cost. In this setting, an insurance manager might choose to offset this distorted incentive by adding coverage that pays for the better diet. In this way, this determinant of health is "socialized" within the insurance plan. In effect, switching to the costlier but healthier diet by the individual provides spillover benefits to others in the plan.

Some goods improve the health of those who use them but generate minimal externalities or spillover effects. Nourishing food is an example. Lower-income persons affected by SDOH may confront food insecurity or poor diets. There is an element of community benefit in the presence of a grocery store selling good food, if consumers will use it, but the majority of the benefit from a better diet accrues to the family using it. If improved health has large medical cost offsets, as discussed in the previous section, the entity paying medical claims (insurer in the case of fee-for-service, health system in the case of capitation) may gain from offering and paying for good food. In this case, insurance covers the private good "my health" to the public good "my insurance claims." It would be important before implementing such a program to determine that it is more effective for health or health claims than the same amount of money paid to families as cash; the evidence does show that unrestricted transfers can have important effects on health. If designed and targeted programs work better, there may be a case for insurers or health systems to foster these health-improving private goods if they can generate external funding to do so.

Levels of Intervention

Managers of health systems may implement interventions across a range of levels to improve SDOH (Exhibit 15.2). Each of these interventions has a range of evidence.

Exhibit 15.2 Levels of intervention

Type	Example(s)
Screening and referring	– A primary care office screening for food insecurity and referring patients who screen positive to community resources
Hiring new team members	– Hiring community health workers and social workers to integrate into a practice – Diversifying the healthcare workforce (e.g., hiring more Black doctors to build trust with Black patients) – Increasing pay for lower-wage workers[25]
Partnering with community organizations and investing in the community	– Conducting blood pressure screenings in barber shops – Making required community benefit spending evidence-based (e.g., investing in lead remediation)[26]
Providing services	– Boston Medical Center Preventive Food Pantry – Independence Blue Cross FareRx grocery delivery – Geisinger food pharmacy – CHOP Medical Financial Partnership – Transportation vouchers – Reach Out and Read
Disparate impact monitoring	– Health systems measuring their outcomes broken down by socioeconomic groups to identify opportunities for intervention
Change payment incentives	– Risk-adjust capitated payments for beneficiaries with higher social needs

[25] Matta, S., Chatterjee, P., & Venkataramani, A. S. (2024). Changes in health care workers' economic outcomes following Medicaid expansion. *JAMA*, *331*(8), 687–695.

[26] Billings, S. B., & Schnepel, K. T. (2018). Life after lead: Effects of early interventions for children exposed to lead. *American Economic Journal: Applied Economics*, *10*(3), 315–344.

First, a primary care practice or an emergency department may screen patients for SDOH and refer them to social services. This might entail having all patients in the waiting room fill out a form asking questions about areas such as housing, food, employment, and transportation. Evidence has demonstrated that screening successfully increases referrals.[27] However, there is not yet robust evidence that screening and referring alone has an ultimate effect on health – there are many places where patients can fall off the truck before connecting with, accessing, and utilizing the services.

At the next level, practices could hire team members such as social workers, case managers, and community health workers to help patients connect to social services. Community health workers are:

> lay members of the community who work either for pay or as volunteers in association with the local health care system in both urban and rural environments . . . CHWs [community health workers] give informal counseling and guidance on health behaviors, provide culturally appropriate health education and information, help people get the care they need, advocate for individual and community health needs, and provide some direct services such as first aid and blood pressure screening.[28]

Community health workers are receiving increasing attention for their effectiveness in improving patient knowledge, empowerment, and care utilization, and Medicaid programs have begun to reimburse for their services.[29] In randomized clinical trials, CHWs have been found to decrease recurrent readmissions and total hospital days as well as improve utilization of post-hospitalization care.[30] There is also preliminary evidence for improvement in

[27] de la Vega, P. B., Losi, S., Martinez, L. S., Bovell-Ammon, A., Garg, A., James, T., . . . & Kressin, N. R. (2019). Implementing an EHR-based screening and referral system to address social determinants of health in primary care. *Medical Care, 57*, S133–S139.

[28] National Heart, Lung, and Blood Institute. (2020). Role of community health workers. www.nhlbi.nih.gov/education/heart-truth/CHW/Role.

[29] Medicaid and CHIP Payment and Access Commission (MACPAC). (2022). Medicaid coverage of community health worker services. www.macpac.gov/publication/medicaid-coverage-of-community-health-worker-services/; Haldar, S., & Hinton, E. (2023). State policies for expanding Medicaid coverage of community health worker (CHW) services. Kaiser Family Foundation. www.kff.org/medicaid/issue-brief/state-policies-for-expanding-medicaid-coverage-of-community-health-worker-chw-services/.

[30] Kangovi, S., Mitra, N., Grande, D., White, M. L., McCollum, S., Sellman, J., . . . & Long, J. A. (2014). Patient-centered community health worker intervention to improve posthospital outcomes: A randomized clinical trial. *JAMA Internal Medicine, 174*(4), 535–543; Kangovi, S., Mitra, N., Norton, L., Harte, R., Zhao, X., Carter, T., . . . & Long, J. A. (2018). Effect of community health worker support on clinical outcomes of low-income patients across primary care facilities: A randomized clinical trial. *JAMA Internal Medicine, 178*(12), 1635–1643.

health outcomes such as measures of diabetes, BMI, and blood pressure among patients randomly assigned to CHWs.[31]

In addition to hiring CHWs, social workers, and case managers, hiring racially concordant clinical team members such as nurses and physicians can make a difference. Building trust with patients of low SES is critical to promote adherence. Experimental evidence in the *American Economic Review* found that a racially concordant provider could improve utilization of preventive care in primary care settings.[32] Partnering with racially concordant community groups as well, such as conducting blood pressure screening in barber shops, offers another option to mitigate SDOH.[33]

Beyond referring and connecting people to services, health systems themselves may be the providers of those services. Hospitals such as the Boston Medical Center and Massachusetts General Hospital,[34] as well as insurance companies such as Independence Blue Cross,[35] are increasingly providing food pantries and grocery delivery services to patients and staff. The goal is that providing healthy food, especially to patients with chronic disease such as diabetes or heart failure, removes barriers to purchasing and preparing healthy meals and reduces downstream hospitalizations. Early evidence has found that these types of programs can improve measures of diabetes and cardiovascular health as well as reduce utilization of costly care.[36] The

[31] Kangovi, S., Mitra, N., Grande, D., Huo, H., Smith, R. A., & Long, J. A. (2017). Community health worker support for disadvantaged patients with multiple chronic diseases: A randomized clinical trial. *American Journal of Public Health, 107*(10), 1660–1667.

[32] Alsan, M., Garrick, O., & Graziani, G. (2019). Does diversity matter for health? Experimental evidence from Oakland. *American Economic Review, 109*(12), 4071–4111; Frakes, M. D., & Gruber, J. (2022). Racial concordance and the quality of medical care: Evidence from the military. National Bureau of Economic Research, Working Paper No. w30767.

[33] Victor, R. G., Lynch, K., Li, N., Blyler, C., Muhammad, E., Handler, J., . . . & Elashoff, R. M. (2018). A cluster-randomized trial of blood-pressure reduction in black barbershops. *New England Journal of Medicine, 378*(14), 1291–1301.

[34] Mirsky, J. B., Zack, R. M., Berkowitz, S. A., & Fiechtner, L. (2021). Massachusetts General Hospital Revere food pantry: Addressing hunger and health at an academic medical center community clinic. *Healthcare, 9*(4), 100589.

[35] FareRx. (2023). Independence Blue Cross grocery delivery program with FareRx. https://farerx.com/delivery-program/.

[36] Seligman, H. K., Lyles, C., Marshall, M. B., Prendergast, K., Smith, M. C., Headings, A., . . . & Waxman, E. (2015). A pilot food bank intervention featuring diabetes-appropriate food improved glycemic control among clients in three states. *Health Affairs, 34*(11), 1956–1963; Berkowitz, S. A., Delahanty, L. M., Terranova, J., Steiner, B., Ruazol, M. P., Singh, R., . . . & Wexler, D. J. (2019). Medically tailored meal delivery for diabetes patients with food insecurity: A randomized cross-over trial. *Journal of General Internal Medicine, 34*, 396–404; Rivera, R. L., Adams, M., Dawkins, E., Carter, A., Zhang, X., Tu, W., . . . & Clark, D. O. (2023). Delivering food resources and kitchen skills (forks) to adults with food insecurity and hypertension: A pilot study. *Nutrients, 15*(6), 1452; Hummel, S. L., Karmally, W., Gillespie, B. W., Helmke, S., Teruya, S., Wells, J., . . . & Maurer, M. S. (2018). Home-delivered meals postdischarge from heart failure hospitalization: The GOURMET-HF

American Heart Association is launching a new "Food Is Medicine" initiative to continue to gather evidence on the importance of diet as a determinant of health.[37]

In addition to providing food services, hospitals provide other services such as medical-financial partnerships, transportation vouchers, and books. The Medical-Financial Partnership at the Children's Hospital of Philadelphia helps families file their taxes, save for college, pay off debt, and navigate public benefits.[38] Transportation vouchers have been found to improve patient health outcomes when delivered concordantly with other social services.[39] The Reach Out and Read program provides books to pediatric primary care patients at well-child visits. It has demonstrated improvements in children's literacy and the family's healthy engagement with the child.[40] Improving the home environment for children can improve immediate health outcomes and reduce violence or mistreatment.

Insurers may improve care for patients of low SES through a suite of "value-based" payment models (see Chapter 9). For example, the goal of risk-adjusting capitated payments to providers who care for patients with high SDOH is to reduce the risk of providers dropping high-risk patients from their panel and to fairly compensate them for caring for these patients. The accountable care organization: realizing equity, access, and community health (ACO REACH) model makes such adjustments.[41] Adjusting spending targets for these patients may also improve providers' ability to care for them because of their greater needs.[42] Finally, incentives that reward equity in

pilot study. *Circulation: Heart Failure, 11*(8), e004886; Berkowitz, S. A., Terranova, J., Hill, C., Ajayi, T., Linsky, T., Tishler, L. W., & DeWalt, D. A. (2018). Meal delivery programs reduce the use of costly health care in dually eligible Medicare and Medicaid beneficiaries. *Health Affairs, 37*(4), 535–542.

37 Volpp, K. G., Berkowitz, S. A., Sharma, S. V., Anderson, C. A., Brewer, L. C., Elkind, M. S., . . . & American Heart Association. (2023). Food is medicine: A presidential advisory from the American Heart Association. *Circulation, 148*(18), 1417–1439.

38 Children's Hospital of Philadelphia. Medical Financial Partnership. www.chop.edu/services/medical-financial-partnership.

39 Solomon, E. M., Wing, H., Steiner, J. F., & Gottlieb, L. M. (2020). Impact of transportation interventions on health care outcomes: A systematic review. *Medical Care, 58*(4), 384–391; Starbird, L. E., DiMaina, C., Sun, C. A., & Han, H. R. (2019). A systematic review of interventions to minimize transportation barriers among people with chronic diseases. *Journal of Community Health, 44*, 400–411.

40 Saravillo, S. J. B., & Agapinan-Alfonso, M. L. (2018). Effects of a community-based Reach Out and Read program among low-income urban families with young children. *Pediatrics*, 142(1_MeetingAbstract): 517. https://doi.org/10.1542/peds.142.1MA6.517.

41 Navathe, A. S., & Liao, J. M. (2022). Aligning value-based payments with health equity: A framework for reforming payment reforms. *JAMA, 328*(10), 925–926.

42 Liao, J. M., & Navathe, A. S. (2022). What comes next in prioritizing equity in payment? The ACO REACH model. *Health Affairs Forefront*, April 6.

outcomes offer an opportunity to directly incentivize providers to design their practice to improve equity.

Lastly, improving patients' environment can ameliorate adverse SDOH. Gun violence is a major source of trauma in urban emergency departments. Research from the Urban Health Lab has demonstrated that greening vacant lots and remediating vacant homes reduces neighborhood crime.[43] Health systems can engage in local greening initiatives in order to improve their community's health.

Conclusions for Managers

The punchline is that there can sometimes be an advantage for managers to try to change SDOH. More often they will have to explain why SDOH, not failed managerial actions, are the main reasons for particular adverse outcomes. As usual, staying alert for something that is both effective and cost-effective – so far absent but potentially discoverable – is the price of success.

The most fundamental financial issue is the return on investment to the health system. What is the benefit your health system can capture from improving housing, transportation, nutrition, or safety when government has failed to do so? If the population you treat is covered by capitation, or better yet, capitation or bonuses for good health outcomes, it may well pay to invest in programs that are effective even if much of the benefit to health spills over to lower cost of public services as higher worker productivity. If your system has reserves to invest, local real estate may be a reasonable place, and more housing close by can be helpful to your workforce. At the other extreme, if you are stuck in a large fee-for-service system where the only benefit for improving population health, even when it can be done in a cost-effective way, is to pile up treasure in heaven, you need to be cautious. The best outcome is, of course, significantly better health, but investing in SDOH may still pay off for a chronically ill population if it can reduce the use of costly inpatient care. What is needed is both head and heart to be taken into account.

[43] Garvin, E. C., Cannuscio, C. C., & Branas, C. C. (2013). Greening vacant lots to reduce violent crime: A randomised controlled trial. *Injury Prevention*, *19*(3), 198–203; South, E. C., Macdonald, J. M., Tam, V. W., Ridgeway, G., & Branas, C. C. (2023). Effect of abandoned housing interventions on gun violence, perceptions of safety, and substance use in Black neighborhoods: A citywide cluster randomized trial. *JAMA Internal Medicine*, *183*(1), 31–39.

16 Conclusion: Don'ts, Dos, and Debunks from Economics

Introduction

Management of innovations in healthcare delivery systems and insurance primarily involves common sense: look around, gather evidence, talk with stakeholders, and think about pros and cons. It isn't rocket science – but, as in rocket science, there sometimes are decisions that are important and nonobvious. And sometimes otherwise unanticipated effects come at the end of a long chain of interactions and reasoning. In the case of health and insurance management, this book argues that economic science can sometimes help.

The most obvious help is when economic analysis can marshal facts and theories that help to specify the odds of success of one action compared to another (or compared to no action). It can also help managers to think more clearly about the forces at play affecting any decision, especially when incentives and outcomes matter: Economic models can lead both to clear hypotheses and to rejection of illogical speculation.

In this wrap-up, my goal is to review and summarize what I think are the most important messages from what has gone before – and offer parting shots on what I think, when all is said and done, about what conclusions seem to follow.

It may come as no surprise that economics is most frequently useful at debunking apparently plausible conventional wisdom propositions about cause and effect – like assertions that Plan A will surely produce net benefits. Most of the time the economics message is "not so fast, the evidence isn't there (yet)." Sometimes it is even more fundamental – "there is no logical way this can work without bad side effects." So, in my summary, I will eventually go for full-throated debunking when it is warranted but also play the role of the cautious conscience that warns you to go slowly and look deeply.

I have provided a long menu in this book of economic views on issues in healthcare management and insurance. I have found over the years, by painful experience, that conclusions from economic analysis often fail to take with audiences. To try to avoid this fate, in this concluding chapter I will combine the usual final deep musings about what it all means with a list and some parting words. I have selected, in the spirit of the subtitle of this book, those conclusions which are most unexpected.

So, in what follows, I am going to provide three passes at summarizing hopefully memorable conclusions from economics. The first pass will be at a high level: broad messages about how economists think healthcare and insurance markets work or should work, the lines for the opening parts of your speech on unexpected ideas in management and policy. Next will be a numerical and annotated list of subject-specific findings from health economic research that managers should know when confronted with specific issues. Finally, a list of misperceptions by noneconomists (especially physician and political experts in healthcare) that economics debunks or at least seriously questions. This is the *Freakonomics* of healthcare part of the book and may at a minimum help you if you are assigned the negative in a debate on what should be done in healthcare.[1] And then some concluding thoughts.

General and Moderately Surprising Specific Insights from the Health Economics Mindset

One general group of messages has to do with the facts (or their absence), for those who are devoted to the idea that actions should be based on evidence.[2] Is there evidence on the difference a particular management strategy might make? Not surprisingly, given the vast set of plausible possibilities out there, only a minority of strategies have conclusive evidence that they matter – but those are important. Some do identify things that really can reduce the resource costs of healthcare while not harming health outcomes too much. Only a very few can promise lower cost with little possibility of some adverse impacts.

Of the few strategies in the last set is the implementation of transitional care for hospitalized inpatients. Care provided and coordinated by specially

[1] Levitt, S. D., & Dubner, S. J. (2005). *Freakonomics: A rogue economist explores the hidden side of everything.* William Morrow & Co.

[2] Pauly, M., Winston, F., Naylor, M., Volpp, K., Burns, L. R., Muller, R., . . . & Chartock, B. (2022). *Seemed like a good idea: Alchemy versus evidence-based approaches to healthcare management innovation.* Cambridge University Press.

trained nurses cuts spending by more than a nominal amount by avoiding returns to the hospital for the inevitable flare-ups that need to be managed. So far this is, in my opinion, one of the only coordinated care strategies that has been shown to make an appreciable difference, but it is something you can hang your hat on – and might be extended further.

Another message is that there is overwhelming evidence that charging middle-class people something out of pocket for many kinds of care reduces total spending. However, precisely because this instrument can be so powerful, it should ideally be deployed with caution, discretion, and concern – not for every kind of care, and not for every kind of person, but targeted at those services where nearly free care stimulates low-value use the most. The goal is not to impose direct costs on consumers but to use such costs to discourage low-value choices by patients and their physicians. We know that patient choices are often based on imperfect information, but there is some evidence that they do take account of relative marginal benefits – ironically, perhaps more so before they seek physician advice than after. However, we do have the result that for the majority of participants in the RAND health insurance experiment who were not at high risk, spending and use fell by a lot from cost-sharing but health outcomes were not affected – strong circumstantial evidence that, somehow, consumers were able to choose what care to forego that did not affect their health, the literal definition of low-value care. The alternatives to cost-sharing – imposing higher cost on suppliers of low-value care or mandating heavily managed care – so far have not come anywhere near the empirical effectiveness on spending of patient cost-sharing. But our present arsenal holds too many blunt and unrefined instruments, and the task of gathering evidence on when free care for all is actually the best and when it is the worst still remains – but it remains important and useful. The question of distributing the cost of care between the patient at the point of use and the consumer or taxpayer who pays an insurance premium is one of the most important unsettled questions in health policy. So is the need for physicians to learn how to provide better advice to the large number of middle-class nonelderly insureds who have plans with high deductibles or coinsurance.

A third important empirical message is that competition among firms selling the same or similar medical products and services – whether those firms are drug companies, health systems, or physicians – works to achieve lower levels of spending compared to less competition. The idea, with this cure-all, is that setting up the pattern of incentives that will produce virtuous outcomes from imperfect suppliers is hard to do in many parts of the country, and hard to maintain where it does exist. There is also an understudy who could be substituted for markets: state programs to specify a target growth rate for spending and then do something (though not clear what) to achieve it. This alternative has yet to step on stage for a long enough period of time to judge whether it will be equally boffo.

Value-based payment, patient-centered medical homes, greater emphasis on primary care, and value-based insurance all have compelling rationales but so far have not had much proven success when they have been tried. My advice on making these risky bets is "Don't." Of course, I do not know what your personal odds are on, say, patient-centered medical homes saving money or improving health more than a trifle, so you need not obey. My fallback position on these interventions is that they are unproven, not that we are sure they will never work. (You cannot prove a negative; maybe a pink unicorn will be discovered in Oregon some day.) If you have to do something and spend real resources or lose them, go ahead. As Chapter 2 on the highbrow decision theory said, it all depends on which kind of mistake you most want to avoid.

However, a fundamental semi-solution to which I return over and over in this book is to suggest having a market sort things out. Friedrich Hayek, one of the Nobel-winning patron saints of market economics, always deprecated the usual economic fixation on static efficiency (of perfect competition) in favor of praising a competitive market's ability to draw in the best information and innovation. That is my cue for optimism in healthcare management – if it can be done, somebody will eventually figure out how to do it, as long as there is free entry and undistorted incentives. Not everything "we" want will necessarily be supplied no matter how long we wait; all those medieval wizards trying to transmute lead into gold eventually gave up, and so it may be with the "triple aim" in healthcare or affordable drug prices or other infeasible desiderata. Care that is effective and personal will inevitably use real resources, telehealth visits to the contrary notwithstanding. But in the laundry list of challenges in this book – coordinating care, coordinating physicians and hospitals, reimbursing effectively, and offering middle-class insurance that hits the best combination of affordability, risk protection, and incentives for high-value care – there is a possibility of improvement.

What to Watch For

A good manager should always survey the environment for opportunities for continuous quality improvement (at no increase in cost) or ways to lower cost (without hurting quality too much). But that person should also have a life – so I offer my take on what economics so far says are the best improvement possibilities to watch. What is it that will help you keep your job or even get a raise? I have discussed the topics on the list already in this book, but I am going to give each of them one last shot in hopes that doing so will stimulate both attention and innovation.

Paying more for primary care. For as long as I can remember, all right-thinking people in health policy have bemoaned the fact that primary care doctors have less clout and make less money than specialists. When I joined the Physician Payment Review Commission more than 20 years ago, custodians of the rollout of the resource-based relative-value fee-for-service (FFS) scheme, I thought I was going to preside over a Medicare effort to right this wrong, at long last, as payments for medical services were to be based on work, not credentials – and primary care physicians work as much as specialists. I was wrong; it is still true in Medicare and in private insurance that the heroic lifesaving or life-changing interventions that open heart surgeons and charismatic orthopods make are compensated much more generously than the observation, diagnosis, and care planning that primary care doctors offer. Some of this is a continuation of a caste system in medicine which has proven amazingly durable, but some of it refers to the commonsense idea that you should want to pay more to someone who does something that obviously makes a big difference than to someone whose advice may or may not eventually help you but you will never be able to tell for sure. Evaluation and management are just not that dramatic. It is hard for consumers to see the value (when it exists) in reduction in uncertainty and direction of the pattern of care primary care physicians provide – precisely because the evidence for it is not in the moment but is in the long-term data which managers can see but patients do not.

And yet these primary care efforts may matter more at the population level than anything specialists do for patients in extremis. A possible vehicle for redressing both incentives and rewards here may come from bundled payment if primary care physicians can place themselves in the role of directing how that bundled lump is parceled down the line into individual medical services – if someone will trust them with the money. If data and statistical methods can prove that top-line management improves population health appreciably, income to those managers may follow. After all, there are already many intermediaries in healthcare like pharmacy benefit managers (PBMs) and consultants who supposedly skim millions for much less valuable actions. The missing link so far is evidence that some version of primary care makes a difference (compared to usual care muddling through). That has not happened yet, but watch this space.

Cost-effectiveness results as management tools. There is a whole industry of "health economics and outcomes research" (HEOR) that studies the costs and benefits of medical innovations primarily but not only of pharmaceuticals. The methods or typical assumptions used by HEOR do not always meet the demands of high-level economic theory (e.g., by allowing the value of incremental quality-adjusted life years (QALYs) to decline in dollar value as more of them pile up), but it has had much influence abroad. In the US, historically a cost-effectiveness study was usually a poor relation in the marketing campaign by a drug firm – a way to say something nice about your product. However, the organization Institute for Clinical and Economic Review has now established itself as fashioning cost-effectiveness tools to beat down high launch prices for new drugs. The Institute will tell you what the price should be if the ratio is to get below their assumed threshold at which it makes sense to buy – but that analysis will matter to the profit-seeking drug firm only if people actually refuse to pay its current higher price.

So how can the evidence on cost-effectiveness be fashioned into decision rules for insurance companies and capitated healthcare systems that make sense? I offered a few thoughts earlier – let those consumers whose QALYs are worth more than average make the rational choice to buy the overpriced drug or (more helpfully) provide the evidence on the distribution of marginal health benefits (not just the average) that can tell the drug firm how much more it would sell if it cut the price. Building a product to use this information seems like a golden opportunity for healthcare consultants, so maybe they will find something worth marketing.

Care coordination. We have a toe in the door with the transitional care model (TCM). Here is a form of care coordination that saves big money and helps people. Other forms of care coordination so far do not. Are there elements of TCM that can spread the magic to patients in need of coordinated care in other settings? Is it the use of specially trained nurses? Is it the initiation of care management at a transitional node in the patient's health? So far neither physicians nor community workers have been able to do as well as TCM but still no more general model has emerged. Maybe it will.

Doing something about social determinants of health (SDOH). It has proven far too easy for researchers to show that the social environment affects lifestyle which in turn affects health outcomes. Documenting the causes of bad outcomes has not, however, led to effective and sustainable interventions to change those causes. At present, the key actors to change this system are under-resourced and politically powerless; health system managers may not have the ability to pull up their own bootstraps until local governments pay more attention.

Conventional wisdom hypothesizes a model that puts primary care physicians at the center and imagines they can write prescriptions for expenditures on things associated with social determinants – nourishing food, better housing, community assistance, wellness programs. This is a useful framing of the decision problem, though one may wonder whether medical training (as opposed, say, to social work education with a little econ on the side) better equips providers to know what is cost-effective. Typically, the discussion of SDOH deals with low-income patients who are presumably insured by Medicaid, which is going to have to cover the bill. We have the usual considerations: Is it possible that paying for one of these benefits has a larger cost offset so it reduces total spending? If so, go for it! But more often there is a modest cost offset that will be lost to the insurer if there is turnover. More fundamentally, can the taxpayers (state and federal) who fund Medicaid be convinced to pay up?

That there is no bright line between medical care and other welfare affecting items of consumption is no reason not to follow this discussion; no silos here! There is a choice between a paternalistic, public, and tax-financed model of help to low-income people – guide or incentivize them to do the right thing with all items of consumption – and an alternative cash transfer tax credit model that provides the family money and information, and then lets it decide how to spend. There are also some environmental factors like pollution and local crime that cannot be dealt with effectively by individuals no matter how much money they have – until they have enough to move to a better neighborhood. Maybe the best approach is a competitive model in which consumers can choose their own helping organization, the original idea of managed care. This approach bears watching. If something is found that really works, that will be noteworthy, in more ways than one.

Employment-based health insurance as a part of total worker compensation. In competitive labor markets, a perceptive employer will think of health benefits not as cost to be minimized but as a tool to attract and retain good workers by offering them what they want. Economists think that (with a few minor exceptions) workers pay for their own health benefits through lower cash wages – so there is no reason and no way for employers to try to shift costs to workers (by higher cost-sharing); the benefits department should seek the trade-off between financial risk and incentives for high-value care that workers most prefer. There are plenty of reasons to be concerned about high healthcare costs in the US, but, because they do not increase our total labor costs, potential impacts on international trade are, according to economists, not one of them.

Hospital care in rural areas and small cities. Competition among hospitals in big cities still works to hold down spending without harming quality, according to antitrust economists. The evidence on competition and price restraint is not as voluminous for ambulatory physician and other services, or for specialized care like rehab or dialysis, but there is some evidence suggesting similar effects.

The problem is that, with a service that is rendered face-to-face, high population density is most conducive to a competitive structure. There is no guarantee; the anonymous nature of households in cities that get very big may inhibit the flow of price and quality information among consumers.[3] But for services where there are some economies of scale, like hospitals and specialized physician care, rural areas are going to be challenged. Measures of competition like the concentration ratio are very highly correlated with population size; the (shrinking number of) hospital markets ranked moderately competitive are the top 10 metro areas by population plus Oklahoma City, Seattle, and San Diego. A one-hospital rural town will face a monopoly, but that potential market power has not been sufficient to keep many of these institutions afloat financially. Their costs are higher and perceived quality lower for what they do, and some consumers respond by hitting the interstate and driving to a close big city.

In contrast to urban hospitals, private insurance payments to rural hospitals are often lower than Medicare. Paradoxes abound. More rural hospitals are being acquired by or linked to larger health systems – and then they raise prices. Possibly good for the financial sustainability of the hospital, but why did it take the arrival of the city folk to wield already-present market power?

So, what should be done – either by public policy or by private managers? We should start with our usual mantra: Do what is most cost-effective but take all costs and benefits into account. So, if expanding some service at the local monopoly hospital saves time for crucial treatment or travel time, do it – but not if it would be less costly and almost as good to move people to big-

[3] Pauly, M. V., & Satterthwaite, M. A. (1980). The effect of provider supply on price. In Health Resources Administration (ed.), *The target income hypothesis and related issues in health manpower policy*. Bureau of Health Manpower. US Department of Health, Education, and Welfare (DHEW). DHEW Publication No. (HRA) 80-27.

city facilities rather than move facilities to people. I believe that following this rule will get you a long way toward rationalizing policy toward small cities and rural areas – but what about the people who are stuck there? A network that uses less costly local hospitals and convinces insureds of their quality is a solution – but only if costs are truly lower and quality at least as high.

There may be additional social value (small town life and all that) attached to those who live in Green Acres; some advocate that the goal of exurban hospitals should be "helping rural communities thrive," which goes well beyond health outcomes. Plus, rural states have as many US senators as urban ones. But any choice here should at least be explicit and its cost distributed to those who attach highest value to help.

Virtual care and artificial intelligence. My advisors tell me I could increase the market for this book by having a full chapter on what managers should know from economics dealing with virtual care and its most recent version, artificial intelligence. Looking at the buzz-o-meter, we get a high reading for this topic. However, there is no chapter because as yet, in my opinion, there is no substance: only prospects and hopes, not evidence or models.

As ATMs revolutionized retail banking 20 years ago, we were told that healthcare was going to be next. So far as I know, the robodoctor never materialized, but we still hear that prediction. Some things have definitely changed. Electronic systems now construct and retain medical records, and insurance eligibility and claims are all online. The money flow part of healthcare has been changed (and had knock-on effects on things like prescription drug insurance) but the information flow part of healthcare still remains to be improved.

This is so even though the coronavirus pandemic did revolutionize health services delivery out of necessity, so there is no longer an issue of inertia or inexperience. However, the end of the story there is that, with the exception of mental health care, delivery has returned to a large extent to the former model of mostly face-to-face encounters with virtual care at less than 10% of all care (measured by episodes or billings).[4] That share is multiples of its pre-Covid level, but this is a bump, not a revolution, and may diminish if Congress does not make the costly Medicare "flexibilities" permanent. What has yet to materialize are superior systems for providing care to patients or paying providers for what they do.

[4] Kaiser Family Foundation. (2022). Telehealth has played an outsized role meeting mental health needs during the COVID-19 pandemic. www.kff.org/mental-health/issue-brief/telehealth-has-played-an-outsized-role-meeting-mental-health-needs-during-the-covid-19-pandemic/.

Medical records are a key tool for physicians and other clinicians to manage a patient's health; often the best indicator of something to be done is a change in a metric over time. However, because health is so multidimensional, the medical care system is awash in metrics and data. Electronic medical records are doubtless better at recording and storing, but so far, they have not been shown to help with decisions – refer to Chapter 2 for an explanation of the value of information. Instead, the well-known complaint is that, whereas formerly a physician needed only to write down what is relevant, now systems require all kinds of questions to be entered in the computer. That raises the cost and the ire of patients and doctors. There have been attempts to construct better linked decision support systems but so far no winners. We know that "computerization" is largely helpful in catching oversights – dumb mistakes – but not in generating insights into diagnosis or treatment. Despite substantial regulatory pressure for interoperability of electronic medical records, progress here seems stalled. Part of the problem, according to economists, is that patient data can be the source of market power for providers, and so they are reluctant to share it with competitors, but part of the problem is that the sorting wheat from chaff informational task has not been easy.[5]

In terms of technology for "seeing" patients, there is no doubt that virtual visits represent a change. This has not been an economic boon, however, because, so far, those visits have not proven to have much lower resource cost than face-to-face visits, and because patients have largely added them to in-person visits rather than substituted them, so no payment was saved. In the good old days, patients or their insurer paid for visits to a primary care doctor, partly as compensation for the visit time but also as bundled payment for the opportunity to make and receive free phone advice on the medical issue. Virtual visits, and to an even greater extent patient portal communications, now substitute for phone calls. The problem is that payment has not been permanently reset. Doing so may be part of the ideal bundle, when and if it appears. That pandemic-related telehealth has largely been abandoned when no longer necessary suggests that the advantages so far are not large, except in mental health. Even huge enterprises like Walmart and Amazon have given up on their virtual care plans.

Economists think that the main problem with telehealth and virtual care is patient demand and acceptance, not provider supply. To sum up: We have

[5] Gaynor, M. S., Hydari, M. Z., & Telang, R. (2012). Is patient data better protected in competitive healthcare markets? Paper presented at the 2012 Workshop on the Economics of Information Security (WEIS), Berlin, June 25–26.

a set of technologies searching for years for an effective application. The coronavirus pandemic and the increase in reimbursements jump-started a number of them but so far has not led to a telehealth reckoning. There are no fatal flaws in trying to use virtual care or computerized records or (so far) artificial intelligence, but no breakthroughs either. One can blame insufficient insurance reimbursement for halting the spread, but that low payment is caused by the absence of evidence of serious benefits and is not a cause. As usual, I would want to see cost-effectiveness play a central role in setting goals for the package but with electronic means somehow used to deliver in a superior way. The experts Bimal Desai and Krista Chaiyachati (in a book I edited) have the right conclusion: "The evidence to spur large scale adoption and payment remains in limbo . . . Hopefully we will be entering an incredibly exciting and rapidly evolving time period of better telehealth evidence generation soon; otherwise, the future role of telehealth in the US health care system may be murky."[6]

Managers and Economics: Will a Parting Shot Hit Its Mark?

Economics was born to challenge conventional wisdom (Adam Smith and contemporaries trashed the guild system and mercantilism) and continues to play that role in healthcare. I have tried to filter health economics research in order to capture some insights that tell managers something different from what they already know or think they know.

As a manager, you should apply the same criteria to evaluate these insights as to other kinds of evidence using the model in Chapter 2. If you are told not to raise private prices when Medicare cuts, or to foster competition rather than monopoly, or stop sweating value-based payment, will that information change the expected consequence of a decision you will make? Economists could be wrong, after all, although some of the insights have really good evidence behind them.

You can make up your own mind on whether there is enough waste in the US healthcare system that someone knows how to eliminate to make an appreciable impact on medical spending or its growth. I am not optimistic; we can define a system as broken only if we know how to fix it. There are some moderate-scale improvements possible, although there is a much larger

[6] Chaiyachati, K. H., & Desai, B. (2022). The unmet and evolving need for evidence-based telehealth. In Pauly, M., Winston, F., Naylor, M. et al., *Seemed like a good idea: Alchemy versus evidence-based approaches to healthcare management innovation* (pp. 301–331). Cambridge University Press.

number of ideas for improvement that either have not panned out or have not been tested well. At the macro level, you could imagine, based on recent data, that medical spending growth is coming more in line with growth in the rest of the economy – although breakthroughs in Alzheimer's or genetic treatments could throw that prediction off for a while if they are phased in. Day-to-day attention to detail was how your parents managed your home, and that is good advice for managers generally. Looking for economic explanations and economic evidence may help you seem smarter than anyone else in the room. This behavior may turn out to be cost-effective.

Specific Messages from Health Economics

I have said everything I can say about the messages from economics for managers in the preceding chapters. However, based on experience, I am aware that the audience reaction to any discussion by an economist is often: "What did he say?" Perhaps the best way for me to summarize is to engage in what is for economists the most fun thing they know how to do: debunking. I will distill some messages from what has been said by health economists that (based on my subjective judgment) seem most unexpectedly contrary to what "many people" believe. I may be wrong; it may be that for some of these thoughts the alternative to the piercing economic insight is a straw man and nobody (or only a few foolish people) believes it. If so, objectively that will be good news even if it saps some of the punch from my story.

Here are things some or all health economists say that may be surprising:

(1) *There is no firm evidence that the US healthcare system overall is very wasteful.* I have discussed the "30% estimate" Buz Cooper was concerned about and the 25% estimate we are told "most economists" believe.[7] Waste (or inefficiency) in economics means that there is a way of doing things differently that can yield mutual benefit to all. Ambiguity arises because "can" in theory is often challenging to turn into "can" in practice. The problem with the evidence is that it is best at suggesting *theoretical* waste rather than practical or *actionable* waste.

One thing I remember from high school physics, coming from a family of tinkerers, was the concept of the efficiency of a machine (and the dream of a perpetual motion). Efficiency of a machine is the ratio between inputs and outputs (rather like the definition of value).

[7] Cooper, R. B. (2019). *Poverty and the myths of health care reform.* Johns Hopkins University Press.

There was theoretical efficiency and the applied or field efficiency – and the difference between the two was usually friction. Mechanical efficiency can never reach the ideal of 100%; machines never work as well on the farm as they do in the plans. If only one could get friction to go away, you could make a perpetual clock. But no one (yet) can get friction to go away. The same story applies to the efficiency of the healthcare system: You cannot get all clinics to be as efficient as the lowest-cost one you observe, much less as efficient as an ideally run clinic. If we then turn to evidence on the impact of efforts to improve the efficiency of the healthcare system in practice, we find little reason for optimism – because much of what contributes to inefficiency so far cannot be changed. You have to pick your battles.

One source of inefficiency economists have flagged is the tax subsidy to employment-based health insurance. This source is now in a kind of policy limbo: It could in principle be curtailed, but attempts to do so have failed, most spectacularly in the Affordable Care Act (ACA). But even had efforts (much more politically unpopular) to eliminate the tax distortion entirely succeeded, the US healthcare spending level would fall by less than 10%. That is about as good as it is going to get.

Perhaps more importantly, we have even less evidence, in theory or in practice, that there are ways to lower the growth in spending. Limiting the rate of introduction and use of costly but beneficial new technology and putting a lid on wages and prices in the healthcare sector have so far not been feasible. Regulators keep trying, in some US states and other countries, but so far without noticeable success. The exhortation to the system to lower cost, improve quality, and increase access is asking for the impossible.

(2) *In an efficient healthcare system, all services that are cost-effective should be provided, and no services that are not cost-effective – even if they are effective – should be provided.* We have methods to decide what is or is not cost-effective, but they would have to be validated, either by politics or by the market. But the principle needs to be accepted while we wait for the implementation. With limited resources, services or goods whose marginal benefit is greater than their marginal resource cost should be made available. Often a given service may be cost-effective for some patients and not others, so context matters. Services that definitely would add to health but have high cost should not be provided. This rule means that health status or outcomes, for an individual or a population, should not be maximized because services of low

marginal benefit (flat of the curve) should be withheld even if insurance would cover their cost. The necessity of refusing beneficial care (unless and until its cost can be brought down) makes managing healthcare and health insurance especially challenging, and suppliers need to compete on ways to do so acceptably. The value of health benefits reflects the (correctly perceived or forecasted) value of health improvements to the direct user of care, but in some cases, positive values are attached by other community members to increased use by those who use low amounts because of low income or racism.

(3) *High US healthcare spending relative to other countries does not necessarily reflect inefficiency but does reflect the fact that suppliers of healthcare inputs in the US are paid higher prices and wages than elsewhere in the world. (Higher profits are a part but only a small part of the difference).* In almost all other developed countries, governments control prices and quantities of healthcare inputs; they have the power to keep wages below competitive levels. This often though not always results in smaller quantities (with shortages and waiting lists) as well as lower spending. In the US, market power from patents (for drugs and devices) or local market power (for hospital and physician services, especially in smaller cities) causes prices to exceed marginal costs.

(4) *Profit-maximizing suppliers will not respond to a lower price imposed by some major buyer by increasing prices to other buyers. Discounts obtained by some buyers will not result in higher prices to other buyers. Cost-shifting only occurs if the seller was initially not charging the profit-maximizing price to all buyers.* Sellers that sell to different sets of buyers may charge or be paid different prices by some buyers than others. If the sellers are initially charging the profit-maximizing price to a buyer, having another buyer pay less does not cause that price to increase. It may either fall (in order to bring in the now more profitable business) or remain the same. Hospital organizations that argue against government payment cuts by saying hospitals will then have to charge their commercial customers more are wrong. Discounts on drugs extracted by PBMs will not lead drug sellers to raise list prices to recoup lost profits. Cost-shifting will not increase profit once price is at the profit-maximizing level.

(5) *Positive out-of-pocket payments (cost-sharing) may be beneficial when applied to services on which middle-class patients are well informed about health benefits and for which demand is responsive to such user prices. There should be zero cost-sharing for settings in which medical*

services are cost-effective. If a service is cost-effective on average but is of below average value for some patients, cost-sharing targeted at those patients may be beneficial. Well-informed insurance buyers will prefer policies with well-targeted cost-sharing to more costly policies without cost-sharing. Individuals will prefer such coverage (silver rather than platinum), and employers will use trial and error to find the level of cost-sharing that allows them to offer the wage-coverage package most attractive to workers they want to hire or keep. For middle-class Americans in average health, adverse health effects from income-conditioned cost-sharing are small but total use and cost are lowered – compared to free care with no limits on supply. Consumers choose insurance policies with cost-sharing when and if cost-sharing discourages use of low-value care relative to its cost. They will not be willing to pay higher premiums for more generous coverage even if there is some positive effect on health. Low-income persons may respond to cost-sharing by curtailing use of beneficial care that is valued by others in the community. Often observers decry alleged underuse of beneficial care under cost-sharing (relative to free care) by low-income households but do not indicate where subsidies to pay for such coverage will come from. Subsidies that lead to reduced cost-sharing in insurance by the middle class (such as the tax subsidy to employment-based coverage) are not efficient.

(6) *Providers of healthcare, especially physicians, should furnish information to patients who have insurance with cost-sharing that allows those patients to identify beneficial care that is cost-effective and refuse care that is not. Physicians are not currently trained to provide this kind of advice. If the health plan and its physicians are not going to provide this information, cost-sharing should be zero, managed care should be strict, and capitation or carefully calibrated hybrid payment should be used.* Physicians have an obligation to provide accurate information to patients; that information is often the main service that patients demand. However, physicians (like others) often find it difficult to convey the notion of probability to consumers – even to ones who play poker – but most medical services change the probability of an outcome, not move it from certain to impossible. The idea that patients may have limits to the value they place on improved health, even though it is the core idea of cost-effectiveness analysis, is also challenging because physicians do not know and have trouble eliciting their patient's willingness to trade health for money.

(7) *The ideal form of payment for medical services and drug providers by managers of an insurance plan should be a two-part or hybrid system that takes the form of F + P*Q, where F is a fixed payment, possibly zero (per person or per episode of care), and P* is a marginal price per unit of some service Q.* The definition of the service needs to include either specification of quality or a supplemental payment per measurable unit of quality. Managers of health delivery systems need to plan how to cope with such insurance plans – and incorporate the two-part model into the way they pay physicians if the system is fully capitated. As described in Chapter 9 on value-based payment, the purpose of the fixed payment F is to ensure participation by a sufficient number of providers (depending on the strategy of the plan). The purpose of the P* payment is to offer incentives to supply the ideal quantity of services per person who chooses the insurance plan. As a manager of insurance or care with capitation you should care about paying doctors correctly because this will lead to results consumers most prefer – not too little care, not too much cost.

(8) *The level of P* should be set at the level at which MB = MC for the particular service rendered to the insurer's population.* For example, the desired frequency of joint replacement or obesity treatment per capita in a population should be set at the level at which the price suppliers are willing to accept at that level, enough to cover their marginal cost, just equal to the price that reflects buyer value at that level, just equal to their marginal benefit. The marginal price should be titrated to the level at which the care supplied is the cost-effective level. This can be accomplished at the aggregate level and physician–patient loyalty can channel the volume of services supplied across the patients who will benefit most.

(9) *The price P* described in conclusion 8 is the correct economically defined value-based price – accept no substitutes! It will ordinarily be greater than zero (so pure capitation is rarely ideal) and may be adjusted depending on measurable dimensions of quality or outcome.* To the present, no insurance plan or medical care system has been able to implement a good value-based pricing system, despite aspirations to do so. Note that the ideal value-based system is partially fee-for-service (FFS) but also incorporates fixed dollar payment and attention to quality and outcomes. The health plan or health delivery system that is able to discover and implement a superior payment system for providers will be able to succeed in the market for health plans, whether the private group market, the Obamacare marketplace, or Medicare

Advantage, accountable care organizations (ACOs), and original Medicare. Most experiments in new payment systems (compared say to Medicare FFS) have not shown the ability to lower cost or improve quality by a practically significant amount. When and if that happens, the market will give advantage to the winner.

(10) *Nonprofit hospitals treating a population with given demand and insurance coverage do not make different choices of care volume, cost, quality, price, or charitable care versus a for-profit twin, despite tax advantages. For-profit hospitals locate in local markets where insurance is more generous and generally avoid markets with large numbers of potential patients who are uninsured or on Medicaid. In other parts of healthcare such as nursing homes, hospice, or home health, nonprofit organizations choose to provide higher quality at higher cost or price.* There is no evidence that ownership structure for hospitals is related to either productive efficiency or product quality – especially in locally competitive markets or in hospitals controlled by physicians. The stable coexistence of nonprofit and investor-owned hospitals in many markets is further consistent with the "not a dime's worth" of difference hypothesis.

(11) *Nonprofit hospitals may be incentivized and managed to increase or maximize the incomes of the medical staff.* In this type of model, there are incentives for hospitals to produce hospital services efficiently, since higher hospital prices to cover higher costs would cut into physician income. However, if the hospital–physician combination has market power, pricing and volume of hospital-related physician services will be set at the profit-maximizing level. Physicians will collect the surplus in their revenues. At a minimum, the interests of physicians influence hospital decisions and objectives. Even when physicians are salaried employees, the availability of competitive alternatives and their control of technical knowledge make their financial interests important to the hospital.

(12) *Positive cost-sharing (compared to free care) may impair measurable health outcomes for the minority of the population with low incomes who are also at high risk. Ideally, they should have more generous insurance than the rest of the population; "skin in the game" is not desirable for this minority but it may be both economically and financially appropriate for a large majority of the population.* Design of programs to differentiate coverage with the potential for well-designed cost-sharing for the middle class and those initially without chronic or high-risk conditions while offering incentives for use of services for those at risk is

a challenge. The empirical evidence on cost-sharing indicates that it surely does reduce spending. For those who are not low-income or high-risk, the majority of the population, this reduction in use does not seem to affect measurable population health outcomes even though it does reduce service types that clinicians think to be beneficial. However, the evidence also suggests that plans with high cost-sharing may be harmful to health outcomes for the minority (10%–20%) of the under-65 population with low incomes and high risk – high-deductible health plans are not ideal for those with chronic conditions. Generous subsidies to this subpopulation are available in states that have expanded Medicaid, though not all states have done so. For the remainder of the population, insurers and providers will be challenged to design insurance plans that target cost-sharing at those services of high marginal benefit which are currently underused. Buyers of private insurance will benefit both from a variety of cost-sharing and managed care options and from their effects on financial protection and health outcomes. Free care for middle-class people in current good health is unlikely to be ideal and will offer incentives for excessively high cost, since private sector healthcare spending is driven by the majority with private coverage who are not poor high-risk individuals.

(13) *Right now, federal policy only roughly approximates this ideal insurance outcome.* Very low-income people in most states get free insurance and free care under Medicaid. Subsidies to Exchange plan premiums combined with cost-sharing subsidies lead to premiums and out-of-pocket payments that eventually increase with income. Medicare also has low-income subsidies to premiums and cost-sharing. However, employment group insurance does not at present fit this model since tax subsidies rise (rather than fall) with income and plans with more generous cost-sharing are more frequently purchased by higher-wage workers (because of the tax subsidy).

Debunking 101: Statements Contradicted or Significantly Questioned by Economics

(1) "*Middle-class people do not respond to cost-sharing in health insurance.*"[8] There have been dozens of economic studies that compare

[8] Gladwell, M. (2005). The moral hazard myth. *The New Yorker*, August 21. www.newyorker.com/magazine/2005/08/29/the-moral-hazard-myth. (Emphasis added.)

the spending of middle-class households across different levels of cost-sharing. The overwhelming number show that middle-class consumers spend less on healthcare, other things equal, the more they have to pay out of pocket. Managed care rules can also lower costs at a given level of cost-sharing. However, even though the two policy features can work together to hold down spending and result in lower premiums, they do subject people to more risk – the risk of an unexpected high out-of-pocket payment, or the risk that your managed care plan will not pay for the care you want (but they think you do not need). Significant cost-sharing in insurance chosen by most middle-class people is here to stay, and managers can benefit from finding ways to work with the patients who have such plans, helping them make wise choices about which care is or is not low value relative to its cost. Consumers need to be careful not to choose a plan with cost-sharing that is not tailored to their health needs, preferences about financial risk, and income.

(2) "*Many households do not have enough money to pay cost sharing typical in private health insurance plans.*"[9] How many is "many" is open for discussion, but it does appear that many low-income people mistakenly are assigned to or choose private insurance with cost-sharing levels that, in the worst-case scenario, will strain their ability to pay out of liquid assets. Bankruptcy can usually be avoided by working out a payment plan over time but sometimes happens. The real social problem is that, while Medicaid will usually cover the poor with minimal cost-sharing, lower-middle-income people too well-off for Medicaid can end up with insurance plans with high cost-sharing obligations in (relatively rare) cases of serious illness – for example, by choosing a "Bronze" plan on the Obamacare exchange. Taxpayers have yet to agree to subsidies for more generous coverage for lower-middle-income people that will offset the need to choose high cost-sharing coverage for its low premiums, although the current levels of subsidy to exchange plans should be adequate to choose a protective plan if the household is well informed. Prohibiting lower-income people from choosing low-coverage, low-premium plans would probably provoke a political outcry, unless and until tax-financed subsidies are better targeted. Evidence shows that nonpoor families who choose

[9] Kaiser Family Foundation. (2022). Many households do not have enough money to pay cost-sharing typical in private health plans. www.kff.org/health-costs/issue-brief/many-households-do-not-have-enough-money-to-pay-cost-sharing-typical-in-private-health-plans/. (Emphasis added.)

inadequate but cheap coverage have other troubles in managing their credit cards, medical and nonmedical debt, and discretionary consumer spending. The financial system has a difficult time dealing with these households across the board. Managers of healthcare systems and insurers will also be challenged but should try to offer both advice and products that can protect against avoidable financial distress. For a 40-year-old, an addition to monthly premiums of around 150 dollars can improve the tier from silver to gold for a stressed middle-class household.[10]

(3) "*The 'triple aim' is a framework to help health care systems optimize performance.*"[11] The triple aim is not really an operable framework but rather a set of aspirations for change in healthcare that would improve the health outcomes of populations, improve the experience of receiving healthcare, and lower cost or at least lower its growth altogether relative to the current system. It is not clear how efforts to move on all three fronts simultaneously will "optimize performance." If optimization means choosing practices alternative to current ones that provide more benefit than cost, the challenge is finding such practices. It is by no means established that there are unequivocally better alternatives to current clinical practices, payment systems, or insurance coverage that can, even to a modest extent, achieve the triple aim. It is also unclear whether consumers would want to move in all three dimensions – they might prefer to incur higher cost for a new practice that improves population health in a significant and convenient way.

(4) "*All modern quality theorists think there is a wide terrain opportunity to improve quality, consumer experience, and reduce costs at the same time.*"[12] "*That we have a tremendous opportunity to improve … is largely unquestioned.*"[13] Quality theorists from William Edward Deming onward have primarily functioned as consultants encouraging firms to pay more attention to quality. The evidence that they have advocated schemes shown to reduce waste is weak. Economists usually assume that firms are already driven to technical efficiency by the desire

[10] Forbes Advisor. (2025). How much does health insurance cost in 2024? www.forbes.com/advisor/health-insurance/how-much-does-health-insurance-cost/.

[11] Verywell Health. (2020). An overview of the triple aim: A framework to help healthcare systems optimize performance. www.verywellhealth.com/triple-aim-4174961. (Emphasis added.)

[12] Berwick, D. (2019). The triple aim: Why we still have a long way to go. Institute for Healthcare Improvement. www.ihi.org/insights/triple-aim-why-we-still-have-long-way-go. (Emphasis added.)

[13] Fisher, E. S. (2020). Reforming health care: The single system solution. *NEJM Catalyst Innovations in Care Delivery*, *1*(5). https://doi.org/10.1056/CAT.20.0456. (Emphasis added.)

to increase profits, which means that if an action that improves quality also lowers cost it is an action that the firm should already have taken. Economic models of quality determination emphasize that, given technical efficiency, higher quality will raise cost and prices but may be worth it to consumers.[14] However, competitive equilibrium with varying quality and varying buyer preferences is not assured to be optimal even under competition; mismatch may occur. There is no economic support for many of the recommendations of quality theorists, either because they point to influences that are hard to measure or change (e.g., leadership) or because lower than maximal quality products are often what the market demands. The theory of disruptive innovation outside of healthcare points to the success of products slightly lower in quality but much lower in price;[15] this model has not so far been endorsed for healthcare. The real challenge to management and consumers is to balance expectations with capacity, and the ability to improve quality at lower cost has so far not been shown to exist at present.

(5) "*Fee for service payment doesn't work because we spend more and have worse health outcomes than other countries.*"[16] Many other countries with lower cost than in the US use FFS payment for physician and hospital services. There may be alternative payment models that could be developed that would be associated with lower spending and better outcomes in the US than current levels but reducing spending substantially would require government authorities to set price levels, potentially in FFS.

(6) *Fee-for-service payment in theory encourages overutilization and does nothing to align financial incentives between different providers. It does not try to encourage high-value low-cost care such as preventive care.*[17] Fee-for-service payment incentives depend on the level of payment for a service relative to its cost. "Overutilization" will occur if FFS payments are too high but can be lowered by reducing payments. Fee-for-service

[14] De Vany, A. S., & Saving, T. R. (1983). The economics of quality. *Journal of Political Economy*, *91*(6), 979–1000.

[15] Christensen, C. M. (2013). *The innovator's dilemma: When new technologies cause great firms to fail*. Harvard Business Review Press.

[16] Calsyn, M., & Lee, O. (2012). *Alternatives to fee-for-service payments in health care moving from volume to value*. Center for American Progress. https://cdn.americanprogress.org/wp-content/uploads/2012/09/FeeforService4.pdf. (Emphasis added.)

[17] Ikegami, N. (2015). Fee-for-service payment: An evil practice that must be stamped out? *International Journal of Health Policy and Management*, *4*(2), 57–59.

will encourage preventive care if it sets high enough payments for it. The statement perhaps describes current Medicare FFS payment structure but that is not the only possible and surely not the best model of payment per unit of service.

(7) "*Savings and quality gains from value-based payment models are consistent and substantial.*"[18] The evidence suggests that, compared to FFS alternatives, value-based payment systems have been inconsistent in improving quality or lowering cost. Any spending reductions so far have been very modest, especially once you account for the cost and bother of setting up and running such systems.

(8) "*Health care delivery cannot simply be for profit.*"[19] Some portions of the healthcare system are largely dominated by for-profit firms, such as prescription drugs, cosmetic surgery, and home health care. Nonprofit hospitals appear to behave in ways very similar to their for-profit counterparts, charging the same high prices when they can and providing similar amounts of charity care. Their main shortcoming in theory is the inability to raise equity capital from investors. While it would be a major and probably unnecessary transition to sell existing nonprofit hospitals to investor-owned firms, the resulting proceeds could be used to create charitable foundations whose returns would pay for more charity care than is currently furnished by those hospitals. The main beneficiaries of nonprofit ownership are physicians and other personnel who use such organizations and middle-class patients whose charges, while high relative to government plans, are probably lower than they would be under full and fully taxed investor ownership.

(9) "*When federal and state health policies give consumers more control over their health care dollars, they can use that power to demand greater value.*"[20] This statement represents an aspiration, not a proven fact. The evidence suggests that consumers with high deductibles often do not choose to shop among competing providers for greater value or choose the most cost-effective treatment given its price. Higher cost-sharing

[18] Werner, R. M., Emanuel, E. J., Pham, H. H., & Navathe, A. S. (2023). The future of value-based payment a road map to 2030. Leonard Davis Institute of Health Economics, February 17. (Emphasis added.)

[19] Bedzow, I. (2020). Should we beware of the for-profit hospital? *Forbes*, December 9. www.forbes.com/sites/irabedzow/2020/12/09/should-we-beware-of-the-for-profit-hospital/. (Emphasis added.)

[20] US Department of Health and Human Services, US Department of the Treasury, & US Department of Labor. (2018). Reforming America's healthcare system through choice and competition. www.hhs.gov/sites/default/files/Reforming-Americas-Healthcare-System-Through-Choice-and-Competition.pdf. (Emphasis added.)

among the middle class does reduce spending compared to free care in ways that do not adversely affect health overall, though some undervalued cost-effective services can be reduced.

(10) "*A single unified provider payment and insurance system that contains incentives aligned to reward population health while reducing opportunities to shift costs [is needed].*"[21] There is substantial empirical evidence that consumers in the US have widely varying preferences for different kinds of insurance and different kinds of medical care delivery systems. There is no evidence to establish the superiority of one model of insurance incentives over another. Economics generally rules out cost-shifting to other insurance plans by profit-maximizing providers who were previously charging profit-maximizing prices.

(11) "*With FFS still the dominant force, no one should be surprised by price growth. The existence of multiple unaligned payment systems makes it possible to resist cost pressure from one payer by shifting costs to others.*"[22] There is no economic theory or evidence that would predict that FFS payment (compared to some alternative such as capitation), if implemented in US healthcare financing, would lower the growth of spending. At most, transition away from FFS would produce a one-time reduction in the level of spending, but the comparative effects of FFS versus capitation on the rate and form of introduction of new beneficial but cost-increasing new technology are not known. Managed care plan spending growth largely parallels FFS spending growth and has not been shown to influence growth in unit prices, other things equal.

(12) "*The high cost of the US health care system is its biggest weakness.*"[23] That an economist would pick cost as the most important problem, rather than health outcomes or consumer satisfaction, is perhaps not surprising. I know of no evidence to support this statement of priority. Higher prices paid to suppliers of medical goods and services in the US transfer income from users of medical care to suppliers of medical care but that is not necessarily a weakness; it depends on the reason for the transfer and the subsequent use of the funds. To the extent that higher prices lead to less comprehensive consumer-chosen insurance, there

[21] Fisher, E. S. (2020). Reforming health care: The single system solution. *NEJM Catalyst Innovations in Care Delivery*, *1*(5). https://doi.org/10.1056/CAT.20.0456. (Emphasis added.)

[22] Fisher, E. S. (2020). Reforming health care: The single system solution. *NEJM Catalyst Innovations in Care Delivery*, *1*(5). https://doi.org/10.1056/CAT.20.0456. (Emphasis added.)

[23] Buntin, M. B. (2021). Confronting challenges in the US health care system: Potential opportunity in a time of crisis. *JAMA*, *325*(14), 1399–1400. (Emphasis added.)

will be more financial distress, while higher prices for public insurances mean either higher taxes or cuts in other spending. These are real harms, but they are not necessarily the biggest. Real resource costs of US healthcare are probably not higher than in many other developed countries. Health outcomes are worse, but those adverse outcomes are primarily related to adverse social determinants of health in the US, not to high medical costs or prices. Prices in excess of competitive levels can in economics cause reductions in welfare but the reduction depends on the responsiveness of use to those higher prices and the consequent effect of lower use on health outcomes. Evidence suggests that these magnitudes are small. The case can be made that the biggest weaknesses in the US health system are an inability to offset adverse SDOH and a lack of care coordination. The poster child for high prices in healthcare is the drug industry, but its share of total spending remains small. Depending on how lower spending is achieved, it might harm health outcomes or leave them largely unchanged.

(13) "*Health care is a right not a privilege.*"[24] Economists need to be careful here since there is no economic concept of either "right" or "privilege." Politicians need to be careful because it is easier to assert a right than it is to pay for the care associated with doing so. The answer to the question is based on the subjective judgment of members of the community, and those preferences are neither empirically known nor clearly stated. In the US, rights guaranteed by the Constitution are primarily limits on government intervention, such as the right to free speech or whatever religion you choose. There are no obvious rights that involve the reallocation of resources to some activity or the specification of how the costs should be distributed. Bauchner and colleagues mention some costly public goods like education and fire protection as rights,[25] but these local public goods are not federally guaranteed and depend on the willingness of taxpayers in different areas to choose whether to fund them and to what extent. Possible economic guidance to the answer to this subjective question would begin with the assumption that there is or could be a consensus that all persons have some baseline level of insurance coverage. (This is despite the repeal of the individual mandate in Obamacare; right now, Americans have the right to be uninsured and must deal with the

[24] Bauchner, H., Fontanarosa, P. B., & Maddox, K. J. (2021). Health care is a right, not a privilege: A new series on US health care and health policy. *JAMA*, *325*(3), 227–228. (Emphasis added.)

[25] Bauchner, H. (2017). Health care in the United States: A right or a privilege. *JAMA*, *317*(1), 29.

consequences.) The key insight economics can offer is a suggestion of how to define the *rightful amount* of either insurance coverage or care use conditional on illness. Platitudes like "affordable high-quality insurance" do not help. Medicaid provides coverage for some low-income people (varying across states) that is free of out-of-pocket payment by insureds but generally has low provider payments that limit access to all physicians in a community; compared to commercial insurance, a two-tier system has been accepted for years and is unlikely to change. An economic definition of the rightful amount of care use and the coverage that facilitates it would be to define that amount as the cost-effective level. For well-off citizens, this level would generally be as much as they were willing to insure and use on their own, with the possible exception of immunizations against contagious disease. For lower-income people, the money valuation of health-improving care would include both their own valuation and that of others in the community concerned about their health outcomes. A similar structure would apply to financial risk protection – whatever you would pay for on your own if you are not poor but with possible tax-financed supplementation if you are low-income and low-wealth.

My opinion is that this economic definition could be helpful, but it has surely not yet been adopted as consensus nor has the information needed to produce a sample description been generated. Presumably, treatments which change the probability of survival from zero to one would be covered, but most treatments only change that probability marginally and/or affect quality of life. Efforts to achieve consensus on public support for cost-effective care, as in the state of Oregon in the 1990s, have so far failed. It seems that economics says that, so far, the question of healthcare in the US as a right is at best poorly defined and at worst a silly question. What taxpayers are willing to pay for the care of lower-income people is obviously expressed through revealed political choices now; information on further health benefits from further spending (like child tax credits) may move this consensus or may not. Most of the 8% of the population currently uninsured who are citizens are eligible for heavily subsidized coverage but have either not applied for it or been unwilling to pay the nominal explicit premiums for employment-based coverage mandated by the ACA. The individual mandate would have closed this gap but was rejected politically. The US could establish some level of health insurance as a right but has so far chosen not to do so for every citizen. Managers of health delivery systems and insurance plans need to be aware of the ambiguity of the current consensus and, to the extent possible, determine the cost-effectiveness of care or insurance designs in deciding whether to subsidize or furnish charity care.

The idea of subsidized and mandated basic minimum coverage, with additional coverage as a self-financed option, has been around for a long time. Most discussions imagine that both the coverage and the subsidy will be more generous for lower-income people; it will be income-related catastrophic coverage.[26] Any attempts to require coverage of specific services beyond cost-effective preventive care and contraception failed in the debate over the ACA, so coverage generosity was limited to an actuarial value calculation with a patchwork of subsidies to cost-sharing for some lower-income people. Evidence can contribute cost-effectiveness evaluations to guide any future efforts – do cost-sharing subsidies improve health? But progress toward a comprehensive design seems unlikely to happen anytime soon.

(14) "*The RAND experiment proved that cost sharing causes all patients to risk going without needed care.*"[27] This is not correct. For the 86% of subjects who were not low-income high-risk individuals, the experiment found large reductions in cost and use but no difference in health outcomes (over a wide range of care-sensitive measures) associated with being in the cost-sharing group, with cost-sharing as high as 15% of income. One interpretation is that, on average, patients were discerning enough to reduce care of low benefit even in categories labeled effective. Regardless of the explanation, this result suggests that cost-sharing-induced reductions do not on balance harm health outcomes for most people. *Not* having cost-sharing led patients to seek *more* medical care but they were unable to find much evidence that, for the average patient, *more care* led to better health outcomes.[28] In contrast, insurance with cost-sharing may be undesirable for low-

[26] Feldstein, M., & Gruber, J. (1995). A major risk approach to health insurance reform. *Tax Policy and the Economy*, 9, 103–130; Pauly, M. V. (1971). *Medical care at public expense: A study in applied welfare economics*. Praeger Publishers; Einav, L., & Finkelstein, A. (2023). *We've got you covered: Rebooting American health care*. Penguin.

[27] Sanghavi, D. (2008). The high price of a medical miracle: If health care costs are trimmed, who will be deprived of treatment. *Washington Post*, May 27. (Emphasis added.)

[28] US Congress (1993). Benefit design in health care reform: Patient cost-sharing. Office of Technology Assessment, Background Paper, OTA-BP-H-112. www.princeton.edu/~ota/disk1/1993/9310/931004.PDF.

income high-risk individuals unless their only alternatives are no insurance or unsubsidized unaffordable generous coverage.

Final Thoughts: Can Economics Help Management?

The economic target for management at all levels should be one of doing everything cost-effective and nothing that is not. This is a useful antidote to viewing high health spending or costs (remember, the two are different) as an unqualified objective. There are worse things than high cost. The concept of net benefit provides a framework for explaining the goals of a health delivery or insurance organization. Not all readers may appreciate cost-effectiveness as a defining principle, but (other than platitudes about the right care at the right cost) what is the alternative?

Skepticism of cheerleaders for value-based payment of care, high-deductible consumer-driven health plans, or triple advocates adds realism and can reduce frustration. Some of the cute tricks in health economics – about cost-shifting, econometric cost functions, and nonprofit firms – will sometimes be helpful. Despite it being a dark story so far, the need for and failure at improved care coordination provides a target for those willing to take a chance.

There are some strategic redirections that may work. One is to come to terms with managing care and information for customers with substantial out-of-pocket payments. Can they be helped to judge the expected benefits from costly medical interventions (taking account of the probability of success or failure) and compare them with the costs of other consumption foregone? In principle, evidence-based cost-effectiveness analysis (with a correct measure of opportunity cost) can be a valuable tool if results are presented in a graceful way. Another help is to rekindle the force of competition in a setting where consumers pay out of pocket and are helped to shop for better deals. Still a third is to make greater use of cost-effectiveness analysis in designing managed care protocols and to differentiate insurance plans based on the value they place on health outcomes. If the $150,000 per QALY health maintenance organization (HMO) sweeps the market, that will tell us something.

However, it is fair to say that economic theory and economic analysis have not yet identified actions that can be shown to make major reductions in costs guaranteed to leave quality unaffected. Fee-for-service payment still dominates health system reimbursement, with at most minor quality footnotes, and payment at the individual physician level is still largely based on volume or revenue. Adjusting levels of fees to offer incentives for higher-value care (effective but underused preventive care) and discourage low-value care (expensive specialty tests and drugs) has yet to happen. Care coordination still is a struggle; medical homes do not show large improvements, and primary care physician incomes are stagnant even as workload is burdensome. Careful targeting of patient cost-sharing to reflect imperfect information and price responsiveness is in its infancy. Health systems grapple with how or whether they could gain from investing in SDOH, and effective programs to reduce disparities are scarce. Nonprofit hospitals are torn between a charity mission and the need to cover costs and make investments in financially stressful markets – competitive in some big cities and monopoly but impoverished in rural areas. The tax burden of subsidizing care is growing, as more become eligible for Medicare and Exchange subsidies are extended up to middle-income consumers, while the tax exclusion for group insurance bleeds federal and state revenues. Employers so far manage to provide coverage workers find attractive but are challenged to cover rising prices, even for better treatments.

Economic theory and evidence explain much of this dark picture: The interventions are poorly designed and the opportunities to reduce waste in a way that does more good than harm are limited. Perhaps realism is all we can expect unless and until some better way of paying for or coordinating care is invented. It has not happened yet, and wishing does not make it so.

Despite a general pattern of inertia, there have been two fairly major changes in the healthcare and health insurance systems that can be partially explained by economics and that may signal future developments. One is the movement of physician payment to salary (as long as salaries are not driven primarily by relative value units), and the other is the risk of private managed care plans in both Medicare (Medicare Advantage) and Medicaid (Medicaid managed care) markets. The final and perhaps the greatest challenge is to deal with a political system, one that includes lobbyists, campaign donors, and populists, not necessarily attuned to the messages from welfare economics.

The most obvious subset of physicians now paid salaries rather than as owners of private practices are those who are hospital employees. Another equally important but often ignored subset are those who are salaried members of physician group practices. In the latter case, the owners of the practice (who bear and receive risky profits) are other physicians or increasingly outside investors.[29] In Coase's theory of the firm, workers who are salaried rather than owners give up managerial control over their actions in return for the assurance of regular income.

This model seems too simplistic for salaried hospital physicians. Powerful department chairs in the medical staff often can dictate hospital management policy, and salaries are often adjusted for individual physician performance in terms of revenue generated for the health system, patient satisfaction, and other measures of quality, and the outcomes of bargaining in a competitive market for physicians. Physician employees are not powerless members of the proletariat – perhaps necessarily so because of the independence in judgment needed for them to manage a set of patients with varying conditions and preferences. College professors are salaried, but they plan their own courses and give their own grades; physicians who are salaried also can choose their own actions and the other services they order for their patients and judge their own success.

There are some urban legends to explain the growth of salaried practice – it is due to a desire for better work–life balance, especially among female physicians; there has been an atrophy of the entrepreneurial spirit among younger doctors; they all need help from a health system in wrangling with insurers – but no complete explanation. The data show fairly dramatic changes over the last decades – now only 16% of doctors are in solo practice and more than half are salaried.[30] The detailed picture is more opaque, however, since 70% of physician payments are FFS, and more than half of physicians are compensated by multiple methods (principally a mix of salary and productivity),[31] while a large fraction of salaried physicians report that their salary this year depends on their productivity last year.[32] There are even 23% of physicians who say they are hospital employees but are paid no salary, only billings.[33]

[29] Abelson, R., & Sanger Katz, M. (2023). Who employs your doctor? Increasingly, a private equity firm. *New York Times*, July 10. www.nytimes.com/2023/07/10/upshot/private-equity-doctors-offices.html.

[30] American Medical Association. (2019). Employed physicians now exceed those who own their practices. www.ama-assn.org/about/ama-research/employed-physicians-now-exceed-those-who-own-their-practices; Physicians Advocacy Institute (2022). COVID-19's impact on acquisition of physician practices and physician employment 2019–2021. http://bit.ly/45KyuyT.

[31] American Medical Association. (2017). Despite APM participation, fee-for-service still dominates. www.ama-assn.org/practice-management/payment-delivery-models/despite-apm-participation-fee-service-still-dominates.

[32] Henry, T. A. (2022). Single source of pay becoming less common for physicians. American Medical Association, October 17. www.ama-assn.org/about/research/single-source-pay-becoming-less-common-physicians.

[33] Rama, A. (2022). Physician compensation methods: The combination of salary and bonus continues to dominate through 2020 as physicians are increasingly paid by multiple methods. American Medical Association, Policy Research Perspectives. www.ama-assn.org/system/files/2020-prp-physician-compensation-methods.pdf/.

Should this transformation from independent practice to salary (at a hospital or large medical group) matter? Economic theory is not much help; it says "it all depends" on how the alternative compensation is structured and on the extent to which physicians respond to financial incentives. The empirical evidence does not suggest much of an impact of compensation per se; organizational changes like the substitution of hospitalists for community physicians making rounds and taking calls seem to matter more. A study of switching compensation from salary to FFS in Norway does suggest an expansion of volume.[34] More generally, however, the details on how salary is determined and the extent to which it is accompanied by managerial pressures to see patients make general conclusions difficult. There could be a delayed response here: At first, a physician converting to salary will practice in the same way as when an owner but over time may be more subject to external pressure and whatever form salary determination takes. There is a complicated simultaneity problem here because the payment structure that will be offered in a tight market has to be one acceptable to all participants – despite the complaints about burnout. Overall, up to the present it does not seem that the nominal but widespread transformation in how American doctors are paid has been matched by a transformation in what they do or the outcomes of what they do. Time may tell.

The other recent significant change has been the emergence of the managed care model from the shadow cast over it by the private insurance HMO backlash into growing popularity in publicly financed schemes: Most Medicare beneficiaries are now in private Medicare Advantage plans, and most of those in Medicaid have been turned over to contracted privately run Medicaid managed care plans.[35] The next round of managed care backlash is waiting for Medicare Advantage plans if they cannot hold down their enrollment fees. The obvious inference is that choosers of insurance coverage prefer private administration of managed care to public administration of FFS. In both cases, FFS plans in Medicare suffer from the effects of low reimbursements – 22% of physicians reject or limit Medicare payments and 32% do the same for Medicaid patients.[36] In Medicare Advantage, private plans have been

[34] Brekke, K. R., Holmås, T. H., Monstad, K., & Straume, O. R. (2020). How does the type of remuneration affect physician behavior? Fixed salary versus fee-for-service. *American Journal of Health Economics, 6* (1), 104–138.

[35] Pauly, M. V. (2019). Giving competition in medical care and health insurance a chance. Mercatus Research Paper. www.mercatus.org/research/research-papers/giving-competition-medical-care-and-health-insurance-chance.

[36] Heritage (2019). More Medicare, less health care: How Medicare for all threatens patient health. August 22. www.heritage.org/insider/summer-2019-insider/more-medicare-less-health-care-how-medicare-all-threatens-patient.

able to get high enough public capitation payments that they can offer more attractive benefits (including dental and preventive) compared to pure FFS.[37] However, in both cases, the current system is on a political thin edge; advocates of more government control would like to reduce the cost these private plans extract from the government. The clash in ideology between competition and choice, on the one hand, and a single same plan for all insureds and all providers, on the other, will never go away. Hence the main challenge to managers is political rather than conventionally economic.

[37] Better Medicare Alliance. (2021). Medicare Advantage payment structure. Fact Sheet. https://bettermedicarealliance.org/wp-content/uploads/2020/03/BMA_OnePager_Payment_Structure_2017_10_18-2021-Update.pdf.

Index

For EU product safety concerns, contact us at Calle de José Abascal, 56–1°, 28003 Madrid, Spain or eugpsr@cambridge.org.

www.ingramcontent.com/pod-product-compliance
Lightning Source LLC
Chambersburg PA
CBHW080129010426
42068CB00092B/714